Sixth Edition

Research Methods for Generalist Social Work

Christine R. Marlow
University of New Mexico

WAVELAND
PRESS, INC.
Long Grove, Illinois

For information about this book, contact:
Waveland Press, Inc.
4180 IL Route 83, Suite 101
Long Grove, IL 60047-9580
(847) 634-0081
info@waveland.com
www.waveland.com

Contents

Preface

My reason for writing this text is not unusual. After several years of seeking a social work research methods text and unsuccessfully trying a new text each year, I gave up and started to write. From teaching the same course repeatedly, I developed a number of ideas of what a text needed: more of a focus on the type of research undertaken by social workers rather than academic social scientists; a more global perspective; and presenting research concepts in such a way that students can see the connection between research and social work practice. These ideas became crystallized through many discussions with students and colleagues and through my experiences with the Council on Social Work Education (CSWE) accreditation process. This text is intended for both undergraduate and graduate students taking a research methods course for the first time.

Themes and Organization

A focus on generalist practice. Undergraduate and foundation graduate courses in social work programs are usually taught from a generalist perspective. Research methods must also be taught within this framework; hence the emphasis in this text on generalist social work practice. *Emphasis on the practice-research link.* When the parallels between generalist practice and research are emphasized, research becomes more accessible because practice is often perceived as more intuitive and understandable. Consequently, the text illustrates these parallels. Throughout the text, examples emphasize the link between research and practice by presenting real-life social work studies.

Discussion of production and consumption. The text presents research methods from the perspective that social workers can be both producers and consumers of research. This also ensures compliance with the CSWE accreditation requirements for the research curriculum. The emergence of evidence-based practice in the last decade provides an effective model for the role of research in social work.

Agency focus. In line with ensuring the relevance of research methods, the text discusses the application of research methods in agency rather than academic settings, because agencies are where the majority of social work graduates will be employed. The focus of the text is on needs assessments, program evaluation, and evaluating individual practice.

Ethics content. Ethical issues are included for each stage of the research process; that is, they are integrated into each chapter and not viewed as separate, discrete topics.

Human diversity content. Similarly, issues concerning human diversity as they relate to research methods are included. Although partly addressed through discussions of alternatives within and to the scientific method, this content (as with the ethics content) is considered for each stage of the research process.

Discussion of the different approaches to research. This text includes coverage of different research approaches: both qualitative and quantitative. A beginning text in research methods cannot engage in complex epistemological debates; what is important for the student to understand is that research can be conducted using different methods and within different paradigms, and that they have a choice.

Global perspective. As universities become increasingly conscious of internationalizing their curricula, social work programs are also adopting global perspectives. Many of the examples are drawn from research studies conducted throughout the world.

This text is written so that each chapter can stand independently if necessary.

Key concepts appear in the text in boldface type and are defined there. These terms are also included in the glossary at the back of the text. Each chapter includes a reference section, as well as a summary and study/exercise questions. If possible, students should complete the exercises as a group; a group effort often provides a richer educational experience.

New to the Sixth Edition

- Research examples updated with an increasing emphasis on **global examples**

- Increased emphasis on **evidence-based practice**

- Updating of the **use of technology** in research, e.g., web-based surveys, database searches, and the use of tablets and cell phones

- Research **examples with updated content** including COVID-19, Black Lives Matter, and other current issues of relevance to social work

- Additional and revised **exercises** in each chapter

- Greatly expanded and updated **appendix on library resources**

- **Updated photographs** at the beginning of each chapter

Ancillaries

Study and exercise questions are provided at the end of each chapter for group activities or homework. Finally, a test question bank and instructor's manual are provided.

Acknowledgments

Completion of this new edition depended on many people (too many for me to name them all), but I would like to thank the following specific individuals and groups: First, I thank Joe Buenker, Associate Librarian at Arizona State University for the extremely thorough and practical Library Appendix. The late Yosikazu (Yoshi) DeRoos, Professor Emeritus, revised the chapter on the analysis of quantitative data for the fifth edition. I am so sorry he is not still with us to enjoy the fruits of his labor, he was a much valued colleague during my tenure at New Mexico State University. I very much appreciate his widow Leigh DeRoos giving permission to publish his work. Colin Van Rooyen, regional director of an international organization for South

Asia and Africa created Chapter 11. Colin has been my friend for many years and his understanding of how social workers can impact people throughout the world has always impressed me. Finally, many thanks to Don Rosso of Waveland Press who convinced me to complete the sixth edition and gave me support throughout the process of publication.

Also, many thanks to all the social work students who, over the years in New Mexico, the United Kingdom, South Africa, Zimbabwe, and Uganda gave me instruction, intentionally and unintentionally, on how research methods should be taught and what should be included in a social work research text.

1

Science and Social Work

The social work research methods course was the one I dreaded the most. I didn't want to take it.

—Social Work Student

INTRODUCTION

The attitude reflected in this student's statement is not unusual in social work classrooms. Social workers often express inherent suspicion or even a phobia about research. Have you ever skimmed over articles in social work journals because you were intimidated by the language and the displays of results? Have you ever shuddered at the thought of undertaking a research project? If so, you are not alone. Because research is typically associated with mathematics, you may not be enthusiastic about applying what is perceived as a cold, impersonal approach to human needs and problem solving. After all, most social workers want to work with people, not numbers. Research, however, is simply a means of gaining knowledge. In social work practice, we need all the knowledge we can muster to be optimally responsible to ourselves, our clients, and our agencies.

Once you understand the research process, you will have access to a vast amount of information in the literature. Articles that once eluded you with discussions of "validity" and "correlation coefficients" will not only become accessible, but will make available information that you can apply to your practice.

When equipped with the knowledge and skills to apply research methods, you will also know how to answer the questions arising in your role as a generalist social worker, such as these:

- Are my visits to Mrs. Garcia helping her cope with the death of her husband? What was her experience with grief counseling?

- How effective is the Change for Families Agency in providing services that support and protect victims of domestic violence? What are the experiences of the clients receiving these services?

- What are the needs of adolescent African American fathers in Detroit? What are the experiences of these fathers?

This book emphasizes the strong links between the processes of research and practice, helping you answer these types of questions and understand social work research. The generalist social work practice steps have their equivalents in social work research. Thus, the following chapters help you learn the research steps in a process similar to the way you learn the practice steps.

Certain themes of this text will help explain research methodology and its relevance to your practice as a generalist social worker:

- Connecting the research process and generalist practice

- Producing research by developing appropriate research questions derived from the literature and practice
- Consuming research using skills to critique and evaluate research
- Choosing qualitative and/or quantitative methods and understanding the associated reliability and validity issues
- Engaging in participatory research whenever possible
- Understanding ethical issues are associated with each stage of the research
- Articulating human diversity issues that include anti-racist and anti-oppressive perspectives that can impact how research is conducted and interpreted
- Understanding social work's role from a global perspective

These overlapping themes support the mission of the book: to present research methods within a generalist social work framework following CSWE's latest Educational Policy and Accreditation Standards (2022).

We introduce many concepts in this book. When first defined, these terms are boldfaced and listed in the glossary at the end of the book. Each chapter includes an overview, a summary, and study/exercise questions.

LEARNING OBJECTIVES

The learning objectives for this chapter are:

1. To identify and describe the different types of understanding and thinking about human behavior

2. To gain a beginning understanding of a positive/quantitative approach to science

3. To gain a beginning understanding of the interpretive/qualitative approach to science

Common Types of Understanding

This section describes the types of understanding that we use to think about the complexity and richness of human behavior. These types of understanding include values, intuition, past experience, authority, and science. Social work can involve any or all of these types of understanding, and it is essential to know about them and their role in generalist social work practice.

Values are beliefs about right and wrong and are closely tied to our respective cultures. For example, among many cultures, a strong value is placed on children's having respect for their elders. Likewise, formal education is highly valued, whereas among others, family-based education is stressed.

Values can be institutionalized by religion. For example, specific values characterize Christianity, such as the Protestant belief that work is a means of gaining societal and individual worth. Buddhists value reincarnation, which affects how people live their present lives. Other religions involve a form of ancestor worship, whereas others strongly value the natural world around them, revering the plants and animals that make up their worlds.

Although values may be fundamental to a culture's tradition, these traditions can change over time. For example, many people now recognize that women should have the same career opportunities as men. This belief was not the case a hundred years ago, or even ten years ago in some countries.

Social work as a profession is based on certain values. These include fundamental notions about the most desirable relationships between people and their environment. In addition, social work values include respect for the individual's dignity and uniqueness; recognizing the client's right to self-determination; and confidentiality. These values are incorporated in the National Association of Social Workers (NASW) Code of Ethics and firmly guide the practice of social work.

Intuition can be defined as a form of insight: When we intuitively know something, we understand it without recourse to specialized training or reasoning. Intuition may also be based on past experiences. In some cultures, intuition is a powerful tool for understanding and explaining the world. People with solid intuition are often seen to have magical powers. If they also exhibit experience and skills, they may enjoy special status in a culture. An example is a *curandera*, a woman perceived to possess healing powers in cultures in the Southwest and Mexico. Similarly, in South Africa among the Zulu people, the *sangoma* is thought to understand the world using special intuitive powers.

Sometimes we call upon intuition in social work practice, which is a valuable source of professional understanding. Although it's unlikely we would act on intuition alone, we might use it to give ourselves some ideas to investigate further. For example, we might have an intuition that a child is being sexually abused. It may be hard to explain this feeling rationally, but the insight can provide a base or starting point for gathering information, which may or may not support intuition.

Experience is the firsthand, personal participation in events that provide a basis for knowledge. You often use this experience to guide present and future actions, particularly when the experience had a successful outcome (even though you may not understand why it was successful). These experiences vary from individual to individual and according to the situation. Experience is highly valued in most cultures. Elders are often highly regarded because of their experience; employers often use experience as a criterion for assessing job applicants. In the practice of social work, this experience is often referred to as practice wisdom. Although highly valuable as a source of knowledge, it is risky to use practice wisdom as the sole guide to practice and the only resource for making practice judgments.

Authority refers to understanding events and circumstances by referring to outside sources of knowledge on specific topics. The authority is credited with an understanding we do not directly possess. Thus, in place of direct understanding—whether obtained through values, intuition, or experience—we accept an explanation by virtue of our confidence in authorities.

Who or what authority depends upon the nature and context of the problem. In practice, social workers rely on authority in several ways. First, we identify experts in different practice fields and seek their opinions and knowledge, either by consulting or reading their publications. There is a vested authority in the social work professional organizations, such as the National Association of Social Workers (NASW) in the United States and the National Institute of Social Work in Great Britain. We use their authority to direct us in different areas, such as adhering to a prescribed code of ethics.

Science refers to both a system for producing knowledge and the knowledge produced from that system. Science dominates the thinking in many countries throughout the world. However, both now and in the past, it has not been universally accepted. For example, Greek rationalism once dominated Western thought, offering logic as the test of truth and not relying on scientific evidence. In the United States, some groups have downplayed the dominance of science. For example, many Conservatives along with the lobbyists for fossil fuel companies decried the existence of climate change despite scientific evidence to the contrary. Similarly, many denied the science surrounding COVID-19, refusing vaccinations and the use of masks.

Despite this variation in the acceptance and role of science, science plays a significant role in how people understand the world today. Moreover, many individuals and organizations across the globe depend on science. For example, the medical profession relies on knowledge derived from the application of science. Likewise, businesses use scientifically based theories and strategies. Social work is no exception; the profession has historically recognized the contributions of the scientific approach.

Science involves using the **scientific method**, which has the following characteristics (Neuman, 2006):

Universalism. Regardless of who conducts scientific research or where it is conducted, it is judged solely on its scientific merit. If a project adopts the scientific method built on systematic, objective observation, then the characteristics, qualifications, national origin, or other researcher characteristics are irrelevant. The research findings are viewed independently from the researcher. This strategy is very different from bestselling novels; here the author is often important (in terms of previous books written, nationality/ethnicity, perhaps gender, etc.) to the writing of the novel. It certainly involves craft and skill, is generally viewed as an artistic endeavor rather than a scientific one, and is viewed accordingly.

Organized skepticism. All scientific evidence should be challenged and questioned. All scientific research is closely scrutinized to ensure the scientific method was followed. There are several generally accepted procedures for doing this. The first is to complete a research methods course; part of this often includes undertaking a research project under the guidance of the research instructor. Later, as a graduate student, you may complete a thesis or dissertation, which is even more closely examined and subject to questioning by your committee and advisor. Ultimately, you may publish in "refereed journals," which means your work in the field will be reviewed by scholars who do not know who wrote the article. They provide feedback on the research to the researcher/author.

Disinterestedness. Scientists should be able to accept other scientific evidence that runs against their position. For example, suppose you have worked in an agency developing a behavioral intervention program with substance abusers. In that case, you might read a research report that disclosed less than satisfactory results using this type of intervention. Your first impulse is to dismiss the study because it runs counter to your beliefs and perhaps even counter to some research you may have undertaken. However, the research should be considered on its merits, and hopefully, the findings used to enhance your program.

Communalism.   Scientific knowledge must be shared with the public, including the methods used. Research almost always results in some type of report, available to those interested. That is why we undertake research. As discussed above, this may be a class research report shared with your classmates and instructor, an agency evaluation disseminated to the staff and administrators, or a published article in a social work journal.

Honesty.   Scientists demand honesty in all research. A code of ethics guides research in social work. The NASW Code of Ethics includes a specific section relating to conducting social work research. Throughout the research process, the participants must be protected in every way from harm, and the researcher must be scrupulously honest at every step of the research process. Each chapter in this book discusses ethical issues confronted at each stage. A critical section in any research report is the limitations section, where the researcher spells out problems with the research method. This is the ultimate in research honesty, but is often difficult for the researcher to do. A research report or article without a limitations section is subject to question because, as every researcher knows, there are always limitations to all research studies!

As well as being characterized by these norms, science consists of **theories** and **research methods**. Theories describe or explain logical relationships among phenomena in our world. They help guide our thinking about many aspects of social work practice and include theories of human behavior, such as developmental theories and theories underlying practice, such as systems theories.

Examples of theories include transgender theory (Breaux & Thyer, 2021), which explains transgender people and views each individual as an expert on their gender without suggesting pathology or deviance. In addition, new theories are often proposed. One example is the suggestion that social work needs to develop an anti-carceral (i.e., not prison-based) theory (Jacobs, Kim, Whitfield, Gartner, Panichelli, Kattari, Downey, Stuart McQueen, & Mountz, 2021) to align itself with the movement to "defund the police." Instead of coercive and punitive practices often directed at underrepresented minorities, an anti-carceral theory would guide the development of interventions that focus on community-centered and mutual aid alternatives.

Theories are distinguished from values, which are concerned with what should be rather than what is. Instead, theories attempt to understand and explain logical and persistent patterns in phenomena.

Theories cannot stand alone in science. They need to be supported by the other component of science: research methods. Research methods adhere to the following principles:

1. Information is collected from *observing* the world. This observation can be carried out in different ways, but it is different from philosophizing or speculating.

2. The research process steps are *systematic,* not random or haphazard.

3. Studies are *replicated,* repeating studies to see if the same results are found.

People think about the relationship between research methods and theory in different ways. Just as theories explain various phenomena, researchers may use other research methods to explore and examine different topics. The next section of this chapter will describe these different methods and ways of conceptualizing science.

Conceptions of Science

Although science is unified by its shared norms, these days, the actual doing of science varies. Positivism is one model or approach used in the social sciences. (Variations and other terms include logical positivism and empiricism.) This is also known as the **quantitative approach or method in the social sciences.** Positivism, or the quantitative approach, rests on several different principles about how science should be done. One central tenet is that science depends upon the collection of observations that support theories. These observations need to be made objectively. **Objectivity** refers to the condition in which researchers' values and biases do not interfere with their study of the problem to the greatest extent possible. Another principle is that the theories and observations remain separate. A theory ultimately needs to be supported by observations, resulting in laws and rules that help make sense of the world.

Over the years, however, the positivist/quantitative approach and its principles have been questioned. Throughout the social sciences, including social work, positivism's claim to be the same as the scientific method and empirical science has raised skepticism. The questioning derives from two major sources: first, students of the history of science; and second, people who traditionally have been excluded from the scientific community—members of diverse, often minority groups, including women. Each of these sources will be discussed.

Thomas Kuhn explores the nature of science in the classic study *The Structure of Scientific Revolutions* (1970). From studying the history of science, Kuhn concluded that other factors besides specific observations and theoretical necessity lead to the emergence and acceptance of the "best theory." These other factors include values. Kuhn wrote about paradigms, defining a paradigm as "the entire constellation of beliefs, values, techniques and so on shared by members of a given [scientific] community" (Kuhn, 1970). Paradigms function as maps, directing us to the problems that are important to address, the accepted theories, and the procedures needed to solve the problems. Kuhn proposed that paradigms shift over time. Paradigms reflect changing values, countering the idea that you can objectively observe a fixed reality. Objective reality appears to change as paradigms change.

An example of a paradigm shift has occurred in social work during the last one hundred years. In the 1920s and 1930s, the prevailing paradigm or framework for social work practice was psychoanalytic and was tied closely to a medical model. In the 1960s, social work adopted a more ecological systems framework. More recently, the shift is towards empowering individuals, families, groups, and communities, recognizing the impact of racism and oppression. This paradigm shift has important implications for how social workers conceptualize their practice and conduct research. For example, research questions deriving from a medical model differ substantially from those deriving from a systems perspective.

The views of diverse groups, previously denied access to the traditional scientific paradigm, have had an increasing impact on how science is perceived. For example, many argue that the types of questions asked are influenced by the social context of the researcher (Kuhn's point) and that different groups bring different experiences to the research, influencing the types of questions asked.

Participatory action research attempts to address this issue. This research approach has three aims intended to empower clients and open the research process up to allow different voices to be heard. The first aim is to produce knowledge and action directly helpful to groups of people. A second aim is to encourage people to construct and use their own knowledge for empowerment. The third aim is to promote collaboration throughout the research process. Participatory action research originated and grew most rapidly outside the United States, where participatory research historically was restricted in its use to motivate workers to adopt new productivity strategies. For example, in a case study of Xerox Corporation, White (1991) demonstrated how labor, management, and the researcher worked as a team to help increase productivity, instead of simply going in with a plan and recommendations from management's perspective. Although participatory action research (or PAR) is used more widely worldwide, it is far from the dominant research paradigm (Pritchett, Ala'i-Rosales, Cruz, & Cibon, 2021). The sense of exclusion from the research process is felt acutely by those groups already marginalized by society, such as Native Americans in the United States (Innes, 2009) and Aborigines in Australia (Bell et al., 2020).

Usually, the study participants participate actively with the researcher throughout the research process, from the initial design to the final presentation and dissemination of results. The researcher can use several different research methods within the participatory action research framework, including the quantitative or qualitative approach.

In addition to focusing research on women's experiences and addressing gender inequalities, **feminist researchers** have also affected how science is viewed. They argue that men and women experience the world differently and that the objective model of science is more compatible with men's ways of thinking. Because women

---

An Example of Participatory Research

Mountz, Capous-Deyllas, and Sevillano (2020) investigated the educational experiences of LGBTQ youth in foster care, a group that makes up 20 percent of those in care. The youth were directly involved in designing the research. Twenty-five youth were involved in in-depth interviews. Findings revealed that these youth shared educational barriers and challenges common to all youth in foster care, in addition to experiencing chronic bullying and harassment within K-12 educational settings. However, California's network of campus-based support programs for current and former youth in foster care was highly supportive of those who could attend college.

often see the world more in terms of relationships and interactions, feminists think this carries over to the relationship between the researcher and subject. Consequently, this results in them constructing a reality between researcher and subject. This assumption also underlies participatory research. According to feminist researchers and many others, no facts exist that can be objectively observed. This questioning of the principles underlying the positivist approach to science resulted in people in the social sciences adopting alternative research models, including those in social work. Positivism has not been rejected, but researchers now consider other alternatives. **Interpretism** or the **qualitative approach** denotes these alternatives. The positivist/ quantitative and interpretist/qualitative approaches are examined in the following two sections, and the different principles guiding the two methods are discussed.

An Example of Feminist Research

Christensen, Caswell, and Hernandez (2020) studied how Latina college students perceive barriers to help-seeking after experiencing sexual violence. Focus groups and individual interviews collected qualitative data. The primary finding was that the women experienced shame centered around their loss of virginity and prioritizing family as barriers to seeking help.

This is a good time to bring up some other types of alternative approaches that lie outside the scientific paradigm but have been embraced as legitimate approaches to methods of inquiry within social work, both in the past and present. Namely, using an historical method. This method is particularly valuable in carrying out policy research and analysis. See Dybicz (2021) for a full discussion of the role of historical research in social work as it is beyond the scope of this text focussed on the scientific method.

The Positivist/Quantitative Approach to Science

Positivism and the quantitative approach are traditionally equated with science and used predominantly in the natural sciences. Some principles of this approach were described in the previous section; here, they are presented in more detail.

According to the quantitative approach, observations of the world can and must be carried out objectively. The researcher must eliminate as many biases and values as possible. Positivist research methods are designed for this purpose, relying on a clear distinction between the researcher and the subject. Contact between the two is strictly formalized. In quantitative research, the subject becomes the object of study. The science is researcher-driven (Guba, 1990); the subjects have little say about how to conduct the research.

The primary goal of the quantitative approach to science is to search for causes of phenomena. Such a search is possible because it is assumed that the world has an order to be discovered. In other words, positivist researchers strive to identify factors that lead to specific events. For example, if it is determined that if a family lives in a rural area, has more than four children, and is headed by a single parent, there is a decreased likelihood that there will be parental involvement with the children's school system. This information can then help guide social work practice.

Causality means that changes in factors (A) produce variations in another factor or factors (B). Causality can be challenging to establish because it must ensure that *all* the following conditions have been met.

- A statistical association has to exist between the factors. (The intricacies of statistical association will be explained later.)

- Factor or factors A must occur prior to factor or factors B.

- The relationship between factors A and B must not be spurious. In other words, the relationship must not disappear when the effects of other factors are taken into consideration. Due to the complexity of human behavior, this condition is challenging to establish, and many factors impact lives. In reference to the example of the causes of parental involvement with a child's school system, besides parental status (single parent), rural or urban location, or the number of children, there may be other factors that were not considered, such as distance from the school, the grade levels of the children, or educational level of the parent. Unless the researcher considers these factors and assesses their potential impact, it is impossible to establish causality.

The quantitative researcher uses a deductive approach to build knowledge. **Deduction** involves drawing conclusions from the general to the particular. A theory generates questions; these questions are then compared with observations. A day-to-day example of deduction is that because many people do not work at their regular employment on the weekends, the stores will be busiest on Saturdays and Sundays. Observing the numbers of people shopping during the week and weekends would support this deduction, or not. Deducing that an older car will be more likely to develop mechanical problems than a car less than two years old, the researcher can also make observations to support or refute this deduction. In social work, an example of deduction could be applying Piaget's theory of child cognitive development across cultures and then testing this through observations. The researcher then feeds these results back into the theory. Similarly, the more recent theories discussed earlier in this chapter, such as anti-carceral practice and transgender models, can be tested and further developed.

The researcher creates categories of the phenomenon under study before investigation and data collection begin. Numbers are assigned to these categories, which are then statistically analyzed.

The quantitative approach requires studying large numbers of subjects because a central concern is that one should be able to **generalize** the research results to as large a group as possible. Findings from a study can be generalized if they can be applied to other groups rather than being specific to those in the current research. For the results to be generalized, the subjects or participants need to be representative of the groups to which the researcher wants to generalize the findings. The researcher uses specific techniques to ensure this representativeness by selecting or sampling the participants in a certain way. Large groups are also needed because the statistical tests used to analyze the quantitative information usually gathered by positivist research are designed for large numbers of subjects.

As discussed earlier, the quantitative approach has come under increasing criticism in recent years, particularly in the social sciences. In general, critics have questioned whether using this approach to the exclusion of others is appropriate when studying human beings. Therefore, the following section offers alternative approaches to science.

An Example of a Quantitative Study

Telitsyna, Arakantseva, and Zavodilkina (2020) studied the different perceptions about the role of mentors between youth who are at risk and institutionalized versus those who are family-based in the Russian Federation. The present study was conducted using a survey questionnaire with respondents between the ages of fifteen and twenty-three years in Moscow. Data analysis was performed on 1,110 responses using different statistical methods. Results indicated that institutionalized and at-risk youth, more than their family-based peers, perceived the mentor to be their friend. On the other hand, the mentor was perceived as a professional who taught them specific educational and vocational skills for family-based respondents.

The Interpretive/Qualitative Approach to Science

There are several branches of interpretive science, including hermeneutics, ethnomethodology, constructionism, phenomenology, naturalistic inquiry, and qualitative methods. Here we need not be concerned with the distinctions among these approaches (see Patton, 2014, for a good discussion), but rather with their overall assumptions and methods of interpretation.

For the interpretive/qualitative researcher, reality is based on people's definitions of it rather than on something externally present. Therefore, the **subjective** experience, rather than the objective, needs to be studied. Observation takes on a different quality for the qualitative researcher than for the quantitative researcher. People's behavior cannot be observed objectively; instead, the researcher and subject create a reality through their interaction. Because reality is perceived as interactive and constructed, the subject's role in the research process is more active. Instead of being researcher-driven, as in the positivist/quantitative approach, the research process is subject-driven. Subjects, or participants, become partners with the researchers and are empowered in the process. In addition, the qualitative researcher explicitly acknowledges the researcher's biases and values. These are stated explicitly rather than ignored.

Qualitative researchers are primarily interested in **description** rather than explanation. Because of the assumption that reality is socially constructed and is in a state of being mutually shaped, the researcher cannot always establish causality. Instead, the interactive reality is discovered and described.

Qualitative researchers usually build knowledge inductively. **Induction** uses observation to examine the particulars of a phenomenon and then develop generalizations to explain or describe relationships among the attributes. Inductive reasoning involves finding patterns common to separate phenomena.

A social work practice example is that of the school social worker who may see certain similarities in children with behavioral problems. After collecting case examples, the social worker develops a theory that states the children have other characteristics besides behavior problems. For example, the majority may be new immigrants whose parents do not speak English. Their behavioral issues may result from teachers' failures to appreciate the children's difficulty transitioning from home to school. Thus, a theory is built from observations rather than developed by generating questions answered through observations. Qualitative approach or qualitative researchers usually collect **qualitative** data. Qualitative information involves the non-numerical examination of phenomena, using words instead of numbers, and focuses on the underlying meanings and patterns of relationships. Often these underlying patterns are disguised if categories are formed before numerical observations are made. Analysis of qualitative information consists of creating categories after the verbal material is collected. When qualitative data are collected, the number of participants in the study is often small because the focus is on collecting in-depth information to understand the participant's subjective experience of the phenomena under investigation.

An Example of a Qualitative Study

Maria José da Silva Rebelo, Mercedes Fernández, and Carmen Meneses (2020) showed that hostility and anger towards migrants are increasingly documented along with the rise of right-wing views in North America and Europe. The literature repeatedly confirms that discrimination harms the general well-being of migrants while often weakening their trust in helping professionals. This qualitative study in which the migrants were interviewed was conducted in Madrid (Spain). Findings revealed that Muslims and Blacks face the most intense racial hostility. Emotions like fear, sadness, learned helplessness, frustration, rejection, anger, and general mistrust were emphasized by participants. In addition, some migrants highlighted harmful coping mechanisms like isolation, aggressive impulses, approaching mafias, and risky behavior, leading to further rejection from host societies. Suggestions for social workers based on the results include: (a) to use their field experience to raise awareness about racial hostility towards this population, and (b) help identify migrants who may rely on negative coping strategies and so prevent adverse consequences.

See Figure 1.1 to illustrate the relationship between the interpretist/qualitative and positivist/quantitative approaches. Remember that the distinction between the two approaches here is somewhat crude. As mentioned earlier, different terms are often used in different ways, and what they denote is subject to considerable debate. The complex field of the philosophy of science is beyond the scope of this book.

The Choice of a Scientific Approach in Social Work

Having described two basic approaches to science, how do you decide which one to use for social work? There has been quite a debate in social work about this very question. Some professionals argue that social work will lose its credibility as a social science if it abandons the positivist or quantitative approach. They say this is the only method that develops sound knowledge on which to base social work practice. Others defend and promote alternative perspectives, arguing that only they can capture the essence and meaning of social work, reminding us that human behavior is complex and not consistently observable and measurable. Furthermore, they argue that the basic principles underlying the interpretive, alternative approaches are more compatible with social work. They empower the subjects and reflect the diversity of opinions and perspectives within the field more accurately.

The position in this book is that both positivism and interpretivism offer the potential to build knowledge in social work. Different models exist to guide practice, each offering its strengths and weaknesses, so in research, various methods have advantages and disadvantages. Each method is a response to different perceptions of reality. Neither the quantitative nor the qualitative approach can offer the ultimate "truth."

An Example of Using Both Qualitative and Quantitative Approaches

Sahota (2019) examined kinship care in American Indian/Alaska Native communities, reviewing qualitative and quantitative studies. Key findings included: (1) there are disparities in the rates of kinship care placement for children who are AI/AN compared to those who are not AI/AN; (2) existing research focuses on grandparents who are AI/AN and are caring for grandchildren; and (3) qualitative studies show there is a striking depth of emotional connection between these grandparents and grandchildren.

Because both approaches offer advantages, the question becomes which one to use when. The decision depends on the type of inquiry. Some problems are more suited to a quantitative research method, and some to a qualitative one. Take the three questions at the beginning of this chapter:

- Are my visits to Mrs. Garcia helping her cope with the death of her husband? What was her experience with grief counseling?

- How effective is the Change for Families Agency in providing services that support and protect victims of domestic violence? What are the experiences of the clients receiving these services?

- What are the needs of adolescent fathers in Detroit? What are the experiences of these fathers?

At least in the first two questions, the focus is on explanation—in other words, whether and how the programs and interventions are working. These questions intend to produce information that is as objective as possible so that the agencies can make funding decisions and develop programs .

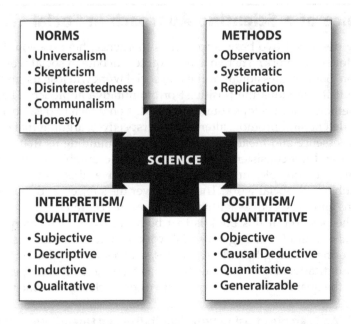

Figure 1.1   Different approaches to science

The second part of each question focuses more on the subjects' experiences, and the goal is to understand rather than explain. As a result, these questions are less concerned with objectivity and the ability to generalize the findings.

Sometimes, the type of question to ask and subsequently the kind of approach to use depends upon our knowledge about the area under study. Qualitative research can help formulate the different aspects of the concept, whether it be the intervention itself, the problem or strength of the client, or the outcome itself. In this way, theories are developed and tested using a quantitative approach. Thus, the generation of knowledge is cyclical, with both approaches integral to developing concepts and theories.

In this book, both approaches will be described, and you will be given guidance about times when one might be more appropriate than the other. Both methods require specific skills, experience, and planning. The suitable choice depends upon the question under study and the overall purpose of the research. As with practice—where, for example, behavioral interventions require a different knowledge base and are appropriate to different circumstances from psychodynamic interventions—no one approach is always better or correct.

Summary

This chapter describes different types of understanding, including values, intuition, experience, authority, and science. The positivist/quantitative and interpretist/

qualitative approaches to science offer advantages in addressing the different types of research questions asked in generalist social work.

STUDY/EXERCISE QUESTIONS

1. List the five different types of understanding presented in this chapter and discuss how you use each of them in your practice. Give specific examples.

2. Go to a public place and observe the people for fifteen minutes. Report back to your class. Note the similarities and differences in what each student observed. Discuss the implications of these observations for the concept of objectivity.

3. Give an example of deduction and induction that you used today outside of the classroom.

4. Identify the instances when you have used the term "cause" during the last few days. Share these instances in class. Did any of them meet the criteria for causality listed in this chapter?

REFERENCES

Bell, S., Angleton, P., Lockyer, A., Ferguson, T., Murray, W., Silver, B., Kaldor, J., Maher, L., & Ward, J. (2020). Working with Aboriginal young people in sexual health research: A peer research methodology in remote Australia. *Qualitative Health Research, 31*(1), 16–28. https://doi.org/10.1177%2F1049732320961348

Breaux, H., & Thyer, B. (2021). Transgender theory for contemporary social work practice: A question of values and ethics. *Journal of Social Work Values and Ethics, 18*(1), 1–71.

Christensen, M., Caswell, C., & Hernandez, F. (2020). Contextualizing barriers to help-seeking after sexual violence: A critical feminist study with Latinx college women. *Affilia, 36*(1), 97–112. https://doi.org/10.1177/0886109920906782

Dybicz, P. (2021). The unfulfilled promise of scientific inquiry in advancing social work knowledge and practice. *Social Sciences & Humanities Open, 3*(1). https://doi.org/10.1016/j.ssaho.2021.100117

Guba, E. G. (Ed.). (1990). *The paradigm dialog.* Newbury Park, CA: Sage.

Innes, R. A. (2009). "Wait a second. Who are you anyways?" The insider/outsider debate and American Indian studies. *American Indian Quarterly, 33*(4), 440–461. https://www.jstor.org/stable/40388481

Jacobs, L., Kim, M. E., Whitfield, D. L., Gartner, R. E., Panichelli, M., Kattari, S. K., Downey, M. M., McQueen, S. S., & Mountz, S. E. (2021). Defund the police: Moving towards an anti-carceral social work. *Journal of Progressive Human Services, 32*(1), 37–62. https://doi.org/10.1080/10428232.2020.1852865

Kuhn, T. (1970). *The structure of scientific revolutions.* Chicago: University of Chicago Press.

Mountz, S., Capous-Desyllas, M., & Sevillano, L. (2020). Educational trajectories of youth formerly in foster care who are LGBTQ: Before, during, and after emancipation. *Child Welfare, 97*(6), 77–100. https://www.jstor.org/stable/48626317

Neuman, W. L. (2006). *Social research methods: Qualitative and quantitative approaches.* Boston: Allyn & Bacon.

Patton, M. Q. (2014). *Qualitative research and evaluation methods.* Thousand Oaks, CA: Sage Publications.

Pritchett, M., Ala'i-Rosales, S., Cruz, A. R. (2021). Social justice is the spirit and aim of an applied science of human behavior: Moving from colonial to participatory research practices. *Behavioral Analysis Practice.* https://doi.org/10.1007/s40617-021-00591-7

Sahota, P. C. (2019). Kinship care for children who are American Indian/Alaska Native: State of the evidence. *Child Welfare, 97*(2), 63–78. https://www.jstor.org/stable/48623644

Telitsyna, A., Arakantseva, T., & Zavodilkina, O. (2020). The perception of mentors and mentorship among youth at risk in the Russian Federation. *Child Welfare, 98*(1), 23–50. https://www.jstor.org/stable/48623678

2

Research and
Generalist Social Work

INTRODUCTION

One problem in understanding the research process is that it is often viewed in isolation rather than closely linked to practice. This chapter will explore the link between research and practice, emphasizing the central role of **evidence-based practice** and drawing parallels between the practice process and the research process.

LEARNING OBJECTIVES

This chapter includes the following learning objectives:

1. To describe generalist social work practice

2. To understand the purpose of research in generalist social work practice

3. To identify the research roles in generalist practice

4. To be able to articulate the similarities between the processes in social work research and practice

5. To gain a beginning understanding of the ethical and human diversity issues in research and practice

Generalist Social Work Practice

Social work has been committed to addressing individual competencies and implementing social change from its inception. Today **generalist social work practice** is the form of social work practice taught in undergraduate programs in the United States and many other parts of the world as a basis for professional social work education.

Over the years, various views have developed about what constitutes generalist practice. The Baccalaureate Program Directors (BPD) webpage defines generalist practice as:

> . . . work with individuals, families, groups, communities, and organizations in various social work and host settings. Generalist practitioners view clients and client systems from a strength's perspective to recognize, support and build upon the innate capabilities of all human beings. They use a professional problem-solving process to engage, assess, broker services, advocate, counsel, educate, and organize with and on behalf of clients and client systems. In addition, generalist practitioners engage in community and organizational development. Finally, generalist practitioners evaluate service outcomes to continually improve the provision and quality of services most appropriate to client needs. The NASW Code of Ethics guides generalist social work practice. It is committed to improving the wellbeing of individuals, families, groups, communities, and organizations and furthering the goals of social justice. (The BPD Website)

Building on this definition, in addition to the concepts presented in the Educational Policy and Accreditation Standards developed by the Council on Social Work Education (CSWE, 2015), Kirst-Ashman and Hull (2018) propose five concepts underpinning generalist social work practice. First, it adopts a theoretical approach in which individuals, families, groups, organizations, and communities are viewed as systems in the environment. Second, generalist social workers use problem-solving to resolve issues. Third, ethical principles focus on human well-being, human rights, and social and economic justice. Fourth, social workers assume a wide array of roles, and fifth, they select the most effective interventions and evaluate their work.

You may use a slightly different definition in your social work practice courses; however, all will usually have the elements identified by BPD and Kirst-Ashman and Hull.

The Purpose of Research in Generalist Social Work Practice

Research plays a prominent role in generalist social work in many different ways. Several of these are related directly to the generalist social work practice elements described previously.

First, research helps generate scientific knowledge for use in practice. This is known as **evidence-based practice**. Second, social workers need to be knowledgeable about research to conduct **ethical practice**. Third, research provides an essential tool in ensuring the **fiscal accountability** of practice. Fourth, research can provide an avenue for the **empowerment** of clients. In turn, we will discuss each of these ways in which research supports social work practice.

Evidence-Based Practice

Scientific knowledge is built by using research methods to develop and refine theories. In the last chapter, we discussed two different research approaches. Each builds knowledge somewhat differently from the other. The quantitative approach uses the deductive method of building theory, deducing premises from the theory and testing those premises. The qualitative approach uses the inductive method, in which the researcher makes observations and builds theories from those systematic observations.

The development of knowledge through research is a central function of research in social work. This knowledge about the extent, nature, and causes of social problems, and the effectiveness of various interventions and programs, significantly enhances social work practice. In recent years, **evidence-based practice** has emerged as a critical approach in social work. This approach "depends on critical thinking to identify empirically validated methods for helping clients" (Briggs & Rzepnicki, 2004, p. xii). The roots of evidence-based practice run deep into social work history. In 1917, in *Social Diagnosis*, Mary Richmond stressed the importance of using empirically based information to understand social problems. In the 1970s, there was a renewed interest in ensuring that social work practice was based on research, and social workers were encouraged to conduct research as a part of their practice (fully discussed in Chapter 7). In addition, other professions are increasingly emphasizing evidence-based practices, particularly in the medical and nursing fields. Thyer (2004) describes a comprehensive history of science and evidence-based social work practice. However we choose to conceptualize evidence-based practice, there is no doubt that it is a present driving force in social work.

Critical thinking is a vital element of evidence-based practice. Such a stance means moving away from "authority-based practice" (Gambrill, 2001) and some other sources of understanding described in the last chapter.

For example, if you were employed in Child Protective Services as an investigator, a critical part of how you would make decisions on family intervention would be based on assessment tools. These tools are based on previous research and are tested using scientific methods. Without such tools, your decision might be based on your authority as an investigator, your intuition, values, or experience—all essential components in the final decision but weakened by the absence of the scientific or evidence-based component.

Entire programs are developed based on research. For example, early intervention programs for new parents are based on research indicating that parent training and support can help reduce the incidence of child abuse and neglect. In addition, the training itself is based on theories of child development that are supported by research.

Similarly, new programs are developed by assessing the needs of certain problems among specific populations. For example, Franchino-Olsen et al. (2020) examined the prevalence of the sex trafficking of children and adolescents in the United States, prompting the planning of new services and interventions to assist this overlooked population.

Once programs are formed, they need to be regularly evaluated to ensure they continue to benefit clients and to identify ways in which the programs need to be changed. For example, Narendorf et al. (2020), in a qualitative combined with a quantitative study, examined the factors that assisted in the success of a mentoring program for youth exiting foster care, and their findings can help shape new programs or adjust those that already exist. Overall, the mentoring appeared successful. Somewhat surprisingly, the difference in cultural and socioeconomic factors did not seem to affect the quality of the mentoring. However, some implicit biases from the mentor's language pointed to further mentoring training.

Evidence-based practice is more feasible now than previously, as accessing the information through such search engines as Google Scholar and ProQuest results in evidence-based practice being more accessible to social work practitioners.

Ethical Issues

Social workers also need to be knowledgeable about research for ethical reasons. Social workers are ethically responsible for providing the best possible services to their clients. In the United States, the NASW (2021) Code of Ethics specifically devotes an entire section to "Evaluation and Research."

- Social workers should monitor and evaluate policies, the implementation of programs, and practice interventions.

- Social workers should promote and facilitate evaluation and research to contribute to the development of knowledge.

- Social workers should critically examine and keep current with emerging knowledge relevant to social work and fully use evaluation and research evidence in their professional practice.

- Social workers should educate themselves, their students, and their colleagues about responsible research practices

In addition to the above guidelines, the NASW Code of Ethics includes several ethical practices that should guide social work research, including informed consent, protection from harm, and maintaining confidentiality and anonymity. We will discuss each of these in further chapters.

Fiscal Accountability

As long as social work practice is predominantly funded by government and charitable contributions, accountability will be a critical issue in the field. In recent years, fiscal accountability has become even more critical. Funds allocated to human services are decreasing rapidly, and different organizations must compete for smaller and smaller pools of money.

We must consider two aspects of social accountability. First, social workers must demonstrate that they are spending money responsibly—this includes the assurance that a social program's goals are met and that funds are distributed most efficiently. The agency or the individual practitioner may be responsible for this accountability. Second, generalist social workers are often called upon to establish new services and programs, particularly in rural areas. To do so and solicit funds for this purpose, you need to substantiate your claim by providing clear evidence of need and a strong basis in research for the proposed program.

Empowering Clients

Not only can research be indirectly empowering to clients—through building knowledge and ensuring fiscal and ethical accountability—but specific research methods can be directly empowering as well. Subjects or participants (often clients) can be directly involved in the research process from planning to implementation. Some research strategies involve clients more than others. For example, in the last chapter, we discussed how the interpretive approach tends to be more subject- rather than researcher-driven. This tendency derives partly from the assumption that meaning emerges from the interaction of subject and researcher rather than from the researcher's objective observations alone. It is possible that through the interpretive approach, clients become empowered because they are not being used as subjects but instead as direct participants in the research. This involvement of the subjects is also possible when using the quantitative approach to research, as discussed in the previous chapter.

An Example of Participatory Research

Gillard et al. (2021) studied the impact of COVID-19 on people with pre-existing mental health conditions in the United Kingdom, using in-depth qualitative methods. In a participatory, coproduced approach, researchers with lived experiences of mental health conditions conducted interviews and analyzed data as part of a multi-disciplinary research team. Existing mental health difficulties were exacerbated for many people. They struggled for social connectedness and had inadequate access to mental health services. Some found new ways to cope and connect to the community. New remote ways to access mental health care, including digital solutions, provided support for some but presented barriers for others. People from Black, Asian, and minority ethnic (BAME) communities experienced heightened anxiety, stigma, and racism associated with the pandemic, further impacting their mental health.

Research Roles/Competencies in Generalist Practice

As we have seen, generalist social work practice is based on research, and practitioners must assess or examine their practice in terms of research. The Council on Social Work Education in the United States Educational Policy and Accreditation Standards (2022) clearly defines the different research roles or competencies social workers must assume. Two of the nine competencies (Competency 4 and Competency 9) directly address the research roles of social workers.

Competency 4: Engage Practice-informed Research and Research-informed Practice

Social workers use ethical, culturally informed, anti-racist, and anti-oppressive approaches to research and to build knowledge. First, social workers use research to inform their practice decision-making and articulate how their practice experience informs research and evaluation decisions. Second, social workers critically evaluate and critique current, empirically sound research to inform practice, policy, and programs. Third, social workers understand the inherent bias in research and evaluate design, analysis, and interpretation using an anti-racist and anti-oppressive perspective. Fourth, social workers know how to access, critique, and synthesize the current literature to develop appropriate research questions and hypotheses. Fourth, social workers demonstrate knowledge and skills regarding qualitative and quantitative research methods and analysis, and they interpret data derived from these methods. Third, social workers demonstrate knowledge about methods to assess reliability and validity in social work research. Fourth, social workers can articulate and share research findings in ways usable to various clients and constituencies. Finally, social workers understand the value of evidence derived from interprofessional and diverse research methods, approaches, and sources.

Social workers:

- Apply research findings to inform and improve practice, policy, and programs; and

- Identify ethical, culturally informed, anti-racist, and anti-oppressive strategies that address inherent biases for use in quantitative and qualitative research methods to advance the purposes of social work.

Competency 9: Evaluate Practice with Individuals, Families, Groups, Organizations, and Communities

Social workers understand that evaluation is an ongoing component of the dynamic and interactive process of social work practice with and on behalf of diverse individuals, families, groups, organizations, and communities. Social workers evaluate processes and outcomes to increase the effectiveness of practice, policy, and service delivery. Social workers apply anti-racist and anti-oppressive perspectives in evaluating outcomes. Social workers understand theories of human behavior and person-in-environment and interprofessional conceptual frameworks and assess critically and apply this knowledge in evaluating outcomes. Social workers use qualitative and quantitative methods for evaluating outcomes and practice effectiveness.

Social workers:

- Select and use culturally responsive methods for evaluation of outcomes; and

- Critically analyze outcomes and apply evaluation findings to improve practice effectiveness with individuals, families, groups, organizations, and communities.

These competencies include reference to the two research roles undertaken by social workers.

The Consumer

As was discussed earlier, the scientific approach is essential in building a knowledge base for social work and directly informs practice through the use of the evidence-based practice approach. This approach currently drives the social work researcher as a consumer.

To use this knowledge in an informed manner, social workers need to understand research methods to evaluate the extent of a theory's research base. Even if the theory has been validated and supported by research, there is no guarantee this research is of high quality. Moreover, the research can include racist and oppressive assumptions that bias the research.

A social worker who is knowledgeable about research can better evaluate the quality of that research base. Unfortunately, many mistakes and errors occur even in published research. Your research instructor can undoubtedly confirm this statement.

Critical research analysis is also helpful in the social worker's assessment of specific practice techniques. For example, generalist practitioners often provide home-based services, and there exists a whole body of literature and research about these services. The practitioner informed about research can turn to this research for practice guidelines. For example, using research in this way, the practitioner may be able to answer a question such as "How do I know whether home visits to eighty-five-year-old Mrs. Garcia will help prevent her placement in a nursing home?"

Gambrill (2004) describes the steps of evidence-based practice as follows:

1. Converting information needs related to practice decisions into answerable questions

2. Tracking down, with maximum efficiency, the best evidence with which to answer questions

3. Critically appraising the evidence for its validity, impact (size of effect), and applicability (usefulness in practice)

4. Applying the results of this appraisal to practice and policy decisions. This involves deciding whether evidence found (if any) applies to the decision at hand (e.g., Is a client similar to those studied? Is there access to services described?) and considering client values and preferences, as well as other applicability concerns, in making decisions.

5. Evaluating the effectiveness and efficiency in carrying out steps 1–4 and seeking ways to improve them in the future.

This text will give you the tools to conduct each of these steps and provide you with a foundation on which to guide practice.

The Producer

The second reason social workers need to know about research methods is the most obvious. Armed with this knowledge, social workers can then use the methods directly in their practice to answer questions that arise. This ability to use research methods is vital whenever answers cannot be found in the existing literature, as is frequent in social work, whether or not the social worker is engaged in generalist practice. For example, social workers often need to research the effectiveness of many interventions they use. In addition, generalist social workers are usually required to demonstrate the need to provide new services or improve existing services. Clearly, this type of inquiry also demands knowledge and the implementation of research methods.

In sum, generalist social workers, acting as producers of research, can build new knowledge for practice. This aspect of research is key to the overall concept of evidence-based practice. Though the production of research may seem overwhelming to you at this point, this book will describe how to produce research step-by-step. This text will provide you with the tools to become a critical and intelligent consumer of research and an active and engaged producer of research.

Remember that social workers routinely use many of the skills and techniques described in this book without formal research training or education. Social workers act as consumers of the literature, for example, when they read reports and gather relevant information. As producers, social workers collect data from multiple sources. In addition, they document progress toward clients' goals, write reports, and engage in many other activities that, as we will see, are all included in the larger activity of research.

Research and Generalist Practice Processes

Social workers are often intimidated by research because they think it involves types of knowledge and skills that are very different from those of practice. As we are about to see, the processes of practice and research are very similar, particularly for generalist social work practice.

As discussed earlier in this chapter, although the generalist perspective is conceptualized in different ways, authors of generalist social work texts are in basic agreement on a general process for practice. This process is usually conceptualized sequentially, consisting of progressive stages leading to specific goals. This concept originated with one of the founding mothers of social work practice theory, Helen Harris Perlman (1957), who proposed "operations" as part of the practice process. Others later modified these operations; for example, Pincus and Minahan (1973) described "guideposts for the process"; Schulman (1992) and Egan (1994) proposed "stages" or "phases"; and Kirst-Ashman and Hull (2018) "planned change steps." For our purposes in this chapter, we will refer to the processes outlined by Kirst-Ashman and Hull.

Engagement

A critical step in social work practice is building the relationship between the social worker and the client, a relationship that respects the client's uniqueness. Kirst-Ashman and Hull describe engagement as "the initial period where you as a practitioner orient yourself to the problem at hand and begin to establish communication and a relationship with others also addressing the problem" (p. 43).

Also critical in social work research is the establishment of a relationship. Traditionally there was a clear distinction between the researcher and the "subject," and a relationship was not part of the equation. However, more recently, it has become apparent that developing a more meaningful relationship and developing a sense of engagement between the researcher and the "participant" more fully informs the research and can serve as a means of empowerment for the client. Participatory action research provides the framework for this relationship and is rapidly becoming the preferred approach to social work research. For example, suppose your agency wants to assess some of the problems and difficulties faced by migrant adolescents. In that case, an essential first step is establishing relationships with some professionals and any family members who have contact with these adolescents. In this way, they can become partners in your research.

Assessment

According to Kirst-Ashman and Hull, assessment refers to "the investigation and determination of variables affecting an identified problem or issue as viewed from micro, mezzo, or macro perspectives" (p. 45) and involves four steps:

1. Identify your client

2. Assess the client in situation from micro, mezzo, or macro and diversity perspectives

3. Cite information about client problems and needs

4. Identify client strengths

Parallel steps occur in research from *deciding on the question* (see Chapter 3), *writing the literature review,* and *identifying the variables* (see Chapter 4). During these research processes, a form of assessment occurs in that the research question is formulated based on an analysis and greater understanding of its larger context. This analysis also helps frame the type of research undertaken.

For example, consider the issue of migrant adolescents. Instead of simply conceptualizing the question as "the problem of migrant adolescents," greater clarity needs to be sought. Instead, the researcher states: "To what extent are the needs of migrant adolescents met?" And then framing from a strengths perspective, "What are some of the strengths of this population?" As we proceed with the research and begin to explore previous research through conducting a literature review, new insights occur, and further information is gathered, which may lead to a reformulation of the research question. For example, the question may change to focus on evaluating the services of a specific agency: "To what extent is program X serving the needs of migrant adolescents?" This question may then become even more explicit: "How effective is program X in advocating for migrant adolescents?" Or from more of a strengths perspective:

"What are some of the characteristics of programs that successfully serve migrant adolescents?" After this period of study specific variables in the research question can be identified and defined.

In our example on migrant adolescents, we would need to define the term "advocating." How does the agency see this role, and how can it be defined so that all concerned agree? What do we mean by "effective" or "successful"? That all migrant adolescents referred to the agency receive advocacy services? Half of the adolescents? How are migrant adolescents defined? What ages will be included in this study? From what country did the adolescents originate? All these questions need to be answered during this research stage, just as they need to be answered in practice.

Planning

The next step in practice, according to Kirst-Ashman and Hull, is "specifying what should be done" (p. 47) involving the steps of

1. Work with the client

2. Prioritize problems

3. Translate problems into needs

4. Evaluate levels of intervention for each need

5. Establish goals

6. Specify objectives

7. Specify action steps

8. Formalize a contract (p. 47)

A very similar step occurs in the research process, in the designing of the research. The *research design* depends on the type of research question being asked (see Chapters 5, 6, and 7). The design lays out, just as in practice, what needs to be accomplished for the completion of the research.

In our migrant adolescents example, the research design might include a comparison group of adolescents who do not receive services from program X—which provides services specifically to migrants—but instead receive services from a more generic type of agency.

Another aspect of the plan is deciding who will be the participants in the research, known as *sampling* (discussed in Chapter 8). The sample in the migrant adolescents research might be relatively small, maybe only ten or so, so their selection will need careful consideration. Arrangements would also need to be made for an interpreter if the researcher does not have the necessary language skills.

Implementation

According to Kirst-Ashman and Hull, the next stage in practice is implementing or "doing" the plan. Research too has its "doing step," notably the *data collection* (discussed in Chapter 9). In this stage, data would be collected from the sample according to the research design, using one or more data collection methods. In the migrant adolescents example, the researcher may interview the adolescents using an open-ended interview schedule.

Evaluation

Kirst-Ashman and Hull stress the importance of this stage in practice as one that determines the effectiveness of the interventions. In part, of course, this is the overall goal of the research. However, we can also identify a parallel step in the research process, namely the *analysis* stage (Chapters 10, 11, and 12). Here the data collected during the implementation stage is subject to close examination using several different techniques depending upon whether the researcher undertakes a qualitative or quantitative approach. If quantitative data are collected, statistical methods are used. However, the information is sorted and categorized with qualitative data, so meaning emerges. As in practice, the analysis step is carried out systematically and conscientiously to avoid misinterpreting the results. Specific techniques are used to ensure bias-free results. Results often generate new questions and issues, much as the social worker generates plans in practice.

Analysis of the data about migrant adolescents may reveal that those in program X thought they had received more advocacy services than those from the comparison program Y. Still, those in program X were less satisfied with the types of medical services available to them. Another phase of the research might include examining the source of this dissatisfaction from program X.

Termination

In generalist practice, the social worker cannot just walk away once the intervention has been implemented and evaluated. Instead, the social worker needs to identify the progress made and communicate this. Similarly, in research, the final stage is the *writing of the report*, which formally presents the analyzed results along with a description of the research method (see Chapter 13).

The research report includes a complete description of the research steps and recommendations for further research. An essential part of the report in social work research is the discussion of the limitations of the research, which in the migrant example might include the adolescents not fully understanding the questions even though an interpreter was present. They may have underplayed some of their problems. Thus, the answers were biased, making the program appear more effective than it really was. The report also includes a section on the research implications for practice: How can the findings help social workers in the field? The researcher may recommend further research into the reasons for the dissatisfaction of the adolescents.

Follow-up

The last step in practice is often known as follow-up. Kirst-Ashman and Hull point out that this stage tends to be the most neglected in practice and involves "checking to find out whether clients have maintained progress and are still functioning well on their own" (p. 52). Not only does a parallel step occur in research, but it also tends to be neglected. In research, this step involves *disseminating findings and utilizing research*; the researcher can do this in a variety of ways, such as publishing a report and distributing to organizations that serve adolescent migrants nationally and internationally. Again, there are a multitude of ways of disseminating the results electronically.

It is important to note that disseminating research findings and their ultimate utilization is a critical step in evidence-based practice. This comparison of research and practice processes brings us full circle from the producer to the consumer of research discussed earlier in this chapter. See Table 2.1 for a comparison of these steps of research and practice

TABLE 2.1 The Relationship Between Research and Practice

Practice	Research
Engagement	Using participatory methods
Assessment	Deciding on the question, writing the literature review, and identifying the variables
Planning	Research design and sampling
Implementation	Collection of data
Evaluation	Data analysis
Termination	Writing the report
Follow-up	Dissemination and utilization of the research findings

Values and Ethics in Research and Practice

Besides the similarities in the processes of research and practice, there is a similarity in their values and ethics. Social workers' ethical codes reflect values relating to social workers' conduct and responsibilities to their clients, colleagues, employers, profession, and society. In the United States, the NASW Code of Ethics (2021), which you can find in Appendix C, includes ethical standards that apply to research. Many of these ethical standards are directly related to the ones underlying practice, such as confidentiality, privacy, and self-determination. Some of these standards were listed earlier in this chapter. Here are the remaining standards with reference to the chapters where we will consider them in more detail:

- Social workers engaged in evaluation or research should carefully consider possible consequences and should follow guidelines developed to protect evaluation and research participants. In addition, the researcher should consult the appropriate institutional review boards (Chapter 9).

- Social workers engaged in evaluation or research should obtain voluntary and written informed consent from participants, when appropriate, without any implied or actual deprivation or penalty for refusal to participate; without undue inducement to participate; and with due regard for participants' well-being, privacy, and dignity. Informed consent should include information about the nature, extent, and duration of the participation requested and disclosure of the risks and benefits of participation in the research (Chapters 6 and 8).

- When using electronic technology to facilitate evaluation or research, social workers should ensure that participants provide informed consent for the use of such technology. Social workers should assess whether participants can use the technology and, when appropriate, offer reasonable alternatives to participate in the evaluation or research (Chapters 6 and 8).

- When evaluation or research participants are incapable of giving informed consent, social workers should provide an appropriate explanation to the participants, obtain the participants' assent to the extent they are able, and obtain written consent from an appropriate proxy (Chapters 6 and 8).

- Social workers should never design or conduct evaluation or research that does not use consent procedures, such as certain forms of naturalistic observation and archival research, unless a rigorous and responsible review of the research has found it to be justified because of its prospective scientific, educational, or applied value and unless equally effective alternative procedures that do not involve waiver of consent are not feasible (Chapters 6 and 8).

- Social workers should inform participants of their right to withdraw from evaluation and research at any time without penalty (Chapters 6 and 8).

- Social workers should take appropriate steps to ensure that participants in evaluation and research have access to appropriate supportive services (Chapter 9).

- Social workers engaged in evaluation or research should protect participants from unwarranted physical or mental distress, harm, danger, or deprivation (Chapter 9).

- Social workers engaged in the evaluation of services should discuss collected information only for professional purposes and only with people professionally concerned with this information (Chapter 9).

- Social workers engaged in evaluation or research should ensure the anonymity or confidentiality of participants and of the data obtained from them. Social workers should inform participants of any limits of confidentiality, the measures that will be taken to ensure confidentiality, and when any records containing research data will be destroyed (Chapter 9).

- Social workers who report evaluation and research results should protect participants' confidentiality by omitting identifying information unless proper consent has been obtained authorizing disclosure (Chapter 9 and 13).

- Social workers should report evaluation and research findings accurately. They should not fabricate or falsify results and should take steps to correct any errors later found in published data using standard publication methods (Chapters 11 and 12).

- Social workers engaged in evaluation or research should be alert to and avoid conflicts of interest and dual relationships with participants, should inform participants when an actual or potential conflict of interest arises, and should take steps to resolve the issue in a manner that makes participants' interests primary (Chapter 5).

Research and Human Diversity

By human diversity, we mean the whole spectrum of differences among populations. The Council on Social Work Education in the United States Educational Policy and Accreditation Standards (2022) address the issue of human diversity in their Competency 3: "engage anti-racism, diversity, equity and inclusion in practice." This states:

> The dimensions of diversity are understood as the intersectionality of factors including but not limited to age, caste, class, color, culture, disability and ability, ethnicity, gender, gender identity and expression, generational status, immigration status, legal status, marital status, political ideology, race, nationality, religion and spirituality, sex, sexual orientation, and tribal sovereign status.

In practice, we recognize the importance of understanding and appreciating group differences, so we will not impose inappropriate expectations; we must also account for these differences in research. In research and practice, we must always be aware of the different assumptions we may be making. If we are not mindful of our assumptions regarding specific groups, these assumptions can be disguised and undisclosed, causing biases in the research itself. Clarifying assumptions is only one way researchers should consider human diversity issues in the research process.

The issue of these assumptions is closely linked to the issue of ethics in research and practice. Unfortunately, in the past, there have been many unethical violations committed in the name of research, usually with vulnerable populations including prisoners, the homeless, victims of domestic violence, and other groups. In 1978, in response to these violations, the Belmont Report (National Commission for the Protection of Human Subjects of Biomedical and Behavioral Research, 1978, revised in 2017) was issued, outlining right and proper research conduct, particularly with vulnerable populations. The principles included in the report are:

1. Respect for persons: We recognize the personal dignity and autonomy of individuals, and we should provide special protection to those persons with diminished autonomy

2. Beneficence: We have an obligation to protect persons from harm by maximizing anticipated benefits and minimizing risks of harm

3. Justice: The benefits and burdens of research should be distributed fairly

The NASW Code of Ethics draws from the Belmont Report in guiding the conduct of research among all groups. As with ethics, each chapter in this book will discuss human diversity issues as they relate to research.

Summary

In conclusion, research and practice follow parallel processes in approaching problems. When research methods are viewed in this way, they appear far less intimidating. We all know that practice can be frustrating; in truth, so can research. Just as practice has its great rewards, however, so does research. The road at times is a rocky one, but ultimately we all benefit.

STUDY/EXERCISE QUESTIONS

1. Discuss some of how you may find yourself engaged in research as a generalist social worker.

2. Select a research article from a social work journal. How could the findings from this research help you in your practice?

3. Select a research article from a social work journal. How would you change the research to make it more participatory?

4. Imagine you were asked to evaluate the program where you were working (use your field placement as an example). How would you justify the importance of this research to a fellow student?

5. Select one of the standards relating to research in the NASW Code of Ethics. Select a partner in the class. One of you will argue why this standard is essential, and the other will provide a counterargument.

6. Give a specific example of how you might use evidence-based practice in your present field placement.

REFERENCES

Briggs, H., & Rzepnicki, T. L. (Eds.). (2004) *Using evidence in social work practice*. Chicago: Lyceum.

Council on Social Work Education. (2022). *Educational policy and accreditation standards*. Available online at https://www.cswe.org/accreditation/standards/2022-epas/

Egan, G. (1994). *The skilled helper: A problem management approach to helping*. Pacific Grove, CA: Brooks/Cole.

Franchino-Olsen, H., Chesworth, B. R., Boyle, C., Rizo, C. F., Martin, S. L., Jordan, B., et al. (2022). The prevalence of sex trafficking of children and adolescents in the United States: A scoping review. *Trauma, Violence, & Abuse, 23*(1), 182–195. https://doi.org/10.1177%2F1524838020933873

Gambrill, E. (2004). Contributions of critical thinking and evidence-based practice to the fulfillment of the ethical obligations of professionals. In Briggs, H. & Rzepnicki, T. L. (Eds.), *Using evidence in social work practice* (pp. 3–19). Chicago: Lyceum.

Gillard, S., Dare, C., Hardy, J., Nyikavaranda, P., Rowan Olive, R., Shah, P., Birken, M., Foye, U., Ocloo, J., Pearce, El., Stefanidou, T., Pitman, A., Simpson, A., Johnson, S., & Lloyd-Evans, B. (2021). Experiences of living with mental health problems during the COVID-19 pandemic in the UK: A coproduced, participatory qualitative interview study. *Social Psychiatry and Psychiatric Epidemiology, 56*(8), 1447–1457. https://doi.org/10.1007/s00127-021-02051-7

Kirst-Ashman, K. K., & Hull, G. H. (2018). *Understanding generalist practice* (8th ed.). Boston: Cengage.

Narendorf, S. C., Boyd, R., Mytelka, C., Vittoria, K., & Green, M. (2020). Bridging the transition. *Child Welfare, 97*(6), 205–232. https://www.jstor.org/stable/48626323

National Association of Social Workers. (2021). NASW Code of Ethics. Available online at https://www.socialworkers.org/About/Ethics/Code-of-Ethics/Code-of-Ethics-English

National Commission for the Protection of Human Subjects of Biomedical and Behavioral Research (1978). *The Belmont Report: Ethical principles and guidelines for the protection of human subjects of research*. Washington, D.C.: Department of Health Education and Welfare.

Perlman, H. H. (1957). *Social casework: A problem-solving process*. Chicago: University of Chicago Press.

Pincus, A., & Minahan, A. (1973). *Social work practice: Model and method*. Itasca, IL: Peacock.

Richmond, M. (1917). *Social diagnosis*. New York: Russell Sage Foundation.

Schulman, L. (1992). *The skills of helping individuals, families, and groups*. Itasca, IL: Peacock.

Thyer, B. A. (2004). Science and evidence-based social work practice. In Briggs, H., & Rzepnicki, T. L. (Eds.), *Using evidence in social work practice* (pp. 74–90). Chicago: Lyceum.

3

Deciding on the Question

INTRODUCTION

"How do I know whether this is a *real* research question? Is this what a research question should look like?" You will find yourself asking these kinds of questions when first confronted with deciding on the research question. As a generalist social worker, you may not always decide on the question; the agency often makes this decision before your involvement in the research. You need to be familiar with the procedure involved in deciding the question to understand (as in practice) how one step in the process leads to the next. You also need to learn about this research stage to evaluate your own practice, a process that is described later in this chapter.

As discussed in Chapter 2, one of the early steps in the research process—deciding on the question—is equivalent to one of the first steps in practice: assessment. In research, as in practice, this step is one of the most challenging, and the process is ongoing and involves continuously reworking and reevaluating.

LEARNING OBJECTIVES

This chapter includes the following learning objectives:

1. To identify the factors that help in the formulation of a social work research question

2. To understand the three main research strategies: explanatory, exploratory, and descriptive research

3. To describe the three types of research questions used in social work: program evaluations, needs assessments, and practice evaluations.

4. To understand the role of the agency in deciding on the research question

5. To analyze the ethical and human diversity influences on deciding on the research question

Sources of Questions

For generalist social workers, research problems or questions usually are determined by the agency; and they direct these questions to solve issues arising in practice and are aimed at practical outcomes. This type of research is known as **applied research**. On the other hand, when we focus on satisfying our intellectual curiosity, even if the results will eventually be applied to help solve practice problems, this is known as **pure research**.

An example will help clarify this definition. You are employed in an agency where a large proportion of the clients are victims of spousal abuse, and you see this as a growing problem. A pure research question would concern the causes of spousal abuse per se. As a generalist social worker employed in the agency, however, you would ask applied research questions, such as how well your agency serves the victims or what other services this client population needs.

If this distinction between pure and applied research still seems difficult to understand, some would argue that the distinction does not exist in social work. However, social work is an applied field, so any question related to social work in any way will be some type of applied question.

Personal experiences also come into play in the formulation of research questions. For example, you may find yourself working with some physically challenged young adults in the agency. You become aware that these clients have some specialized housing needs. After consulting with your supervisor, you want to determine if the need is extensive enough to justify advocating for increasing housing opportunities in the community. Your interest also may have stemmed partly from the fact that a member of your family is physically challenged.

The following is a checklist you can use to test whether the question you are considering can be successfully answered.

- Does this topic really interest me? (For example, am I choosing this topic to please someone else, or do I have a genuine interest in it?)   Yes____   No____

- Do I think this problem is appropriate for scientific inquiry? (For instance, if the question is along the lines of whether child abuse is morally wrong, the question may not be a suitable topic for scientific inquiry, as we discussed in Chapter 1.)   Yes____   No____

- Do I have enough resources available to investigate this topic? (For example, will the topic require many time-consuming interviews or large samples that will be costly to access? Do other people or I have the time and money to pursue the topic appropriately?)   Yes____   No____

- Will this topic raise ethical problems? (For instance, will the questions to be asked of participants arouse potentially harmful emotions? Will the participants in the research, feel coerced in any way?)   Yes____   No____

- Will I be able to secure permission—from the agency, community, clients, and so on—to carry out this research?   Yes____   No____

- Will the research be able to address human diversity issues?   Yes____   No____

- Will the participants be involved in the design and implementation of the research?   Yes____   No____

- Are the research results going to be useful and have implications for the practice of social work?   Yes____   No____

Note that research questions are constantly under review and can change at any time, given the availability of new knowledge or new resources. For example, it might be that a local politician recently became interested in housing for the physically challenged and is asking about community support for the development of special facilities. Hence the focus of your research might shift to community attitudes. Alternatively, in a recent issue of *Social Work*, you read about a study identifying some of the housing difficulties confronting the physically challenged. This, too, may change the focus of your research.

Research Strategies

Once you decide on the main thrust of the research question, you can then begin to think about the type of research strategy you will use to answer the question. In many ways, the initial question drives the process, which is determined by three factors: (1) the intent or goal of the research; (2) the amount of information we already have on the topic to be investigated; and (3) the intended audience. There are two main strategies: descriptive and explanatory.

Descriptive Research

Descriptive research describes records and reports phenomena. Descriptive research can provide important fundamental information for establishing and developing social programs, but it is not primarily concerned with causes. Many surveys trying to determine the extent of a particular social problem—for example, the extent of child sexual abuse—are descriptive. An entire approach to research, called **survey research**, focuses on describing the characteristics of a group; this type of research will be discussed further in Chapter 5. Descriptive research can use either the quantitative or qualitative approach.

The researcher can produce detailed descriptions of phenomena using the qualitative approach, carefully selecting the participants. However, if the intention is for the results to be generalized to broader populations and used as the justification for new or expanded services, the quantitative approach would probably be more suitable. Here, it would be of more benefit to collect relatively objective quantitative data describing the phenomena (rather than seeking people's subjective experiences) and select the research participants according to how well they represent the population under study.

You will encounter descriptive research in social work journals. A considerable amount of policy evaluation and analysis is of this type. As a generalist practitioner, you may also engage in descriptive research. For example, you could be asked

---

An Example of Descriptive Research

Using survey research, Watson et al. (2022) described the needs and difficulties of K–12 students and their families during the COVID-19 pandemic. The researchers surveyed 1,275 school social workers during the spring 2020 school closures. The findings indicated that the children and families they served had significant unmet basic needs, including food, healthcare, and housing. Poverty and mental health compounded pandemic difficulties associated with the sociodemographic makeup of schools. In addition, student engagement in social work services during the closures was significantly lower than pre-pandemic levels. Several policies and practice implications arose from these findings, including a need for additional services for students and families, a plan to address structural inequities in schools and communities, and coordinated outreach to reengage missing students. In addition, they recognized the vital work done by school staff coupled with a need for additional support and resources to combat persistent inequality.

to present some descriptive data relating to your agency (number of clients served, types of problems, and so forth) or to your community (the proportion of the population living below the poverty line, for example). Your supervisor may also require you to keep a journal describing your activities in the agency.

Explanatory Research

Explanatory research aims to provide explanations of events to identify causes rather than simply describe phenomena. For example, a descriptive study might examine the extent of self-mutilating behavior among teenage girls. In contrast, an explanatory study would try to identify the factors associated with the causes of this phenomenon. Explanatory research requires the formulation of a **hypothesis**, which is simply a statement about the relationships between certain factors.

An Example of Explanatory Research

Mogro-Wilson and Cifuentes (2021) studied Latino fathers' parenting. They examined the relationship of six Latinx cultural constructs—familismo, simpatia, personalismo, respeto, traditional machismo, and caballerismo—on the parenting style of Latino fathers. In addition, the researchers examined data from 309 Latino fathers on the relationship between authoritative, authoritarian, and permissive parenting styles and cultural values. Using statistical analysis, the researchers found that higher levels of personalismo and caballerismo and lower levels of traditional machismo were associated with authoritative parenting. Whereas higher levels of simpatia, respeto, and traditional machismo and lower personalismo and caballerismo were associated with authoritarian parenting, higher levels of familismo, simpatia, respeto, and traditional machismo and lower levels of personalismo and caballerismo were associated with permissive parenting.

Hypothesis

Hypotheses usually have an "if x, then y" structure. For example, "If the ethnicity of the group leader is the same as the client, then success in the group will be more likely." Or "If a teenage girl's mother experiences major health problems, then the girl is more likely to engage in self-mutilating behavior."

As discussed in Chapter 1, certain conditions need to be met to establish causality, central to explanatory research. These three conditions are rigorous and often challenging to establish. First, *two factors must be associated with one another.* Usually, this association is established empirically. For example, you might determine a relationship between the grade B.S.W. students received in the practice class and their grade in the field. That relationship, however, does not necessarily mean that the practice grade caused success in the field. The other conditions of causality also need to be met. The second condition is that *the cause precedes the effect in time.* For example, you need to demonstrate that students completed their practice courses before entering the field in our example. The third element of causality is that *other factors cannot*

An Example of Hypothesis
Lamothe, Geoffrion, and Guay (2022) tested the hypothesis that if Child Protective Services workers are victims of psychological and physical acts of aggression perpetrated by their clients, then this places the workers at greater risk for subsequent victimization as they become emotionally unavailable to their clients. The researchers administered questionnaires to 173 CPS workers who had suffered acts of aggression within the last month. Additional questionnaires were administered two, six, and twelve months later. Statistical analysis of the responses took into account sociodemographic factors and supervisor support. The results indicated that the workers were more likely to be victimized in the short term if they did not take sick leave, but not in the long term. Supervisor support did not seem to impact this outcome.

explain the relationship between the factors. In our example, it is possible that other factors, such as past experience, had as much impact on field performance as the practice course grade.

In each step of the research process, explanatory research tries to address these conditions of causality. In reality, meeting all three conditions is often extremely difficult; the best we can expect is that only one or two of the conditions will be met. A positivist approach is often most appropriate when testing hypotheses and carrying out explanatory research. Qualitative data, however, can often be used to add depth and detail to the findings and assist in accepting or rejecting the hypothesis.

As generalist social workers, you may be directly involved in explanatory research. Usually, you would not undertake such research alone but would participate as a team member. For example, a typical project would be to determine the effectiveness of a particular program or agency.

Exploratory Research

Beyond the strategies of explanatory and descriptive research, another strategy, **exploratory research,** deserves mention. You adopt this strategy when you know very little about the topic. Such studies can adopt either an explanatory or a descriptive strategy. A qualitative or quantitative approach is appropriate with exploratory research, although exploratory research is often associated with the former. Exploratory research often determines a study's feasibility and raises questions to be investigated by more extensive studies using either the descriptive or the explanatory strategy.

For example, you might suspect that the ethnicity of a group leader is essential for success in the support group you have organized for children of alcoholics. However, the group leader is Puerto Rican. After interviewing some of the clients in the group to get their opinions, you find that the Puerto Rican clients were more likely than the others to state that the group was successful. Based on these results from the exploratory study, you plan to undertake more extensive research to evaluate the impact of the group leader's ethnicity on clients' perceptions of success.

An Example of Exploratory Research

Sicora, Lu, and Lei (2020) carried out an exploratory comparative study investigating errors made by social work practitioners. Two groups of social workers, one in Italy and one in mainland China, answered questions about the causes and effects of mistakes, professional errors, and reactions to mistakes made by their colleagues. They also looked at the influence of intuition on the decision-making process that generates mistakes and errors of professional judgment. The biggest differences between the Italian and Chinese respondents were their willingness to talk about their mistakes and their confidence in training. A longer social work tradition in Italy helps practitioners in that country to feel stronger and to engage in a reflective learning process rather than defensive actions. On the other hand, as members of a new and not yet fully recognized profession, social workers in Mainland China are more likely to blame external circumstances for adverse outcomes. However, both groups shared the same positive consideration of intuition and the risk of losing service users' trust.

Types of Questions

This section will explore the different types of applied research questions asked in generalist practice. The following questions from Chapter 1 provide examples of these different types of questions.

Practice evaluations evaluate the effectiveness of individual practice:

1. How effective is the grief counseling I am providing to Mrs. Garcia in helping her cope with her husband's death?

2. How is Mrs. Garcia experiencing the grief counseling I provided?

Program evaluations evaluate the effectiveness of a program:

1. How effective is the Change for Families program in providing services that support and protect victims of domestic violence?

2. What are the experiences of the clients who receive services from Change for Families?

Needs assessments describe the extent of a social problem

1. What are the needs of adolescent fathers in Detroit?

2. What is it like to be a teenage father in Detroit?

Note that two examples are offered for each type of question. As we discussed in Chapter 1, the first example for every kind of question is asked in a more appropriate way for the quantitative approach—for example, "Program X received additional funding for next year. How can we show our program is effective and deserves more money?" The second example for each type of question is more appropriate for the qualitative approach—for example, "In what areas could our program be improved and what are our clients' experiences with the program?" The choice of the type of question depends on the knowledge already existing on the topic under study as well as the overall purpose of the research.

These types of questions, practice evaluations, program evaluations, and needs assessments, represent the different types of applied research encountered by generalist social workers in their practice. In addition, the researcher can undertake other types and forms of research, but as discussed earlier in this chapter, they are less applied. For example, a more "pure" social science research question might ask, "What are the factors associated with (or the causes of) teenage fatherhood?" While this can generate essential new knowledge, it generally is not the type of research question a generalist social worker would undertake, but perhaps the type of question you would ask if you were writing a thesis or a dissertation in social work.

We will now discuss the different types of questions in more detail.

Practice Evaluations

One type of research question that often occurs in social work practice is concerned with the effectiveness of an individual social worker's practice. Practice evaluations usually involve only one case, subject, or client system and require social workers to use specific criteria and methods in monitoring their own practice cases. For the generalist social worker, these cases include individuals, families, groups, or communities. Whatever the type of client system, you only evaluate one in a practice evaluation. This type of research can be either descriptive or explanatory and quantitative or qualitative.

Practice evaluations are recognized as an integral element of social work practice. In part, this recognition has resulted from social workers seeking a method of evaluation that could easily integrate into their practice. In addition to being easily integrated into practice, practice evaluations offer the generalist practitioner the advantages of low cost and immediate feedback (to the client). In addition, they cumulatively provide important information that helps develop evidence-based practice (Byiers, Reichle, & Symons, 2012). Practice evaluations will be discussed more fully in Chapter 7.

Program Evaluations

Program evaluation research questions are asked extensively in generalist social work practice and involve assessing a program's overall functioning rather than individual practitioners' effectiveness. This type of question relates directly to the generalist social work function of promoting the effective and humane operation of the systems that provide resources.

Program evaluations play an increasing role in today's social work practice. During the federal government's War on Poverty of the 1960s and early 1970s, funding for social programs was high. Unfortunately, however, there was little accountability to funding sources regarding social programs' effectiveness in meeting client needs. Fischer (1976) reviewed casework practice in social work. He concluded that approximately half of the clients receiving casework services either deteriorated to a greater degree or improved slower than subjects who did not participate in the programs. Fischer's study jolted social workers and others into the awareness that adequate funding did not ensure a program's effectiveness. Fischer's work also disclosed that many of his reviewed studies contained various methodological problems. As a result, the profession realized the necessity for more sophisticated research methods to assess service effectiveness and conduct program evaluations so that positive or negative findings would be reliable.

Program evaluation is primarily concerned with determining a program's effectiveness, which can be accomplished using three different strategies: formative, summative, or cost-benefit approaches. First, the **formative program evaluation** approach, or **process analysis**, examines a program's planning, development, and implementation. This type of evaluation is often performed as an initial evaluative step and is generally descriptive. Often the interpretive approach is used because it allows for a fuller understanding of the processes at work within the agencies and can address these processes from multiple perspectives—those of the client, the worker, and the administrator.

A Formative Program Evaluation

De Souza and Vongalis-Macrow (2021) carried out a formative evaluation of an education-to-work program for adults with Down syndrome in Australia. It was conducted to understand the need for a two-year Education-to-Work training program, the quality of its content, and the views that eight parents, five facilitators, and four students had about changes attributable to the program after its first year. Findings from the evaluation highlighted the potential usefulness of post-secondary education (PSE) transitioning programs to secure longer-term employment for adults with Down syndrome. The researchers made specific recommendations to improve the quality of the program.

The **summative program evaluation** approach, or **outcome analysis**, determines whether goals and objectives were met and the extent to which program effects are generalizable to other settings and populations. This type of research is usually explanatory. Usually, the quantitative approach is more appropriate with summative evaluations since the purpose is to establish causality (the program's effect). Often these types of evaluations are required by funding organizations, which are more interested in the kind of research evidence (generally quantitative) produced by quantitative studies.

A Summative Program Evaluation

Edwards, Siller, and Wheeler (2021) examined the effectiveness of a six-session (twelve-hour) empowerment self-defense classroom-delivered curriculum among American Indian girls. The girls were selected from high schools and middle schools in two cities. One city provided the intervention, and the other did not.

Girls exposed to the program reported significant increases over time in effectiveness to resist a sexual assault and knowledge of effective resistance strategies. In addition, the girls who received the program reported significantly fewer types of sexual assault and sexual harassment at follow-up than girls in the comparison group. However, the researchers found no effect on physical dating violence. These data suggest that empowerment self-defense is a promising approach in preventing sexual assault and sexual harassment among American Indian girls.

Needs Assessments

Needs assessment questions are concerned with discovering the characteristics and extent of a particular social problem to determine the most appropriate response. This type of research is usually descriptive and, as previously mentioned, is also known as survey research. This kind of question is related to the practice function of linking people with systems.

An example of this type of needs assessment is the following: "I have talked to a couple of clients who need an alternative living situation for their developmentally delayed adult children. I wonder if there is a great enough need in the community to start a group home for developmentally delayed adults?"

Reporting hearsay, citing individual cases, or simply acting on a hunch does not provide enough evidence for funding sources. Usually, a funding source, whether a voluntary organization, a private foundation, or a state government, requires documentation of the need for the program with evidence that the needs assessment has been performed scientifically.

Often, a quantitative approach is used for a needs assessment since most needs assessments are concerned with the generalizability of results rather than an in-depth understanding of how people experience social problems. Sometimes, however, a qualitative approach can provide some critical insights and new directions for assessing the needs of specific populations. In addition, you can design needs assessments differently; these design issues are discussed in Chapter 5.

An Example of a Needs Assessment

Yang and Bechtold (2021) conducted a qualitative needs assessment exploring the educational needs and experiences of twenty-seven adults between the ages of thirty and fifty who were emancipated from foster care as youths. Key findings from this study are that the majority of emancipated youth desire to obtain a post-secondary education but developmental difficulties such as an incomplete transition into emerging adulthood, lack of knowledge about post-secondary education, and lack of financial resources prevented enrollment in higher education. However, many emancipated youths can return to a post-secondary institution later in life and graduate with a bachelor's degree or higher. The primary supportive factor is a positive relationship and additional developmental maturity.

Although the types of research questions appear quite different, they all follow essentially similar research steps and strategies. Nevertheless, some differences in approach are sometimes required, particularly in the design stage. Thus, a separate chapter is devoted to each of the three types of research questions (Chapters 5, 6, and 7).

The three types of research questions described here are not the only types of research questions social workers ask. If you look through any social work journal, you will find other types of research questions. For example, you may find some pure research questions or historical studies. In addition, some articles may be theoretical and conceptual rather than empirical.

This book focuses upon practice evaluation, program evaluation, and needs assessment questions simply because these are the types of research questions you will be most likely to encounter as generalist social workers. Remember, though, that many other types of questions are possible in social work.

Ethical Issues in Deciding on the Question

As we discussed earlier, except when conducting practice evaluations, you may have little or no choice in the research you will be doing as a generalist social worker. For example, the question may have already been decided, and your task instead may be to conduct a needs assessment to help build a case for developing a new program in your community. Or perhaps your program's funding source demands that you undertake an evaluation for funding to continue. As a result, you may find that you often have little opportunity to decide on research strategies or types of questions.

Two ethical issues are central to the stage of the research process concerned with deciding on the question: the question's applicability to social work practice and the availability of funding.

Applicability of the Question to Social Work Practice

One concern when you are deciding on a research question is whether and how the answer to the question will contribute to the field of social work. Usually, applicability to practice is not too much of an issue, particularly for generalist social workers, because most questions derive directly from our practice in an agency. If your question has evolved from your personal experiences, however, you must ask whether answering the question will assist the clients you serve. To determine the appropriateness of the question, discuss it with colleagues.

You must recognize that research is almost always a team effort, particularly at the stage of deciding on the question. Consult with agency staff, clients, and the community to determine what they want from the evaluation or needs assessment. Don't forget to confer with those providing the funding for the project. These are the elements of participatory action research first introduced in Chapter 2.

One strategy for ensuring that those affected by the research or its findings participate more fully in the research is **focus groups**. A focus group is generally a group

---

An Example of Participatory Action Research

Keller, Miller, LasDulce, and Wohrle (2021) examined parental engagement in their children's education. Engagement was shown to positively affect children's academic outcomes; thus, learning ways to increase parental engagement can be beneficial for students. The researchers used community-based participatory research (CBPR) for the data collection. The study took place in an economically and ethnically diverse school community. Social workers and social work students facilitated focus groups with parents and community stakeholders to explore ways to increase parental engagement in their children's school and identify engagement barriers.

composed of people who are informed about the topic or will be impacted by it some-how. You can use a focus group at any stage of the research process, from helping to develop the research question to providing the data to assisting with its analysis and disseminating the findings. The focus group is relatively informal and is generally composed of anywhere from six to twelve individuals, with the researcher asking a series of open-ended questions to the group. A recorder can assist in taking notes.

An Example of the Use of Focus Groups

Obasi (2022) carried out a study in the north of England that examined the issues confronted by Black social workers. The researcher gathered the data from six semistructured interviews and two focus groups. The responses included identity, race, and racism and how these contributed to positions of visibility, invisibility, and hypervisibility within the social work setting. The article calls for social work educators, practitioners, and the wider academic field to centralize anti-racist approaches to challenge racism in social work.

In addition to focus groups, agencies often use task forces to help formulate research questions. Task forces are usually made up of representatives of the agency and sometimes representatives from the community, including clients. Task forces often assess needs or develop strategic plans. These activities are often the starting point for developing research questions that concern the agency.

Availability of Resources

In agencies, research projects may be conducted because funding is available for these projects. Specific issues may be a priority at the local, state, or federal level, and funds consequently become available. You should be aware of the reason you re conducting research on these particular issues—namely, at least in part, the avail-ability of funds. Presumably, it was already established that this topic is a deserving one. Still, you need to realize that other issues are probably equally worthy, and you should not ignore them because of the convenience of funding. In other words, you should continue to act as advocates for those issues, regardless of the extent to which they are receiving fiscal support.

An Example of the Use of a Task Force

Bosnjak et al. (2021) reported on a Joint Psychological Societies Preregistration Task Force consisting of the American Psychological Association (APA), the British Psychological Society (BPS), and the German Psychological Society (DGPs), supported by the Center for Open Science (COS) and the Leibniz Institute for Psychology (ZPID). The goal of the Task Force was to provide the psychological community with a consensus template for the preregistration of quantitative research in psychology adapting to specific journals, disciplines, and researcher needs. The article covers the structure and use of the PRP-QUANT template while outlining and discussing the benefits of its use for researchers, authors, funders, and other relevant stakeholders.

In addition, you may sometimes want to confirm for yourself whether a research program deserves an investment of time and money. Again, the literature and your colleagues are the best sources for this type of information.

Human Diversity Issues in Deciding on the Question

Researcher Characteristics

During the stage of deciding on the question, you need to pay attention to human diversity issues. You should be aware that the researchers' characteristics can influence their research and that agencies may also promote biases. Many claim that the characteristics of the researcher are vital in conducting culturally responsive research. In the past, most social work research was conducted by a relatively homogenous group, resulting in an inherent bias in the types of questions asked and the research methods. Now there is greater diversity among those undertaking research and a corresponding diversity of topics and methods. This diversity expresses itself in many ways.

However, it is important to note that the problem of "researcher identity bias" can still exist. The discussion of the characteristics of those undertaking the research tends to focus on either ethnic/racial diversity or gender diversity, ignoring another critical source of researcher bias: socioeconomic status. Hodge (2003) points out this potential discrepancy between client and social worker, but a similar social class and subsequent value disparity can also exist between researcher and participant. Although socioeconomic status is interrelated to other aspects of diversity, particularly race/ethnicity, the researcher is most likely to be well educated and middle class, and the participants are more likely to be poorer and less educated. This aspect of diversity results in a whole set of socioeconomic values that will drive the research from the initial research question through to the interpretation of the findings.

One strategy for addressing this issue is for the researcher to undertake a participatory approach. For example, suppose the research participants are directly involved in planning, designing, implementing, and disseminating the research results. In that case, the identity of the researcher and their associated biases become less influential in the research itself. Instead, the "subjects" drive the direction of the research, a philosophy that is directly compatible with the empowering approach of social work in general.

A final point concerning who conducts the research relates to the potential problem of people's studying themselves—an issue when members of an organization or agency evaluate their performance. Although the input and participation of organization members are essential, these evaluations do need to be counterbalanced by outsiders' evaluations.

Access to Participants

Human diversity issues also interface with a researcher's access to participants. Specific individuals, groups, and communities are more accessible than others and can lead to a particular bias on who and what is "studied." For example, you might want to compare the perceptions of those living in an inner city with those trying to propose and plan new housing schemes. These proposers and planners may well be the city mayor, counselors, or other political officeholders. Interviewing the politicians will generally result in much greater challenges than interviewing the residents of the inner city. In addition, access is generally more limited to those with more privileged (whether by money, ethnicity/race, social class, political views, or other) status.

Bias in the Agencies

Most of our research questions derive from practice in agencies. However, we need to be aware that bias can also exist in agencies and influence decisions about research questions. Although these biases can exist in many forms, every agency may develop its own "culture" that determines how it conducts business, including the type of research. For example, an agency's homophobic attitudes may ignore the needs of lesbian clients, even though that group may require substantial social support. As a result, your supervisor may dismiss your request to conduct a needs assessment of this particular group. Other biases may be related to the agency's mission and the underlying philosophy. For example, the focus may be more on identifying and treating individual pathology than community organizing and identifying broader societal issues. Hence, any research will be driven by these assumptions.

Watch for these biases; be aware that presuppositions and prejudices may influence your agency's operation.

Summary

This chapter described two research strategies: descriptive and explanatory. There is a distinction between applied research and pure research. Generalist social workers usually engage in three types of applied research: practice evaluations, program evaluations, and needs assessments.

Usually, research questions have already been decided on in agencies, but it is vital to ensure maximum input from those affected by the research and the resulting services. Focus groups help ensure this input, and participatory action research is recommended. Other ethical issues in deciding on the research question include assessing the question's applicability to social work practice and funding availability. Human diversity issues include the researcher's characteristics and the agency's biases.

STUDY/EXERCISE QUESTIONS

1. Look through a social work journal such as Social Work Research and Abstracts or Affilia and identify studies that adopt the research strategies described in this chapter (practice evaluations, program evaluations, and needs assessments).

2. Ask your field placement supervisor about any program evaluations or needs assessments recently carried out by the agency. Find out why the evaluation or needs assessment was carried out. Who suggested it? Who was involved in that decision? Present the results of this discussion in class.

3. Form a focus group (or groups in your research class to help identify a research question that will guide a class project).

4. In your field placement agency, identify one or two aspects of the agency that may bias the decision about the research undertaken.

5. In small groups, develop a list of the three types of research questions discussed in this chapter: practice evaluations, program evaluations, and needs assessments.

REFERENCES

Bosnjak, M., Fiebach, C. J., Mellor, D., Mueller, S., O'Connor, D. B., Oswald, F. L., & Sokol-Chang, R. I. (2022). A template for preregistration of quantitative research in psychology: Report of the joint psychological societies preregistration task force. *American Psychologist, 77*(4), 602–615. https://psycnet.apa.org/fulltext/2022-06923-001.html

Byiers, B., Reichle, T., & Symons, F. (2012). Single-subject experimental design for evidence-based practice. *American Journal of Speech and Language Pathology, 21*(4), 397–414. https://doi.org/10.1044/1058-0360(2012/11-0036)

De Souza, D., & Vongalis-Macrow, A. (2021). Evaluating a pilot education-to-work program for adults with Down syndrome. *Studies in Educational Evaluation, 70*(2), 1–10. DOI:10.1016/j.stueduc.2021.101016

Edwards, K. M., Siller, L., Wheeler, L. A., Charge, L. L., Charge, D. P. L., Bordeaux, S., Herrington, R., Hopfauf, S. L., & Simon, B. (2021). Effectiveness of a sexual assault self-defense program for American Indian girls. *Journal of Interpersonal Violence, 37*(15–16). https://doi.org/10.1177/0886260521997942

Fischer, J. (1976). *The effectiveness of social casework.* Springfield, IL: Charles C. Thomas.

Hodge, D. R. (2003). Value differences between social workers and members of the working and middle classes. *Social Work, 48*(1), 107–120. https://doi.org/10.1093/sw/48.1.107

Keller, J. G., Miller, C., LasDulce, C., & Wohrle, R. G. (2021). Using a community-based participatory research model to encourage parental involvement in their children's schools. *Children & Schools, 43*(3), 149–158. https://doi.org/10.1093/cs/cdab015

Lamothe, J., Geoffrion, S., & Guay, S. (2022). Investigating the cyclical hypothesis of client aggression as a 'loss spiral': Can child protection worker distress lead to more client aggression? *Health and Social Care in the Community, 30* (1). https://doi.org/10.1111/hsc.13401

Mogro-Wilson, C., & Cifuentes Jr., A. (2021). The influence of culture on Latino fathers' parenting styles. *Journal of the Society for Social Work and Research, 12*(4), 705–729.

Obasi, C. (2020) Black social workers: Identity, racism, invisibility/hypervisibility at work. *Journal of Social Work, 22*(2), 479–497. https://doi.org/10.1177%2F14680173211008110

Sethy, S. S. (2021). *Introduction to logic and logical discourse.* Singapore: Springer, Nature. https://doi.org/10.1007/978-981-16-2689-0

Sicora, A., Lu, W., & Lei, J. (2020). Exploring mistakes and errors of professional judgment in social work in China and Italy: The impact of culture, organization, and education. *Journal of Social Work, 21*(5), 1065–1083. https://doi.org/10.1177%2F1468017320919879

Watson, K., Astor, R., Benbenishty, R., Capp, G., & Kelly, M. (2022). Needs of children and families during Spring 2020 COVID-19 school closures: Findings from a national survey. Social Work, 67(1), 17–27. https://doi.org/10.1093/sw/swab052

Yang, J. L., Bechtold, S. (2022). The educational journey of former foster youth: A dream deferred. *Journal of Social Work, 22*(2), 498–517. https://doi.org/10.1177%2F14680173211008369

4

Writing the Literature Review and Identifying the Variables

INTRODUCTION

Suppose your supervisor asked you to conduct a needs assessment to establish a health promotion program for a local business. You have some implicit assumptions about what the program will include: seminars and information dispersal on wellness. However, after consulting with the company's staff, you find that they define a health promotion program more broadly. Their idea of a health promotion program includes other services, such as revising the business's health insurance coverage and providing discounts to local health clubs, counseling information and referral, and so forth.

This chapter will describe the research stage of developing the question, equivalent to the practice stage of assessment described in Chapter 2. Developing the question involves clarifying the research question once you initially formulate it. This clarification can help make explicit some initial assumptions inherent in research, in much the same way as is necessary in practice.

Developing the research question involves searching the literature related to the topic and determining the key components you need to include in your research.

LEARNING OBJECTIVES

This chapter will include the following learning objectives:

1. To understand the role of the literature review in developing the research question

2. To learn techniques for accessing library resources

3. To identify strategies for critiquing and assessing the literature

4. To gain the skills to write a literature review

5. To understand and identify units of analysis, levels of measurement, variables, and values

6. To articulate ethical and human diversity issues when developing the research question

As discussed in the last chapter, the research question often has been decided on before your involvement. For example, the agency may have been asked by one of their funding sources to evaluate the services, and you are to help with planning and implementing the study. Similarly, many of the stages discussed in this chapter may have been completed by the time you are involved. Nevertheless, it is still crucial for you as a team member in the project to understand the rationale behind these stages and, if you have the opportunity, to develop them yourself.

Note that the central assignment in a beginning social work research methods course is writing a research proposal. This text takes you through that process step by step. At this point, you may want to refer to Chapter 13, where there is a complete discussion of research writing, from the research proposal through to the final report.

The Literature Review

When conducting applied research—whether a program evaluation, a needs assessment, or a single system study—we need to consult other sources of information.

Sometimes information can come from colleagues who have had experience with the questions we are trying to answer. Our usual source of other information, however, is written material. Increasingly common are **scoping reviews.** Logan et al. (2021) describe this relatively recent methodology, and Munn et al. (2018) provide guidelines on using a scoping versus a literature review. You can undertake a scoping review before a more thorough literature review (sometimes referred to as a systematic review). The scoping review takes a very broad look at the extent, range, and nature of research in an area, and you can think of this as exploratory.

An Example of a Scoping Reviews

Mason et al. (2017) examined the involvement of social work in global environmental change. They searched five electronic databases: Social Work Abstracts (SWA), ProQuest Social Services Abstracts, ProQuest Environment Abstracts, SCOPUS, and Web of Science Social Sciences Citation Index, selecting issues/articles for "social work" in addition to a list of global environmental change topics. Inclusion criteria were: (a) published since January 1, 1985; (b) published in a peer-reviewed journal; (c) is empirical; (d) is social work research; and (e) examines at least one topic related to global environmental change. They identified 112 studies to include. About one third of studies examined hurricanes and typhoons, and most were conducted in the United States, Canada, or Asia. Many described consequences or coping with change, and although more than one third of studies examined a formal response/intervention, there was little in the way of outcomes-focused research.

Undertaking a **literature review** means consulting with the written material relevant to a research problem and is more specific than a scoping review. You can find written material in various places, including libraries, both public and private; city, state, and federal buildings; social agencies; private collections; and political, professional, social, and interest group organizations such as the NASW. Almost all are available online, and there are several different databases relevant to social work (see Appendix A).

This section will discuss the specific uses of the literature review, accessing the information, and writing the literature review.

Using the Literature Review

The literature review assists with developing the question in the following ways:

- connecting the research question to theory
- identifying previous research
- giving direction to the research project

Consulting the literature is beneficial in conducting research and guiding practice, mainly if the literature is based on research.

Connecting the Research Question to Theory

As discussed in Chapter 1, science consists of both theories and research methods. Consequently, the connection to theory must be made clear in any research. In pure research, connecting a question to theory is a fairly obvious step. For example, if you are investigating the causes of spousal abuse, you need to be apprised of the human behavior theories that attempt to explain spousal abuse.

You can find this theoretical base in the existing literature. However, this step is not so apparent in applied research, and you can easily overlook it. We will clarify this step by giving illustrations of the use of the literature review for linking different types of social work research questions to theory.

Practice evaluations.   When evaluating your own practice, you need to understand the theoretical base underlying your use of a particular intervention. For example, if you are using positive reinforcement to help a parent learn disciplining skills, you need to be familiar with the theory behind positive reinforcement—namely, behavior theory. Then it is necessary to consult the literature on behavior theory. In addition, you need to understand the theoretical link between positive reinforcement in disciplining children and its appropriateness and effectiveness for this purpose, again turning to the literature for this information.

Program evaluations.   Recall that program evaluation can take several forms: summative, formative, or cost-benefit analyses. We need to consider how the research question links to theory for each form. For example, you may be examining whether the agency where you are employed meets one of its goals in providing support services to the homebound elderly. You consult the literature to ascertain the theoretical basis for this type of care and examine existing studies. You may also find some of this material in the initial program proposal.

Needs assessments.   When assessing the need for a program, you can also consult the literature to provide some theoretical substance. For example, in conducting a needs assessment to determine the number of homeless women and children in our community,

---

An Example of Connecting the Research Question to Theory: Program Evaluation

Han et al. (2020) explored the theoretical base underlying prison-based dog training. The study interviewed twenty-one dog training staff to examine the utility of empowerment theory as a theoretical framework for understanding mechanisms of change for the participants. Six themes were found: (1) finding purpose and meaning, (2) enhanced self-concept, (3) skill development, (4) greater perceived control, (5) increased community engagement, and (6) positive post-release outcomes. These outcomes aligned with the constructs of empowerment theory. Consequently, programs may benefit from using empowerment theory as a guiding framework in program design and training of program staff. Prison-based dog training programs may be of particular interest to social workers in correctional settings.

a theoretical perspective and context can be gained by consulting the literature and determining the risk factors and problems experienced by homeless women and children.

Identifying Previous Research

When you choose or are assigned a research question, it is helpful to determine whether a similar or identical question has already been answered. If it has, you may wish to reconceptualize the research question. For example, in conducting your needs assessment, you may find a report on a survey conducted in your community two years previously. This information will probably be helpful since the survey was recent. However, if the survey was undertaken ten years ago, you would need to replicate or repeat the study. Similarly, in a program evaluation, you may find that other evaluations of comparable programs had already been conducted, and thus your evaluation might not necessarily contribute new and valuable knowledge. Alternatively, you may find that the evaluations were conducted in communities very different from the one your agency serves, which suggests your evaluation would be helpful.

An Example of Identifying Gaps in the Literature

Quan-Haase et al. (2021) investigated research focused on the #MeToo movement. Through a synthesis review covering sources from 2006 to 2019, they learned that only twenty-two studies examined participation on social media such as Twitter and Facebook in this time period. The authors concluded that more research needs to be conducted, particularly qualitative studies. While #MeToo is a global movement, the omission of any reference to geography or a lack of geographic diversity suggests a narrow focus on scholarship based in the Global North. They suggested a need for more cross-cultural analysis to understand the movement better as it evolves over time and moves into different spaces.

Note that when writing a **thesis,** you will be required to include a clear discussion of the relationship between your research topic and its theoretical framework.

Giving Direction to the Research Project

Although the concern here is primarily with the role of the literature review in developing the research question, you should also note that the literature review can give overall direction and guidance to the entire research project. You can, for example, review the literature to find out how researchers set up comparison groups in similar projects or get ideas about how you can select samples. Using the literature review in this way, particularly in the early step of developing the question, can save considerable time later and avoids "reinventing the wheel."

Accessing Information

In today's information age, thousands of resources are available to anyone searching for information. The question becomes how to locate the best, most reliable information promptly. Librarians often can supply some insight into research questions and let you know about services that you might not know existed.

Libraries have for centuries housed extensive collections of materials. They often specialize in different materials, and the scope of the material available can vary widely. The selection of materials usually reflects the mission of the library.

Most libraries will provide Interlibrary Loan (ILL) to patrons. ILL permits libraries to borrow specific materials from other institutions across the country. It is also possible for a librarian to bring in materials from Special Libraries. In addition, government agencies and public and private organizations often maintain specialized collections or materials. These materials are increasingly available online.

Academic Libraries

Academic libraries have traditionally provided research literature and the tools for research, including indexes and abstracts. These tools may still be available or incorporated into electronic databases in many cases. Although the internet has transformed the information search process, libraries still play an essential role when accessing scholarly material. The libraries pay for databases to access journals and other scholarly materials. These database collections will vary from institution to institution based on the needs assessment of that institution.

Library sites or their OPACs (Online Public Access Catalog) are often essential links to more than print (books and serials). Library OPACs often provide links to electronic texts and reliable websites. Usually, keyword searching will help you narrow down subjects at the beginning of a search. Of course, you can also search for authors and publications with excellent reputations. Many catalogs provide advanced search features permitting terms to be combined.

The library site also often provides access to databases containing thousands of complete text resources. These resources may be magazines, journals, newspapers (old and current), or recent dissertations. This material is often superior to material located via the web since search engines are usually paid by businesses to have their materials come up first on a search. Also, you may be accessing someone's page. Wikipedia, one very popular web page, is open to editing by the public. It is interesting to look at the history of the page for changes. Wikipedia may provide links to government, educational, or organizational pages. However, it does not provide a reliable research source.

When searching for scholarly materials online or in a database, it is helpful to use an advanced search mode. In scholarly databases, it is easier to do a Boolean Logic search. This type of search permits you to place a different concept on each line and connect those concepts by AND, OR, or NOT. This method allows you to narrow or broaden the search.

Example:

		Native American	**Abstract**
		Indians	Abstract
	OR	Indians	Abstract
	AND	Diabetes	Abstract
	AND	New Mexico	TEXT

- FULL TEXT

- REFEREED, SCHOLARLY, PEER REVIEWED

This search would permit any article with either Native American or the term Indian plus diabetes to be searched. The option often exists in databases to add additional lines to a search. You can refine the above search by adding "AND New Mexico." The quotes around words ensure that the terms are searched adjacent to each other. They help prevent "new" diabetes cases in "Mexico" from being the results.

You are researching women with diabetes who develop a mental impairment. You don't care if it is Alzheimer's disease or a case of dementia that causes the impairment. The use of "OR" permits both terms to be searched. Often you will need to be prepared to reword your search. Therefore, it is helpful to have a list of synonyms prepared before the search. For example, let's say you are researching the effects of videotaping in trials. The search is more fruitful in databases if you use "Videos AND Courtrooms."

Many databases will permit you to search "full-text" articles. If you do not select the full text, be prepared to receive a lot of citations and abstracts. A research institution may provide a tool that permits you to search citations for the database that contains the full-text article you need. This is useful if you have a list of citations you are interested in pursuing. The citations on one excellent article may lead you to a wealth of other articles. If a citation cannot be located in a database, it may be available through ILL. Although ILL may sometimes have a rapid turnover, other times, it can take months to arrive.

Just as most databases permit a full-text search, most offer a choice of the type of material searched. Materials that experts in their field review are usually available. The search can be limited to this type of article by choosing scholarly journals, peer-reviewed articles, or refereed journals. The terms "scholarly journal," "peer-reviewed," or "refereed" are used to show that experts have reviewed the material in the field the journal publishes. This type of authority control is essential in research. Certain organizations, publishers, and authors are known for their authority in their fields. With all the vanity presses and self-published articles today, it is always wise to question the credibility of the material. The literature review will permit you to compare points of value, note exemplary studies, note gaps in the research, and help evaluate authority and objectivity.

Internet Searches

Nowhere is credibility a more critical issue than when using the Internet. The URL (universal resource locator), commonly known as the web address, can provide valuable information. Does it contain a name? Does someone host it? What is the domain? These can all provide helpful information. If there is a name, it may be a personal page, and you need to look closely at the author. Since such web pages are not evaluated through a publisher, it is hard to test the page's authority. There may be more than one author named Joe Smith. Domains can be very valuable when searching or evaluating sites. Look closely at the URL for the domain name.

Common domains:
    .com or .net —available to anyone
    .gov —a government site (beware of political speeches)
    .mil —the military
    .org —organizations (no longer restricted to non-profits)
    .edu —college-level educational organizations
    .museum —museum

The country codes .us, .de, and .uk are not tightly controlled. None of the domains are foolproof but are helpful in evaluating material. Most major search engines provide a full-text search option. This option permits a more tailored search. The domain can be limited, and exact wording searched.

One excellent source of information is a government site entitled PubMed. PubMed Mesh is a part of the National Institutes of Health Public Access Policy. The Mesh database provides an excellent tutorial. Although this may seem like only a medical database, there are excellent articles on abuse and post-traumatic stress topics. This type of publishing and DSpace institutional repositories may hold the future of a lot of scholarly publishing. DSpace is an open-source platform used by many academic institutions for scholarly publishing. DSpace pages may or may not be peer-reviewed. Google Scholar, JSTOR, and Science Direct are also excellent resources. It's not that difficult to identify others.

When searching any online information, it is always necessary to question the validity of the information. For example, who published the material and why? Do they have an agenda? Are they an expert, and can you verify their credentials? Is the information current and up to date? Is the material accurate? It is essential to take the time to evaluate all information. Even census information may not reflect the community in its entirely because of its members' religious, cultural, or legal status. Local authorities can help you sort through information when you realize it does not reflect the community.

Writing the Literature Review

Although writing up your research, including the literature review, is discussed in Chapter 13, some guidelines for writing the literature review are given here.

The literature review is usually the first section of the research to be completed and written. You should complete this section before undertaking other stages of the research.

The literature review places the current research in its historical and theoretical context. It describes the background to the study and the relationship between the present study and previous studies conducted in the same area. The literature review should also identify trends and debates in the existing literature. It provides a link between the past, present, and future and provides a context for discussing the study results.

A literature review places the current research in its historical and theoretical context. It describes the background of the study and the relationship between the present study and previous studies conducted in the same area. It also identifies trends and debates in the existing literature. Here are a few issues to consider when constructing a literature review (van Rooyen, 1996):

- Cite only research you find specifically pertinent to the current study; be selective. Avoid reviewing or referring to sections of articles or texts that are not related to your study.
- Discuss and evaluate the literature you have selected.
- Show the logical continuity between existing literature and your study.
- Identify controversial issues or differences in the literature and your study.
- If there is a choice, cite the more recent literature unless the older citations are needed for additional perspective.
- Write the literature review in the past tense.
- Refer to published studies for examples of literature reviews.

Units of Analysis

After conducting the literature review, which, as we discussed earlier, connects the research to theory, identifies previous research, and gives direction to the research project, it is essential to further develop the question by "breaking it down" into smaller components. This process is all part of engaging in the *systematic* steps of the research process discussed in Chapter 1. In addition, such a breaking down process helps focus the question and ensures that the area of research is not too broad and that there is a shared understanding about what you are investigating. Ultimately, this is more likely to produce more valuable and applicable research and allow the *replication* of the research (also discussed in Chapter 1).

One of the first steps in this process is determining the **unit of analysis**. The unit of analysis refers to what or who is being studied. Three types of units of analysis are used in social work research: individuals, groups, and social artifacts.

Individuals. These are the most common units of analysis. Descriptions of individuals are often aggregated to explain social group functioning. For example, in conducting a needs assessment for a community youth center, you may interview individual youths to assess their needs. You would then aggregate this information to document the needs of the group.

Groups. Groups can also be the unit of analysis. Groups are of different types and include families, organizations, and communities. Families are often the unit of analysis in social work. For example, in an evaluation investigating the impact of a program on family cohesion, the family group would be the unit of analysis.

Social artifacts. These are behaviors or products resulting from human activity. In social work, social artifacts may include books, divorces, birth practices, or ethical violations. For example, your state NASW chapter asks you to investigate unethical social work practice behavior. In your research, you examine the characteristics of those charged: whether they are B.S.W.s or M.S.W.s, the field of practice in which they are employed, and so on. Here the unit of analysis is unethical social work practice.

An Example of Units of Analysis

Wells & Fotheringham (2021) examined whether current government-endorsed violence prevention plans in countries of the Global North included men and boys as a target for primary prevention. One hundred and fourteen plans (the unit of analysis) from fourteen countries were analyzed. The findings revealed that engaging men and boys as primary prevention advocates is still in its infancy and primarily focused on individual change.

Naming the Variables and Values

After identifying the unit of analysis and the level of measurement, the next step in focusing and developing the research question is to identify the factors of central interest in the research. These factors are known as the **variables**.

A variable is a characteristic of a phenomenon and refers to a logical grouping of attributes. Common variables often seen in social work research are income, ethnicity, and stress level. These characteristics vary or have different quantities, and these different quantities of variables are referred to as *values*. Note that our use of *value* in this context is not the usual meaning we assign to that term in social work practice, such as the social work value of self-determination. You can also think about values as the potential answers to questions on, for example, a questionnaire.

Using the examples just given, possible values of income might include the following:

- under $20,000/year
- $21,000–$30,000/year
- $31,000–$40,000/year
- $41,000–$50,000/year
- $51,000 and over/year

Ethnicity values (for New Mexico) might include the following:

- Hispanic
- White non-Hispanic
- Native American
- African American
- Other

Stress level values might include the following:

- high
- medium
- low

The variables and the values used in research studies differ from study to study. For example, in conducting a survey to assess the need for a daycare center for developmentally delayed preschoolers, one variable might be income so that you can determine the extent to which parents could pay for such a service. If you were carrying out the needs assessment in rural Kentucky, you might anticipate that incomes would be low. Consequently, the values included on the survey instrument would also be low; the levels presented in the above example might be too high. However, if you were conducting a needs assessment in Santa Barbara, California, this categorization might be too low, and we would need to add much higher income levels.

In the same survey, ethnicity might also be considered a factor influencing service need and consequently should be included in the study. As a variable, ethnicity is restricted in the values that can be included, but there are still some choices. For example, if the study was carried out in New Mexico, the values for ethnicity listed earlier would need to be included. Alternatively, if the study was conducted in South Africa, completely different values would be used. Again, the values included depend on the purpose and context of the study.

One of the problems with naming values in this way is that you lose information. For example, clustering all individuals in a category such as "Native American" leads to the loss of potentially critical information: the differences between different tribes, places of residence (on or off the reservation, rural or urban areas), and so on. This problem points to the importance of using the qualitative approach to research when appropriate, particularly when you are unsure about the nature of the values to be included in the study.

In qualitative or interpretive studies, the variables and values are not necessarily named before the research but instead emerge from the study. For example, in the study identifying factors that contributed to the maternal response to children sexually abused by the mother's intimate partner, the researcher did not know what the factors were before undertaking the research. Instead, the variables—level of maternal support, maternal history of abuse, nature of the relationship with the partner, and ethnic affiliation—appeared to be important in understanding this phenomenon. However, even in interpretive studies, you need to know what variables are to be studied, even if other variables and their values are added later. In this example, the primary variable studied was pregnancy.

One note of caution about deciding on variables to include in a study: Beware of what is called **reductionism**, or the extreme limitation of the kinds and numbers of variables that might explain or account for broad types of behavior. Reductionism is particularly problematic when using the quantitative approach because all the variables are named before the study, and little allowance is made for discovering additional variables. For example, in a study on spousal abuse, you may take many perspectives to explain this phenomenon. You might focus on economic factors, biological factors, family dynamics factors, or psychological factors, to name a few. According to the literature, all appear to play some role in spousal abuse. Incidentally, the literature review is vital in the selection of these variables. However, time and money constraints often force us to consider only one group of factors. In this case, you may opt for the economic factors because the literature review disclosed these as needing further investigation. Choosing economic factors above the others is not, in itself, necessarily a problem; however, if you then suggest that these are the *only* factors in explaining spousal abuse, you would be guilty of reductionism. When selecting the variables for a study, these variables may represent only one perspective on the explanation; in discussing your results, you need to acknowledge this. Social workers study human behavior, and human behavior is very complex. You cannot expect to come up with a complete explanation; you need to be aware of this limitation from the early stage of question development to the final stages.

The Relationship of Variables

The next step in developing the question is to focus on the relationships between the variables and consider what functions and roles the variables have in the research. The primary distinction is between the roles of the independent and dependent variables. Independent and dependent variables are of primary concern in an explanatory study where you identify specific variables as they contribute to specific outcomes— in other words, the study attempts to establish causality. However, in descriptive studies, such as a needs assessment, independent and dependent variables are often not identified as such.

The **independent variable** is the variable that can affect other factors in the research. For example, if you were studying the impact of social isolation on child sexual abuse, the independent variable would be social isolation. In a program evaluation, the independent variable is the program itself.

You can think of the **dependent variable** as the outcome variable that has presumably been affected by the independent variable. For example, in a summative program evaluation where you are interested in whether the program's goals are being met, the dependent variable would be those goals. In the example of the study attempting to identify the factors leading to child sexual abuse in a community, child sexual abuse would be the dependent variable. For each study, there may be several independent and dependent variables. For example, in the study of child sexual abuse, income level (in addition to social isolation) may be another independent variable. In addition, different types of child sexual abuse might be identified as different dependent variables.

An Example of Independent and Dependent Variables

Van Raemdonck (2021) reviewed two different types of frontline social services for unaccompanied young adult refugees. First, this study examined the impact of intensive case management and specialized educational/occupational orientation services (the independent variables) on young refugees' capabilities to reach the life goals to which they aspired (dependent variables). Both qualitative and quantitative data were collected. The qualitative data are drawn from forty-two in-depth interviews with twenty-four young refugees, one interview, and three focus group discussions with ten service providers.

As with identifying variables and values, the literature review is critical in determining the dependent and independent variables. For example, in the study of child sexual abuse, any related theories need to be found in the literature, and additional variables identified.

Like values, variables are not fixed as dependent or independent; the terminology depends on the study's purpose and context. For example, although child abuse is identified as a dependent variable in the example given, in a study examining the factors determining teenage pregnancy, you might identify child sexual abuse as an independent variable.

Defining and Operationalizing the Variables

Variables need to be defined unambiguously; in much the same way, we need to define concepts in practice. This is equivalent to a part of the assessment process in practice.

A central tenet of the quantitative approach is that you must clearly define variables so that you can measure them.

An Example of Defining Variables in a Quantitative Study

Shovali et al. (2019) examined the relationship between grandparents' level of confidence and outcomes for the school-aged grandchildren under their care ($n = 678$). Each of the variables: performance in school, the number of formal services, financial support, and confidence in using services, were defined. They found that higher levels of grandparents' confidence in obtaining and utilizing community services predicted higher academic performance for grandchildren.

Definition of the variables is less of a priority when using the qualitative approach because often more clearly defining the variables is the purpose of the study. The definitions of concepts or variables emerge as the topic of inquiry is explored. Nevertheless, there should still be some clarity surrounding the concepts or variables included in the study.

For example, in a study exploring beliefs about mental illness, the researcher would have to be clear about defining *mental illness,* even if the study itself ultimately explores and expands this definition by drawing on the participants' responses.

Many variables used in social work practice tend to be vague; they may seem open to several interpretations depending on who uses them. For example, in my first field practicum in a psychiatric hospital in Chicago, I was confused by such terms as *ego strength, depression,* and *independent living skills.* The definitions of these terms were either not provided or varied depending on who was defining them. In social work practice, we must define our terms clearly; otherwise, confusion can result. For example, a worker and client may think they both know what they mean by *independent living,* while their understandings are very different. The client may have in mind "living in my own apartment with no supervision," whereas the worker may mean "living in her own apartment with close supervision." In this example, no matter which definition is accepted, the term *supervision* will also need to be defined—perhaps as "the client's reporting to the social worker twice a week."

One danger of defining variables is that a definition appropriate in one culture may be inappropriate in another. So, you must be particularly careful about using definitions cross-culturally. In addition, be especially careful with definitions when studying people in an unfamiliar culture (with *culture* not limited to describing nationality or ethnicity but also including groups of diverse types, such as single fathers or children of alcoholics). A more qualitative approach might even be advisable so that definitions can emerge from the research.

An Example of Defining Variables in a Qualitative Study

Reid (2021) investigated the types of interventions most effective in supporting wellness and recovery of victims of gender-based violence, particularly those simultaneously experiencing homelessness. This was a qualitative study that explored the experiences of eighteen young women experiencing gender-based violence and homelessness who participated in a community-based, trauma-informed group intervention in Toronto, Canada. Participants completed audio-recorded and transcribed semi-structured interviews, analyzed using thematic content analysis. Participants described valuing the safe, women-only space, shared lived experiences, and tailored psychoeducation. This resulted in improved confidence, coping, health, relationships, and future directedness. Findings suggested that community-based, trauma-informed group interventions can facilitate wellness and recovery in this population, thus helping to define the elements of the intervention more clearly.

When naming the variables earlier, use the literature when defining variables. Consult the previous research and theoretical writings on the topic for approaches to definitions. This can save considerable time and avoids "reinventing the wheel." It is also a sound research practice and facilitates any future replication of the research.

Operationalizations

When using a quantitative approach, the next step after defining the variables is to **operationalize** them—this means specifying how the variables are to be measured. This process is central to the positivist or quantitative approach, in which measuring and quantifying the study's variables is critical. However, an interpretist or qualitative approach is not concerned with this step since the purpose of the study is to understand different dimensions of the variable.

Operationalizing becomes easier once you formally define the variables. Even after definitions have been accepted, however, some ambiguities remain. For example, measuring the extent of a client's independent living would involve clarifying the issue of supervision. Would the client report by using a telephone call or a face-to-face visit? How long would the client need to live independently to be considered successful? What kind of financial status would qualify as independent living? These are only a few of the questions needing to be answered before achieving a satisfactory operational definition of the variable.

Measuring a variable could entail simply recording the presence or absence of a phenomenon. If reporting is defined as telephone contact, either the contact was made or it was not. Or measurement might involve more elaboration, such as specifying the nature of the telephone contact. For example, if a prior arrangement was made about the time of the call and who was to initiate it, were these conditions fulfilled?

Operationalizing variables can be a challenge. Measuring a concept like depression may seem overwhelming to the social worker. A helpful strategy in operationalizing a variable is to look in the literature and determine how others operationalized this concept. We refer to many variables in social work research over and over again. Depression is a good example; many measures of depression are available in the literature. Social workers can adopt many of these measures for evaluating their own practices.

Nevertheless, perhaps none of these measuring instruments is appropriate for the aspect of depression you are interested in examining. *Depression* is generally a label applied to specific behaviors being exhibited; to operationalize a variable like depression, we often must consider the behaviors that led to the label's original application. These behaviors might include excessive sleeping, loss of appetite, and so forth. A person's excessive sleeping is easier to measure than the person's level of depression. Excessive sleeping could be measured by the time spent sleeping.

The processes of defining and operationalizing the variables are closely related and can become circular. For example, after defining a variable, the social worker may find it difficult to operationalize the variable, and consequently, the variable needs to be redefined. This circular process characterizes the entire research process in the same way it characterizes practice.

An Example of Operationalization

Seon et al. (2021) examined the relationship between formal and informal social supports and academic achievement using a sample of forty-six undergraduate students with unstable childhood experiences. The authors operationalized formal support by specifying services and informal support using the Lubben Social Network Scale and the Perceived Social Support Scale. Academic achievement was measured using GPA. Statistical analysis indicated that students who utilized the campus counseling or health centers demonstrated higher academic achievement. Additionally, students with greater numbers of friends in their social networks demonstrated higher academic achievement.

Defining and Operationalizing Goals and Activities

Next we will discuss when the generalist social worker conducts a summative program evaluation to determine whether a program has met its goals. As mentioned previously, it might be most appropriate to use the quantitative approach here, and the program's goals and activities need to be defined and operationalized.

First, you need to specify what is meant by *goal* and *activity*. Unfortunately, people use these terms differently, which confuses the matter. Occasionally, people use the terms *goal* and *objective* synonymously, or they use *goal* to refer to a long-term end product and *objective* to refer to a short-term end product. *Activity*, in this context, refers to how the goal is achieved.

The goals of a program called Adolescent Family Life might be to reduce the rate of high-risk babies born to adolescents and the rate of child abuse and neglect among teenage parents. The activities might include providing prenatal care and parenting classes to adolescent parents.

The next step is to define and operationalize these goals and activities. The first goal—reducing the rate of high-risk babies born to adolescents—requires defining *adolescents* and *high-risk babies*. We might decide to define *adolescents* as those eighteen years old and younger and *high-risk babies* as infants born premature or with low birth weights. Then, of course, we would need to operationalize these last two terms—*low birth weight*, perhaps as under 5.2 pounds at birth, and *premature* as born after a pregnancy lasting thirty-two weeks or less. We would continue defining and operationalizing the other goals and the activities similarly.

Levels of Measurement

Another step in developing the research question, and one concerned with ensuring that the research is focused and carried out systematically, is considering the **level of measurement.** The level of measurement is the extent to which a variable can be quantified and subsequently subjected to specific mathematical or statistical procedures. Quantification involves assigning a number to a variable and it depends on how the variable is being operationalized. Using an example of measuring depression, we could count the number of hours the client sleeps each night, use an already developed measure such as the Generalized Contentment Scale, or have the client note whether she was depressed each day. Each measure involves assigning numbers in different ways, and consequently, they result in different levels of measurement. We can identify four different levels of measurement: nominal, ordinal, interval, and ratio (see Table 4.1).

Nominal measures classify observations into mutually exclusive categories, with no ordering to the categories. Phenomena are assigned to categories based on similarities or differences (for example, ethnicity, gender, or marital status). Numbers are assigned to nominal categories, but the numbers themselves have no inherent meaning. For example, 1 is assigned to Hispanic and 2 to African American, but you could reverse the numbers and lose no meaning. The use of numbers with nominal data is arbitrary. In the example of depression, the client recording the absence (no) or presence (yes) of depression each day would result in a nominal level of measurement, as would other yes/no responses to questions.

Ordinal measures classify observations into mutually exclusive categories with an inherent order. An ordinal level of measurement can often be used when we are examining attitudes. For example, you might ask respondents to a survey whether they agree with a particular statement. In this case, the alternatives are as follows: strongly agree, agree, disagree, or strongly disagree. These responses are ordered in sequence from strongly agree to strongly disagree (or vice versa) and numbered 1 to 4. Nevertheless, although these values are placed in sequence and are meaningful, the distance between each of the values is not necessarily equal and may be somewhat arbitrary.

Interval measures classify observations into mutually exclusive categories with an inherent order and equal spacing between the categories. This equal distance differentiates the interval level from the ordinal level of measurement. A good example of an interval scale is the IQ test: The difference between an IQ of 120 and 130 is the same as between 110 and 120. Nevertheless, the interval level of measurement does not allow one to make any statements about the magnitude of one value in relation to another. For example, it is not possible to claim that someone with an IQ of 160 has twice the IQ of someone with an IQ of 80.

TABLE 4.1   Levels of Measurement

Level of Measurement	Definition	Example
Nominal	Data are assigned to categories based on similarity or difference	Ethnicity, marital status, yes/no response
Ordinal	Data are sequenced in some order	Many attitude and opinion questions
Internal	Data are sequenced in some order, and the distances between the different points are equal	IQ, GRE scores
Ratio	Data are sequenced in some order, the distances between the different points are equal, and each value reflects an absolute magnitude. The zero point reflects an absence of the value	Years of age, number of children, miles to place of employment

Ratio measures possess all the characteristics of the interval level of measurement and reflect the absolute magnitude of the value. Put another way, the value is absent at the zero point or did not occur. Measurements of income, years of education, the number of times a behavior occurs—all are examples of ratio levels of measurement. In the depression example, counting the number of hours of sleep each night would result in a ratio level of measurement. Note that you can define most variables to allow different levels of measurement.

Our example of depression is one case; anger is another. For example, a variable like anger can be measured at various levels. For example, if the question "Do you think your child is angry?" is posed, and possible responses are yes and no, this constitutes a nominal level of measurement. But say the question is, "To what extent do you think your child is angry?" The respondent is offered the following scale: very aggressive, aggressive, not aggressive. This would be an ordinal level of measurement. If you measure anger as one component in a personality test such as the Minnesota Multiphasic Personality Inventory (MMPI), the resulting level of measurement would be interval. Finally, if anger is defined in behavioral components, for example, the number of times the child hit another in an hour, it would be possible to use a ratio level of measurement.

These levels of measurement have important implications for the statistical analysis of research results. We will examine these implications in Chapter 12.

Ethical Issues in Developing the Question

Giving Credit to Contributors

When drawing on information generated by others (for example, using a literature review or consulting with colleagues), you need to give credit to these sources of information when you write the research report. How to do this is discussed in Chapter 13. If you refer to someone else's ideas, particularly their written ideas, and do not give them credit, you may be guilty of plagiarism.

Including Relevant Variables

The major ethical issue at the early stage of the research process is determining what variables and values to include in the research question. You need to be sure you included all the important variables. It might be tempting to leave out some factors that you think may not support the need you are trying to document in a needs assessment. For example, in surveying a community to assess the need for an elder daycare center, you want to leave out variables such as transportation need because, if such needs are great, the eventual funding of the project might be jeopardized. On the other hand, you should include all the variables perceived as necessary to the study. Completeness is particularly critical when conducting positivist research, in which you clearly define the variables before undertaking the research. Including relevant variables is less of a problem with the interpretist approach, when the variables are often identified as part of the study.

Avoiding Reductionism

An associated issue that we discussed previously is reductionism. You need to avoid looking at only one type of variable (for instance, economic factors) and claiming that this variable alone is responsible for the particular outcome if an association is found. Reductionism can be a danger when carrying out program evaluations because it is tempting to look only at the variables associated with the program rather than considering others. For example, if you are evaluating a program intended to enhance self-esteem among high school dropouts, you would undoubtedly include the program-related variables such as length of time in the program and so on. However, you may not consider measuring outside factors that could also influence self-esteem, such as involvement in a local sports activity. These other factors may turn out to have far more impact than the program itself, but you may be reluctant to include them because they jeopardize the demonstrated efficacy of the program. Again, this problem of reductionism is more apparent in positivist research. A tendency to reductionism is one of the significant drawbacks of this research approach. On the other hand, it provides one of the rationales for social work to use more interpretive studies to answer many of the questions confronting social workers.

Human Diversity Issues in Developing the Question

In developing the question, you must look carefully at human diversity issues to ensure that you are not biased against certain groups. The last chapter described the possible bias when only certain groups undertake research in social work. Here the potential bias in the literature will be discussed.

An Example of Bias in the Literature

Drabish and Theeke (2022) conducted a literature search that included stigma, discrimination, prejudice, bias, health, and transgender people. A total of fifteen studies met inclusion criteria for review. Results indicate that transgender people experience high levels of discrimination, prejudice, and bias. When internalized, this victimization leads to decreased psychological health, including increased harmful behaviors such as substance abuse and eating disorders, reduced relationship quality, ineffective coping, lower levels of self-esteem, and increased risk of attempted suicide. Internalized stigma also leads to decreased physical health outcomes stemming from healthcare avoidance, reduced healthcare utilization, decreased screenings, and delayed treatment.

Before you use materials to help guide a particular research project, you need to be aware of bias in the literature. Literature relating to human diversity issues has been scarce, although, in recent years it has increased. For example, one social work journal is devoted explicitly to human diversity issues: the *Journal of Multicultural Social Work*. Generally, though, we need to remember when consulting the literature that historically, most social science research was conducted by white, middle-class men; even when women have contributed, they have tended to be white, middle-class women. Overrepresentation of the views of these segments of the population, to the exclusion of others, constitutes a clear bias. Research questions developed by other groups may take a somewhat different course. For example, until relatively recently, few studies had been conducted on the relationship between women's work and family lives, particularly those of minority women and their families. Studies of family functioning often did not examine women's experiences but instead focused on role relationships or parenting practices.

Another human diversity issue in developing the research question is the influence of cultural factors on each of the processes presented in this chapter. For example, how a variable is defined is heavily influenced by the culture in which the definition occurs. One of the examples discussed earlier, *independent living,* is a culturally laden term. In some cultures, this may involve living with the family and being employed outside the family setting or living with the family and being married. The different possible definitions are as diverse as the number of cultures.

Summary

A critical step in the research process is the literature review, which assists in generating questions, connecting the question to theory, identifying previous research, and giving direction to the project. The unit of analysis needs to be determined at this stage in the research process. You must distinguish between variables and values. The definition and operationalization of variables includes defining goals and activities. Another step in developing the question involves determining the level of measurement: nominal, ordinal, interval, or ratio.

Often the generalist social worker does not influence the development of the research question. Ethical issues include ensuring the identification of relevant variables and avoiding reductionism. Human diversity issues in the development of the question include identifying potential bias in the literature and understanding different cultural definitions.

STUDY/EXERCISE QUESTIONS

1. Look at research articles in Social Work and identify the unit of analysis used in the study. Also, note the independent and dependent variables when appropriate.

2. You are involved in evaluating a support group for parents of children with developmental disabilities.

   a. Identify some possible goals and activities of the group.

   b. Name at least five variables you would need to include in the evaluation.

   c. Define and operationalize these variables.

3. You have been asked to help design and implement a needs assessment for an elder daycare facility in your community. Whom would you consult in the early stages of developing the assessment?

4. If you are in a field placement, talk to your supervisor; if not, talk to someone employed in a supervisory position in an agency in your community.

   a. Discuss with that person who they have involved in research projects at the agency and how they have involved those other people.

5. At your university library, meet with the social work reference librarian.

Practice searching for a specific topic.

REFERENCES

Drabish, K., & Theeke, L. A. (2022). Health impact of stigma, discrimination, prejudice, and bias experienced by transgender people: A systematic review of quantitative studies. *Issues in Mental Health Nursing, 43*(2), 111–118. DOI: 10.1080/01612840.2021.1961330

Han, T. M., Gandenberger, J., Flynn, E., Sharma, J., & Morris, K. N. (2021). Empowerment theory and prison-based dog training programs. *Journal of Social Work, 21*(6),1360–1376. https://doi.org/10.1177%2F1468017320954350

Logan, J., Webb, J., Singh, N., Walsh, B. R. H., Tanner, N., Wall, M., & Ayala, A. P. (2021, April 19). Scoping review search practices in the social sciences: A scoping review protocol. https://doi.org/10.31219/osf.io/cdf9h

Mason, L., Shires, M. K., Arwood, C., & Borst, A. (2017). Social work research and global environmental change. *Journal of the Society for Social Work and Research, 8*(4), 645–672.

Munn, Z., Peters, M. D. J., Stern, C., Tufanaru, C., McArthur, A., & Aromataris, E. (2018). Systematic review or scoping review? Guidance for authors when choosing between a systematic or scoping review approach. *BMC Med Res Methodol 18*, 143. https://doi.org/10.1186/s12874-018-0611-x

Quan-Haase, A., Mendes, K., Ho, D., Lake, O., Nau, C., Pieber, D. (2021). Mapping #MeToo: A synthesis review of digital feminist research across social media platforms. *New Media & Society, 23*(6), 1700–1720. https://doi.org/10.1177%2F1461444820984457

Reid, N., Kron, A., Rajakulendran, T., Kahan, D., Noble, A., Stergiopoulos, V. (2021). Promoting wellness and recovery of young women experiencing gender-based violence and homelessness: The role of trauma-informed health promotion interventions. *Violence Against Women, 27*(9), 1297–1316. https://doi.org/10.1177%2F1077801220923748

Seon, J., Prock, K. A., Bishop, J. D., Hughes, A. K., Woodward, A. T., & MacLean, M. (2019). Formal and informal social support and academic achievement among college students with unstable childhood experiences. *Child Welfare, 97*(1), 21–44. https://www.jstor.org/stable/48623575

Shovali, T. E., Emerson, K. G., & Augusta, M. (2019). School-aged children living in grandfamilies: Grandparent caregiver confidence in community resources matters. *Child Welfare, 97*(2), 79–94. https://www.jstor.org/stable/48623645

Van Raemdonck, L., Clycq, N., Mahieu, R. Using the capability approach in social work with unaccompanied young adult refugees. *Journal of Social Work, 22*(2), 556–578.

Van Rooyen, C. (1996). Taking the leap: A guide to higher degree research study in the Department of Social Work at the University of Natal. Durban, South Africa: The University of Natal, Department of Social Work.

Wells, L., & Fotheringham, S. (2021). A global review of violence prevention plans: Where are the men and boys? *International Social Work.* https://doi.org/10.1177%2F0020872820963430

5

Designing Needs Assessments

INTRODUCTION

This chapter will examine needs assessments, one of the three major types of research questions undertaken in generalist social work, and first described in Chapter 3. Social workers carry out needs assessments before designing a program, and for generalist social workers, the need assessment is probably the most common type of research undertaken.

Needs assessments are often thought of as a type of survey research. Surveys measure people's attitudes, behaviors, or beliefs at one point in time. This chapter will see that the survey is only one type of needs assessment design. This chapter will not include all the information you need to complete a needs assessment. Refer to Chapter 9, where there is information on different data collection methods that you will require to conduct a compelling needs assessment.

LEARNING OBJECTIVES

The learning objectives for this chapter are:

1. To identify the reasons for conducting needs assessments

2. To describe and understand the types of designs for needs assessments

3. To articulate the ethical and human diversity issues in designing needs assessments

Reasons for Conducting Needs Assessments

Sometimes it may seem unnecessary to conduct a needs assessment because it seems obvious that a particular program is needed. For example, a social worker working with children with autism has heard parents for the last year maintaining that increased respite care would help considerably relieve some of the stress for themselves and their families. So why not just go ahead and develop a program? When writing program proposals, you will usually be competing with many other prospective program developers, and one way of strengthening you proposal is to add a well-designed and implemented needs assessment. Thus, although you think you know the needs of the clients, this presumed knowledge is only a subjective opinion and will not carry much weight with your proposed program's potential funders.

In addition, and perhaps more importantly, this results in a more sound and ultimately more effective program because it will be responsive to identified needs.

You can design several different types of needs assessments. Each one has a different purpose or reason. Being clear about the reason for conducting the study is important because that can help you more accurately plan, design, and implement the needs assessment. Five different reasons can be identified (Royse, Thyer, & Padgett, 2016):

1. To determine whether services exist in the community

2. To determine whether there are enough clients

3. To determine who uses existing services

4. To determine what barriers prevent clients from accessing services

5. To document the existence of an ongoing social problem

Needs assessments may be conducted for just one of these reasons or several. Each will be described in turn using the example of respite care for the parents of children with autism as an illustration.

Determining Whether Services Exist in the Community

Just because you do not know of an intervention or program, that does not mean that it does not exist. Again, however, this situation is more likely to be the case if you work in a large metropolitan area than if you are employed in a rural setting.

Use your networking skills, the Internet, or other resources to search for programs to make this determination. First, if your community does not already have a directory of social service agencies and programs, create one. Next, use your research skills to create a directory of services available on computerized databases. This directory can be either a community-wide resource or one explicitly addressing the needs and concerns of the client population with which you work. In our example, this step would involve documenting services already available for families with autistic children in your community.

Determining Whether There Are Enough Clients

One of the more common reasons for conducting a needs assessment is whether there are enough clients with a particular problem to justify a new program. For example, you may hear the need for respite care expressed from the majority of your clients, but your clients may not constitute enough of a need to start a new program. In addition, perhaps your clients are not representative of clients of other agencies or other workers; in other words, your clients may be a nonrepresentative sample. It would help if you systematically documented the extent of the need.

An Example of a Needs Assessment

Winter, O'Neill, and Cook (2021) studied the use and impact of dating apps. They point out that the number of dating/hook-up apps such as Tinder are rising. Although these apps offer some positive benefits (e.g., friendship and romantic relationships), their use is also related to negative body image, which has adverse health and mental health consequences. The researchers were interested in how socioeconomic status (SES) can relate to body image in order to design and implement appropriate interventions and policies. They examined relationships among SES and two measures of body image (i.e., body image self-consciousness and body appreciation). At the same time, they controlled for age, gender identity, and race among a sample of cisgender adults in the United States who used a dating/hook-up app within the last month ($n = 342$). They found SES was significantly related to body appreciation and body image self-consciousness.

Determining Who Uses Existing Services

Just because an agency or community runs a particular program does not mean that those who benefit from it actually use the program. For example, respite services may be available, but parents may think they are ineligible or have not heard of the program. Certain parents may use the program, but others may not; for example, older parents may use the services more than younger parents. Most relied on public transportation to gain access to healthcare services but expressed fear in using this form of transportation.

An Example of a Needs Assessment Determining Who Uses Existing Services

Biegel, Farkas, and Wadsworth (2021) describe selected community-based social services available to older adults in terms of the purpose or goals of the service, the target population and the eligibility requirements, and the location of the service. Using a literature review, they examine the research findings relating to the extent of participation in particular services and data concerning the effectiveness of specific services. The researchers found that older adults are the direct recipients of services provided by adult daycare programs; families also are thought to receive some benefits from the service. In addition, by utilizing self-help experiences, many people become aware of services and may be more inclined to seek them out and use them.

Determining What Barriers Prevent Clients from Accessing Services

Sometimes clients know about services and may be referred to them by social workers but do not use them for various reasons. Identifying these barriers can start the process of redesigning services or developing supplementary services. Often factors such as transportation and childcare work as barriers. In the example of parents of children with autism, one barrier might be parents' feelings of guilt concerning their children. In which case, counseling and support to the families might be necessary before using respite care.

Documenting the Existence of an Ongoing Social Problem

Sometimes it is not clear what problems people are confronting. This is a more fundamental question than documenting how many people need a service. In that case, we assume the nature of the problem is already known. This type of needs assessment focuses on the characteristics of the social problem. In the respite care example, it was not until the parents started speaking out and expressing their need for support and assistance in the care of their children that the need for respite was recognized.

> ### An Example of a Needs Assessment
> ### Determining the Existence of Barriers to the Use of Services
>
> Richert, Svensson, and Johnson (2021) studied the barriers to seeking professional support experienced by the family members of people with drug addiction. In-depth interviews were conducted with thirty-two parents of adult children with drug addiction in Sweden. Parents described problems in encounters with social services and barriers to adequate psychological support for their children. They described feelings of shame and guilt, negative views of social services, and fear of stigma and loss of control that were barriers to seeking professional support. On an interpersonal level, barriers to help were connected to problems in the interaction among parents, children, and social services. On a structural level, barriers pertain to deficiencies in the availability and quality of support measures, inadequate cooperation between authorities, and a shift in responsibility from the state to the individual and the family. The researchers concluded that social services' collaborative approach may decrease parents' self-blame and concern, and then strengthen their role in their children's treatment process.

> ### An Example of a Needs Assessment
> ### Assessing the Nature of an Existing Problem
>
> Barros-Lane et al. (2022) explored the experiences of family reunification for unaccompanied immigrant youth who entered the United States from Honduras, El Salvador, Guatemala, or Mexico. The researchers collected data from thirty youth, six parents, and four school administrators via focus groups and semistructured interviews. Unaccompanied immigrant youth had arrived in the United States during the previous three years. Results showed that the youth struggled to reconnect with their parents due to prolonged separations, which contributed to loneliness and loss. In addition, parent-child attachment disruptions contributed to problems related to relationships among family members, traditional family roles and hierarchies, and new family constellations (e.g., blended families). Results point to the importance of developing interventions to increase trust, empathy, and communication between unaccompanied immigrant youth and their parents.

Types of Designs for Needs Assessments

We usually think of a needs assessment as a descriptive survey, and as discussed in Chapter 3, it does not require the types of explanatory designs needed for program evaluations. Some choices in design do need to be made, however. The first step is to understand why the study is being conducted. Then, use the options outlined in the previous section as a guide. Whatever question is asked (except for the one determining whether services already exist), almost all surveys, including needs assessments, depend on how the participants are selected. A complete description of the selection of the research participants, also known as "sampling," will be thoroughly discussed in Chapter 8.

The next step in deciding what type of design to use is to pose several questions.

1. Whose need is being assessed?

2. Who will have input into the design of the needs assessment?

3. When will the needs assessment be carried out?

4. What type of understanding of the need is required?

5. What level of description is useful?

We will discuss each of these questions next. (See Figure 5.1 for a chart depicting the different reasons for conducting a needs assessment and the different types of designs.)

Whose Need Is Being Assessed?

The first question—whose need is being assessed?—should be answered early on since it determines who will be selected as participants in the research. We can consider four different levels of needs: individual, organizational, communal, and societal. Most needs assessments are concerned with clients' individual needs or potential clients, including basic needs such as food and shelter and needs for social services. However, a significant proportion of needs assessments carried out by social workers are concerned with organizational needs, technical assistance, or training of some type—for example, the need for parental leave.

Needs assessments are also carried out in communities, assessing the community's need for neighborhood development or services—for example, a community's need for a youth program. Societal needs are assessed at an even broader level—for instance, evaluating the need for revisions in Social Security or national policies related to services for the very old.

Who Will Have Input into the Design of the Needs Assessment?

As with program evaluations, you need to determine who will be involved in designing and implementing the needs assessment early on. This determination is partly related to the answer to the previous question—whose need is being assessed? The decision then becomes whether and to what extent participants will have input into planning the project. This book stresses the importance of participatory or action research. Involving the participants in the study design ensures their "ownership" of the results. Suppose participants are involved in designing and implementing a needs assessment. In that case, the results will have greater validity and relevance and will be much more likely to be heard.

When Will the Needs Assessment Be Carried Out?

Two main choices exist about the timing of the data collection. First, the assessment may be cross-sectional or longitudinal. With **a cross-sectional design**, a survey is carried out at one point in time. For example, you ask parents about their need for a respite care program. Even though it may take a few months to collect the data, whether through a questionnaire or interview, data are collected from each parent just once. This is the most common type of design for a needs assessment.

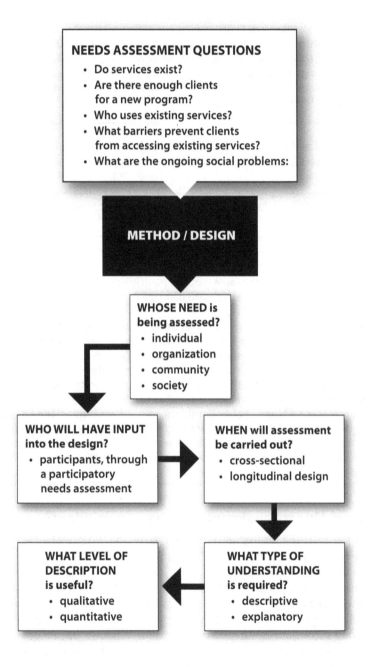

Figure 5.1   Designing a needs assessment

An Example of a Cross-Sectional Study

Dykes, Johnson, and Bamford (2021) carried out a cross-sectional study of the psychological stressors of intensive care healthcare professionals during the COVID-19 pandemic to assess their need for specific support. The researchers assessed the prevalence of anxiety, depression, and post-traumatic stress disorder amongst a cohort of intensive care workers within the United Kingdom. Significant levels of depression, anxiety, and PTSD were reported. However, only three percent accessed mental health services.

A **longitudinal design** might sometimes be necessary. Longitudinal studies are surveys conducted on multiple occasions over an extended period of time.

An Example of a Longitudinal Study

Fridman, Gershon, and Gneezy (2021) examined how attitudes toward vaccination shifted throughout a public health crisis. They carried out a longitudinal study during six months (March 16 through August 16, 2020) of the COVID-19 pandemic that looked at trends in attitudes towards vaccines. The same group of participants completed a survey four times (or in four "waves"). The sample size was 1,018 participants for the first wave and 608–762 for the second, third, and fourth waves.

Contrary to past research suggesting that the increased salience of a disease threat should improve attitudes toward vaccines, they observed a decrease in those who intended to get a COVID-19 vaccine when one became available. They also found a decline in favorable attitudes towards vaccines in general and those who intended to get the influenza vaccine. Analysis of the sample indicated that this decline was driven by participants who identify as Republican, who showed a negative trend in vaccine attitudes and intentions, whereas Democrats remained largely stable. Consistent with risk perception and behavior research, those with less favorable attitudes toward a COVID-19 vaccination also perceived the virus to be less threatening. Differential exposure to media channels and social networks could explain the observed asymmetric polarization between self-identified Democrats and Republicans.

What Type of Understanding of the Need Is Required?

As with other research strategies, you need to decide whether to adopt a positivist or interpretist approach.

Generally, needs assessments adopt primarily a positivist approach. The goal, after all, is to provide documentation of need that will withstand the critical review of a funding organization or other monitoring body. As such, needs assessments usually involve collecting new data through questionnaires (delivered either by mail or face-to-face) or using secondary or already existing data, whether from a government or non-governmental sources. (See Chapter 9 for a discussion of these data collection methods.)

Sometimes, however, a more in-depth understanding of a need is required. It may be necessary to use a qualitative approach in such a case. For example, you may be interested in more detail about what parents of developmentally delayed children have in mind when they express the need for respite care. What is their definition of respite care? What has been their experience of respite care in the past?

Qualitative data collection methods often include interviewing key informants, using focus groups, frequenting a community forum, and observation, all discussed in Chapter 9. These needs assessments depend less on probability sampling because of the different types of understanding sought.

What Level of Description Is Useful?

You may need to determine whether it is necessary to go beyond basic description and examine the relationship between certain variables in the study. These designs are often used in program evaluations and will be described in the next chapter. However, the independent variable is fixed in some needs assessments (unlike program evaluations, where the program itself is the independent variable and can be changed). Therefore, it cannot be altered in any way. For example, you might be interested in the relationship between the age of the child with autism and the expressed need of the parents for respite care. Here the extent of delay cannot be changed as the participants in the study already possess this factor before the study begins. This type of study is known as **ex post facto design** (meaning simply "after the fact"). Common variables in ex post facto designs include gender, ethnicity, age, living situation, and type of problem.

Several problems are associated with the ex post facto design, and it is essential to note that this is not a form of experimental design (see Chapter 6 for a full discussion of experimental designs). The independent variable is simply an attribute, not an experimental manipulation such as random assignment to a program or the group not in the program. In addition, any difference in the dependent variable could be due to many other factors for which this design does not control. Thus, the relationship between the variables is simply an association. You cannot make statements about causality with ex post facto designs. In other words, although there may be a relationship between parents with an older child requesting respite care less frequently, you cannot say that being a parent of an older child with autism *causes* the need for less frequent respite care.

An Example of an Ex Post Facto Needs Assessment

Garcia-Carmona et al. (2021) assessed the needs of caregivers of cancer patients. Caregivers often experience anxiety, depression, and decreased quality of life. Using a sample of sixty-seven informal caregivers of cancer patients, the study examined the mediation effects that perceived emotional support can have immediately after diagnosis and six months later. Participants completed the Medical Outcomes Study 36-Item Short Form (SF-36), the Hospital Anxiety and Depression Scale (HADS) and the Berlin Social Support Scale (BSSS), and a sociodemographic questionnaire. Data were collected between March 2017 and November 2018. The perceived emotional support appeared to assist the caregivers.

Another approach to carrying out a needs assessment using a different description type is to do a **meta-analysis**, which is similar to a literature review. Still, it focuses on actual empirical studies on a particular subject, examines the results from those studies, and looks for similarities or differences in the findings.

An Example of a Meta-Analysist

Sylla et al. (2020) used a meta-analysis to examine the reproductive health outcomes for the millions of women living with female genital mutilation (FGM). The authors searched fifteen electronic databases for studies published between 1 August 1995 and 15 March 2020, reporting maternal and perinatal FGM complications. They included studies comparing women both with and without FGM. Risks were assessed for a range of maternal and perinatal outcomes. They identified 106 unique references, considered 72 full-text articles, and included 11 studies. They found postpartum risks, but these vary according to the subgroup of women.

Ethical Issues in Designing Needs Assessments

A key ethical issue with needs assessments is ensuring that the needs documented in your report are those expressed by the participants in the research rather than the needs the agency or administration would like to see met. Agencies have their agendas; sometimes, there is a temptation to respond more to these agendas rather than the "true" needs of the community. Do not underestimate this temptation. After all, you are employed (as a student or a regular employee) in that organization and must be responsive to your supervisors; it is a dilemma that must be acknowledged and dealt with responsibly.

There is also the temptation to pursue funding sources and have those sources guide your research rather than the needs of the potential or actual clients. Obviously, with limited funding sources, you must be somewhat responsive to any available funds, but not to the point that you move dramatically away from your initial interest. For example, a prominent foundation in your state is interested in funding programs for the visually impaired, and your initial interest was in programs for sexual offenders. Such a radical shift of focus in response to the source of funds may not be advisable, and ultimately the overall quality of the research will suffer. However, sometimes you can shift the emphasis of your research, say from visually impaired children to adults, to respond to a financial source.

Again, as with ethical issues raised previously in this book, you can avoid these issues by ensuring that clients have input into the research. They must direct and design it as much as possible, with the result that the clients come to own it rather than the agency. This approach ensures an appropriate focus for the research and can empower the participants in the study.

An Example of an Empowering (and Participatory) Needs Assessment

Conrad and Scannapieco (2021) used a participatory evaluation approach throughout their study and included: (1) engaging stakeholders in instrument development; (2) obtaining perspectives from all relevant stakeholders; (3) providing translation and interpretation as necessary; (4) using and refining methods that consider cultural sensitivities or preferences, and (5) ensuring communication and research materials are appropriate and accessible to the range of ages represented.

The researchers also made sure that different tribes were represented, recognizing the diversity within the local American Indian population. They included the Choctaw Nation in Oklahoma (29 percent); the Cherokee Nation in Oklahoma; the Muscogee (Creek) Nation in Oklahoma (6.7 percent); the Chickasaw Nation in Oklahoma (6.5 percent); the Navajo Tribe in Arizona, New Mexico, and Utah (5.6 percent); the Comanche Indian Tribe in Oklahoma (4.3 percent); the Mississippi Band Choctaw Indians (3.3 percent); the Seminole Nation in Oklahoma (2.2 percent); the Kiowa Indian Tribe in Oklahoma (1.9 percent); and the Citizen Potawatomi Nation in Oklahoma (1.7 percent).

Human Diversity Issues in Designing Needs Assessments

The primary purpose of a needs assessment is to identify "deficits" or problems to be addressed through new programs or modifications to existing programs. While necessary, identifying needs can lead to certain groups being stigmatized and racially profiled by being consistently associated with specific problems. For example, inner-city African American youths may be associated with crime, adolescent parents with inadequate parenting skills, refugee groups with acculturation problems, and so on. It is important to remember that needs assessments can also assess the strengths of the participants in the research, and this should often be done in addition to presenting the needs.

Summary

Designing needs assessments is a main research activity for generalist social workers. There are five reasons for carrying out needs assessments: (1) to determine whether services already exist; (2) to determine whether there are enough clients to justify a new program; (3) to assess who uses the existing services; (4) to assess the barriers that prevent clients from accessing existing services; and (5) to document the existence of an ongoing social problem. The type of design you adopt depends on the reason for conducting the needs assessment. These reasons include: (1) whose need is being assessed; (2) who will have input into the design (using a participatory design); (3) when the assessment will be carried out (longitudinal or cross-sectional study); (4) what type of understanding is needed (interpretist or positivist); and (5) what type of description is required. Ethical issues include ensuring that participants have maximum input into the needs assessment design. Human diversity issues include the importance of addressing strengths and deficits in the documentation of needs.

STUDY/EXERCISE QUESTIONS

1. Find an article describing a needs assessment in a social work journal and identify:
   a. Any limitations in the methodology
   b. How you would have designed it differently
2. Talk with your fellow students about a service/program need that seems to exist at your university. Design a needs assessment for this issue.
   a. Design one using the quantitative approach.
   b. Design one using the qualitative approach.
3. Ask your field placement supervisor whether a needs assessment would be helpful in the agency, and if so, what its purpose would be.
4. How would you maximize the participatory aspect of a needs assessment?
5. Identify a needs assessment in the literature and suggest how to incorporate a more strengths-based approach.

REFERENCES

Barros-Lane, L., Brabeck, K., & Berger Cardoso, J. A. (2022). "Es como que no los concierge": Reunification of unaccompanied migrant youth with their US families. *Social Work Research, 46*(1), 5–16. https://doi.org/10.1093/swr/svab026

Biegel, D. E., Farkas, K. J., & Wadsworth, N. (2021). Social service programs for older adults and their families: Service use and barriers. In Kim, P. K. (Ed.), *Services to the aging and aged* (pp. 141–178). Philadelphia, PA: Routledge.

Conrad, P., & Scannapieco, M. (2021). Assessing the needs of urban American Indians in North Texas: A community-based participatory research project. *American Indian & Alaska Native Mental Health Research: The Journal of the National Center, 28*(2).

Dykes, N., Johnson, O., & Bamford, P. (2021). Assessing the psychological impact of COVID-19 on intensive care workers: A single-centre cross-sectional UK-based study. *Journal of the Intensive Care Society, 23*(2), 132–138.

Fridman, A., Gershon, R., Gneezy, A. (2021). COVID-19 and vaccine hesitancy: A longitudinal study. *PLOS ONE, 16*(4). e0250123.

Garcia-Carmona, M., Garcia-Torres, F., Jablonski, M., Solis, A., Jaen-Moreno, M., Moriana, J., Moreno-Diaz, M., & Aranda, E. (2021). The influence of family social support on quality of life of informal caregivers of cancer patients. *Nursing Open, 8*(6). https://doi.org/10.1002/nop2.887

Richert, T., Svensson, B., & Johnson, B. (2021). Experiences of Swedish parents seeking social services support for their adult children with drug addiction. *Journal of the Society for Social Work and Research, 12*(4).

Royse, D., Thyer, B. A., & Padgett, D. K. (2016). *Program evaluation: An introduction to an evidence-based approach* (6th ed.). Boston, MA: Cengage.

Sylla, F., Moreau, C., Andro, A. (2020). A systematic review and meta-analysis of the consequences of female genital mutilation on maternal and perinatal health outcomes in European and African countries. *BMJ Global Health, 5*(12). e003307.

Winter, V. R., O'Neill, E., & Cook, M. (2021). An investigation of socioeconomic status and body image among hook-up app users. *Journal of the Society for Social Work and Research, 12*(4).

6

Designing Program Evaluations

INTRODUCTION

This chapter will discuss the design of program evaluations, another type of research question asked by generalist social workers that we first introduced in Chapter 3. As with needs assessments, understanding how to design and implement a program evaluation is critical in ensuring an effective intervention or organization. With the needs assessment, the goal is to establish the program's need and to help guide an appropriate response. Program evaluations assess the program itself and determine how well it is functioning.

There are two different types of program evaluations: formative and summative. We discussed these briefly in Chapter 3. A formative or process program evaluation focuses on description rather than causality. The interpretive or qualitative approach is sometimes more appropriate for these types of evaluations. A summative, or outcome, program evaluation is used to determine the extent to which the program's goals were met—in other words, assessing the extent to which the program caused a specific outcome. Usually, we adopt a positivist or quantitative approach with this type of research. As discussed previously, causality can be difficult to establish because it demands that we meet three basic conditions described in Chapter 1. First, the cause precedes the effect in time. Second, the cause and the effect are related to one another. Third, this relationship cannot be accounted for by other factors.

These three conditions of causality are established by aspects of the summative research design, including the timing of the data collection and the formation of comparison groups. These research designs are called group designs because they assess the program's relationship to a group of client systems rather than to just one client system (referred to as evaluating individual practice, a topic discussed in Chapter 7).

Both formative and summative program evaluations are critical to assessing programs. However, a summative program evaluation is usually required by a funding source, and the establishment of causality can present a major challenge. Therefore, the focus in this chapter will be upon these summative group evaluation designs.

As with other research process steps, you may not be directly involved in designing the research for a program evaluation. However, your agency will undertake such an evaluation at some point, and it is essential that you understand the implications of selecting one type of design over another. In some cases, you may find yourself responsible for initiating an evaluation.

Throughout this chapter, we will use a case example to demonstrate the pros and cons of different designs. Assume you are employed by a program that offers high-risk adolescents a series of six birth control classes to increase knowledge of birth control practices. You are asked to evaluate the effectiveness of the program. During this process, you will need to consider different types of designs.

LEARNING OBJECTIVES

This chapter includes the following learning objectives:

1. To describe and identify formative program evaluations

2. To describe and identify summative program evaluations

3. To understand the different types of summative program evaluation designs

4. To describe internal and external validity

5. To address the problems of randomization and fidelity

6. To articulate the ethical and human diversity issues in program evaluation design

Formative Program Evaluations

Formative evaluations, also known as process evaluations, are generally very descriptive and provide detail about a program's strengths and weaknesses. Interpretive approaches using qualitative data are particularly useful with these types of evaluations.

In the adolescent birth control program, you would undertake a formative evaluation if you were interested in finding out how the adolescents experienced the program: What did they perceive as its limitations and strengths? Alternatively, a formative evaluation might examine how the parenting classes were conducted, how the syllabus was developed, and whether the syllabus was being followed.

Formative evaluations do not attempt to establish any type of causality—in other words, no claim is made that the program resulted in specific outcomes. Also, no attempt is made to generalize the findings. Consequently, there are no dependent and independent variables, and the sampling is generally purposive rather than random. The focus is on in-depth description and analysis to improve and strengthen the program. Thus, much of the emphasis in a formative program evaluation is on assessing quality.

In understanding the adolescents' experiences with the birth control classes, you might conduct an in-depth interview to elicit the youths' reactions to the program. You could observe the classes, interview the facilitator to understand how the classes were implemented, and identify areas needing development.

Often, we can strengthen formative evaluations by comparing various factors, such as males and females, ethnic groups, socioeconomic groups, etc.

Formative evaluations are beneficial in the first year of a program's implementation since findings from such a study can provide immediate feedback for improvement and growth. In addition, thorough formative evaluations can lay the groundwork for later summative evaluations.

Summative Program Evaluations

Summative program evaluations, also known as outcome evaluations, are primarily concerned with causality. However, as discussed in earlier chapters, causality is

---

An Example of a Formative Program Evaluation

Bui, Coyle, and Freeman (2021) carried out a formative evaluation of the Age-Friendly Boston Initiative's Senior Civic Academy (SCA). This self-advocacy course aimed to engage older residents in advocacy training to incorporate their voices in local policy and planning. The formative evaluation used mixed methods to evaluate the program's impact on the participants ($N = 49$). Lessons learned from the SCA serve as a guide for other communities to develop programs that encourage civic engagement and advocacy among older adults.

---

difficult to establish in social work (and social science research in general). Therefore, the concept of validity is a central issue. There are two main types of validity when considering the validity of a research design: internal validity and external validity.

Internal validity is the extent to which the changes in the dependent variable(s) are a result of the introduction of the independent variable(s) and not some other factor(s). For example, was the knowledge of birth control a result of the adolescents' participation in the birth control classes, or were other factors responsible for this increase in knowledge? This is an attempt to establish causality. However, to ensure internal validity in the birth control question, the three aspects of causality described in the previous section need to be addressed.

The first two conditions—that the cause precedes the effect and that there is a relationship between cause and effect—can be met by one aspect of the research design: the data collection time. You can measure the adolescents' knowledge about birth control before and after the classes. If you find that their knowledge level is low before the classes and high after the classes, this establishes that the classes preceded the increase in knowledge level.

The two measures also allow you to assess the extent of the relationship between a change in knowledge levels and participation in the classes. For example, 80 percent of those in the classes had a high level of knowledge after their participation. We use statistical tests to decide whether this is a significant relationship (these will be discussed in Chapter 13). Even if you determine that the relationship is significant, you still cannot say the classes caused a change in knowledge level because other factors could explain the connection. For example, the adolescents may have received some instruction at school on birth control at the same time as you were collecting data, which contributed to the change in knowledge level. This is where the second aspect of research design, **comparison groups**, as it relates to causality becomes so important. Comparison groups either go through another type of program or else receive no type of bona fide intervention. These comparison groups can help strengthen causality claims. For example, suppose the increase in knowledge level is greater among those who attended the classes than among those in the comparison group. In that case, you can begin to narrow down the factors responsible for that change to the classes. See Figure 6.1 for an illustration of internal validity.

The comparison groups must be otherwise equivalent to the group involved in the program under study. The most reliable way of ensuring equivalence of the

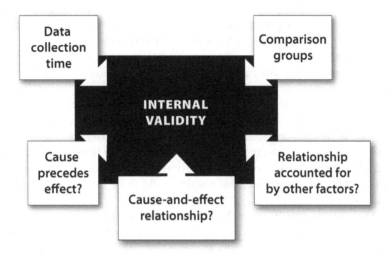

Figure 6.1   Internal validity in group design

groups is to use random assignment of subjects into an **experimental group** (the group that receives the intervention being evaluated) and a **control group** (the group that does not receive the intervention being evaluated). **Random assignment** means that every subject has an equal chance of being assigned to either group. Equivalency of the groups is important because you cannot determine whether the disparity in outcome between the two groups is due to the treatment or the difference between the two groups. Later in this chapter, we will discuss some problems associated with random assignment and alternative strategies for setting up comparison groups.

Do not confuse random assignment with random sampling. Random sampling and random assignment may or may not be used in the same study. They are independent procedures and have different implications for the findings. Random sampling involves creating a sample from a population. It is concerned with the representativeness of the sample. In other words, to what extent the sample reflects all the characteristics of the population. This is important to know when you want to generalize the research results gained from the sample to the entire population. (See Chapter 1 for a more detailed discussion of generalizability.) There are several different ways to select a random sample, and we will discuss these in detail in Chapter 8. On the other hand, random assignment is concerned with the equivalence of the experimental and control groups and establishing causality.

External validity is the other type of validity of concern in a group design. As with the type of sampling method selected (random or not), it is concerned with the generalizability of the research results to the wider population. In other words, how effective is the birth control program with adolescents in general? The generalizability can also be affected by the type of sampling method again. Refer to Chapter 8 for a description of sampling methods.

External validity and generalizability depend on two conditions: first, ensuring the equivalency of the groups, and second, ensuring that nothing happens during the evaluation to jeopardize the equivalence of the groups.

The first condition for external validity is to ensure the *equivalency of the groups* being compared. For example, you may decide that randomly assigning the comparison group is not feasible and that instead, the comparison group should be made up of adolescents who are not eligible for the classes. However, this type of comparison group is problematic because individuals in the comparison group might possess different characteristics from those who entered group therapy. Consequently, not only would any outcome showing differences between the two groups have a lower internal validity, but in addition, the population to which the results could be generalized would be limited. Therefore, the results could only be generalized to those eligible for the classes.

The second condition influenced by the research design that affects external validity is ensuring that *no interference* occurs during the evaluation, which may decrease the distinction between the experimental and control groups. Interference of this kind is sometimes called **treatment diffusion**. It can happen in three different ways. First, the adolescents may discuss the class with their peers, who may be in the comparison group. Then a comparison between the two groups becomes problematic. Second, the distinction between the program group and the comparison group can be difficult when the program is not clearly defined. (This often points to the need for a formative evaluation to define the program components more clearly.) Finally, treatment diffusion can result from reactivity effects. Changes occur when people are aware they are participants in a study that blurs the distinction between the program and comparison groups. Finally, treatment diffusion leads to problems in generalizing the initial results to the wider population. See Figure 6.2 for an illustration of external validity.

Types of Summative Program Evaluation Designs

In this section, different types of research designs, with their relative validity problems or threats, will be examined. Three main types of design can be distinguished: the pre-experimental design, the quasi-experimental design, and the experimental design. The experimental designs are the strongest in establishing causality in that they have the least threats to external and internal validity. See Table 6.1 for a summary of the threats to internal and external validity for each type of group design.

Pre-experimental Designs

A pre-experimental design is a group design that is often the only feasible design to adopt for practical reasons. It uses comparison groups rather than control groups or no type of comparison or control group and thus, as we will see, has limited internal and external validity. Hence the name "pre-experimental."

TABLE 6.1   Group Research Designs: Threats to Internal and External Validity

Type of Design	Threats to Internal Validity	Threats to External Validity
One-group posttest only	Selections, history, mortality	Selectioni = treatment interaction, history-treatment interaction
One-group pretest-posttest	History, maturation, testing, instrumentation, regression to mean, interaction of selection, and other threats	History treatment interaction, reactive effects
Static-group comparison	Selection and mortality	Selection-treatment interaction
Time series	History	History-treatment interaction, reactive effects
Pretest/posttest comparison	Selection and maturation	Selection treatment interaction, maturation treatment interaction, reactive effects
Pretest-posttest control group	None	Reactive effects
Posttest-only control group	None	None

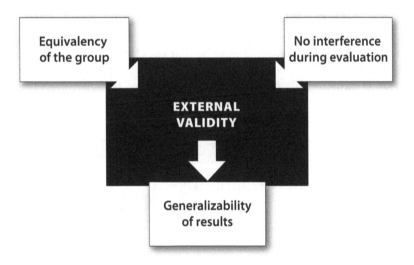

Figure 6.2   External validity in group design

One-Group Posttest-Only Design

The one-group posttest-only design consists of one group (so that there is no comparison group) with only one point of data collection (after the intervention). Figure 6.3 shows how this design might be visualized. Sometimes this design is referred to as a one-shot case study. Although the term *test* is used in the name of this design, this simply refers to the point at which data collection occurs. The data collection method may be any of the types discussed in Chapter 9, such as observing behavior or administering a questionnaire.

The one-group posttest-only design can help gather information about how a program is functioning. This design can answer several questions. For example, how well are participants functioning at the end of the program? Are minimum standards for outcomes being achieved? This type of design is often used for **client satisfaction surveys**, in which clients are asked about how they experienced or perceived the program.

The one-group posttest-only design is very limited in its ability to explain or make statements about whether a program caused particular outcomes for clients and whether the results can be generalized to other client populations. Consequently, this design is viewed as having numerous threats to its validity—both internal and external.

Threats to Internal Validity

Remember that internal validity refers to whether it can be determined if the program caused a particular outcome. So, with the case example, we need to ask whether it was, in fact, the provision of birth control information that led to an increase in knowledge.

If you use the one-group posttest-only design, this will result in the following threats to internal validity.

Selection.   The kinds of people selected for one group may differ from those selected for another. For example, it may be that the clients who enrolled in the program were already highly motivated to learn about birth control. However, there was no pretest to measure this potential predisposition of the clients, so this possibility of **selection** threatens internal validity.

Figure 6.3   One-group posttest-only design

History.   **History** involves those events—other than the program—that could affect the outcome. For example, participants' high levels of knowledge about birth control may result from classes held in school or from some other factor. Without a comparison group, this possibility cannot be assessed.

Mortality.   Subjects may drop out of the groups so that the resulting groups are no longer equivalent; this possibility is called **mortality**. For example, some adolescents may have attended one class on birth control and then dropped out; however, they are still considered members of the experimental group. As a result, the group that ultimately receives the posttest is biased and perhaps shows a higher success rate than would be the case if the success rates of those who dropped out were also monitored. Consequently, the outcome of *all* participants must be assessed, which cannot be done without some type of pretest.

Note that mortality and selection are a little like mirror images. Mortality is the bias introduced by those who drop out of the program once they have begun. Selection is the bias involved when people initially choose to participate in the program.

As for our case example, because the data collection only occurs once (after the intervention) and because there is no comparison group, the extent to which we can say the program caused a change in knowledge is limited with this design. Consequently, this is the least desirable type of research design.

Threats to External Validity

The one-group posttest-only design poses some threats to the external validity and generalizability of results. Possible problems include the following.

Selection-treatment interaction.   Selection-treatment interaction occurs when the ability to generalize is limited because the sample is not randomly selected or there is no pretest, so you cannot determine how typical the clients are. In our example, the adolescents may be highly motivated to learn about birth control before enrolling in the program, so whether they complete the classes is irrelevant.

History-treatment interaction.   History-treatment interaction occurs when other factors may contribute to the outcome and might affect the generalizability of the results (for example, if the positive outcomes resulted from a massive media campaign on pregnancy prevention rather than from the program). The program might have a negative outcome if the evaluation were carried out at a different point in time.

One-Group Pretest/Posttest Design

Another pre-experimental design, the **one-group pretest/posttest design** (Figure 6.4) is similar to the preceding design except that a pretest is added. In the case example, the pretest might consist of a questionnaire given to all clients asking about their birth control knowledge before attending the classes.

This design helps you answer several questions: how well participants are functioning at the end of the program, whether minimum standards of outcome are being achieved, and how much participants change during their participation in the

Figure 6.4   One-group pretest/posttest design

program. This is a helpful design and is often used in program evaluations. It is also a valuable design when no comparison group is feasible.

You can gain additional information from this type of design that can enhance statements of causality. The pretest allows selection to be ruled out as an alternative explanation because you can identify any preexisting information on birth control. In the long run, however, this design often poses even more threats to validity than the one-group posttest-only design.

An Example of a Pretest/Posttest Design

Petering et al. (2021) looked at the impact of a peer-based mindfulness and yoga intervention as a way of reducing interpersonal violence in a network of homeless young adults (YAEH). A group of YAEH (*n* = 58) who accessed homelessness drop-in services in Los Angeles, CA, completed a baseline (pretest). Twelve YAEH were identified and invited to participate in the Mindfulness and Yoga Peer Ambassador Training for Health (MYPATH). The training consisted of a three-hour intensive followed by seven weekly one-hour sessions. The training introduced mindfulness and yoga as tools and practices to increase emotion regulation and reduce impulsivity. Follow-up data were collected two months after the pretest. Results revealed increased mindfulness and yoga practice frequency and reduced violence-engagement behaviors in the network of YAEH.

Threats to Internal Validity

The one-group pretest/posttest design poses the following threats to internal validity.

History.   Because there is no comparison group, there is no way to tell whether other events apart from the birth control classes resulted in increased knowledge.

Maturation.   Even though a change may be detected between the pretest and the posttest, this change may be due not to the subjects' participation in the program but rather to **maturation**. This refers to the participants changing, in this case, by acquiring knowledge about birth control over time due to lifelong learning rather than program effects. With adolescents and children, especially, the possibility of maturation is a potentially serious threat to internal validity.

In the case example, the adolescents' level of knowledge would have changed regardless of the program. Maturation is a potential threat if the participants are young or if a long time has passed between the pretest and the posttest. A comparison group helps control for maturation effects.

Testing.   The **testing** threat to validity may occur when the subjects are exposed to a measuring instrument more than once. For example, if the pretest included information that could increase the adolescents' knowledge of birth control, this effect cannot be separated from the effect of the classes. However, a comparison group can help control these testing effects because they exist for both groups if they do exist. Consequently, if the knowledge of the clients in the experimental group changed more than those in the comparison group, the researcher would be more confident in concluding that the intervention, rather than the pretest, was responsible for this change.

Instrumentation.   How the variables are measured, known as **instrumentation**, may change during the evaluation. For example, a questionnaire may change between its first and second administration. Sometimes these changes are difficult to avoid. For example, the context in which the questionnaire is administered may vary, as may the person administering it. This change, rather than the intervention, may account for any difference in the results. A related concept is that of the reliability of the instrument. We will discuss this in Chapter 9.

Regression to the mean.   In the example, if eligibility for the birth control classes was determined by a test on birth control knowledge (those with low knowledge levels would be eligible), then a posttest after the classes could exhibit regression to the mean. This may occur because most people tend to perform close to their averages, but they may score exceptionally high or low on some days. When they retake the test, they will regress to the mean or be closer to their average score. Thus, any change in score between the pretest and the posttest would not necessarily reflect the program's influence but could simply be a **regression to the mean.**

Interaction of selection and other threats.   Even if none of these previously discussed threats to internal validity apply to the general population, the threats may be relevant for those selected to participate in the study. To take maturation as an example, it may not be the case that women, in general, become more knowledgeable about birth control as they mature. However, adolescents who desire to receive more information through counseling may also be more likely to become more knowledgeable due to their age. Again, this represents the **interaction of selection and other threats**—in this case, maturation.

Threats to External Validity

History-treatment interaction.   History-treatment interaction may be a problem with the one-group pretest/posttest design.

Reactive effects.   Reactive effects can occur when subjects change their behavior because they know they participate in the study. As a result, the resulting outcomes may be distorted and cannot be generalized to a broader population. These reactive effects are challenging to overcome in any design because you cannot ethically engage in research without gaining participants' consent. We will discuss consent later in this chapter.

Static-Group Comparison Design

The static-group comparison design is the third type of pre-experimental design. An extension of the posttest-only design includes a comparison group with a posttest (Figure 6.5). In this design, the groups are nonequivalent, in that the comparison group was not randomly assigned, and there is no way of knowing how the groups are different or similar.

Several strategies can be adopted to achieve some equivalency for the comparison group even if the random assignment does not occur. These strategies include baseline comparison, matching, cohort groups, and overflow comparison.

An Example of a Static-Group Comparison Design

Siria et al. (2021) examined sexual offending youth's recidivism in Spain. Seventy-three adolescent sexual offenders were divided into two groups: sexual reoffenders (SR, $n = 34$) and non-reoffenders ($n = 39$). Data collection included reviews of official files, interviews with professionals in charge, and interviews with the offenders who were administered the Interpersonal Reactivity Index (IRI). The groups were compared statistically. Results showed that SR had 12.95 times the odds of sexual victimization, 6.91 times the odds of having lived in a sexualized family environment, and 3 times the odds of bullying victimization. Deviant sexual fantasies were exclusively present among SR (44 percent). Significant differences between groups were also found in some sexual crime variables but not on the empathy scale. This is a static group comparison design, but it is also an ex post facto design used in needs assessments.

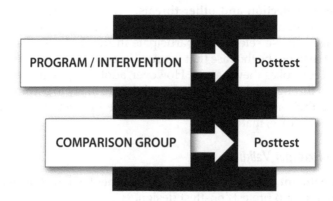

Figure 6.5   Static-group comparison design

Baseline Comparison

Baseline comparison occurs when the comparison group is composed of cases handled before introducing the program. The problem with this approach is that it is difficult to determine whether cases identified as eligible in the absence of a program would have been referred to the program.

Matching

Matching involves selecting specific characteristics that are thought to impact outcomes substantially—for example, gender or ethnicity—and ensuring that each group's characteristics are equally represented. In the example, because of previous research and our own experience, you may think ethnicity, such as Latinx, is essential in determining the program's effectiveness. Consequently, you ensure that the program group has the same proportion of Latinx adolescents as the comparison group.

One drawback to matching is that you need to be sure that the variables you consider in the matching are, in fact, key variables. Often, it is difficult to determine the critical variables because of the lack of previous research or other sources of information to guide these decisions.

An Example of Matching

Keller Hamilton et al. (2021) studied electronic cigarette (e-cigarette) use among adolescents and its association with increased risk of subsequent cigarette smoking. The researchers compared e-cigarette smokers to those that had never used e-cigarettes. Boys from urban and Appalachian Ohio ($N = 1220$; ages 11–16 years at enrollment) reported using e-cigarettes at baseline and every six months for two years. One e-cigarette user was matched with two similar e-cigarette non-users. The data analysis revealed that e-cigarette users were more than twice as likely to initiate cigarette smoking later.

Cohort Groups

Cohort groups provide another strategy for compiling comparison groups. A variation on matching, cohort groups are composed of individuals who move through an organization at the same time as those in the program being evaluated do, but who do not receive the program's services. For example, you compare adolescents in the same class at school. Some are enrolled in the birth control class program, and others are not, or one entire class is enrolled, and another class is not. Cohort groups can also be combined with matching.

Overflow Comparison

Sometimes people are referred to a program, but a waiting list is created because the slots are filled. The **overflow comparison group** of people on the waiting list can serve as a comparison group.

Regardless of how the comparison groups are formed in the static-group comparison design, they are all non-equivalent, not randomly assigned. This design offers one advantage over single-group designs: The threat from history is eliminated because external events that may affect the outcome will be occurring in both groups. However, the static-group comparison design still has other threats to internal and external validity.

Threats to Internal Validity

Selection.   The major threat to the static-group comparison design's internal validity is selection, which results from not randomly assigning the groups and having no pretest. Consequently, it is impossible to determine how similar the two groups are. As a result, any difference occurring between the two groups may not be due to the presence or absence of the intervention. Instead, it may be due to other differences between the groups.

For example, if the experimental group consists of adolescents who elected to enroll in the birth control classes and the comparison group is made up of adolescents who did not want to attend the classes, the comparison group may differ from the experimental group. The experimental group may later have greater birth control knowledge than the comparison group, but this may be less a function of the classes than the experimental group's greater motivation to learn about birth control. The equivalency of the groups is not assured because there is no random assignment or a pretest.

Mortality.   Because of the absence of a pretest and a randomly assigned comparison group, mortality is still a problem with the static-group comparison design.

Threats to External Validity

Selection-treatment interaction.   Selection-treatment interaction is a problem with this design.

Reactive effects.   Reactive effects threaten the external validity of this design.

Quasi-Experimental Designs

These designs eliminate more threats to internal and external validity than pre-experimental designs. Still, they either measure one group over time or use comparison groups (non-equivalent groups) rather than control (equivalent) groups. Thus, they are ultimately not as strong as experimental designs in establishing causality.

Time Series Design

A **time series design** overcomes some of the problems of the designs discussed previously, measuring several times before the intervention and then several times after the intervention (Figure 6.6). For example, the adolescents might be tested on their knowledge of birth control several times over several months before the classes. Then the same test is given several times after the classes. The test might also be provided during the time of the classes.

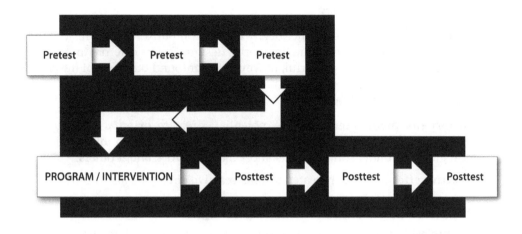

Figure 6.6   Time series design

The advantage of the time series design is its ability to detect data trends before and after the intervention. In effect, this discounts the problems of maturation, testing, and instrumentation associated with the single pretest/posttest design because any trends in these effects could be detected. For example, if maturation affects the adolescents' knowledge of birth control, that effect will be seen in a difference between the pretest scores.

An Example of Time Series

Gabrhelik et al. (2020) investigated the association between cannabis use during pregnancy and birth outcomes. Data from the Norwegian Mother and Child Cohort Study (MoBa), a prospective pregnancy cohort, were used. Participants were recruited from all over Norway between 1999 and 2008. Nine thousand, three hundred and twelve women with 10,373 pregnancies who reported the use of cannabis before or during pregnancy were included in the study. Women reported illegal drug use before pregnancy, between weeks seventeen and eighteen of pregnancy, at week thirty of pregnancy, and at six months postpartum. In 10,101 pregnancies, women had used cannabis before pregnancy but not during pregnancy. In 272 pregnancies, women had used cannabis during pregnancy, and among these, in sixty-three pregnancies, women had used cannabis in at least two periods. Only cannabis use during at least two periods of pregnancy showed statistically significant effects on birth weight. The results may indicate that prolonged use causes more harm, whereas short-term use did not indicate adverse effects on birth outcomes.

Threats to Internal Validity

History.   Because of the absence of any type of comparison group, history is a major threat to internal validity in the time series design. Events external to the evaluation would have to be fairly powerful, however, to confound the effect of the classes.

Threats to External Validity

History-treatment interaction.   A potential threat to external validity is history treatment interaction, as history interacts with the classes. An intervention that appears to work under some circumstances may not work under others.

Reactive effects.   With repeated testing, reactive effects are also a problem.

Pretest/Posttest Comparison-Group Design

The pretest/posttest comparison-group design combines the static-group comparison and the one-group pretest/posttest design (see Figure 6.7). The comparison group is still not randomly assigned. However, this design can adopt various methods used to set up comparison groups mentioned for the static-group comparison design. By combining features of both the static-group comparison and the one-group pretest/posttest design, this design becomes less problematic than either of them. For example, history is controlled due to the comparison group, and the pretest identifies, to a certain extent, differences or similarities between the groups.

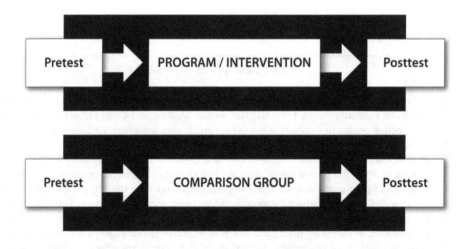

Figure 6.7   Pretest/posttest comparison-group design

An Example of a Pretest/Posttest Comparison-Group Design

Han and Kim (2021) conducted a quasi-experimental study to assess the effectiveness of two empathy enhancement programs on 105 social workers working with older adults in South Korea. The experimental group ($n = 52$) received a simulation-based empathy enhancement program along with a brief mindfulness practice session, and the comparison group ($n = 53$) watched a thirty-minute-long educational video about empathy. Data were collected just before and two weeks after the intervention. The experimental group showed significantly lower psychosocial stress levels than the comparison group. It also showed significantly higher levels of cognitive empathy and considerably lower levels of compassion fatigue at posttest. Also, the comparison group demonstrated significantly higher levels of a unidimensional factor of empathy, compassion satisfaction, and caring efficacy at posttest.

The authors recommended that a further randomized controlled trial study be needed to examine the program's effectiveness.

Threats to Internal Validity

Selection and maturation interaction.   In the example, the pretest may indicate that the group that received classes had more knowledge about birth control than the comparison group before the intervention. Suppose the posttest also shows this difference between the groups. In that case, maturation may have been the cause of the treatment group's greater knowledge over time, whether they received the classes or not. This potential problem with internal validity depends significantly on how the comparison group is selected and what the results indicate.

Threats to External Validity

Selection-treatment interaction.   A potential problem is a selection-treatment interaction, which can affect the generalizability of the results.

Maturation-treatment interaction.   Another potential problem is maturation-treatment interaction.

Reactive effects are also a problem with the pretest/posttest comparison-group design.

Experimental Designs

These designs result in findings that can make the most substantial claim for causality and eliminate most of the threats to external and internal validity.

Pretest/Posttest Control-Group Design

The difference between the **pretest/posttest control-group design** and the previous design is that the comparison and experimental groups are randomly assigned. When this occurs, we refer to the comparison group as a control group (see Figure 6.8). In the example, you might randomly assign participants in the control or experimental group from among high-risk students in a high school class. As a result of a

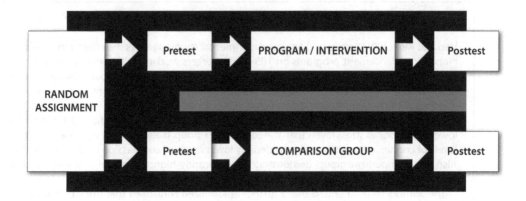

Figure 6.8   Pretest/posttest control group design

randomly assigned control group, the threats to the internal validity of history, maturation, mortality, selection, regression to the mean testing, and instrumentation are all virtually eliminated.

An Example of a Pretest/Porsttest Control-Group Deesign

Budge et al. (2021) compared the effectiveness of two interventions in addressing minority stress (a contributor to mental health status) among transgender, nonbinary, and gender-nonconforming individuals. Transgender individuals ($n = 20$) were recruited to participate in a randomized controlled trial comparing the two psychotherapy interventions: (a) Transgender Affirmative psychotherapy (TA), and (b) Building Awareness of Minority Stressors + Transgender Affirmative psychotherapy. Gender-related stress and resilience were assessed before, immediately after, and six months following the intervention; the researchers assessed psychological distress and working alliance at these three points in time and weekly during the intervention. Exploratory analyses indicated improvement in both groups based on general outcome measures; targeted outcome measures indicated a trend of improvement for internalized stigma and non-affirmation experiences.

Only one potential external validity problem with the pretest/posttest control-group design remains. This involves the possible reactive effect of the pretest.

Despite the strength of this design, there are some difficulties in its implementation. These problems are similar to those encountered in setting up nonrandomly assigned comparison groups. We will discuss ethical issues with this design later in this chapter.

Posttest-Only Control-Group Design

One way of eliminating the threat to external validity posed by the previous design is to eliminate the pretest. In the **posttest-only control-group design** (see Figure 6.9), the two groups are again randomly assigned and consequently should be equivalent, and there should be no need for the pretests. Some researchers, however, are reluctant to eliminate what is essentially a safety measure to ensure the groups' equivalency, and published examples of the use of this design are few and far between.

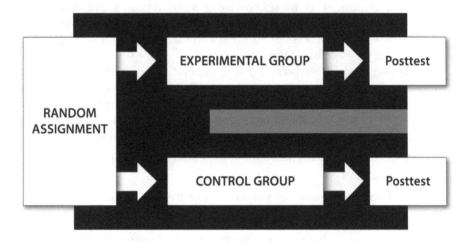

Figure 6.9   Posttest-only control-group design

Table 6.1 summarizes each of the summative group designs and their threats to internal and external validity, as discussed in this chapter.

The Challenge of Randomization

It should be clear from this chapter that it is preferable to use experimental designs with randomly assigned control groups if you are interested in establishing whether a program or intervention and not some other factor or factors was responsible for a specific outcome. As generalist social workers, however, you may find that the textbook research examples are not practical, nor are they necessarily preferred. So don't be discouraged if you can't use random assignment; it may be that one of the other designs will give you the kind of information you need.

The challenge is for us to develop *feasible and appropriate designs for the research question.* Not only are these alternative strategies compatible with agency practice, but if the comparison groups received services or treatments (including part of the intervention being provided to the experimental group), many of these strategies become even more feasible and attractive to agencies. This approach is beneficial to crisis-oriented or court-ordered services.

Another strategy that may result in the greater participation of agencies involves using unbalanced designs with fewer subjects assigned to the comparison or control group. Consequently, clients referred to the agency are more likely to receive services.

Finally, do not overlook the importance of formative program evaluations. They have an essential role in the development of programs and should be the evaluation of choice for new programs. In addition, certain types of practice simply do not lend themselves to experimental designs (for example, community organization and policy practice).

Most important is to acknowledge your design's drawbacks and address them in the reporting of the evaluation. If we conduct research in this practical and responsible way, the process of building knowledge in social work can progress with a solid agency-based foundation.

Having made these points, it is important to emphasize that randomized controlled studies are an essential foundation for evidence-based practice as a consumer of research. Use the following standards provided by the journal *Evidence-Based Mental Health* for assessing acceptable randomized controlled trials (experimental designs):

- Random allocation of participants to comparison groups
- Follow-up end point assessment of at least 80 percent of those entering the investigation
- The outcome measure of known or probable clinical importance
- Analysis consistent with study design
- Assessment or diagnosis of clients conducted with demonstrated reliability, using a reasonably reliable system and reports of interrater agreement (see Chapter 9)
- Assessments were conducted blindly, without assessors knowing the clients' group assignment

Thyer (2004) pointed out that these types of studies provide the best type of scientific evidence on which to base social work practice.

The Challenge of Fidelity

Fidelity in research methods has a similar meaning to how we use it—and its variant, "infidelity"—in everyday language. Fidelity in research essentially means that a program is true to its form: how much of the prescribed program to be evaluated is actually performed or implemented. Were substitute interventions adopted, or modifications made that were not communicated to the researcher? This can provide a political and social challenge in the agency context. One approach to ensure fidelity is to track the social workers as they implement the intervention. This can be logistically challenging and resisted by the social workers if they perceive this tracking as "looking over their shoulders" or "micromanaging." Again, you can partially alleviate these problems by adopting participatory approaches and maximizing input and ideas from all the parties involved in the program evaluation.

An Example of Fidelity in Research

Thyer and Bloomfield (2021) examined the fidelity of two intervention methods: developmental, individual differences relation-based therapy (DIR) and creative arts therapy (CAT). Both have had positive effects for individuals with autism spectrum disorder (ASD). This study evaluated them in combination, with an emphasis on ensuring the fidelity of each of the interventions and the outcomes.

Pretest and posttest quantitative standardized measures were used for data collection and analysis. The study also collected data from treatment logs to document the fidelity to the treatment model. The study was conducted in a non-profit, parent-founded private day school in a large city on the East Coast of the United States. Twenty-one students (ages 5–21 years old) participated in the program of weekly individual and group-based dance, music, and art therapy sessions across six months. Children who participated experienced moderate increases in social/emotional skills.

Ethical Issues in Program Evaluation Design

Two major ethical issues are related to group design, both associated with control or comparison groups. First is the issue of whether establishing a comparison or control group involves denying services to clients. Second is whether the subjects' informed consent should be obtained so that a comparison group can be established.

Assignment to the Comparison or Control Group

The NASW Code of Ethics (2021) states that social workers should take appropriate steps to ensure that participants in evaluation and research have access to appropriate supportive services. You should always assure the participants in the research of some services. Though whether they will be assured of those services is an issue when participants are assigned to comparison or control groups.

This research strategy could be viewed as a denial of services justified in the name of science; it poses an ethical dilemma that can have implications for the administration of the evaluation. The personnel may see the creation of comparison or control groups as a way of manipulating clients that could consequently influence the evaluation. For example, in a situation where the comparison group is receiving a variation of the intervention to be evaluated, the staff—if they disagree with the creation of the comparison group—may not adhere to the guidelines governing this variation in an attempt to bring legitimate services to the subjects in the comparison group. In addition, clients simply may not be referred to the project.

There are two arguments that using comparison or control groups does not always pose a serious ethical problem. First, deciding who receives services in an agency is often arbitrary and political. For example, program services may run on demand, and the deprivation of services is not uncommon. Moreover, as Bloom (2005) points out, random assignment treats sample members equally in that each has a sense of being assigned to the experimental or control group.

Second, by suggesting that clients are denied valuable treatment, we assume that the evaluation intervention is effective. Often, though, that assumption has no empirical basis. If it did, there would be little reason for carrying out the research in the first place. As in practice, however, the situation in research is often not this clear-cut. Usually, some evidence—perhaps a combination of practice wisdom and research findings—indicates that the treatment is helpful to some extent. The purpose of the evaluation is then to determine how valuable it is. Consequently, our concern that we are violating subjects' rights by possibly denying them beneficial treatment involves other factors, such as individual judgments and values about how detrimental the denial could be. This is another example of the vital role of values in the scientific process.

The seriousness of the problem probably governs decisions relating to establishing control or comparison groups. Under most circumstances, it would be hard to justify establishing a control group of emotionally disturbed children involved in self-destructive behaviors. In addition, the use of waiting lists and cohort groups, baseline comparison groups, and assignment to other types of interventions or programs can help alleviate some of the potential ill effects of being assigned to the comparison or control group.

Informed Consent

Informed consent involves both informing potential subjects fully of their role and the consequences of their participation in the research and seeking their permission. The NASW Code of Ethics (2021) states:

- Social workers engaged in evaluation or research should obtain voluntary and written informed consent from participants, when appropriate, without any implied or actual deprivation or penalty for refusal to participate; without undue inducement to participate; and with due regard for participants.

- Informed consent helps ensure well-being, privacy, and dignity. Informed consent should include information about the nature, extent, and duration of the participation requested and disclosure of the risks and benefits of the involvement in the research.

- When evaluation or research participants are incapable of giving informed consent, social workers should provide an appropriate explanation to the participants, obtain the participants' assent to the extent they are able, and get written consent from an appropriate proxy.

- Social workers should inform participants of their right to withdraw from evaluation and research at any time without penalty.

Notice with the third bullet that reference is made to "assent to the extent they are able." **Assent** is a critical concept to understand when research participants cannot provide the necessary informed consent and it involves a more straightforward explanation about the nature of the research that might affect their decision as to whether they want to participate. For example, consent is needed in the case of people with dementia and with children. In addition, consent is necessary because it allows a more diverse group of people to participate in research.

Informed consent is an issue because of the difficulty of forming comparison groups. In seeking a comparison group, you may be reluctant to fully inform potential participants that they will not be receiving a service. In attempting to ensure their participation, you may justify your failure to inform them on the grounds that their consent is not necessary if they are not receiving the service. Informed consent is less of a problem with control groups. Participants will be randomly assigned to the control and experimental groups and will therefore be told that they may or may not be receiving the service. *Consent must be gained at all times for any participation,* whether it is in the experimental group, comparison group, or control group.

As discussed in the previous section, the effects of being in the control group can be improved somewhat by adopting alternative strategies—waiting lists, alternative programs, and so forth. These strategies can also help with the consent issue. In other words, the researcher will not be so tempted to avoid seeking informed consent in anticipation of the potential subject's refusing to participate, because ultimately, the client will receive some type of intervention. The second issue relating to informed consent is the possibility that informing the subjects of the evaluation details will jeopardize the validity of the findings. For example, suppose the experimental group knows they are the experimental group and the control or comparison group knows they are the control or comparison group. In that case, expectations can be set up that affect outcomes. For example, the experimental group may expect to change and, regardless of the actual impact of the intervention itself, may show improvement. This threat to validity was discussed earlier in the chapter as a reactive effect. Given the possibility of this threat, it is tempting to avoid giving subjects all the details of their participation. Informed consent should still be obtained, however. One way of dealing with the reactive problem is to inform the subjects that they will either be placed in a control, comparison, or experimental group, yet they will not be told which of the groups they will join to protect the validity of the findings. Of course, this is only an option if the control or comparison group receives at least some type of intervention, whether it is a variation of the one being evaluated or another intervention altogether.

If such intervention is not feasible, the researcher needs to acknowledge possible reactive effects rather than simply not informing the subjects.

Human Diversity Issues in Program Evaluation Design

When developing a program evaluation and making decisions about the research design, the central issue relating to human diversity is ensuring that certain groups are not being exploited to establish comparison groups. Sometimes such exploitation can occur unintentionally. For example, in social science research, the tendency is to assign disadvantaged people such as the poor, minorities, women, and others to comparison groups. (This is not an issue for control groups when randomly assigning subjects.)

There is a danger that the choice of particular comparison groups demonstrates the scientist's "implicit theoretical framework." These theoretical frameworks can be biased against certain groups such as women or other groups. "Knowing" what variables to include entails biases that can favor certain groups over others. The choice of the comparison group defines the perspective that will dominate the research and, in turn, influence the findings.

Parlee (1981) cited a study in which a matched comparison group of women was sought for a study of aging among twenty-year-old men. One alternative was to match the women according to intelligence, education, and occupation. Another might argue for matching according to physiological similarities, by, for example, including the men's sisters. The former represented the social scientists' perspective, while the latter reflected that of biomedical scientists. These two alternatives involved two different perspectives on the underlying causality of aging and would probably result in different conclusions being drawn from the study.

It is critical to recognize this potential bias in comparison group selection. To counterbalance this problem, we should involve diverse people in conceptualizing the research, particularly if the program evaluation impacts diverse populations. This way can incorporate alternative viewpoints and perspectives into the group design.

Summary

There are two main types of program evaluations: formative and summative. Formative evaluations are primarily descriptive, whereas summative evaluations focus on causality. When designing summative program evaluations, it is necessary to select a group design. Each design poses various threats to internal and external validity. Internal validity is the extent to which the changes in the dependent variable are a result of the independent variable. External validity refers to the generalizability of the research findings to a broader population. There are also the dual challenges of randomization and fidelity.

Ethical issues relating to group design include potentially denying services to clients when establishing comparison or control groups and obtaining informed consent from clients. Human diversity issues include not exploiting certain kinds of people for use as comparison groups.

STUDY/EXERCISE QUESTIONS

1. The family service agency where you are employed is planning to evaluate its services. As the leader of a support group for parents of children with Asperger's, you are asked to design an evaluation.

   a. What design could you develop that would be feasible and maximize the validity of your findings?

   b. Under what circumstances would a formative evaluation be appropriate, and how would you carry this out?

2. Review an issue of Social Work Research and Abstracts and select an article that used one of the research designs described in this chapter.

   a. What are the threats to internal and external validity?

   b. Were these threats explicitly discussed?

   c. Propose an alternative design that would be feasible.

3. You are asked to help implement an early childhood intervention program evaluation. The program is funded by a large international aid organization and requires that you use a full experimental design that involves the random assignment of the participant families. What ethical/political/social arguments will you present in favor of this type of design?

4. As a class, identify a program to evaluate. Then, break into small groups, with each group developing a different design for the evaluation and presenting its advantages and disadvantages to the entire class.

5. You are asked to evaluate a work readiness program for developmentally challenged adults. What would be some of the informed consent issues you would need to address?

REFERENCES

Bloom, M., Fischer, J., & Orme, J. (2009). *Evaluating practice: Guidelines for the accountable profession* (6th ed.). Boston: Allyn and Bacon.

Bui, C. N., Coyle, C. E., & Freeman, A. (2021). Promoting self-advocacy among older adults: Lessons from Boston's Senior Civic Academy. *Journal of Applied Gerontology, 40*(4), 452–458. https://doi.org/10.1177%2F0733464820902628

Budge, S. L., Sinnard, M. T., & Hoyt, W. T. (2021). Longitudinal effects of psychotherapy with transgender and nonbinary clients: A randomized controlled pilot trial. Psychotherapy, 58(1), 1–11. https://psycnet.apa.org/doi/10.1037/pst0000310

Gabrkelik, R., Mahic, M., Lund, O., Bramness, J., Selmer, R., Skovlund, E., Handal, M., & Skurtveit, S. (2021). Cannabis use during pregnancy and risk of adverse birth outcomes: A longitudinal cohort study. *European Addiction Research, 27*, 131–141. https://doi.org/10.1159/000510821

Han, A., & Kim, T. H. (2021). Effectiveness of empathy enhancement programs for social workers working with older adults: A quasi-experimental study. *Journal of Social Work, 21*(4), 913–930. https://doi.org/10.1177%2F1468017320940591

Keller-Hamilton, B., Lu, B., Roberts, M. E., Berman, M. L., Root, E. D., & Ferketich, A. K. (2021). Electronic cigarette use and risk of cigarette and smokeless tobacco initiation among adolescent boys: A propensity score-matched analysis. *Addictive Behaviors, 114*, p. 106770.

Parlee, M. B. (1981). Appropriate control groups in feminist research. *Psychology of Women Quarterly, 5*, 637–644.

Petering, R., Barr, N., Srivastava, A., Onasch-Vera, L., Thomson, N., & Rice, E. (2021). Examining impacts of a peer-based mindfulness and yoga intervention to reduce interpersonal violence among young adults experiencing homelessness. *Journal of Social Work and Research, 12*(1). https://doi.org/10.1086/712957

Siria, S., Echeburúa, E., & Amor, P. J. (2021). Adolescents adjudicated for sexual offending: Differences between sexual reoffenders and sexual non-reoffenders. *Journal of Interpersonal Violence.* https://doi.org/10.1177/08862605211015209

Thyer-Bradley, F., & Bloomfield, S. (2021). An evaluation of a developmental individual differences relationship-based (DIR®)-creative arts therapies program for children with autism. *The Arts in Psychotherapy, 73*, [101752]. https://doi.org/10.1016/j.aip.2020.101752

7

Designing the
Evaluation of Practice

INTRODUCTION

During the last twenty years, social workers have experienced increased pressure to evaluate their practice. In part, this pressure stems from studies done in the 1960s and early 1970s, which suggested that social work practice was not as effective as many had expected. However, on closer examination, the research studies themselves were found to have significant methodological problems, raising questions about whether the findings from the studies should be viewed seriously and as an accurate reflection of the state of social work practice.

First, the research studies often used no type of comparison group, which led to questions about the internal and external validity of the results. Second, group designs used in program evaluations pooled the results from both successful and unsuccessful programs to determine average results. However, they could not determine what worked with whom and with what kinds of problems. Consequently, the results were often of little use to the practitioner. Third, the group designs generally relied on only two measurements—one taken before and one after. There was no way of knowing what happened between these two measurement points. For example, a posttest may indicate that the target problem has not decreased in severity. However, some decreases may have occurred after the intervention but before the posttest. It could not be determined why such an effect occurred because of how many of these studies were designed.

In addition to these methodological problems, other problems relating to ethical and social issues characterized these early studies. First, it was and is often difficult to get the support of agency personnel in assigning clients to control or comparison groups because of the ethical issues discussed in Chapter 6. Second, it was also often impossible for agencies to access the funds for a full-scale evaluation of even a moderately sized program.

As a consequence of these problems and the continuing demand for accountability of the social services, social workers were increasingly required to evaluate their practice. Different ways of implementing these evaluations emerged. At first, emphasis was on an approach adopted from psychology, a technology known as **single-system** or **single-subject designs** or **studies**. These studies tried to assess the impact of interventions on client systems.

Single-system designs relied heavily on collecting empirical behavioral data grounded in the positivist tradition. They grew in popularity as they produced results identifying how specific interventions were effective with particular clients with specific types of problems.

Later, departments and schools of social work taught single-system designs. However, single system technology came under criticism partly because of lack of agency support, the intrusiveness of the designs, and an unrealistic expectation of the social worker. As a result, alternative approaches to evaluating practice began to emerge. Instead of the single-system design approach of assessing the impact of interventions on client systems (explanatory designs), descriptive methods were developed to monitor client progress and intervention. These methods used interpretive and qualitative approaches, differing significantly from the positivist approaches associated with single-system studies. In addition, program administrators began to use a group of single-system studies to evaluate entire programs.

These more recent ways of evaluating practice give the social worker choices about which approach to use. As stressed in Chapter 1 and throughout this book, the choice depends on the researcher's question. Practice evaluation involves three major questions. First, how can the intervention be described? Second, how can the client's progress be monitored? Third, how effective is the intervention in bringing about client change? The first two questions are primarily descriptive, whereas the third is explanatory. Regardless of the practice evaluation adopted, both emphasize assessing change over time, rather than (as with the group designs) comparisons with other groups.

With the increasing emphasis on evidence-based practice discussed in Chapter 2, practice evaluations, in conjunction with program evaluations, play an essential role in providing evidence on the effectiveness of social work practice.

LEARNING OBJECTIVES

This chapter will include the following learning objectives:

1. To describe and understand the role and types of descriptive designs for practice evaluation

2. To describe and understand the role and types of explanatory designs for practice evaluation

3. To gain a beginning understanding of the analysis of practice evaluation data

4. To understand the strengths and limitations of practice evaluations

5. To articulate the ethical and human diversity issues in practice evaluation

Descriptive Designs for Practice Evaluation

As just discussed, two types of questions in practice evaluation require descriptive designs: questions that focus on the nature of the intervention and questions that focus on monitoring any client change. We will present each of these in this section.

Monitoring Interventions

The researcher/practitioner can often examine and reflect on the intervention, referred to as **monitoring interventions**. Evaluation then becomes a process of discovery rather than an experiment. For example, as a student social worker, you may be asked to evaluate how you apply an intervention and describe your activities to your supervisor. You can use various strategies to evaluate an intervention. For example, you can use three methods to monitor interventions: process recordings, practice logs, and case studies.

Process Recordings

Process recordings are written records based on notes or a transcription of a recording (audio or video) of interactions between the worker and clients. These qualitative data then become an important source of information for improving practice.

Suppose you are just beginning your employment with Child Protective Services, and your supervisor has given you the go-ahead to visit a family alone. However, you are still unsure whether you are conducting the interview appropriately. Consequently, immediately after the home visit, you sit down and record the major interactions that occurred. You later share this process recording with your supervisor. This process can help identify the strengths and weaknesses in your interviewing skills; if you continue this type of monitoring for several cases, you may see patterns emerging.

Practice Logs

A variation on the process recording is an ongoing **practice log**, in which you use self-reflection and analysis to understand how you and the client worked together in resolving the issues raised. Practice logs go beyond a process recording. Here the writer self-reflects and comments on their use of the intervention and practice experience. You may be required to keep practice logs in your field practica. As a form of data collection, we will discuss these in Chapter 9.

An Example of Reflecting on Practice

Zuchowski et al. (2021) described and explored e-placements that engaged social work students in the first semester of 2020 due to placement disruption after the emergence of COVID-19. The term "e-placement" describes a placement undertaken off-site by the placement organization or agency. Students at James Cook University (JCU) in Queensland, Australia, who could not continue in on-site placements were offered the opportunity to participate in a Community Connector Project (CCP) to complete their placement. These were online supported placements delivering a comprehensive and interactive learning experience. The students worked with the community to explore community needs during the pandemic, share and distribute existing information and resources, and develop further information and resources. Twenty students chose to participate in the CCP. The project included biweekly meetings, small group work, and individual work. Much of the data involved practice reflections by field education staff, students, and a service provider. These practice reflections were carried out on the project and the project's outcomes, challenges, and learning.

For example, say you are trying to organize a community center for youths, but this is an entirely new experience for you. Consequently, you carefully record all your activities, impressions, and thoughts connected with this endeavor, and you share this information with a more experienced community organizer you met at an NASW chapter conference the previous year. In this situation, your practice log gives you a systematic record of what occurred so that you don't have to rely on anecdotes and your memory. Moreover, this record can provide potential data for a more explanatory design you might want to attempt later, in which you try to determine whether your strategy had the anticipated outcomes.

These evaluations are rarely published since they are used primarily by individual workers and agencies to enhance practice.

Case Examples

Case examples/studies involve a complete description of the application of the intervention. They tend to be more "objective" and less self-reflecting than the process recordings or practice log approaches. Detailed case studies of unusual, successful, or unsuccessful cases can yield vital information. The type of information generated may either support existing practice principles or suggest new approaches and principles. You can use a single case study or multiple case studies.

An Example of a Case Study

Datta et al. (2020) explored family resiliency by focusing on the indigenous concepts of resistance and reconnection. This family case study discussed family interaction, social distancing, and isolation during the COVID-19 pandemic. It highlighted how indigenous elders, knowledge-keepers, and ancestors' stories helped build resistance and reconnection to be active, hopeful, and joyful during the pandemic.

An Example of Multiple Case Studies

Rémillard-Boilard, Buffel, and Phillipson (2020) investigated how age-friendly cities and communities have become in light of the World Health Organization's (WHO) push to improve the quality of life for older people living in urban areas. As a result, the WHO developed the Global Network of Age-Friendly Cities and Communities, connecting 1,114 (2020 figure) cities and communities worldwide.

To learn about the progress made in more detail, this study compared the experience of eleven cities located in eleven countries. Using a multiple case study approach, the study explored the key goals, achievements, and challenges faced by local age-friendly programs and identified four priorities the age-friendly movement should consider to further its development: (1) changing the perception of older age; (2) involving key actors in age-friendly efforts; (3) responding to the (diverse) needs of older people; and (4) improving the planning and delivery of age-friendly programs.

One significant advantage of monitoring interventions using any of the three approaches described here is that it provides a means for practitioners to reflect on and study their practice. The reflective method "would encourage practitioners to examine professional activity and the knowledge reflected in that activity against empirically based theory as well as against their practice wisdom and tacit knowledge, using a range of methodologies" (Millstein, 1993, p. 257).

An Example of a Reflective Method

Lotty (2020) described the author's journey of pursuing a Ph.D. as a social work practitioner, researcher, and doctoral candidate. First, she described her study, which designed, developed, and evaluated a psychoeducational intervention for foster carers in Ireland. Then, she discussed her reflections on her position in the research and how she theoretically framed her study, discussing the challenges of a practitioner and doctoral candidate. Finally, she concluded that her position as a practitioner and doctoral candidate probably enhanced her research.

Monitoring Client Progress

Not only can you monitor an intervention, but also the client's progress. Information is gathered on the client while the intervention is taking place. As a result, decisions can be made about whether the intervention should be continued, modified, or stopped. These data can be either qualitative, in the form of notes and narrative, or quantitative, in the form of behavioral observations or the different rapid assessment instruments described in Chapter 9. Whichever data collection method you use, you must clearly specify the client's goals.

For example, in working with a group of adolescent mothers, you may decide to monitor the clients' progress both during the months when the group meetings are held and after they stop. The change goal was to learn parenting skills, the maintenance goal was to practice those skills, and the prevention goal was to avoid future reporting for child abuse or neglect. The goals were monitored monthly for two years. This type of practice evaluation is rarely published, although it is crucial for evaluating practice as an ongoing activity. Moreover, the information gained from descriptive evaluations of individual practice can often help formulate hypotheses for future practice evaluations. Consequently, you can view descriptive studies as an inductive mode of building knowledge (as discussed in Chapter 1).

Explanatory Designs for Practice Evaluation

Explanatory designs examine the impact of the intervention on the target behavior. These designs are now also called single-system designs or single-system studies. They involve three elements that help establish causality: a baseline, clear identification of the intervention, and target behaviors that can be operationalized and repeatedly measured. Wong (2010) gives an excellent overview of the strengths and weaknesses of the different designs.

An Example of Using Logs for Reflection

Ferguson (2018) examined social workers' logs and their responses to questions after their interactions with clients and observation to examine how reflection develops their practice. The findings showed that practitioners often reflect in action by elevating their minds above the interactions they are having to think critically about and adjust to what they are doing. However, there are times when reflection is either limited or nonexistent because practitioners defend themselves against the sensory and emotional impact of the work and the high anxiety they are experiencing. In other words, "the self is protected." This has important implications for practice.

Baseline

Rather than depending on control or comparison groups in their search for causality, single-system designs rely on target behaviors measured time and time again. In effect, the client system serves as its own control. A similar principle is in effect here as that used in the time series designs discussed in Chapter 6; with that group design, however, a group of client systems is monitored, whereas the single-system study monitors only one client system. The repeated measurement before the intervention is known as the baseline. The baseline allows you to compare target behavior rates before and after the intervention, thus assessing the intervention's impact on the target behavior. This repeated measurement or baseline can take different forms. For example, it could be the frequency of a behavior, its duration, or its intensity. The choice depends upon the focus of the intervention. Figure 7.1 demonstrates how results from explanatory single-system designs are usually displayed. The X-axis records the incidents of the target behavior, and the Y-axis shows the time interval over which the behavior is recorded. The vertical line represents the point at which the intervention was introduced.

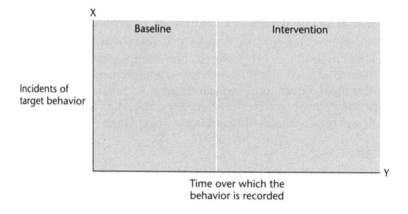

Figure 7.1   Displaying the results from explanatory single-system designs

For the assessment to have some validity, you need to establish a stable baseline before implementing the intervention. Fluctuations may occur, but this should constitute a stable baseline as long as they happen with some regularity. An unstable baseline makes it difficult to interpret the study's results. A problem with interpreting the findings also occurs when the baseline is stable but moves toward the desired outcome before the intervention's implementation (see Figure 7.2).

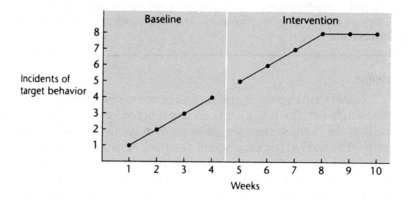

Figure 7.2   Example of a baseline moving in the direction of the desired outcome

Clearly Defined Intervention

Explanatory designs also require a clearly defined intervention, and the point at which it is introduced must be presented.

Operationalization and Repeated Measure of Target Behavior

Explanatory designs also require that the target behaviors that are the focus of the intervention be clearly defined. For example, rather than a target behavior's being defined as a child's inattentiveness, a more precise definition would be the number of times a question is repeated to a child before they answer. In addition to being clearly defined, you must repeatedly collect data about the target behavior.

We will now describe different types of explanatory designs.

AB Design

The **AB design** is the simplest of the single-system designs. First, you collect data on the target behavior before the intervention, which constitutes the design's baseline or phase A. Then, the B phase consists of measurements of the target behavior after you introduce the intervention. Finally, the effectiveness of the intervention is determined by comparing the A measure to the B measure.

Let's look at the problem of a family's low attendance at a parenting class. The goal or target behavior of the intervention is to increase attendance. The A phase would be the number of times the family attends the class before the intervention. The class is held twice a week, and data are already available on the family's attendance over the previous three weeks. You can use these data as a baseline.

The point at which the intervention is introduced marks the beginning of the B phase. For example, the intervention might be to arrange for another family to help with transportation to the class. You then record the frequency of the target behavior for several weeks after intervention.

An Example of an AB Design

Callender, Trustey, Alton, and Yuan Hao (2021) conducted an exploratory AB single case research design to assess the effectiveness of a twelve-week mindfulness-based mobile intervention to reduce burnout and increase mindfulness and self-compassion. The participant was one fifty-five-year-old White woman employed as a substance abuse counselor at a medium-sized treatment facility in a midwestern state. Three weeks of baseline data were collected, followed by a twelve-week intervention using the Calm© app, and then self-reported scores on the Copenhagen Burnout Inventory, Freiburg Mindfulness Inventory, and the Self-Compassion Scale across baseline and intervention phases. Data analyses indicated that using the Calm© app across twelve weeks may decrease burnout and increase mindfulness levels but it provided no evidence for increased self-compassion.

An illustration of how these data might look if charted is given in Figure 7.3. The results can be analyzed by simply viewing the chart. An increase in attendance is evident.

One of the advantages of the AB design is its simplicity. In addition, the design can easily be integrated into the practice process, giving important information about those interventions that appear to work with particular client systems.

Some problems are associated with this design, however. The major problem is that you do not control extraneous factors or the history threat to internal validity. In

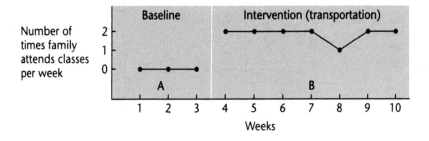

Figure 7.3   Example of an AB design

our example, it was possible that the classes suddenly became more attractive to the family or that the mother had convinced the father—who was exhibiting the most resistance to attending—of the benefits of the class. Or the results might have been due to a multitude of other factors. Thus, the AB design is restricted in its information about causality.

ABC Design

The **ABC design** is also known as the **successive intervention design** because the C phase represents the introduction of another intervention. Others can also be added on as D or E phases. The ABC design is simply the AB design with the addition of another intervention. With this design, the target behavior continues to be measured after the introduction of each intervention.

The ABC design can be convenient because it often reflects the reality of practice. We introduce one intervention, and if it seems ineffective, we implement another intervention. The ABC design adds an empirical element to this common practice.

To continue with the example, we have been using, transportation assistance did not increase attendance for another family. After further assessment, it was found that the parents—although they spoke English—were native Spanish speakers and were having difficulty following the class. Consequently, a second intervention was the organization of a class conducted in Spanish for several Spanish-speaking families in the community. The families' attendance was monitored following this intervention and it showed an increase. See Figure 7.4 for an illustration of how these results would be displayed.

Although the ABC design nicely reflects the reality of practice, this design has the same types of problems associated with the AB design. You have no way of knowing whether the intervention or some other factor accounted for any change in the target behavior. This validity issue is complicated in the ABC design by not knowing whether it was the C intervention that resulted in the final outcome or a combination of the B and C interventions. Although you may not know precisely which intervention influenced the outcome, you do know about the effect of some combination of the interventions—a finding that in itself can enhance your practice and service to clients.

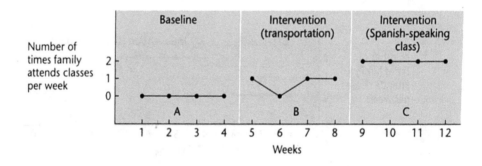

Figure 7.4   ABC single-system design

An Example of an ABC Design

Doll, Livesey, McHaffie, and Ludwig (2007) evaluated an intervention to improve employees' cleaning behaviors at a ski shop. The baseline lasted four weeks. Seven cleaning behaviors were monitored during this time, five of which were later targeted in the B and C interventions. The B intervention involved a task clarification session and a posted checklist of tasks to be completed. Following this phase, cleaning behaviors increased by 52 percent. The C intervention involved providing employees with daily task-specific feedback, resulting in another cleaning behavior increase of 12 percent.

ABAB Design

The **ABAB design** is also known as the **reversal design** or the **withdrawal design**; it consists of implementing the AB design and then reversing—withdrawing the intervention and collecting baseline data again before implementing the intervention a second time. For example, suppose a school social worker constantly works with the problem of absenteeism. In the past, she has made regular home visits to the families involved, and she has a sense that this is working. So she decides to test the intervention, starting with a single case of a twelve-year-old boy.

The social worker monitors his attendance at school over three weeks and then starts the home visits—which include counseling, information, and referral—twice a week. Next, she collects data on attendance for another three weeks and then stops the visits, again monitoring attendance for another three weeks. Finally, she once again introduces the intervention. The results, displayed in Figure 7.5, indicate that the intervention appears to impact the student's school attendance.

The great advantage of the ABAB design is its ability to tell us about the impact of the intervention versus the impact of other possible factors; in other words, its ability to explain and imply causality is greater than those of the AB or the ABC designs.

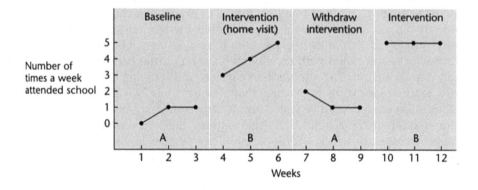

Figure 7.5   ABAB reversal single-system design

> ### An Example of an ABAB Reversal Design
>
> Hanashiro-Parson and Miltenberger (2021) compared the effectiveness of token reinforcement and monetary reinforcement for increasing physical activity among adults with intellectual challenges. They used an ABAB design with an alternating treatments design to compare the token and monetary reinforcement. The participants chose between the two reinforcement conditions in the second intervention phase. Results showed that both reinforcement conditions increased physical activity.

The ABAB design has a few problems. First, you cannot apply it to all target behaviors and all types of interventions. Some interventions cannot be reversed, particularly those involving teaching a new behavior. For example, suppose you identify the target behavior as a second grader's tardiness. Next, you assess that the problem results from the mother's not being assertive about getting ready for school. The intervention consists of the social worker's teaching the parent how to be assertive with the child. This would be a problematic intervention to reverse since you cannot reverse the mother's learned behavior.

Even if the intervention seemingly could be reversed, some residues of the intervention might remain. In the example of the twelve-year-old boy's absenteeism, the home visits might have resulted in some carryover effects even after they were halted; in fact, this seems to have been the case. The interpretation of the results and the precise impact of the intervention then becomes more difficult.

With any explanatory single-system study, and particularly with the reversal design, you must spell out the details and possible consequences for the clients before the intervention is instituted. This procedure is similar to obtaining clients' informed consent before engaging in a group study.

Multiple Baseline Designs

A **multiple baseline design** involves replicating the AB design by applying the same intervention to two or more target behaviors, to two or more clients, or in two or more settings at different points in time. For example, a child is exhibiting problems at school; you identify the target problem as the teacher's concern that the child is not verbally participating in class. After the assessment, it becomes apparent that this behavior is associated with the child's Navajo cultural background, which discourages speaking out. The intervention consists of discussing cross-cultural issues with the teacher, including suggesting that she use some Navajo examples in teaching. This intervention could be tested *across client systems* by using the intervention with three different Navajo children. Alternatively, the intervention could be used *across target problems*, in which additional problems such as low grades and low socialization might be identified. You could monitor this behavior both before and after the implementation of the intervention. The intervention could also be tested *across settings* by, for example, looking at changes in one of the target problems at the daycare center and at home in addition to the school setting.

Often multiple baseline designs are further strengthened by introducing interventions at different points on the baseline. As the intervention is introduced for the first behavior, client, or setting, the others are still at the baseline phase. This aspect of the design strengthens the internal validity of the design in that if an external event occurs at the same time as the introduction of the intervention, the baseline will pick up the potential impact of this event. However, if the intervention is responsible for the change, this change will occur on each graph at the point corresponding to the intervention's introduction. Figures 7.6 and 7.7 show how data from a multiple baseline design might be displayed.

The multiple baseline design offers a great deal of potential for examining the effectiveness of particular interventions and can allow us to be more confident in our belief that the intervention was responsible for any measured change. In effect, the multiple baseline design involves the principle of comparison groups in group design, using another client, another setting, or another target problem as a comparison. For example, if you find that the same intervention for the same target problem for the same setting was effective for two different clients, you would be more confident of the intervention's effectiveness than if you had simply examined one client.

An Example of a Multiple Baseline Design

Kenyon et al. (2021) investigated the effects of power mobility training provided to children with cerebral palsy on (1) parenting stress, (2) parents' perceptions of their children, and (3) children's attainment of power mobility skills using a multiple baseline AB single-subject research design with three participants. First, the target behavior was changed in the magnitude of parenting stress as measured by the Parenting Stress Index–Short Form. Parents' perceptions of their children were assessed using the Caregiver Priorities and Child Health Index of Life with Disabilities Questionnaire and a parent interview. Finally, children's attainment of power mobility skills was assessed using the Canadian Occupational Performance Measure (COPM), the Assessment of Learning Powered Mobility Use, and the Wheelchair Skills Checklist. Power mobility training was provided twice a week for eight weeks using an alternative power mobility device. After intervention, positive and negative changes in both magnitudes of parenting stress and parents' perceptions were identified. All participants gained power mobility skills.

Nevertheless, there are some limitations on how you can hold the intervention responsible for any change in the target problem even with these designs. For example, when applying the multiple baseline design across clients, even if the change in the target problem resulted in a positive outcome for both clients, there is still no guarantee that the intervention and the intervention alone resulted in the specific outcome. The validity limitations are similar to those associated with many nonexperimental designs discussed in Chapter 6.

As mentioned earlier in this chapter, you can use the multiple baseline design to evaluate entire programs. You can put together the results from a number of these designs to assess an intervention's effectiveness.

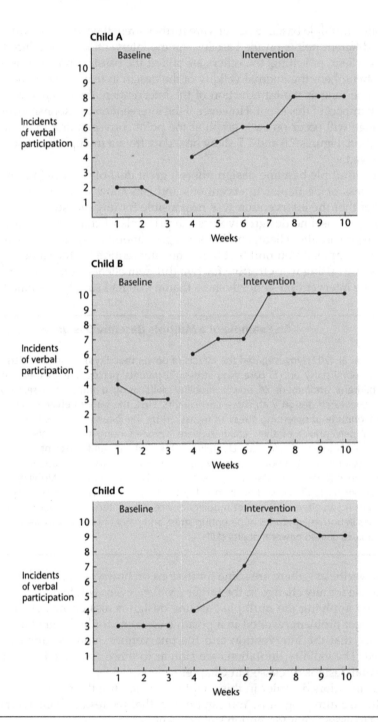

Figure 7.6   Multiple baseline design

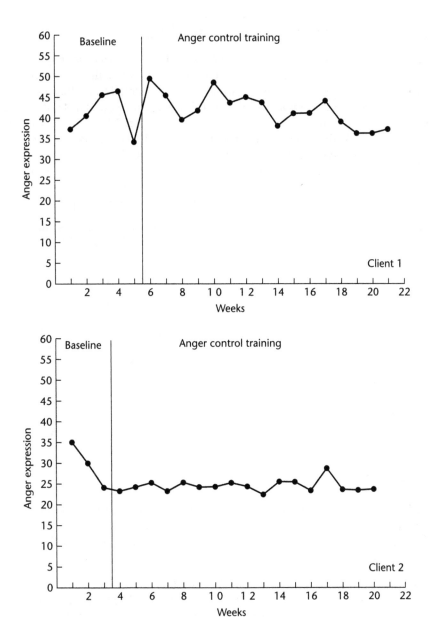

Figure 7.7   Weekly anger expression scale scores for Clients 1 and 2

Source: From "Validating school social work: An evaluation of a cognitive-behavioral approach to reduce school violence," in G. W. Whitfield, 1999, *Research in Social Work Practice, 9*(4), 399–426.

Analysis of Practice Evaluation Data

After collecting the data using the designs described in this chapter, it becomes necessary to make sense of the results. In later chapters, we will discuss the data analysis
from group designs. When quantitative data are collected from these designs, statistical
analysis is required (do not throw away this book quite yet, as it is not as painful as you
might think). Statistical analysis is included in Chapter 12. We also use other data analysis methods. Although not statistics, this type of data analysis is very challenging and
potentially time-consuming. Qualitative data analysis is discussed in Chapter 11. Here
though, we will discuss ways of presenting the results from single-system studies.

The first step is to describe the findings, which is best done visually. You can
think of practice evaluation data charts as possessing specific properties, including:

Level. The magnitude of data is the level. Differences in levels can occur between
the baseline and the intervention. A change in level is called a **discontinuity** (see
Figure 7.8).

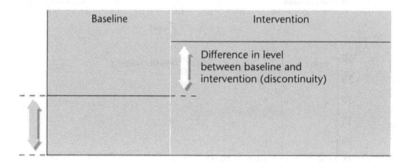

Figure 7.8   Levels of data

Stability.   Where there is precise predictability from a prior period to a later one, the
data are stable. Stability occurs if a mean line can easily represent the data. Data lines
can still be stable even if they change in magnitude. See Figure 7.9 for two examples
of data stability between baseline and intervention periods.

Trends.   A trend is present where the data tend in one direction—whether the pattern is increasing or decreasing. Trends are called **slopes** when they occur within a
given phase and **drifts** when they happen across phases. See Figure 7.10 for variations of trends.

Improvement or deterioration.   Specific comparisons between the baseline and intervention periods can improve or worsen the target behavior. Of course, determining what constitutes improvement and what constitutes deterioration depends on
whether greater or lesser magnitudes of the behavior are desired. Figure 7.11 illustrates this idea.

Other factors that we need to consider when describing findings from the charts include the following:

The timing of the effects. Sometimes effects occur immediately after the baseline and sometimes they are delayed (Figure 7.12).

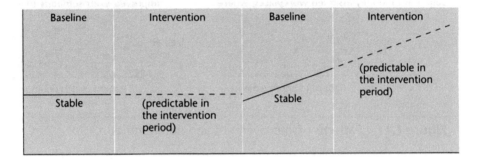

Figure 7.9   Stability of data between baseline and intervention

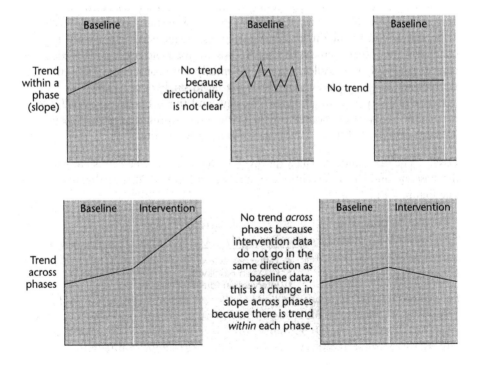

Figure 7.10   Trends within and across phases

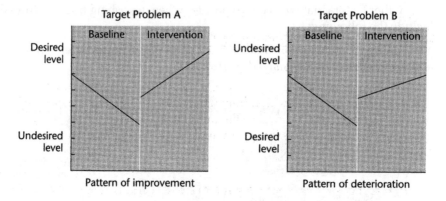

Figure 7.11   Patterns of improvement and deterioration

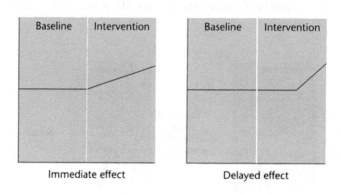

Figure 7.12   Immediate and delayed effects

The stability of the effects.   The effect of the intervention may wear off. If so, implementation of a different intervention is indicated (Figure 7.13).

Variability in the data.   This often happens but needs to be treated cautiously, particularly when the variability occurs during the baseline period. For example, in both examples in Figure 7.14, it is difficult to interpret the effects due to variability in the baseline data.

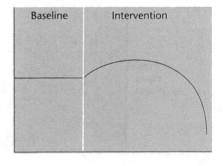

Figure 7.13   Unstable effects

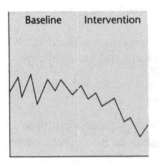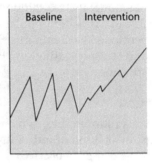

Figure 7.14   Variability in data

The Strengths and Limitations of Practice Evaluations

Much has been written about the relative strengths and limitations of practice evaluations and specific designs and their applicability to practice and agency settings. These strengths and limitations include the following.

Strengths

Strengths include feedback to the client, knowledge building for practice, and low cost and time factors.

Feedback to the Client

One benefit of practice evaluation is that you can provide feedback to the client. The intervention-monitoring and client-monitoring designs offer consistent feedback. With single-system designs, you can give the client tangible evidence that the intervention does or does not appear to impact behavior. Feedback can result in longer-term effects and the clients' adopting self-help measures, avoiding further social work intervention.

Knowledge Building for Practice

The activity of monitoring interventions or client progress can enhance workers' knowledge of their practice by allowing workers to critically examine the values and assumptions underlying the use of theories and their associated interventions in practice. Questions that are critical in developing a knowledge of practice include: Am I doing what I think I'm doing? If not, what am I doing? What does my work tell me about how I make meaning of practice? What ways of knowing do I use?

The single-system explanatory studies offer information about the efficacy of specific interventions. You can gain further knowledge by replicating or repeating the single-system studies—testing interventions with other clients, other target behaviors, and other settings. Replication increases internal validity (it is the intervention and not something else affecting the outcome) and external validity (the results are generalizable to a broader population).

As mentioned earlier in this chapter, you can build knowledge through single-system studies by integrating single-system and group approaches in evaluating program effectiveness.

Time and Cost

Unlike group studies, which often require additional funds, you can easily incorporate evaluation of individual practice into practice with no extra expense or excessive time commitment.

Limitations

Evaluation of individual practice offers some advantages in agency settings, but arguments can also be made against the use of such evaluations in agencies. They possess some limitations, including limited application, limited validity, and limited data analysis.

Limited Application

Historically, single-system explanatory designs were used almost exclusively to test the effectiveness of behavioral intervention techniques. In part, their application was limited because of the emphasis in behavior theory on defining behaviors clearly so that any changes in the behaviors can be easily recorded. As a result, many social workers, including generalist social workers, are deterred from using single-system studies because they have assumed the design is appropriate only for behavioral intervention and clearly observable and recordable behaviors. You can use designs that monitor intervention and client progress with various interventions and target behaviors.

In addition, some designs, such as the withdrawal and multiple baseline designs, are often simply not practical. As a result, it is rarely possible to withdraw an intervention.

Finally, it is often challenging to select a design when just beginning to work with a client; instead, designs are determined as practice evolves. This is less of a problem with the monitoring designs described in this chapter, which are sensitive to the process of practice.

Limited Validity

Internal and external validity is a problem with the explanatory single-system designs, even when results are replicated. Single-system studies simply are not as valid as well-designed group designs used in program evaluations. As discussed in Chapter 6, however, well-designed group studies are rare. More often, less satisfactory designs (in terms of causality) are used, resulting in internal and external validity problems. Consequently, in many instances, single-system studies can be considered worse in terms of validity than many group designs and are certainly better than no design at all.

Another validity issue is the extent to which self-report instruments, designed to measure subjective aspects of the client's problems, actually result in therapeutic reactive effects.

Analysis of Results

Another potential drawback of evaluating practice in agencies is that the analysis of findings is essentially a matter of judgment, so their applicability is limited. Some statistical analyses can be carried out for single-system designs, but this is beyond the scope of this text.

Ethical Issues in Practice Evaluation

Issues relevant to other types of social work research, such as confidentiality and informed consent, are obviously applicable here, although they have other implications when applied to practice evaluations. Two additional ethical issues are specifically related to practice evaluation: the use of the reversal design and the issue of interference with practice.

Informed Consent and Practice Evaluations

Rzepnicki (2004) points out how the combination of social work practice and evaluation poses ethical challenges to the clinician. Responsibility for the conduct of ethical practice and evaluation rests on the clinician's integrity, so it is essential for practitioners to understand the legal, ethical, and procedural standards that protect their clients from harm. The author emphasizes effective communication to enhance client understanding of how changes in their problems will be evaluated. Major goals of informed consent are to ensure (1) that clients understand what is being asked, (2) that clients can make knowledgeable decisions regarding their participation in the service, and (3) that consent is given voluntarily, with no coercion and no negative repercussions for refusal.

Reversal Design

As we discussed in the reversal design section, one could argue that withdrawing an apparently effective intervention is unethical. The counterargument is that withdrawal of the intervention will allow us to determine whether the intervention is responsible for any change in the target problem. This determination enhances the worker's knowledge of the intervention's effectiveness and demonstrates its effectiveness to the client. As a result, the intervention may have a more prolonged effect; parent training is a good example.

Interference with Practice

The second issue—the idea that practice evaluation procedures interfere with practice—has been raised consistently. One response to this position is that practice evaluation studies can enhance practice and help direct and inform social workers in their day-to-day contact with client systems. For example, determining the data collection method may offer other insights and prompt further exploration with the clients regarding the target problem.

In addition, the client's involvement in the research, particularly in the data collection, can result in the client being engaged in the change process to a greater extent, simultaneously limiting the problems with confidentiality and informed consent. This effect constitutes not so much interference as an enhancement of practice.

In conclusion, because of the joint participation of worker and client in several of the methods used in this chapter, ethical violations are far less likely than in group designs for program evaluations.

Human Diversity Issues in Practice Evaluation

Throughout the process of evaluating individual practice, you need to pay attention to human diversity issues. This effort includes more studies on diverse clients, recognizing that what may be effective for one type is not necessarily effective for another. Practice evaluations provide an excellent opportunity for exploring the richness of human diversity. However, practice evaluations may also introduce a bias because opportunities exist for the imposition of cultural assumptions about the types of behaviors tracked and their expected outcomes. Particular attention needs to be paid to researcher-participant matching as a precaution against undue cultural bias—a bias that is often undetectable. This issue also points to the importance of maximizing participatory approaches to research, whether a group or a single design is adopted.

Summary

There are two major approaches to evaluating practice: descriptive and explanatory. Descriptive methods include monitoring interventions and monitoring client progress. Explanatory approaches, or single-system designs, include the AB design, the ABC design, the ABAB design (reversal), and the multiple baseline design. Evaluating individual practice in agency settings is advantageous because of the opportunity for direct client feedback, knowledge building for practice, and time and cost factors. However, some problems are also associated with the evaluations, including limited analysis, limited validity, and limited application. Because of the partnership required between client and social worker, ethical violations are less likely than with group design. Evaluations of individual practice offer many opportunities for exploring the great diversity among different groups.

STUDY/EXERCISE QUESTIONS

1. You are working with a family with an adolescent who is not attending school regularly. You want to evaluate your intervention with the adolescent and collect data on her school attendance. What would be the advantages and disadvantages of the following designs for this evaluation?

    a. AB design

    b. ABC design

    c. ABAB design

    What would be the ethical issues in this case?

2. You would like to evaluate your practice as a generalist social worker in a hospital, but your supervisor objects, saying it would be too time-consuming. Support your request and address her concerns.

3. Find an article in a social work journal that examines practice evaluation, then summarize the main points.

4. You have been facilitating a support group for teenage parents. The goal is for the group to continue without a facilitator. You will be monitoring attendance at the group as an indicator of its effectiveness. How would you do this?

5. Your supervisor asks you to monitor your practice, focusing on the interventions you use. How would you do this?

REFERENCES

Callender, K., Trustey, C., Alton, L., & Hao, Y. (2021). Single case evaluation of a mindfulness-based mobile application with a substance abuse counselor. *Counseling Outcome Research and Evaluation, 12*(1), 16–29. https://doi.org/10.1080/21501378.2019.1686353

Datta, R., Chapola, J., Datta, P., & Datta, P. (2020). The COVID-19 pandemic: An immigrant family story on reconnection, resistance, and resiliency. *Journal of Comparative Family Studies, 51*(3/4), 429–444. https://doi.org/10.3138/jcfs.51.3-4.016

Doll, J., Livesey, J., McHaffie, E., & Ludwig, T. (2007). Managing cleaning behaviors at a ski shop. *Journal of Organizational Behavior Management, 27*(3), 41–60.

Ferguson, H. (2018). How social workers reflect in action and when and why they don't: The possibilities and limits to reflective practice in social work. *Social Work Education, 37*(4), 415–427. https://doi.org/10.1080/02615479.2017.1413083

Hanashiro-Parson, H., & Miltenberger, R. G. (2021). An evaluation of token and monetary reinforcement on physical activity exhibited by adults with intellectual disabilities in a group home setting. Behavior Analysis: Research and Practice, 21(3), 184–194. https://psycnet.apa.org/doi/10.1037/bar0000215

Kenyon, L. K., Aldrich, N. J., Farris, J. P., Chesser, B., & Walenta, K. (2021). Exploring the effects of power mobility training on parents of exploratory power mobility learners: A multiple-baseline single-subject research design study. *Physiotherapy Canada, 73*(1), 76–89. DOI: 10.3138/ptc-2019-0045

Lotty, M. (2021). Reflections on navigating the Ph.D. journey as a social work practitioner. *Qualitative Social Work, 20*(3), 851–865. https://doi.org/10.1177%2F1473325020921926

Millstein, K. H. (1993). Building knowledge from the study of cases: A reflective model for practitioner self-evaluation. *Journal of Teaching, 8*(1/2), 255–277.

Rémillard-Boilard, S., Buffel, T., & Phillipson, C. (2020). Developing age-friendly cities and communities: Eleven case studies from around the world. *International Journal of Environmental Research and Public Health, 18*(1), 133. https://doi.org/10.3390/ijerph18010133

Rzepnicki, T. L. (2004). Informed consent and practice evaluation: Making the decision to participate meaningful. In Briggs, H. E., & Rzepnicki, T. L. (Eds.), Using Evidence in Social Work Practice: Behavioral Perspectives (pp. 273–290). Chicago: Lyceum Books.

Wong, S. E. (2010). Single-case evaluation designs for practitioners. *Journal of Social Service Research, 36*(3), 248–259, DOI: 10.1080/01488371003707654

Zuchowski, I., Collingwood, H., Croaker, S., Bentley-Davey, J., Grentell, M., & Rytkönen, F. (2021). Social work E-placements during COVID-19: Learnings of staff and students. *Australian Social Work, 74*(3), 373–386. https://doi.org/10.1080/0312407X.2021.1900308

8

Selecting the Participants

INTRODUCTION

Now that you've decided on your research question and the type of design, who will be the participants? In social work research, **sampling** involves choosing the participants in the study. Sampling is necessary because you usually cannot include everyone in the study, just as in practice, you cannot interview or meet with all those involved in a situation. For example, you may be interested in determining the need for an afterschool program in your community, and you want to identify and get opinions from all the families in the city who have children twelve years and under in age. Even in a small city, this could be a large number of families, but you have a limited budget and only two months to complete the project. Consequently, you need to select a smaller group of participants, or **sample**, from this large group or **population** that is made up of all possible cases you are ultimately interested in studying (see Figure 8.1). Note that the population is a theoretical construct and refers to people with specific characteristics that the researcher is trying to understand.

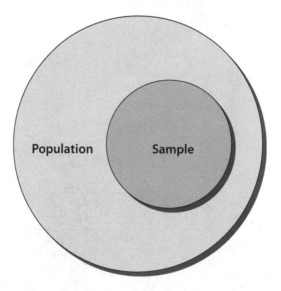

Figure 8.1   Population and sample

Sampling should be a familiar concept to you as a generalist social worker. You often need to collect information relating to a target problem from a large number of people. When you cannot contact all relevant people because of time and other constraints, you select a sample. There are specific ways to select a sample; the particular method we use depends on the nature and accessibility of the population and the type and purpose of the study we are undertaking.

As with the research process steps already discussed, you may not be directly involved in sampling decisions. However, knowledge of the process is essential for two reasons: First, sometimes you will be involved in the sampling decision; second, you need to understand how sampling can affect the use of the research findings in your practice.

LEARNING OBJECTIVES

This chapter has the following learning objectives:

1. To understand the key concepts in sampling

2. To identify the types of sampling methods

3. To learn the implications of sample size

4. To articulate the ethical and human diversity issues in sampling

Key Concepts In Sampling

One of the key concepts of sampling is the extent to which the sample is representative of the population. A **representative sample** means that the sample has the same distribution of characteristics as the population from which it is selected. For example, in assessing the city's need for an afterschool program, you are interested in making statements applicable to the entire city, so your sample needs to be representative. Thus, in this case, it is essential that the sample not be biased in any way. One way bias occurs is if only one neighborhood is selected.

Neighborhoods tend to have specific socioeconomic and ethnic characteristics—for example, upper-middle-class suburbs, African American inner-city neighborhoods, retirement communities, and small rural settlements. As a result, they are not usually representative of the entire city population, at least not in terms of socioeconomic and ethnic structure. The neighborhood is only one example of possible bias. Other groupings, such as schools and churches, may not represent the larger community.

If your sample is representative of the population, then you can generalize the findings from your sample to that population. Although it is important to remember that it is the population of most interest to the researcher, the sample is used because it is more accessible and convenient than studying the entire population. When you generalize, you claim that the sample's findings can be applied to the population. For example, suppose you discover in your representative sample of families from your city that 70 percent express an urgent need for an afterschool program. In that case, you then generalize that 70 percent of the families in your city (that is, your population) will also express this need. In needs assessment studies such as this, you must be able to generalize your findings. Thus, a quantitative approach, which emphasizes the generalizability of the results, is taken when conducting many needs assessments.

Generalizability and representativeness, however, are not such important issues in other studies. For example, rather than looking at the extent of the need for an afterschool program, you might be more concerned with exploring the experiences of families with children who spend part of the day unsupervised. Here you might use a qualitative approach. Then there would be less concern with the representativeness of the sample and the generalizability of the findings. In an interpretive study, the key concept is that the sample is **information-rich**; that is, the sample consists of cases from which you can learn about issues central to the research question.

Before describing different sampling strategies, you need to become familiar with two other general sampling concepts. First, an **element** in sampling refers to the item under study in the population and sample. In generalist social work research, these items or elements may be the different client systems we work with—individuals, families, groups, organizations, or communities. The element depends upon the unit of analysis. Elements may be more specific than these basic systems. In our example, families with school-age children twelve and under are a more specific element than simply families.

The second concept is the **sampling frame**. This consists of a list of all the elements in the population from which the sample is selected. In the above example, the sampling frame would consist of a list of families in the city with school-age children under the age of twelve.

As you confront the realities of compiling a sampling frame, you may need to redefine the population. For example, you might have decided on families with children aged twelve and under as your element because the state in which you are conducting the study legally mandates that children of this age cannot be left without adult supervision. However, when you compile a sampling frame, you run into problems because you find it very difficult to identify families with children of this age and younger. Instead, you discover that you can more easily identify families with children in the first through the seventh grades through the school system. You may end up with a few thirteen-year-olds, but this isn't a problem if you redefine your population as families with children in the first through the seventh grades. Remember that the population and the sampling frame are not the same thing. The population is more of a theoretical construct, whereas the sampling frame is a tool used to select the sample.

Types of Sampling Methods

You can select the sample in two major ways: probability and nonprobability sampling. **Probability sampling** allows you to select a sample in which each element in the population has a known chance of being selected for the sample. This type of sampling increases the sample's representativeness and should be strived for when using the quantitative approach to research.

Instead of a probability sampling method, you may choose **nonprobability sampling**. This approach allows you to handpick the sample according to the nature of the research problem and the phenomenon being studied. As a sampling method, nonprobability sampling is limited in terms of representativeness. This is because the probability of each element of the population being included in the sample is unknown. However, it is often the sampling method of choice in qualitative studies, where the generalizability of results is less important.

We will present probability and nonprobability sampling in more detail in the following sections.

Probability Sampling

Probability sampling occurs when every element in the population has a known chance of being selected; thus, its representativeness is assured. In addition, no subject can be selected more than once in a single sample. There are four major types of probability sampling: (1) simple random sampling, (2) systematic random sampling, (3) stratified random sampling, and (4) cluster sampling. Table 8.1 includes each probability sampling method and its associated potential generalizability.

TABLE 8.1 Probability sampling methods and generalization of findings

Sampling Method	Generalizability
Simple random	Can generalize; limitations minimal
Systematic random	Can generalize; limitations minimal—note how the elements are listed in the sampling frame
Stratified random	Can generalize; limitations minimal—make sure the strata involved are reflected in the analysis of the data
Cluster	Can generalize, but some limitations possible—note the characteristics of the elements because there is a possibility of sampling error with this type of probability sampling

Simple Random Sampling

Simple random sampling is the easiest of the sampling methods. The population is treated as a whole unit, and each element has an equal probability of being selected in the sample. Because the sampling is random, each element has the same chance of being selected. When you toss a coin, there is an equal chance of its being heads or tails. In the afterschool program needs assessment example, a simple random sample would involve assigning identification numbers to all the elements (families with children in first through seventh grades) and then using a table of random numbers generated by a computer. Most software packages for the social sciences can generate random number tables.

Simple random sampling is the most straightforward probability sampling method. However, it can often be challenging to implement in social work research and does have some drawbacks, which will become apparent as the other types of probability sampling are discussed.

An Example of Simple Random Sampling

Ware and Cagle (2021) studied the extent to which hospice social workers are paying attention to patient pain, whether physical, psychological, social, emotional, or spiritual. The researchers randomly sampled 248 hospices nationally, requested blank social work psychosocial assessments, and reviewed their pain-related content. A total of 105 hospices responded (a response rate of 42.3 percent). Less than half (47.6 percent) of the agencies included pain assessment content in their assessment. No associations were observed between having pain assessment content and agency characteristics. None of the assessments included content about three barriers to pain management: tolerance, overdose, stigma, and fatalism. Few agencies included other barriers to pain management: addiction (1 percent), burden (1 percent), nonadherence (3.8 percent), and stoicism (18.1 percent). Agencies that had pain assessment content mainly included other dimensions of pain: psychological (80 percent), emotional (74 percent), and social (78 percent). The researchers concluded that hospice social workers could do more to assess and address pain concerns—especially along the psychological, social, and emotional dimensions.

Systematic Random Sampling

Systematic random sampling involves taking the list of elements and choosing every nth element on the list. The size of n depends upon the size of the sampling frame and the intended size of the sample. For example, if you had four hundred elements in your sampling frame and needed a sample of one hundred, you would select every fourth element for the sample. On the other hand, if you need a sample of two hundred, you will select every second element.

An Example of Systematic Random Sampling

Adhikari et al. (2021) conducted a patient satisfaction survey in a hospital in Nepal. To recruit participants for the study, they applied a systematic random sampling method with a sample size of 204. The researchers used a validated Patient Satisfaction Questionnaire III (PSQ-III) developed by the RAND Corporation, including sociodemographic characteristics. The results indicated a wide variation in patient satisfaction across seven dimensions. About 39 percent of patients were generally satisfied, 92 percent were satisfied in an interpersonal manner, and 45 percent were satisfied in accessibility and convenience. Sociodemographic factors such as age, gender, and ethnicity were associated with the patients' general satisfaction. However, other sociodemographic variables such as education, occupation, and religion were associated with a majority of the dimensions of patient satisfaction. Age was the strongest predictor of patient satisfaction in five out of seven dimensions.

Generally, systematic random sampling is as random as simple random sampling. However, one potential problem with systematic random sampling arises when the ordering of elements in the list being sampled follows a particular pattern. As a result, a distortion of the sample may result. In the afterschool program example, students from the school district may be arranged into class lists of approximately thirty students, with all students who moved to the community within the last six months placed at the end of the lists. In some communities, these recent additions may primarily be the children of migrant workers. Consequently, if you were to select every tenth, twentieth, and thirtieth element in each class list, your resulting sample would be made up of a disproportionate number of migrant workers' children. Even though each class has only three or four such students, they are more likely to be the thirtieth element in a class list.

Problems with ordering elements can usually be identified quite easily, and you can take precautions to guard against them. For example, systematic random sampling may be easier than simple random sampling when lists are available because it avoids assigning identification numbers to the elements.

Stratified Random Sampling

Stratified random sampling is a modification of the previous two methods; the population is divided into strata, and subsamples are randomly selected from each stratum. Sometimes you need to ensure that a certain proportion of the elements (sometimes this sampling method is referred to as Proportional Stratified Sampling) is represented. Stratified random sampling provides a greater chance of meeting this goal than systematic or simple random sampling.

In the afterschool program study, you may be concerned about representing the different ethnic groups of the families with children in first through seventh grades. For example, you identify 10 percent of the families as Native Americans.

With a simple or systematic random sample, your sample should include 10 percent Native American families if it is truly representative. Unfortunately, due to the workings of probability theory, this is not always the result. At this point, we cannot delve into the depths of probability theory, but if we toss a coin twenty times, we might expect to end up with ten heads and ten tails. Often, however, results vary. We might end up with twelve heads and eight tails.

To ensure that Native American families are represented in the sample, you can use proportional stratified random sampling. Stratified random sampling requires two preconditions. First, you must be sure that membership in the group whose representation you are concerned about impacts the phenomenon you are studying. In our example, do you think Native American families' viewpoints on afterschool programs will differ from those of other families? If not, their adequate representation in the sample may not be that important. Second, you need to know the proportion of this group relative to the rest of the population. In our example, 10 percent are Native American.

Stratified random sampling involves dividing the population into the groups or strata of interest; in this example, you would divide the population into Native

Americans and non-Native Americans. (Note that you can create more than two strata if necessary. For example, you might also be concerned that Hispanic families be assured adequate representation in the sample. Knowing they make up 40 percent of the population, you would create three strata: Native Americans, Hispanics, and others.) After creating the strata, simple or systematic random sampling is then carried out from each stratum in proportion to the stratum's representation in the population. In our example, to end up with a sample of forty, you would randomly select four from the Native American stratum, sixteen from the Hispanic stratum, and twenty from the other stratum (see Figure 8.2).

Although stratified random sampling may be an improvement over simple random sampling, the disadvantages are the two preconditions described earlier. In other words, the certainty that the characteristics you are concerned with will impact the outcome and that you know the proportions of these characteristics in the population before the sampling.

Sometimes it may be necessary to use a variation of stratified random sampling referred to as disproportionate stratified random sampling. For example, with the proportionate stratified random sampling example discussed earlier, only a small proportion of Native Americans are included in the sample, reflecting their proportion in the population. This is not a problem if we are interested in an overall assessment of the afterschool program. However, you might be interested in comparing the experiences of the different ethnic groups; if that were the case, you would need to take equal proportions of each ethnic group (thirteen from each group for a total sample size of thirty-nine).

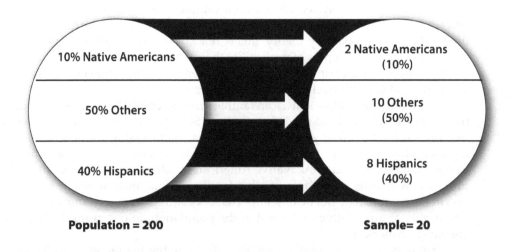

Figure 8.2   Stratified random sampling

An Example of Stratified Random Sampling

Day, Smith, and Tajima (2021) examined whether former foster youth are more likely to stop out (i.e., students who withdraw temporarily but reenroll at a later date) of a four-year university than low-income, first-generation students who did not experience out-of-home care. A stratified random sample of 803 students was selected. Students were enrolled at a large, public, four-year university in the Midwest over ten years, including 438 former court wards identified on the Federal Application for Student Aid and a comparison group of 365 low-income, first-generation college students who did not identify as court wards. Findings indicated that foster youth are more likely to transfer to another college or university, stop out, experience stop-outs earlier in their academic career, and are less likely to graduate than their low-income, first-generation peers. Foster youth also took longer to graduate than the comparison group.

Cluster Sampling

Cluster sampling involves randomly sampling a larger unit containing the elements of interest and then sampling the elements to be included in the final sample from these larger units. Cluster sampling is often done in social work research because it can be used when it is difficult to get a sampling frame, yet it is still a form of probability sampling. In the afterschool program example, suppose you are required to obtain the lists of students from each school rather than from the school district office. This could present a lengthy undertaking in a large school district with many schools. Or the lists may not be available either from the school or the school district. In these cases, cluster sampling might provide a feasible solution.

In cluster sampling, you take a random sample of a larger unit; in this case, the schools in which first through seventh graders are enrolled. This random sampling can be either simple, systematic, or stratified. In the afterschool program example, you use simple random sampling to select four schools. Then a random sample (again, either simple, systematic, or stratified) of the first through seventh grades in these four schools

An Example of Cluster Sampling

Sigurdardottir et al. (2021) examined older people's views and experiences of family relations in Iceland. The goal was to explore the frequency and kinds of contact and the support older people received from their adult biological children and stepchildren. Cluster sampling was carried out at community centers nationwide in Iceland. The questionnaire was answered by 273 older people, including 193 women (75 percent) and 64 men (25 percent). The average age was 79 years. About 200 (74 percent) lived in the capital area of Reykjavik, while 70 (26 percent) lived in the countryside. Older people received more support from biological children than stepchildren in frequency and contact quality. The results revealed gender differences, with daughters offering more help and support than sons. Older women have more frequent contact and closer relationships with their biological children than with stepchildren. Relationships with stepchildren were weaker.

would be selected (Figure 8.3). Alternatively, if a student list is not available, you would include all first through seventh graders in the four schools in the final sample.

Cluster sampling can be useful in an agency setting, for example, when an agency serves many clients yearly (for example, 8,000 clients are referred). Instead of randomly selecting from this large sampling frame, three months (every fourth month) may be systematically and randomly sampled from the year, and the clients referred during those three months included in the sample. Each month represents a cluster.

Cluster sampling has one potential problem. When only a few units are sampled (for example, four schools), there is a greater probability that the sample will differ from the population (see the discussion later in this chapter about sampling error). For example, the four schools may consist of three white middle-class schools, whereas the students' population (in ten schools) is a 50/50 mix socioeconomically. Consequently, the sample would favor white middle-class students, and other groups would be underrepresented.

Nonprobability Sampling

Nonprobability sampling allows the researcher to intentionally select information-rich elements, making it the sampling method of choice in qualitative studies. In the afterschool program example, you may decide you are more interested in learning about the problems and experiences of families who need afterschool care than in finding out the proportion of families who need afterschool services.

There are several different types of nonprobability sampling methods. Described here are seven of the most commonly used in social work: typical case, key informants, criterion, quota, snowball, purposive, and availability. See Table 8.2 for the different types of nonprobability sampling methods.

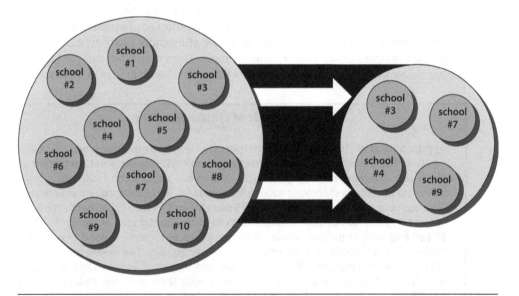

Figure 8.3   Cluster sampling

TABLE 8.2 Nonprobability Sampling Methods

Method	Characteristics
Purposive	Is one whose characteristics are defined for a purpose that is relevant to the study.
Typical cases	Those with "typical" characteristics
Criterion	Participants selected according to some eligibility criteria
Key informants	Those with expertise in the research topic
Quota	Certain proportions of participants from different groups selected according to specific characteristics
Snowball	Some participants identified: these participants then identify others with certain characteristics
Availability	Those selected because they are available

Typical Cases

Typical case sampling is often used as a method of purposive sampling. You can find typical cases using the literature, previous research, or consultation with relevant groups. For the afterschool program example, you would contact families who appear typical in their need for services through a local agency or the schools.

Key Informant Sampling

Key informant sampling relies on people in the community identified as experts in the field of interest.

An Example of Key Informants

Nyahunda et al. (2021) selected social workers serving two villages as key informants in studying the impact of COVID-19 and drought upon women in Zimbabwe. Focus groups were also conducted, eliciting responses from the women. The women experienced increased domestic violence, increased food shortages, and discrimination by the authorities. The key informants disclosed that climate change is the new normal in rural communities and women are suffering from its impacts.

Criterion Sampling

Criterion sampling involves picking all cases that meet some criteria, for example, including all families in an agency who meet eligibility criteria to receive services from that agency.

The researchers found a lack of geographical and platform diversity, an absence of reflexive dialogue, and little engagement with critical race perspectives.

An Example of Criterion Sampling

Matamoros-Fernández and Farkas (2021) looked at recent developments in the study of racism and hate speech in the subfield of social media research. They systematically examined 104 articles, and they had three research questions: Which geographical contexts, platforms, and methods do researchers engage within studies of racism and hate speech on social media? To what extent does scholarship draw on critical race perspectives to interrogate how systemic racism is (re)produced on social media? What are the primary methodological and ethical challenges of the field? They established five sampling criteria for publications: (1) to be in the form of scholarly articles; (2) written in English; (3) primarily focused on racism or hate speech against ethnocultural minorities; (4) primarily focused on social media platforms, and (5) published between 2014 and 2018.

Quota Sampling

Quota sampling involves a certain proportion of elements with specific characteristics to be purposively included in the sample. In some respects, quota sampling is similar to stratified random sampling, except that no randomness is involved in selecting the elements. For example, when examining families' experiences with unattended school-age children in an interpretive study, you might be interested in ensuring that you interviewed families from all ethnic groups in the community. Like stratified random sampling, quota sampling requires you know the proportion of these ethnic groups in the population. The problems associated with this form of sampling, as with stratified random sampling, are that the researcher needs to ensure that the categories or variables selected are essential and that the proportions of these variables are known in the population. It may be that ethnicity is not a key variable that needs to be included.

An Example of Quota Sampling

According to Lazar et al. (2021), the social work profession in Romania was reestablished in the early 1990s after being completely abolished for three decades during the country's communist period. This article reported findings from the first national survey of Romanian social workers, which studied characteristics of social workers and their roles, tasks, and types of services provided. In addition, it explored how burnout, income, and efficacy were associated with social workers' plans for leaving the profession or country through a seventy-three-item online survey tool to collect data from 1,057 social workers from across Romania using a quota sampling strategy. Romanian social workers tend to be young, female, and members of Romanian ethnic groups. While Romania has a large rural population, social workers primarily practice in urban areas. Social workers had reasonably high levels of job satisfaction and feelings of self-efficacy and were most likely to be working in child and family protection using direct practice methods.

Snowball Sampling

Snowball sampling involves identifying some population members and then having those individuals contact others in the population. This is a very useful strategy to adopt with less accessible populations like the homeless. However, it could also be used with the example of families with children who are unsupervised after school. You might identify and contact a few families and then ask them to contact others they think are having problems.

An Example of Snowball Sampling

Cote et al. (2022) analyzed the evolution of practices in Quebec, Canada, from their development in the 1970s to today, focusing on the participants' work with children. Forty-eight semi-structured individual interviews were conducted between December 2014 and June 2015. The participants were classified into pioneers, veterans, and workers. *Pioneers (n = 8)* were women who, between 1975 and 1985, either opened a domestic violence shelter, contributed to the development of the first coalition of shelters, or developed intervention guidelines for domestic violence shelter workers. *Veterans (n = 7)* were women who, between 1975 and 1985, were involved as employees, volunteers, interns, or activists in a domestic violence shelter but did not "fit" the criteria for the pioneers as defined above. As the pioneers and veterans constituted a small group of women in the province of Québec, they were recruited through a snowballing sampling technique. *Shelter workers (n = 33)* who had between six and twenty-eight years of experience at the time of the interview and were either doing direct work in a shelter or employed in an umbrella organization were also sampled. They were recruited voluntarily as a purposive sample.

Purposeful/Purposive Sampling

A **purposeful sample** is one whose characteristics are defined for a purpose that is relevant to the study. Specific criteria need to be met. The study's findings based on purposive (and convenience/availability) sampling can only be generalized to the (sub)population from which the sample is drawn and not to the entire population.

An Example of Purposeful Sampling

Elsherbiny & Maamari (2021) examined game-based learning (GBL) effectiveness among social work students. They explored the use of GBL through mobile phone apps and looked at its effectiveness in enhancing learning for social work students. The researchers used a purposeful sample of forty-eight social work students registered in two Generalist Practice in Social Work course sections. The two sections were compared using both pretests and posttests. Although there was a strong similarity between the experimental and control groups before the GBL intervention, there was a significant difference between them after it, which indicates that digital GBL might have the potential to enhance learning in social work.

Availability/Convenience Sampling

Availability or **convenience sampling** is used extensively in social work research and involves including available or convenient elements that are easily accessible to the researcher. This is the weakest form of sampling. Sometimes availability sampling is confused with random sampling because it appears superficially random. A typical example of availability sampling is interviewing people in a shopping mall in an attempt to get a sample of the community. Alternatively, you are asked to conduct a program evaluation in an agency. The funds for the evaluation are available now, and you have two months to collect the data. Consequently, you decide to include clients referred to the program in your sample during the next thirty days. The population under study is all those referred to the program.

Research findings from availability samples cannot be generalized to the population under study. In the shopping mall example, you will be able to include in your sample only people who shop at the mall—it may be a small and not very representative sample of the community as a whole. In the program evaluation example, the clients referred to the agency in the month of the sampling may be different from clients referred at other times of the year; December may not be a very representative month of the entire year. Consequently, the sample is biased, making it difficult to generalize results to the community as a whole. Availability sampling is also problematic because it does not possess the advantages of a purposive sampling method. The elements are not picked for their information richness but selected based on convenience. Availability samples, however, often present the only feasible way of sampling.

Availability sampling is often the sampling method to use when evaluating your practice. One case or more is selected, and the effectiveness of the intervention is assessed. We discussed this type of research in more detail in Chapter 7.

An Example of Availability/Convenience Sampling

Lee et al. (2021) conducted a study examining parent-child dynamics during initial COVID-19-related school closures. It used a cross-sectional survey that used a convenience sampling approach. Data were collected in April 2020, approximately five weeks after the World Health Organization declared the coronavirus a pandemic. Participants (N = 405) were parents (69 percent mothers and 31 percent fathers) recruited throughout the United States with at least one child 0–12 years of age. Most parents (78 percent) were educating their children at home due to COVID-19. Most (77.1 percent) reported using online tools for at-home education, including educational apps, social media, and school-provided electronic resources. More than one-third (34.7 percent) of parents said their child's behavior had changed since the pandemic, including being sad, depressed, and lonely. Most parents were spending more time involved in the daily caregiving of their children since COVID-19. Two out of every five parents met the criteria for major depression or severe major depression (40 percent) and for moderate or severe anxiety (39.9 percent). Content analyses of open-ended questions suggested that school closures were a significant disruption, followed by lack of physical activity and social isolation. The study results indicated that parents' mental health might be an important factor in at-home education and child well-being during the pandemic.

Studying Complete Populations

Sometimes, particularly when conducting program evaluations, it is possible to study the entire population rather than a sample, especially when it is relatively small. For example, if the clients served during a specific period (say, six months) could be defined as the population, and all could be studied. (Remember, the definition of the population is in part up to you.) Or, if the program is new, it might be quite feasible to study the entire population—namely, all who have been served since its inception. It is also possible to study the entire population if it is quite specific—for example, children with Down's syndrome in a medium-sized city. Finally, you may also be able to study an entire population if every element is identifiable. For example, all clients currently being served or who have been served in a specific agency.

An Example of Complete Populations

Siette et al. (2020) studied services that supported social participation for older adults in Australia. Participants were those aged ≥60 years (*n* = 1,141) who completed a social participation tool with their care coordinator as part of routine assessments from March 1, 2016, to December 30, 2018. The researchers included all community aged care clients living in New South Wales and the Australian Capital Territory during the study period. They completed the assessment tools as part of a routine needs assessment. As a result, two participation profiles were identified: (a) connected, capable, older rural women and (b) isolated, high-needs, urban-dwelling men.

Sample Size

Statisticians devote a considerable amount of energy to determining how large or small samples should be. However, some kinds of research that generalist social workers usually conduct, such as program or practice evaluations, do not require you to decide sample size because the sample is fixed—namely, a small program or your own practice.

The sample size depends on its homogeneity or the similarity among different elements. If you can be assured that the characteristics of the sample elements are similar to the dimensions you are interested in studying, then the sample can be smaller. In the example of unsupervised children, if all the children are similar in the characteristics you are interested in—ethnicity, socioeconomic status, and family configuration—the sample size can be small. If, however, you are interested in comparing the afterschool program needs of different types of families—for example, across family configuration, income, and so on—then you would probably need a larger sample to ensure that you have enough subjects in each category. As we saw in Chapter 3, a minimal number of cases is required in each category to allow specific statistical analyses to occur.

The size of the sample also depends on the research approach used. In positivist studies using probability samples, sample sizes usually must be quite large. In interpretive studies, the sample size is small, and the information-richness of the cases is essential. In interpretive studies, the sample size is no larger than that needed to gather the information of interest.

Also, when deciding on sample size it is important to consider the issue of sampling error. **Sampling error** is the extent to which the values of the sample differ from those of the population. The margin of error refers to the precision needed by the researcher. A margin of error of 5 percent means the actual findings could vary in either direction by as much as 5 percent. For example, a client satisfaction survey finding 55 percent of clients were "very satisfied" could have actual results anywhere from 50 percent to 60 percent. If the sample is large enough, you can reduce the sampling error and margin of error. With one hundred tosses of a coin, you are more likely to end up with 50 percent heads and 50 percent tails than you are with twenty tosses. Therefore, it is important to report the extent of sampling error in reporting the results of large-scale surveys.

A number of quite complicated formulas can assist in determining sample size. If you have concerns about your sample size, consult with a statistician or refer to a good statistics text (see Chapter 12 for some references).

Table 8.3 gives different sample sizes and their associated margin of error. The margin of error reported in this table is 5 percent. This means the actual findings could vary as much as 5 percent, either positively or negatively. Another way to view this is to state that the findings, using the sample sizes in the table, have a 95 percent confidence level, which expresses how often you would expect similar results if you repeated the research. For example, in a sample with a 95 percent confidence level (or alternatively stated, a 5 percent margin of error), the findings could be expected to miss the actual values in the population by more than 5 percent only five times in one hundred surveys. Use the table as a guide and not a strict formula for sample size determination.

When deciding on the sample size, a final consideration is to recognize that sample size can impact statistical analysis. We will discuss this more in Chapter 12. The smaller the sample, the more likely statistical analysis will yield positive results. This, in turn, then influences the generalizability of the results. Findings from a large sample can be generalized to the wider population.

TABLE 8.3   Size of Sample Required at 5% Margin of Error

Population Size	Sample Size	Population Size	Sample Size	Population Size	Sample Size
50	44	400	196	10,000	370
75	63	500	217	15,000	375
100	80	750	254	20,000	377
150	108	1,000	278	25,000	378
200	132	2,000	322	50,000	381
250	152	4,000	351	100,000	384
300	136	5,000	357	1,000,000	384

Ethical Issues in Sampling

Two ethical issues relate to sampling: first, responsible reporting of the sampling method, and second, obtaining the subject's consent to the research.

Reporting the Sampling Method

When reporting research findings—whether in a journal article, a report, or a presentation—it is the researcher's responsibility to ensure that the research methods used in the study are described as accurately as possible. We will describe reporting in Chapter 13. First, however, some discussion is necessary here because inaccuracies and ambiguities in research reports often concern the sampling method.

Sometimes authors write about supposedly random methods of sampling that are really just a matter of participant availability or some other form of nonprobability sampling. When reading reports and articles, look for an explicit description of the sampling method along with a frank description of the generalization limitations, particularly if a nonprobability sampling method is used. It is unethical to claim that the results of a nonprobability sample are generalizable to a broader population. Such a claim is misleading and can have some serious negative implications.

As discussed earlier in this chapter, nonprobability and probability sampling methods have different purposes.

Informed Consent

Whenever any social work research is undertaken, it is critical that no coercion is exerted and the subject voluntarily agrees to participate. You must always tell the participants about the purpose and goals of the research. As discussed in Chapter 6, voluntary, informed consent should always be obtained from the participants. Fortunately, the researcher is assisted in gaining informed consent by the existence of Institutional Review Boards (IRBs). All organizations that do research and receive federal funds must have an IRB that reviews the procedures adopted in treating human subjects and protects the participants from harm. The IRBs provide guidelines that the researcher should follow and include the information in a consent form. IRBs will be discussed further in Chapter 9.

Many organizations that support a large number of research studies—like, for example, the National Institutes of Health (2021)—have specific guidelines for the content of the consent documents. These guidelines include:

- A statement that the study involves research
- An explanation of the purpose of the research, an invitation to participate, an explanation of why the participant was selected, and the expected duration of the participation
- A description of the procedures to be followed and an explanation of the use of randomization and placebos
- A description of any foreseeable risks or discomforts to the participants and the steps to be taken to minimize these

- A description of any benefits to the participant
- A disclosure of any appropriate alternative procedures that might be advantageous to the participant
- A statement describing the extent to which the records will be confidential
- For research involving more than minimal risk, and explanation of any compensations or medical treatments available
- An explanation of who to contact for questions about the research
- A statement that participation is voluntary and there will be no penalties for refusing to participate
- A statement indicating that the participant is deciding whether or not to participate

Figure 8.4 is an example of a consent form. In addition, cover letters used in mailed questionnaires, which are discussed in Chapter 9, often also include content on informed consent.

Many ethical guidelines present dilemmas. For example, you may feel that disclosing information about the research project to the participant will jeopardize the research results. For example, if you use observation to collect data about a specific behavior and if participants know they are being observed, their behavior might change considerably. Another problem arises when you inform participants that their involvement in the research is voluntary: A certain number may choose not to participate. The researcher then does not know whether the results from the participants who agreed to participate are different from those who refused.

Sometimes—and these times are *not* frequent—the voluntary participation ethical standard may need to be modified. If this is necessary, you must clearly understand and explain the reasons. In particular, you must take care that researchers do not use their power or authority to exploit the participants. For example, suppose a professor researching students' experiences of sexual harassment requests that all the students in her class complete a questionnaire that she estimates will take about fifteen minutes. She states that participation is voluntary, but those who choose not to participate will be required to write a five-page research paper. This is a form of coercion, with the professor using her authority to force participation. A similar situation can be envisioned with a social work researcher requiring the participation of individuals who are dependent upon the social worker for services. You must carefully consider any decision to forgo the participant's consent to ensure no blatant coercion.

Another way of viewing the issue of the subject's consent is to modify our perspective on the distinction between researcher and participant. The relationship between researcher and participant can be seen as egalitarian, rather than viewed, as it has been traditionally, as a relationship in which researchers wield power and authority over subjects. When an even footing is adopted, the question of the participant's consent becomes a nonissue. Instead, researchers make their research skills accessible to participants; participants become active contributors and each gain from being involved. Emphasizing the egalitarian relationship between researcher and participant is one way

**THOUGHTS AND FEELINGS OF TEENAGE MOTHERS
WHO HAVE HAD PREMATURE INFANTS**

CONSENT FORM

PRINCIPAL INVESTIGATOR
Dr. John Doe
Associate Professor, Department of Psychology
NEW MEXICO STATE UNIVERSITY
(505) 646-xxxx

DESCRIPTION

I am interested in the thoughts and feelings of teenage mothers of premature infants. You, as the mother of a newborn premature infant, are the best person to describe these thoughts and feelings. This research study will involve one or two interviews with you, each lasting approximately 30 minutes. The interviews will be recorded using a digital recorder. The recordings will be typed out as word-for-word transcripts of the interviews. The recordings will then be erased.

CONFIDENTIALITY

Your name will not be attached to your interview responses. Your name and any other identifiers will be kept in a locked file that is only accessible to me or my research associates. Any information from the study that is published will not identify you by name.

BENEFITS

The results of this study may benefit other teenage mothers of premature infants by influencing the health care they receive. There will be no direct benefit to you from participating in this study.

RISKS

It is possible that the discussion of thoughts or feelings about the birth of your baby may make you feel sad or uncomfortable. However, there are no other know risks to you.

CONTACT PEOPLE

If you have any questions about this research, please contact the principal investigator at the phone number listed above. If you have any questions about your rights as a research subject, please contact the Office of the Vice Provost for Research at the New Mexico State University at (505) 646-0000.

VOLUNTARY NATURE OF PARTICIPATION

Your participation in this study is voluntary. If you don't wish to participate, or would like to end your participation in the study, there will be no penalty or loss of benefits to you to which you are otherwise entitled. In other words, you are free to make your own choice about being in this study or not, and may quit at any time without penalty.

SIGNATURE

Your signature on this consent form indicates that you fully understand the above study, what is being asked of you in this study, and that you are signing this voluntarily. If you have any questions about this study, please feel free to ask them now or at any time throughout the study.

Signature _____ Date _____

A copy of this consent form is available for you to keep.

Figure 8.4 A form for obtaining participants' informed consent

of incorporating this connectedness into research methodology. This relationship can be created using sampling methods such as the key informant, the focus group, and the community forum. Community members have an opportunity to serve both as participants and as contributors. An egalitarian relationship between researcher and participant is a characteristic of participatory research, as discussed in previous chapters.

When evaluating individual practice, you must be careful how you present the research to the client. For example, if you present the research as something unique, different, or separate from practice, the client will see it that way and often resist being involved (or used) in a research project. But suppose you stress the integration between research and practice and point out how the client will benefit from feedback on the relative effectiveness of the intervention. In that case, you will be more accurately depicting the whole idea of evaluating practice. In addition, you will be engaging in a true partnership with the client, benefiting all involved.

Breaking down the distinction between researcher and participant has other advantages apart from the issue of the participant's consent. First, it addresses the concern that research is not always responsive to the needs of oppressed groups. When a partnership between researcher and participant is created, responsiveness is more assured. Second, the validity of the research may be enhanced.

The more traditional relationship between researcher and participant, which emphasizes separateness, may result in a greater likelihood of the participant giving invalid responses out of a lack of understanding of the researcher's intent. You can avoid this problem by building a partnership. Third, this approach seems to be particularly compatible with social work practice, where the emphasis is placed on establishing a relationship with the client.

Creating an egalitarian relationship between participant and researcher thus seems a reasonable approach to adopt and offers several advantages.

Human Diversity Issues in Sampling

Unfortunately, the social science literature before the early 1970s does not provide many examples of studies with heterogeneous samples. Instead, there was a tendency to study only white males and college students. The samples were homogeneous, but the findings from these samples were generalized to the population as a whole—populations that included women, minorities, an people who were not college students. You should never make these generalizations because the samples were simply not representative of the populations.

Kohlberg's (1969) study of the development of morality provides a classic example of this problem. In his initial study, he selected a sample of male Harvard graduates. Based on this study, Kohlberg developed a model and theory of moral development that he used as a template to assess the moral development of *all* individuals. Moreover, applying this model to women, he concluded that women often did not reach the higher level of moral development and were, therefore, morally deficient. Later, Gilligan (1977) challenged these conclusions and studied moral development in a sample of women. As a result, she proposed alternative moral developmental stages for women, concluding that women were neither deviant nor deficient in their moral development but simply followed a different course.

Similar assumptions and erroneous generalizations have been made relating to minority populations. White middle-class samples have been studied, and the findings have been generalized and presented as the norm to evaluate minorities. Such improper generalizations are not always made explicitly by the researchers themselves, but often by others who draw assumptions from the findings and apply them to other groups.

Historically, such generalizations have been made about the effectiveness of social programs. If a program is demonstrated to be ineffective with a minority urban sample, the researchers may conclude that the program would be ineffective with all minorities. It is critical that we also recognize diversity within minority groups. Program ineffectiveness with some urban minorities does not mean program ineffectiveness with other minorities or rural minorities.

The danger of improper generalizations can be avoided if research consumers enhance their knowledge. This includes you. As discussed in the previous section, researchers can also help by being explicit about the limitations of their sampling method. However, it is often easier to be critical of existing studies than to avoid such pitfalls in our research. Kohlberg's erroneous assumptions seem almost obvious now, but that is because we have an increased sensitivity to gender issues.

Additionally, there is an increasing awareness of ethnic and racial diversity when applying research methods. However, be cautioned that other dimensions of diversity are less evident. For example, ageism and homophobia are still pervasive in our culture, even among social workers. Sometimes we are not even aware of all the dimensions of diversity. The issue goes beyond consciously excluding a particular group.

An Example of Gender in Sampling

Mooney et al. (2008) designed a study in response to the lack of women in prior substance abuse and prison inmate research samples, which traditionally focused on men. One hundred women prisoners participated in interviews that explored how their perceived stress, impulsiveness, and beliefs in the efficacy of drugs related to their self-reported drug use severity. Findings indicated that while substance abuse severity was not related to demographic characteristics, it was positively related to impulsiveness and beliefs.

Summary

Key concepts in sampling are representativeness, generalizability, and information richness. The two different types of sampling strategies are probability and purposive methods. Probability sampling includes simple random sampling, systematic random sampling, stratified random sampling, and cluster sampling. Purposive sampling includes typical cases, criterion sampling, focus groups, key informant sampling, community forums, quota sampling, snowball sampling, and availability sampling.

Ethical issues include accurate reporting of the sampling method and the subject's consent. Human diversity issues relate to whether the sampling represents diverse populations adequately.

STUDY/EXERCISE QUESTIONS

1. A local agency has asked you to help them conduct a survey to determine whether the city needs an elder daycare facility. The population of the city is 65,000. About 20 percent of the city's population lives below the poverty level. Anyone over the age of sixty would be eligible for the center.

   a. Define the population.

   b. Will probability sampling be possible? If not, why not? If so, what method would you use?

   c. Discuss the pros and cons of each of the following suggestions made by various members of the board of the agency:

      (i)   Interview elders who frequent the local shopping mall early in the morning for exercise

      (ii) Mail questionnaires to members of the local branch of the American Association of Retired Persons (AARP)

      (iii) Carry out a web survey of local AARP members

2. Review an issue of *Social Work* and answer these questions about the research articles:

   a. What was the sampling method used?

   b. What are the limitations with each of the sampling methods?

   c. Were these limitations made explicit in the articles?

   d. How was informed consent obtained?

REFERENCES

Adhikari, M., Paudel, N. R., Mishra, S. R., Shrestha, A., & Upadhyaya, D. P. (2021). Patient satisfaction and its sociodemographic correlates in a tertiary public hospital in Nepal: A cross-sectional study. *BMC Health Services Research, 21*, 135.

Cote, I., Damant, D., & Lapierre, S. (2022). Children in domestic violence shelters: Does the feminist perspective collapse? *Journal of Social Work, 22*(2), 422–439.

Day, A., Smith, R., & Tajima, E. (2021). Stopping out and its impact on college graduation among a sample of foster care alumni: A joint scale-change accelerated time analysis. *Journal of the Society for Social Work and Research, 12*(1), 11–39.

Elsherbiny, M. M., & Al Maamari, R. H. (2021). Game-based learning through mobile phone apps: Effectively enhancing learning for social work students. *Social Work Education, 40*(3), 315–332.

Gilligan, C. (1977). In a different voice: Women's conceptions of self and of morality. *Harvard Educational Review, 47,* 481–512.

Kohlberg, L. (1969). *Stages in the development of moral thought and action.* New York: Holt, Rinehart & Winston.

Lee, S. J., Ward, K. P., Chang, O. D., & Downing, K. M. (2020). Parenting activities and the transition to home-based education during the COVID-19 pandemic. *Children and Youth Services Review, 122.*

Lazăr, F., Lightfoot, E., Iovu, M. B., & Dégi, L. C. (2021). Back from the ashes of communism: The rebirth of the social work profession in Romania. *The British Journal of Social Work, 51*(1), 340–356.

Matamoros-Fernández, A., & Farkas, J. (2021). Racism, hate speech, and social media: A systematic review and critique. *Television & New Media, 22*(2), 205–224.

Mooney, J. L., Minor, K. I., Wells, J. B., Leukfeld, C., Oser, C. B., & Tindall, M. S. (2008). The relationship of stress, impulsivity, and beliefs to drug use severity in a sample of women prison inmates. *International Journal of Offender Therapy and Comparative Criminology, 52*(6), 686–697.

National Institutes of Health, U.S. Department of Health and Human Services (2021). *Policy for Informed Consent.*

Nyahunda, L., Chibvura, S., & Tirivangasi, H. M. (2021). Social work practice: Accounting for double injustices experienced by women under the confluence of COVID-19 pandemic and climate change impacts in Nyanga, Zimbabwe. *Journal of Human Rights Social Work, 6,* 213–224.

Siette, J., Berry, H., Jorgensen, M., Brett, L., Georgiou, A., McClean, T., & Westbrook, J. (2021). Social participation among older adults receiving community care services. *Journal of Applied Gerontology, 40*(9), 997–1007.

Sigurdardottir, S. H., Juliusdottir, S., & Karlsson, T. (2021). Family relations of older people: Personal and practical support. *Journal of Social Work, 21*(3), 533–550.

Ware, O. D., & Cagle, J. G. (2021). The assessment of pain and barriers to pain management: A content analysis from a national sample of hospice psychosocial assessments completed by social workers. *American Journal of Hospice and Palliative Medicine®, 38*(3), 260–265.

9

Collecting the Data

INTRODUCTION

Now that you have decided on the research design and how participants will be selected, you need to gather the data. Do you go out and interview people directly? Do you use forms and questionnaires to collect data, or do you need to observe?

As discussed in Chapter One, there are two types of data, qualitative and quantitative; both can be collected in various ways, which will be the focus of this chapter.

In generalist practice, you must also decide how to collect the information after defining and conceptualizing the problem. In both practice and research, this information is referred to as **data** (singular **datum**), and they are collected using a **measuring instrument** or data collection method. These methods include questionnaires, observation, logs and journals, interviews, scales, and secondary data. We will describe all of these in this chapter.

As a generalist social worker, you may or may not actually collect the data. The plan and perhaps even the data collection may have already been implemented. Even if you don't direct the data collection, and certainly if you are responsible for collecting data, you will need to know what instruments are used under what circumstances.

LEARNING OBJECTIVES

This chapter will include the following learning objectives:

1. To understand the different ways in which data can be collected

2. To understand who should collect the data

3. To understand the conditions under which data collection methods can be combined

4. To distinguish between the reliability and validity of data collection methods

5. To articulate the ethical and human diversity issues associated with data collection

Ways of Collecting Data

This section will describe six major methods of collecting data or measuring instruments (see Figure 9.1): interviews, questionnaires, observation techniques, logs and journals, scales, and secondary data. All these methods can include both qualitative and quantitative data, except logs and journals, which are generally qualitative, and scales that are quantitative.

At this point, note that you can either construct your data collection instrument using one or more of the methods listed here or else use an already existing measure. Whenever possible, use an existing measure, particularly if it is standardized.

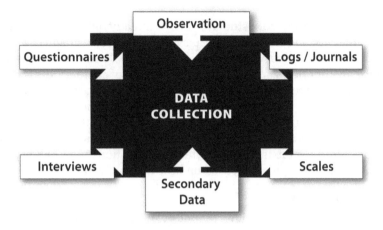

Figure 9.1   Methods of data collection

A standardized instrument is uniform throughout. It includes items uniformly administered and scored according to an agreed-upon procedure. This instrument is convenient and has established reliability and validity, two measurement concepts discussed at the end of this chapter.

As we describe, each of the six methods will be assessed for both **neutrality** and **applicability**. Patton (2014) proposed the term *neutrality* as an alternative to either *objectivity* or *subjectivity.* Objectivity is one of the central premises of the quantitative approach. However, as discussed in Chapter 1, objectivity is virtually impossible to achieve, and even the quantitative researcher admits it is a problematic term. Qualitative research is more concerned with the subjective experiences of the subjects in the study. *Subjective,* however, is also a problematic term, with negative connotations implying bias and relevance only to specific topics. Therefore, *neutrality* appears to be a more helpful term. Patton defines it as characterizing research in which "the researcher does not seek to prove a particular perspective or manipulate the data to arrive at predisposed truths" (p. 55).

Patton suggests adopting the term *empathetic neutrality* for the qualitative approach. Here, though, we maintain that *neutrality* is a useful term for both the quantitative and qualitative perspectives.

Apart from neutrality, the other criterion by which the data collection methods will be discussed in the next section is applicability. The applicability of a measuring instrument is whether it is appropriate and suitable for a particular type of problem. For example, observation would typically not be a useful method to employ if we were collecting information on child abuse but would be suitable for collecting information on child behavior problems. Each data collection method will be described, along with a discussion of its strengths and weaknesses in terms of neutrality and its relative applicability for the kinds of research questions we encounter as generalist social workers.

Interviews

As a generalist social work student, you are already quite skilled at conducting interviews. Interviewing is an integral part of social work practice; Kirst-Ashman and Hull (2018) refer to interviewing as a key micro skill. Kadushin and Kadushin (2013) describe an interview as "The simplest definition of an interview is that it is a conversation with a deliberate purpose that the participants accept. An interview resembles a conversation in many ways. Both involve verbal and nonverbal communication between people during which they exchange ideas, attitudes, and feelings" (p. 4). For research purposes, it is helpful to divide interviews into three types: structured, semistructured, or unstructured. Often, the questions may be very similar, but the interviews are distinguished based on how they are conducted.

Structured Interviews

In a **structured interview**, the interviewer knows in advance the questions to ask and, in many cases, is simply administering a verbal questionnaire. Often this questionnaire is already developed by the agency workers.

An Example of a Structured Interview

Litman et al. (2021) conducted a study aimed to understand how one participatory action research (PAR) team (comprised of university and community researchers) navigated power dynamics. This qualitative study used loosely structured interviews and journaling with all members of the PAR team ($N = 5$) to explore how the team navigated power throughout the PAR process. This study found that PAR team members navigated the PAR process using values, especially in negotiating power and resource realities and distinguishing equity from equality.

Semistructured Interviews

In a **semistructured** interview, the interviewer has more freedom to pursue hunches and improvise with the questions. Semistructured interviews often use interview schedules consisting of general questions, but they are not a questionnaire. Sometimes semistructured interviews are referred to as open-ended interviews.

An Example of a Semi-Structured Interview

Birger and Nadan (2021) explored the relationship between social workers and adult Eritrean refugee service users experiencing a hostile political climate and restrictive state policies. The study examines the implications of politics and policies on forming this relationship. The researchers conducted a qualitative study in Israel and Germany. Semistructured in-depth interviews were conducted with thirty-eight participants—sixteen Eritrean refugees and twenty-two social workers who work with refugees. Two main themes emerged in both countries. First, the relationships were more "informal." Second was the emergence of a different power relationship, more like a friendship or a parent-child dynamic.

A context in which semistructured interviews can take place is in focus groups. These were discussed in Chapter 3.

An Example of Focus Groups

Currin-McCulloch et al. (2021) compared the similarities and differences of breast cancer survivors' experiences between posters on Reddit and focus groups. First, posts from a breast cancer-specific Reddit community were extracted and analyzed. Then, investigators performed a thematic analysis of two focus groups of breast cancer survivors ($N = 18$). Finally, the themes derived from each analysis method were compared. The Reddit posts resulted in seven themes: diagnosis, treatment process, social support, existentialism, risk, information-seeking, and surgery. Focus groups revealed the same four initial themes along with additional themes of disclosure, coping, and fears.

The authors concluded that extracting information from the Reddit posts could offer a cost-effective way of collecting data.

Unstructured Interviews

Completely **unstructured interviews** can also be used. This type of interview is like a conversation, except that the interviewer and interviewee understand it to be an interview. In addition, the interviewee has information of interest to the interviewer. In unstructured and semistructured interviews, probes are often necessary; follow-up questions are agreed upon before the interview or may be developed on the spot. However, probes mustn't bias the participant by suggesting a particular response.

Group Interviews

Group interviews can take several different forms. Two of these were discussed in Chapter 3, as they can also serve as a mechanism for participatory research. First, group interviews can take the form of a focus group. They can also take the form of a **community forum**. Here a meeting is publicized, the individuals are briefed on a topic, and then they are asked for input. Finally, a group interview can also simply be where the interview is conducted with several participants in the research.

Neutrality

Although structured and semistructured interviews are more neutral than unstructured interviews, asking specific questions minimizes some bias—in general, the neutrality of interviewing is limited. We know that we respond differently to different people depending on how we are approached. The answer to an interviewer's question will be influenced by several factors: the interviewer's age, gender, ethnicity, and dress; the context in which the interviewer approaches the interviewee; the manner in which the interviewer speaks; and so forth. In addition, these characteristics will not have a constant effect on all the interviewees. Instead, each interviewee will respond differently to these characteristics depending on previous experiences, and there is no way of knowing exactly how these responses differ. We refer to this as the *reactive effect:* the interviewer influences the interviewee, and the interviewee responds in a particular way, which will then have a feedback effect on the interviewer. With the quantitative approach, the reactive effect can be a serious limitation and can jeopardize the data collection method's objectivity, which, as you will remember, is important when using the quantitative approach.

If you are using the qualitative approach, reactivity is not necessarily a problem since the method involves recognizing that the relationship between the researcher and the subject exists and enhances the quality of the data and can itself create the data. Using the interpretive/qualitative approach, the researcher and subject explore the topic together, each contributing to the process and working differently.

Thus, when using the qualitative approach, you must acknowledge that objectivity will be lost. Neutrality is still essential, however. In fact, qualitative researchers often state "up front" the type of relationship they strive for with their subjects. For example, Gregg (1994), in her study of pregnancy, stated:

> I continued (quite consciously) to refrain from developing friendships with the women during the course of the study, even though this sometimes seemed artificial and contrived. I did not want them to feel they had to continue with the study or to feel that they were obliged to reveal things to me out of loyalty or friendship . . . . When I ran into someone I had interviewed, we would say hello, I would ask her how she was, and we would go on. These encounters were awkward for me. (p. 55)

You can overcome some of the problems undermining the neutrality of interviews by training the interviewers. They can be given an explicit protocol or format that they must follow. As a generalist social worker, you may be required to conduct interviews of this type. Also, audio recordings allow the interviews to be reviewed. However, recording can sometimes inhibit the interviewees, resulting in a distortion of their responses.

The advantage of interviews is that they allow ambiguous questions to be clarified. This opportunity does not exist when questionnaires are administered, particularly by mail. Then respondents interpret the question in their own way, which may differ from the researchers' intention when they developed the questions. Interviewing can also positively affect the **response rate** and the proportion of people who respond to a questionnaire or interview questions. We have all been asked to participate in research—on the telephone, on the street, or through the mail. Sometimes we agree, and sometimes we refuse to participate.

For researchers, a problem arises when many people refuse to participate because these people might be very different from those who do. For example, if you send out one hundred questionnaires asking about people's experiences of childhood sexual abuse, and only twenty-five people respond, yet all the respondents stated they were not abused as children. You have no way of knowing whether the nonrespondents were all abused and were reluctant to disclose this on their questionnaire, or were not abused and decided not to respond, or were distributed between abused and not abused. Because you do not know, you must be cautious and assume that the results may well be biased. Interviews, however, generally obtain a high response rate. This is particularly true for face-to-face interviews, less so for telephone interviews.

Nevertheless, the high response rate of even face-to-face interviews is not always assured. The response rate does not just depend on the data collection method; other factors include the characteristics of the subjects, the purpose and nature of the research question or project, and the characteristics and training of those applying the data collection instruments.

One form of interviewing involves focus groups. These were described in Chapter 3 to develop the research question and Chapter 8 as a sampling method. You can also use them to collect data.

Applicability

Interviewing may be preferred to other techniques in the following circumstances:

- You are interested in a high response rate.

- You want to gather in-depth information. Interviewing is one of the primary methods for collecting qualitative data and is a critical data collection method in many qualitative studies. The focus is on gathering information that discloses the richness of the participant's or informant's experience.

- Anonymity is not of primary importance. Suppose your research involves a sensitive issue—such as the incidence of spousal abuse in a community—and the community is relatively small. In that case, anonymity may be necessary, and interviewing would not be an appropriate data collection method. People are less reluctant to share such sensitive information with strangers.

- Time and money are of no great object. Interviews are time-consuming, particularly if you are interested in getting responses from a large geographic area. In addition, interviewers often need to be trained. Consequently, this data collection method is expensive. If the budget is low and the sample large, interviewing would not be the data collection method of choice.

- The respondent is not comfortable with writing or is illiterate.

Questionnaires

In general, questionnaires have many advantages that interviews do not have; at the same time, they lack the strengths of interviews. There are several types of questionnaires.

Mailed Questionnaires

Mailing questionnaires is one method of distributing questionnaires. Agencies often use this method to survey their clients as part of a program evaluation or needs assessment. The disadvantages are cost and often a low participation rate. Mailed questionnaires have been used less recently, as online data collection instruments usually result in a higher response rate. However, mailed questionnaires do offer the advantage of a greater assurance of anonymity.

An Example of a Mailed Questionnaire

Abendstern et al. (2022) studied the current role of social workers in Community Mental Health Teams (CMHTs) in England. A national survey of CMHT team managers (44 percent response rate) was carried out by mailing questionnaires. The analysis focused on membership, roles, tasks, and change within the previous twelve months. Social workers were found to undertake various generic roles and tasks but were reported to do so less often than nurses. A large minority were involved in non-traditional social work tasks such as monitoring medication. In one-fifth of teams, managers thought they had too few social workers. Managers valued social workers for their social perspective and expressed concern regarding their removal, seeing this as harming service delivery.

Telephone Surveys

We have probably all been asked to participate in a **telephone survey**. Have you noticed that the calls are often made in the early evening? This is intentional, of course, to maximize the possibility that people are at home. The disadvantage compared with other survey forms is cost (telephone surveys take time to administer). Many people no longer have "landlines" but rely more on mobile telephone service, making finding telephone numbers challenging. In addition, much of the population now screen their calls, resulting in problems when trying to obtain a high response rate for the survey.

Face-to-Face Questionnaires

Face-to-face questionnaires may be administered much the same as structured interviews. However, structured interviews are simply verbally administered questionnaires. Consequently, they confront the same problems as interviews.

Group Questionnaires

Group questionnaires are administered to groups, much like a focus group is a form of group interview. For example, if you are interested in getting feedback on a foster parent training session, you might administer questionnaires to the entire group at one time. The challenge with this type of administration is that sometimes participants can be influenced by others in the group, even just by non-verbal behaviors, resulting in them completing the surveys differently than if they were alone.

Web or Online Surveys

An increasingly popular method of conducting surveys using a questionnaire is through **online surveys.** Online surveys offer several advantages: they are easy to complete and submit, cost-effective, and allow for easy data analysis and rapid feedback and dissemination of results.

A disadvantage is that not everyone has convenient access to the internet or email. Two examples of online survey tools include:

- **Alchemer** (https://www.alchemer.com/survey) is an online survey tool for designing surveys, collecting data, and performing analysis. This tool supports a variety of online data collection methods, including online surveys, online quizzes, questionnaires, web forms, and landing pages.

- **SurveyMonkey** (http://www.surveymonkey.com/) enables anyone to create professional online surveys quickly and easily.

- **Google Forms** is also a valuable tool to help build your questionnaire online.

An Example of Assessing the Effectiveness of Web-Based Surveys

Oliveri et al. (2021) examined the effectiveness of online surveys in eliciting responses from a highly vulnerable population (lung cancer patients) about their preferences. The researchers found advantages, including the possibility of reaching a wider and geographically distant population in a shorter timeframe while reducing the financial costs of testing, the greater flexibility offered, and the reduced burden on the patients. However, some limitations included the potential lack of inclusiveness of the research, the lack of control over who is completing the survey, a poor comprehension of the study material, and therefore, a lower level of engagement with the study.

Neutrality

Questionnaires are relatively neutral. Interviewer bias is absent, and the responses are clear and usually unambiguous. However, the neutrality of the responses depends a great deal on the care with which the questionnaire was constructed. You can minimize ambiguities by stating questions as clearly and simply as possible. For example, avoid questions containing double negatives, such as "Do you disapprove of the refusal to build a daycare center in your neighborhood?" Also, avoid double-barreled questions or two questions in one, such as "How many children under the age of twelve do you have and do you have problems with childcare?"

In addition, avoid leading and biased questions that indicate to the respondent how you want the question to be answered. For example, "There is a great deal of community support for the new youth center; are you in favor?" Also, ask only questions respondents can answer in that they have some knowledge of the issue being researched. Try not to ask questions about future intentions; instead, focus on the present. Finally, to maintain maximum neutrality, avoid response sets. These are questions phrased in such a way that the answers will probably all be the same (for example, all yes answers or all no answers). This is because people tend to become set in a certain way of responding.

Just as interviews generally have high response rates, questionnaires—particularly those that are mailed—have low response rates. You can take some precautions to help improve the response rate, though. Such safeguards include taking care with the questionnaire's directions, length, the structure of the questions, timing, the content and order of the questions, the format of the questionnaire, the cover letter, and the follow-up.

Directions.   You need to give the respondents to the questionnaire very clear directions. This is particularly important with mailed questionnaires. For example, if you need a checkmark placed in a box, say so. If you need a sentence response, say so.

Length.   Make the questionnaire as short as possible and eliminate unnecessary questions. When constructing a questionnaire, for each question ask yourself, "How is this question relevant to my research question?" If you cannot come up with a good answer, drop the question.

Structure of the questions.   Questions can be structured in two ways: closed-ended and open-ended. A closed-ended question gives the respondent a limited number of categories to use as answers. For example:

> Name those who help you with childcare:
> _____ parents
> _____ older children
> _____ other relatives
> _____ daycare center
> _____ family daycare
> _____ unrelated babysitter
> _____ other

These are easy for the researcher to understand once the questionnaire is returned. Still, it is essential to ensure that all possible categories are included for the respondent. Closed-ended questions result in quantitative data.

An **open-ended question** leaves it up to the respondent to create a response. No alternatives are given. For example:

> What kinds of improvements would you suggest the daycare center
> make in this next year?
> _____
> _____
> _____

Open-ended questions can be intimidating to respondents and they may be put off by them but this type of question ensures that respondents can answer in ways that accurately reflect their views—that is, they are not forced to respond using the researcher's categories. Open-ended questions are particularly useful when you do not know a great deal about the subject that you are investigating. They also provide a way of collecting qualitative data.

The content and order of the questions.   One strategy for increasing the response rate is to limit sensitive and very personal questions or embed them within the questionnaire if you need to include them. It would help if you were also careful about ordering opinion questions; you should ask these first before the factual questions. Otherwise, the factual questions may influence the opinions. For example, if you are interested in assessing the need for respite care for foster parents, ask questions about need first, then follow with such questions as the number of foster children they have living with them and demands on the foster parents' time. Also, people like to state their opinions. They are not so interested in demographic questions such as gender and educational level. So instead of starting the questionnaire with these questions, place them at the end.

Format and appearance of the questionnaire. The overall packaging of the questionnaire can also enhance the response rate. Make sure it is free of typographical and spelling errors. Ensure that the layout is clear and uncluttered. Make it inviting to complete.

Cover letter. If you are mailing the questionnaire, include a **cover letter** that very briefly describes the purpose of the study and encourages the person to respond. An example of a cover letter is shown in Figure 9.2.

The cover letter should include how you will maintain confidentiality (confidentiality is discussed later in this chapter). You may want to include a small incentive, such as money. This can increase the return rate anywhere from 10 to 15 percent.

New Mexico State University
School of Social Work
MSC 3SW
Box 30001
Las Cruces, New Mexico 88003

We are carrying out a study on stress in the workplace and you have been randomly selected from a list of all employees at the university. Your answers will assist the university in planning programs to support its employees. This is the only survey you will be sent.

We would very much appreciate your filling out this brief survey; it should take only about five minutes to complete. Please return the survey in the enclosed addressed envelope.

Your participation in this research is entirely voluntary.

Please do not write your name on the survey as all the responses are completely confidential and anonymous. Your return of the survey indicates your willingness to participate in the study.

If you would like to receive the results from this survey, or have any questions, please e-mail me at cmarlow@nmsu.edu, or send me a note using the address above, or call me at 555-4984.

Thank you.

Christine Marlow, Ph.D.
Professor and Principal Investigator of the Employee Survey

Figure 9.2 Example of a cover letter

Of course, the person should never be coerced to respond. Always include a self-addressed, stamped envelope. Ideally, use an actual postage stamp rather than a bulk mailing stamp. This makes the request appear more personal, and hence the participant may be more likely to respond.

Follow-ups. Second mailings can enhance the response ratio of mailed questionnaires by about 10 percent to 15 percent, but they add to the project's cost. Ideally, you should use two follow-ups. When the initial responses drop off, you should send another letter and another copy of the questionnaire.

A checklist for constructing a questionnaire or an interview schedule is given in Table 9.1.

Even with a carefully designed and administered questionnaire, response rates can still suffer. As we discussed with interviews, other factors besides the instrument's structure or administration can influence the response rate. These factors include the topics and variables included in the research itself.

Applicability

Questionnaires can be used in preference to other data collection techniques when

- a high response rate is not a top priority
- anonymity is important
- budgets are limited (although extensive mailings of questionnaires can also be expensive)
- the respondents are literate

TABLE 9.1   Checklist for Constructing Questionnaire and Interview Questions

___ The questions are short.	___ Consent has been given to answer the questions.
___ There are no double-barreled questions.	
___ The questions are clear and focused.	___ Anonymity and confidentiality have been assured.
___ There are no sensitive questions.	If mailed (snail or e-mail):
___ There are no leading questions.	___ A cover letter or explanation of the research is included.
___ The respondents are capable of answering the questions.	
___ The questions are focused on the present.	___ The questionnaire is clearly formatted.
___ There are no questions containing double negatives.	___ The questionnaire is short.
	___ There are mostly closed-ended questions.
___ The response categories are balanced.	___ There is a return date.
___ The questions are in a language that can be understood by the respondent.	___ A stamped, addressed envelope is included or return e-mail address clearly specified.

Email Surveys - Please see manuscript. Delete?

Observation Techniques

Not all phenomena can be measured by interviews or questionnaires. Examples of these types of phenomena include illegal behaviors or children's behavior. If we are interested in a child's behavior in the classroom, interviewing or administering a questionnaire to the child would probably not elicit objective responses. As a social work student, you probably realize that observation is an integral part of social work practice, and you have already learned to be a good observer. Observation can be structured or unstructured.

An Example of Observation

Ferguson (2016) used observation to study social worker home visits in England. He spent three months in each local authority, staying on site for two to three days per week. The researcher accompanied the social workers on their journeys to see service users, interviewing the workers about their plans and feelings. For example, when parents gave consent, he followed the worker into the family home and observed and audio recorded their practice encounters with children, parents, and others present. On the way back to the office or on the next visit, he interviewed the workers about their experience of the visit.

Structured Observation

When behaviors are known and categorized before the observation, and the intention is to collect quantitative data, **structured observation** is the method of choice. This method categorizes behaviors before the observation according to their characteristics, including their frequency, direction, and magnitude. These categories can then be quantified.

Take the example of measuring a child's inattention in the classroom. First, inattention needs to be clearly defined, perhaps as talking with other children without the teacher's permission. Frequency would be the number of occasions during a specified period (for example, one hour) that the child talked with other children without permission. Duration would be the length of time the child spoke. Magnitude would be how loudly the child talked within a specified period. The selection of the observation method depends on the behavior being measured, how the behavior is defined, and how often it occurs.

Unstructured Observation

When you don't know much about the observed behaviors, or when an interpretive approach is adopted, and the goal is to focus primarily on collecting qualitative data, you need to use unstructured observation. This strategy for collecting data is known as **participant observation**. Participant observers can adopt slightly different roles.

At one extreme, the participation takes precedent over the observation. In other words, the researcher fully participates in the activity under study. The advantage of this approach is that the researcher has an understanding of the phenomena under investigation that would be impossible to achieve through other means. For example, studying the stressful experiences of a child protective social worker might be best understood by "becoming" a CPS worker for a period of time and recording the experiences. Without adopting this role, the workers may never disclose the kinds of stresses they are experiencing to the researcher. Of course, the disadvantage of this approach is that the line between researcher and participant becomes very blurred, and roles confused, making even an interpretive approach tricky to undertake. In addition, it often involves a fairly lengthy time commitment, which is not always an option to the researcher.

At the other extreme, the participant-observer may emphasize more the observation side of this approach to data collection by not actually engaging in the group's activities but only observing. Clearly, this approach is useful when studying illegal activities such as drug dealing. However, the disadvantage is that often the observation is for a short time, and the knowledge gained about the activity can be limited.

Whether observation or participation is emphasized, there remains an ethical question of how much information the participants receive about the researcher's intentions. This is particularly the case when the role is more as a participant. For example, does the researcher disclose why she is adopting this role to the other workers? If she does, wouldn't this then jeopardize the validity of observations? This is a complex ethical dilemma discussed in the last chapter and needs to be carefully considered when you use participant observation.

An Example of Participant Observation

Meneses-Falcón (2021) describes the difficulties of participant observation in four brothels of female prostitution. The author lived with the women and employees of the brothels in four Spanish cities. She discusses issues arising during the ethnographic work. These issues include the selection of and access to the spaces of interaction, the roles to be carried out by the researcher, the limits of participation, the legal and ethical codes, acceptance by the informants, and the learning of hidden meanings.

Neutrality

Observation varies in its neutrality. The degree of neutrality depends a great deal on the type of observation, the level of training, and the control for reactivity.

Type of observation. Generally, structured observation is more neutral than unstructured observation because, in structured observation, the behaviors are defined beforehand. With unstructured observation, behaviors are not so clearly defined. In addition, in unstructured observation, the observer's involvement in the behavior can further bias the observation.

The level of training. The more training the observers receive regarding the procedures to be followed for the observation, the greater the neutrality. Often, particularly in structured observation, the categories are not immediately apparent, no matter how much care was taken in their development. Therefore, observers may need to be instructed in what is meant by, for example, asking for the participant's opinion.

Control for reactivity. **Reactivity**, or the reactive effect, is the problem of subjects changing their behavior due to the observers observing them. (We discussed this effect earlier in regards to interviewing.) Reactivity can be partly controlled by using one or more of the following four strategies: videotapes, one-way mirrors, time with the observer, and participant observation. Using video to record behavior can be used, but this may further inhibit the subject.

Second, sometimes one-way mirrors can be used, although you must be sure to obtain consent from those being observed. A third method for controlling reactivity is for the observer to spend some time with the subject to become more comfortable with the observation. For example, if you want to observe classroom behavior, sit in the classroom for some time before you make the observation. Finally, you can overcome some reactivity effects with participant observation.

One further comment regarding neutrality is that observation need not always be visual. Sometimes you can gain enough information by listening to audio recordings. Maybe you have already used this method of observation as a means of improving your practice. Remember that since you are then without the nonverbal part of the interaction, neutrality can decrease from a possible misinterpretation of the communication.

Applicability

Observation can be used in preference to other data collection techniques when behaviors are challenging to measure using different techniques, and observers and funds are available for training.

Logs and Journals

Sometimes you can use logs, journals, or diaries to collect data. These could be considered forms of self-observation, but warrant a separate discussion. Logs, journals, or diaries—like observation—can be structured or unstructured. There are two types. First, those kept by the researcher to record their research process. Keeping such a journal or log helps the researcher track their progress, or lack thereof, on a project. It can help them identify barriers and successes that can help guide the current project and any they may undertake in the future. The second type of log or journal is kept by a social worker, client, or participant in the project. This type of log provides data for the research. The client may record their own behavior, or the social worker may record the client's behavior or their own. For example, in Figure 9.3, the social worker assesses her feelings and reactions to a home visit by recording in a journal.

This log is unstructured and allows for a stream-of-consciousness type of data collection; these data types are often very valuable in an interpretive study. Note that social workers can also use these types of journals to provide feedback for their practice. When used for this purpose, they are referred to as process recordings (see Chapter 7). Finally, logs can also be used to collect quantitative data. Service logs are of this type, where the entries involve checking or noting numbers next to categories of behavior or activities.

Neutrality

The neutrality of logs and journals can be limited, particularly if they are not structured or guided in some way. Neutrality can be enhanced by using more structured journals and logs so that the client or worker responds to specific questions. In addition, it is helpful to encourage the client to record behaviors as soon as they occur rather than to rely too much on retrospective information.

SOCIAL WORKER'S JOURNAL RECORD OF A HOME VISIT TO A CLIENT

Thursday, February 15

Tonight I visited Art A. again. The house looked dark when I pulled up, and I felt kind of uneasy. I went through all the safety precautions I had learned previously and then went to the door and knocked. My stomach felt jittery. Finally, after several minutes, I heard footsteps inside and Art opened the door. He looked kind of disheveled and I sensed that he was upset about something, but he asked me very politely to come in and sit down. The house was so dark! I asked him to turn on some lights, and I sat near the door, just in case. Something just didn't feel right. Then it hit me—his dog Spike hadn't barked when I knocked and that dog was his constant companion. 1 didn't want to ask him about Spike because I was sure it was bad. I felt a lump forming in my throat. What a great social worker I am! I'm supposed to be calm, cool, and collected! I guess if I didn't empathize though, I wouldn't have been there in the first place. Sure enough, Spike was dead—he'd been run over by a car.

CLIENT'S LOG OF DRINKING BEHAVIOR

Monday

10:00   I took my break at work and had a couple of sips of George's beer (he brings it in his lunch pail).

12:00   Drank 2 beers with lunch.

5:00   Stopped after work at Charlie's Grill and had 3 beers and 2 or 3 shots of whiskey, which my friends bought for me.

7:00   Jack Daniels before dinner (on the rocks).

8:00   3–4 beers watching the Broncos whip the Cowboys.

11:00   Went to buy cigs and stopped at Fred's bar, had a couple of beers.

1:00   Had a shot of whiskey before bed to help me get to sleep.

Figure 9.3 Examples of journal and log recordings

Applicability

Logs and journals can be used in preference to other data collection techniques when detailed personal experiences are required from participants.

An Example of Using a Mobile Phone Log

Karadzhov (2021) used an innovative method to collect data from a homeless population through a participatory research approach. This population is hard to reach and "hidden." The author used a mobile phone diary with homeless adults with serious mental illnesses. The diaries produced "contextualized and nuanced accounts of the lived experience of homelessness, social isolation, coping, and recovery."

Scales

Most variables are not clear-cut and cannot be contained in one question or item; instead, they are composed of several dimensions or factors. For example, level of functioning, marital satisfaction, and community attitudes are complex types. Composite measures consisting of several items are called **scales**. You can use scales in interviews and questionnaires—sometimes even in structured observation—essential when collecting quantitative data.

Standardized scales are a type of scale that is uniform and tested extensively. Usually, published scales are accompanied by information about what they are intended to measure and with what type of population. Sometimes you may need a scale to measure a specific variable—for example, child well-being or aggression. Whenever possible, as with other data collection methods, try to use existing scales; they can eliminate considerable work. There are some drawbacks to using existing scales, though: They may not be designed to measure the variables in your study. For example, a family coping scale would not be appropriate for measuring family cohesion. The other problem is the temptation to design research around a standardized instrument—for example, changing your study to look at family coping rather than family cohesion.

Scales lend themselves to use in online surveys, and you can elaborate on them by using technologies such as streaming video and sound.

Developing Scales

If you are tasked with developing a scale, you will need to identify sources of scale items. These sources can include your existing knowledge about the topic of the scale, the literature, people who are knowledgeable about the topic, and the people who are the focus of the research.

You need to take the following steps when developing scales:

1. Develop or locate more scale items than you will ultimately need.
2. Eliminate items that are redundant or unclear.

3. Pretest the remaining items for validity or reliability (see discussion below) and eliminate those that do not pass the test

4. Repeat the third step as many times as necessary to reduce the number of items to the required number.

Selecting the scale items.   Each statement is considered for its content validity (see discussion later in this chapter). For example, if you construct a scale measuring adoptive parental attachment to an adoptive child, the items should relate to the attachment. The range of variation of the items needs to be broad and not too narrow. The extremes will only apply to a few respondents. For example, with the level of attachment, an item relating to sexual abuse between the adoptive parent and child would add nothing to the scale. First, the respondents (the parents) would not admit to this, and second, it is very unlikely. Apart from the validity and the range of variation, items also need to be assessed based on their unidimensionality. In other words, the items need to relate to and measure only one variable; otherwise, the scale becomes muddled. As a part of this process, it is essential to distinguish between different variables and aspects of the same variable. Again, with the attachment example, attachment contains several dimensions, including emotional and physical. All the items should be connected or correlated; this can be done by carrying out a pretest.

As you can tell by now, the construction of scales is not an easy process. In addition, certain types of scales have very specific types of requirements. A discussion of the different types follows.

Types of scales.   The most common form for social science research is the **Likert scale**. The respondent is shown a series of statements and is then asked to respond using one of five response alternatives, for example, "strongly agree," "agree," "no opinion," "disagree," "strongly disagree," or some variant of these. Likert scales are designed to avoid certain kinds of response patterns, i.e., the statements vary in form so that the answers are not always the same.

Another type of scale is the **Thurstone scale**. These are constructed using equidistant intervals. These are very rigorously pretested but can be used to generate interval-level data (refer to Chapter 4) and allow the data to be more rigorously analyzed, as we will discuss in later chapters. Both Thurstone and Likert scales require at least twenty or more items to be included.

The **Semantic Differential (SD) scale** is yet another type of scale. The SD Scale includes a format that presents the respondent with a stimulus, such as an event or a person, rated on a scale using adjectives. Unlike the Likert and Thurstone scales, SD scales only require four to eight adjective pairs to provide reliable results.

The last type of scaling in our discussion is the **Guttman scale**. This type of scale ensures that a measurement is truly unidimensional and the items on the scale are progressive, usually relating to the intensity of the variable under study. Generally, they are organized with the "easy" items first and the "harder" ones later. A variation of this type of scale used to enhance both social work practice and research is known as the target problem scale.

An Example of Using a Semantic Differential Scale

Heckemann et al. (2021) compared Swedish and Austrian nursing students' attitudes to those eighty years and over. A pen and ink survey was administered to the Austrian students and an online survey to the Swedish students. The surveys included a four-factor, twenty-six item validated Ageing Semantic Differential scale and demographic questions. One hundred and thirty-six Austrian and two hundred and twenty-two Swedish students responded (88 percent of whom were women). Swedish students were older and had more positive attitudes about oldest-old adults than Austrian students.

TARGET PROBLEM (rated by client)	TARGET PROBLEM RATING						GLOBAL IMPROVEMENT
	Degree of Severity				Degree of Improvement		
	Session #						
	1	2	3	4	Month		
Difficulty in talking about feelings	ES	ES	S	S	S	3	
Getting to work on time	ES	S	S	NVS	NP	5	
Fear of leaving house in daytime	ES	S	S	NVS	NP	5	
					TOTAL	13/3 = 4.3	
							Somewhat to a lot better

Severity Scale			Improvement Scale		
NP	=	No problem	1	=	Worse
NVS	=	Not very severe	2	=	No change
S	=	Severe	3	=	A little better
VS	=	Very severe	4	=	Somewhat better
ES	=	Extremely severe	5	=	A lot better

The global improvement rating is obtained by totaling the change scores and dividing by the number of target problems. This yields a number that reflects the client's overall improvement on all problems.

Figure 9.4   Example of a target problem and global improvement scale for one client

Target problem scales are a means to track changes in a client's target behavior. This type of scale is advantageous when actual outcomes are challenging to identify. The scale involves identifying a problem, applying an intervention, and repeatedly rating the extent to which the target problem has changed. One such target problem scale is shown in Figure 9.5. In addition, this example includes a global improvement scale that summarizes the amount of change in the target problem.

A rapid assessment instrument (RAI) is a standardized series of structured questions or statements administered to the client to collect. Rapid assessment instruments are short, easy to administer, and complete. RAIs are extremely useful for collecting data for the evaluation of practice. The Multi-Problem Screening Inventory (Hudson and McMentry, 1997), or MPSI, is one example. The MPSI can be used with practice to collect data on several variables, including generalized contentment and marital satisfaction. Refer to Fischer, Corcoran, and Springer's (2020) collection of measuring instruments, which provides an excellent reference for the social worker practitioner.

Neutrality

Scales are designed to be as neutral as possible, particularly standardized scales.

Applicability

Scales are useful in studies in which the emphasis is on collecting quantitative data. They are also helpful for measuring multifaceted concepts. Finally, scales are helpful when there is not much time available for data collection.

Secondary Data

Secondary data are data collected for purposes other than the present research. They may be data collected for another research project or data not collected with research in mind.

We use secondary data in generalist practice by consulting case records written by others and referring to agency statistics when writing up reports. This is sometimes referred to as "data-mining." Case records provide an important secondary data source for agency-based social worker research. Other secondary data sources

---

An Example of Secondary Data Use

Hong et al. (2021) looked at the association between bullying victimization and internalizing on foreign-born and U.S.-born Latino/Hispanic and Asian adolescents in the United States. In addition, the study looked at the moderating effects of parental monitoring. Data were from the 2009–2010 Health Behavior in School-Aged Children study. The study sample comprised 3,349 Latino/Hispanic and 681 Asian American adolescents between the ages of ten and seventeen from various locations in the United States. Foreign-born adolescents were more likely to be bullied than U.S.-born adolescents. For both groups, being bullied increased the likelihood of internalizing problems. However, parental monitoring moderated the relationship between bullying victimization and internalizing problems among foreign-born adolescents only.

An Example of Using Records as Data

Taylor et al. (2019) studied the extent of trauma among youth in child welfare. They data-mined case records to explore how trauma manifests in child welfare and how child welfare workers engage youth who have experienced trauma. The case records revealed that youth exhibit many signs and symptoms of complex trauma. However, most did not have a trauma-related mental health diagnosis.

---

include U.S. Census Bureau data and the numerous reports generated by state and federal government, including historical documents.

Agencies—both private and public—are creating data banks in increasing numbers and storing information about their operations, including the number of clients served, types of target problems, outcomes, staffing patterns, and budgets. Additionally, information can be obtained on crime rates, child abuse and neglect rates, and other factors.

An Example of Using Historical Data

Menzies (2019) inspected the historical record to examine the evolving definition of collective, historical, and intergenerational trauma and the value of these concepts in understanding the health and social challenges seen within colonized Indigenous communities, specifically within Australian Aboriginal communities. Programs that focus on reducing the rates of certain variables, including infant mortality, incarceration rates, or school completion rates, are essential but are merely treating symptoms unless the underlying trauma is addressed. Due to the ongoing devastation caused by many years of forced child removal, this is especially important for health, legal, and welfare practitioners within the child protection system and the social work field to break the cycles of family and cultural disruption.

These types of data are beneficial when conducting a needs assessment. Two strategies can be adopted using secondary data in a needs assessment: rates under treatment and social indicators. The rates under treatment approach uses existing data from agencies to determine the needs of a community. The problem with this approach is that existing services may not reflect unmet needs.

An Example of Using Rates Under Treatment

Karlsson & Lundström (2021) examined the rates of children diagnosed with ADHD and medicated in the child welfare population. These rates are very high, creating an "ADHD epidemic." They argue that social workers need to conduct more research in this area, which is dominated by the medical profession. The social work profession can contribute to our understanding of this common phenomenon among children and adolescent clients that is often comorbid with other conditions such as conduct disorder.

The **social indicators** approach selects demographic data from existing public records to predict a community's needs. Existing statistics relating to people's spatial arrangement and facilities in a community, housing patterns, crime patterns, and so on can help us determine where, for example, to place a community center.

It is also possible to use **vignettes** in collecting data. These are hypothetical situations either drawn from a source or developed by the researcher (in which case the vignettes are not strictly secondary data) to elicit specific responses from the participants in the study.

McKinroy and Beer (2020) discuss using digital vignettes simulating social media in internet research. They point out the advantages and disadvantages of this method. This can be a helpful approach with a stigmatized and geographically dispersed population of youth who are highly digitally engaged.

An Example of Using Vignettes

McLaren et al. (2020) used four vignettes from Sri Lanka, Malaysia, Vietnam, and Australia to examine the "intersections between Covid 19 and gendered burdens." They focused on frontline work, unpaid care work, and community activities. The authors demonstrated how these burdens increased during the pandemic.

Indirect Sources

Indirect sources refer to information that is used for research, but was initially collected for some other purpose. Indirect sources include case records, newspapers, and other media reports. For example, we may be interested in studying an agency's attitudes toward the developmentally disabled, so we consult case records. The most common way of dealing with indirect sources is to subject them to **content analysis**. Content analysis is a method of coding communication to a systematic quantifiable form. We will discuss this further in Chapters 10 and 11.

Neutrality

When using secondary data, we need to be aware that sometimes these data have limited neutrality. Indirect sources can often be particularly biased because they were not collected for research purposes. For example, there may be gaps in a record that we are using. In addition, because records were made for another purpose, information relating to our research question may be missing. For example, if we gathered information on agency attitudes toward the developmentally disabled, that information may be missing from case records.

Direct sources are more neutral, but the researcher needs to verify the exact form of the initially asked questions. The structure of questions asked later by the secondary researcher may be different; we need to know what this difference is. For example, you may be interested in the number of juveniles who had a previous record of substance abuse seen by the local juvenile probation office. Your focus may be on alcohol use, whereas the data collected did not distinguish between alcohol and other types of substance abuse. When using secondary data, you cannot assume that the first researcher's questions are similar to yours.

Applicability

Secondary data can be used when available (this is not always the case). Secondary data also can be applied when the definition of the secondary data variables and the form of the questions are the same (or similar) to yours; if not, you must at least be aware of the differences. In addition, secondary data can be helpful when a needs assessment is required, and the budget is limited. Finally, secondary data can yield much information when you are interested in conducting a historical study—for example, the history of an agency or of the way a particular problem has been addressed in the past.

Who Collects the Data

As with the other decisions concerning data collection, who should collect the data depends greatly on the type of research question asked. We tend to think of the researcher as the only person who should collect the data when interviewing or administering a questionnaire.

The client or subject can also collect the data for the research. Participants can use journals or diaries in this way. Questionnaires can be self-administered; mailed questionnaires are the obvious example. Clients can also observe and record their own behavior using scales or checklists. Engaging the client in the data collection is particularly valuable in conducting single-system studies. As we saw in Chapter 7, it can provide feedback on changes in the client's behavior.

Earlier, we discussed reactivity effects. This reactivity effect can also be a problem when clients collect data on their own behavior or use **self-monitoring**. This reactivity can be quite strong, resulting in self-monitoring as an intervention device.

Combining Data Collection Methods

You should use methods and instruments in conjunction with one another. As mentioned earlier in the chapter, you can collect both qualitative and quantitative data. In addition, you can use several different methods in the same study (see Table 9.2).

Combining measures can enrich your study and help ensure that you are tapping a maximum number of dimensions of the phenomenon under investigation. Using several data collection methods is sometimes called triangulation.

Other forms of triangulation include using several different theories, researchers, or research methods—for example, a mix of quantitative and qualitative approaches. Triangulation, particularly in qualitative studies, can help enhance the validity of findings.

TABLE 9.2 Characteristics of Data Collection Methods

	Unstructured interviews	Mailed questionnaire	Participant observation	Standardized observation	Logs	Face-to-face administered standardized scales
High response rate	yes	no	n/a	yes	maybe	yes
Anonymity assured	no	yes	no	no	no	no
Low reactivity effects	no	yes	maybe	maybe	yes	yes
Illiterate subjects	yes	no	yes	yes	no	no
Semilegal or illegal behavior	no	maybe	maybe	no	no	no
Large sample or limited funds	no	yes	no	no	no	yes
In-depth, "thick description"	yes	no	yes	no	yes	no

An Example of Combining Data Collection Methods

Zhu and Andersen (2021) discussed which knowledge areas of digital competence are vital for Norwegian social work education today. The research used different methods to collect data. These included a case study of the Norwegian Labour and Welfare Administration (NAV), a document analysis of Norwegian social work education guidelines and curricula, and a semistructured interview with social work educators. The results indicated minimal integration of digital competence knowledge areas across Norwegian social work education. Therefore, the authors suggest further research to develop a consensus in defining digital competence and its core knowledge areas in social work to prepare future professionals.

Determining Reliability and Validity

Before you use a measuring instrument in the research process, it is crucial to assess its reliability and validity. This is important regardless of whether you use a qualitative or quantitative approach. However, assessing the instrument varies according to the approach and whether the data are qualitative or quantitative. Quantitative data collection instruments—particularly scales and highly standard interview, questionnaire, and observation schedules—lend themselves most readily to the tests for reliability and validity presented here. Standardized scales are always accompanied by the results of validity and reliability tests. However, open-ended, qualitative instruments are more challenging to assess for reliability and validity. That said, you can still use the principles presented here as guidelines with open-ended instruments to improve their validity and reliability.

Reliability

Reliability indicates the extent to which a measure reveals actual differences in the phenomenon measured rather than differences inherent in the measuring instrument itself. Reliability refers to the consistency of a measure. To illustrate, a wooden ruler is a reliable measure for a table. However, if the ruler were made of elastic, it would not provide a reliable measure because repeated measurements of the same table would differ due to the ruler's expanding and contracting. If a client is chronically depressed and you measure the degree of depression at two points in time, the instrument is reliable if you get close to the same score each time, provided the level of depression has not changed. It would help if you established the instrument's reliability before determining actual changes in the phenomena under study.

As a generalist social worker, you need to assess how reliable the data collection instrument is. There are two major ways to determine the instrument's reliability: assessing sources of error and assessing the degree to which the instrument's reliability has been tested. We will discuss each of these in turn.

Sources of Error

When assessing the reliability of an instrument, you need to determine whether there is evidence of certain sources of error. The following are four major types of error: unclear definition of variables, use of retrospective information, variations in the conditions for collecting the data, and instrument structure.

Unclear Definitions of Variables

As we saw in Chapter 4, variables can be challenging to define because many social work terms tend to be vague. If a variable is not clearly operationalized and defined, its measurement lacks reliability: Different social workers can interpret the possible outcome differently. The wording of questionnaires often creates problems with unclear definitions of variables. A question might be phrased so that two individuals interpret it differently and provide two different answers, even though the actual behavior they are reporting is the same. For example, people might ask, "Do you often use public transportation in the city?" In responding, people may interpret the question in different ways. Interpretive studies in which the variables are not necessarily clearly defined and operationalized pose a challenge. Extensive use of interviews in these types of studies overcomes some of the problems because the unstructured data collection method allows exploration of the concepts. If the variable described by the respondent is unclear, the respondent can be asked to elaborate and define. The definition comes from the subjects rather than from the researcher.

Use of Retrospective Information

Retrospective information is gathered through subject recall, either by a questionnaire or an interview. These data are almost inevitably distorted. Moreover, sometimes subject memory is hampered because of the nature of the topic under study—as you might expect if you were investigating an adult's experience of childhood sexual abuse, for example. Case records are one form of retrospective data collection but are subject to considerable error. These types of data usually reflect the idiosyncratic recording practices of the individual social worker. The worker will select certain aspects of the case for recording, resulting in impaired reliability.

Variations in Conditions for Collecting the Data

Interview conditions can also affect reliability when you use interviews to collect data. For example, the subject may respond differently depending on whether the interviewer is male or female (this is the reactive effect we discussed earlier). Similar problems may arise due to the ethnicity and age of the interviewer. Where the interview is conducted may also cause disparities in responses. Even with questionnaires (for example, mailed questionnaires), a lack of control over the conditions under which they are administered can result in low reliability.

Structure of the Instrument

Certain aspects of the data collection method itself may enhance or decrease reliability. An open-ended questionnaire that requires that responses be categorized and coded can present reliability problems.

Testing Reliability

In addition to identifying the sources of error in an instrument, we can also assess the extent to which the instrument's reliability has been tested. As generalist social workers, you will need to understand what reliability tests others have conducted. In addition, you may be able to use these tests on some of the instruments you develop.

Reliability is determined by obtaining two or more measures of the same thing and seeing how closely they agree. Four methods are used to establish the reliability of an instrument: test-retest, alternate form, split half, and observer reliability.

Test-Retest

Test-retest involves repeatedly administering the instrument to the same people on separate occasions. These people should not be subjects in the actual study. The results of the repeated administrations are then compared. If the results are similar, the reliability of the instrument is high. A problem associated with this method of testing reliability is that the first testing has influenced the second.

For example, during the second test, the individuals may be less anxious, less motivated, or less interested. On the other hand, they may simply remember their answers from the first test and repeat them. In addition, they may have learned from the first testing, particularly with attitude questions. To prevent these problems, you should avoid measuring instruments strongly affected by memory or repetition.

Alternate Form

With **alternate form** tests, different but equivalent forms of the same test are administered to the same group of individuals—usually close in time—and then compared. The major problem with this approach is developing the equivalent tests, which can be time-consuming. In addition, this approach can still involve some of the difficulties associated with the test-retest method.

Split Half

With the **split-half method**, items on the instrument are divided into comparable halves. For example, a scale could be divided, so the first half should have the same score as the second half. This testing method looks at the internal consistency of the measure. The test is administered, and the two halves are compared. If the score is the same, the instrument is probably reliable. A major problem with this approach is ensuring that the two halves are equivalent. Equivalency is problematic with instruments other than scales.

Observer Reliability

Observer reliability involves comparing administrations of an instrument performed by different observers or interviewers. To use this method effectively, the observers need to be thoroughly trained; at least two people will code the content of the responses according to specific criteria.

Each of these testing methods for reliability involves comparing two or more results. Usually, this comparison uses some kind of **correlation coefficient**. This statistic measures the extent to which the comparisons are similar or not similar— the extent to which they are related or correlated. We will discuss the concept of correlation in more detail in Chapter 12. For our purposes now in assessing reliability, the correlation coefficient can range from 0.0 to 1.0, with the latter number reflecting a perfect correlation or the highest level of reliability possible. Generally, a coefficient of .80 suggests the instrument is reasonably reliable. Table 9.3 summarizes the criteria you can use to assess an instrument's reliability.

TABLE 9.3   Criteria for Assessing the Reliability of Measuring Instruments

1.	Is the variable clearly defined?
2.	Is retrospective information avoided?
3.	Are there controlled conditions under which the data are collected?
4.	Is the question format closed?
5.	Are reliability tests used? If so, is the correlation coefficient greater than 0.5?

If the answer is yes to most of these questions, then the instrument is probably reliable.

Instruments with High Reliability

The scales included in the Multi-Problem Screening Inventory developed by Hudson & McMurtry (1997) all have a test-retest and split-half reliability correlation coefficients of at least .90. The scales were designed for various behaviors, including child problems, guilt, work problems, and alcohol abuse.

Validity

The **validity of a measuring instrument** reflects the extent to which you are measuring what you think you are measuring. This is a different idea than reliability. To take the example used previously, if a wooden ruler is used to measure the dimensions of a table, it is a reliable and valid instrument. However, if you use the ruler to measure ethnicity, the instrument maintains its reliability, but it is no longer valid. This is because you would not be measuring ethnicity but some other variable (for example, height), which has no relationship to ethnicity as far as we know.

Validity is not as straightforward as reliability because there are different types of validity, and each one is tested in another way. The three main types of validity are criterion validity, content validity, and construct validity. Each type of validity relates to different aspects of the instrument. Each addresses various dimensions of the problem of ensuring that what is being measured is intended to be measured. Therefore, these types of validity will be discussed, along with how each can be tested.

Validity testing can be quite complex, and sometimes entire articles in the social work literature are devoted to testing the validity of specific instruments. For example, Kiehne and Cadenas (2021) developed and initially validated a psychometrically sound instrument to assess how Latinx immigrants are viewed as a threat. Cabrera-Nguyen (2010) offers guidelines to researchers and authors for reporting scale and validation results. As generalist social workers, you will need to understand what type of validity testing has been carried out and, in some cases, the test instruments you have developed.

Criterion Validity

Criterion validity describes the extent to which a correlation exists between the measuring instrument and another standard. For example, to validate an instrument developed to assess a program that helps pregnant teenagers succeed in high school, a criterion such as SAT scores might be used as a comparison. Similarities in scores would indicate that criterion validity had been established.

Content validity

Content validity is concerned with the representativeness of the content of the instrument. The content included in the instrument needs to be relevant to the concept you are trying to measure. For example, the content validity of an instrument developed to measure knowledge of parenting skills could be obtained by consulting with various experts on parenting skills—perhaps social workers who run parenting groups and a professor at the department of social work. They could then point out areas in which the instrument may be deficient.

Content validity is partly a matter of judgment and is dependent upon the knowledge of the experts available to you.

Construct validity

Construct validity describes the extent to which an instrument measures a theoretical construct. For example, a measure may have criterion and content validity but still not measure what it is intended to measure. Construct validity is the most difficult to establish because, as we mentioned earlier, many research variables are challenging to define and theoretically vague. Constructs used in social work include aggression, sociability, and self-esteem, to name just a few. With construct validity, we are looking not only at the instrument but also at the theory underlying it. The instrument must reflect this theory.

For example, in testing the construct validity of an instrument to measure aggression in preschoolers, the associated theoretical expectations need to be examined by referring to the literature and research on the topic. One explanation that may be found is that the highly aggressive children will not be achieving well in the classroom. If the instrument does not reflect this dimension of the topic, the instrument probably does not have construct validity. IQ tests provide an example of a measure with low construct validity. IQ tests were created to measure intelligence. Since their development, however, it has become apparent that they measure only one dimension of intelligence—the potential to achieve in a white middle-class academic system. Other dimensions of intelligence remain untapped by IQ tests, resulting in their limited validity for measuring intelligence.

One way of more fully ensuring construct validity is to define the construct using small, concrete, observable behaviors (Duncan & Fiske, 1977). Such definition helps avoid some of the wishy-washiness associated with many constructs used in social work practice. For example, if both the verbal and nonverbal behaviors of preschoolers are recorded, and certain patterns of these behaviors become apparent in those children previously labeled aggressive, you can be more fully assured that your label does indeed have construct validity.

Once you are familiar with this information on validity and how it can be tested, you are then in a position as a generalist social worker to assess the validity of the measuring instruments you read about or propose to use. Table 9.4 presents a checklist that you can use to determine the validity of instruments.

Feedback

Feedback is an important way of testing the validity of qualitative data, particularly when the intent of the research may well be to define and elaborate on these concepts. However, data must be understandable and relevant to the participants in the research. The participants should be allowed to verify the data. This feedback can be carried out formally (through focus groups or community meetings) or informally (through meetings and informal gatherings with the participants, for example).

TABLE 9.4   Criteria for Assessing the Validity of Quantitative Measuring Instruments

....

1.   Was the instrument tested for criterion validity?

2.   Was the instrument tested for content validity?

3.   Was the instrument tested for construct validity?

4.   Is the variable defined as clearly and concretely as possible?

If the answer is yes to most of these questions, then the instrument is probably valid (that is, if the findings from the tests support the validity of the instrument).

Note that often in the collection of qualitative data, responsibility for validating the data lies directly with the researcher rather than being assured through the use of prescribed methods such as a criterion validity check. Therefore, it is even more critical for the researcher to act responsibly and ethically.

An Example of Testing Reliabilitiy and Validity

Graham et al. (2021) examined numerous intimate partner violence (IPV) risk assessment tools. The reliability and validity of these tools are critical because intimate partners perpetrate one in seven homicides worldwide. The authors conducted a review of these assessment tools from around the world. Forty-two were included and systematically examined for their validity and reliability. Researchers in eight countries have tested eighteen risk assessment tools.

Ethical Issues in Collecting Data

When collecting data for a research study, we need to be concerned about three ethical issues: potential harm to the subjects, anonymity, confidentiality, and research justification.

Harm to the Participants

We need to avoid harming the participants in any way. Strict guidelines governing the potential harm to the participants in the research were developed because of landmark studies in the first half of the twentieth century. For example, in 1963, Milgram published a study showing that 65 percent of participants were willing to give another person electric shocks if prompted by an experimenter (Milgram, 1963). Furthermore, in many of the experiments, the participants displayed severe psychological distress, which Milgram described in his article:

> In the first four conditions, 71 of the 160 subjects showed definite signs of
> nervous laughter and smiling. The laughter seemed entirely out of place,
> even bizarre. Full flown uncontrollable seizures were observed for 15 of

these subjects. On one accession, we observed a seizure so violently convulsive that it was necessary to call a halt to the experiment. (Milgram, 1965, p. 68).

After the experiment, the researchers explained that no electric shocks were given. Milgram's study has been used as a case study in discussions of harm to research subjects.

Another landmark study for the discussion of research ethics is the Tuskegee Study. From 1932 to 1972, the U.S. Public Health Service studied untreated and undertreated late syphilis in 400 African American farm laborers in Alabama. At the time of the study, there was a treatment for late-stage syphilis, although the side effects were harsh. The study intended to compare the untreated syphilis subjects (the farm laborers) with a treated population. The ethical issues in this study involved informed consent, exploitation, and access to treatment. Cave and Holm (2003) analyzed both of these studies and discussed how ethical guidelines for research have been developed as a result.

Consequently, the NASW Code of Ethics (2021) is very clear on these issues and states:

- Social workers engaged in evaluation or research should carefully consider possible consequences and should follow guidelines developed for the protection of evaluation and research participants. Appropriate institutional review boards should be consulted.

- Social workers engaged in evaluation or research should protect participants from unwarranted physical or mental distress, harm, danger, or deprivation.

As simplistic as these mandates may seem, these things are easier said than done on closer examination. When asking questions in whatever form—whether interviewing or using a questionnaire—you often require participants to examine and assess their behavior. For example, questions relating to childhood abuse may be painful for the respondent. Other questions which are challenging to answer concern income and the ability to pay for a proposed service.

Consequently, assessing the extent of discomfort for the participant can be difficult. The **Institutional Review Boards** (IRBs) discussed in Chapter 8 make this assessment for you. All federally funded research and research conducted at universities requires the proposed research to be reviewed by IRBs. If you complete a project as a part of your research class, your proposal will need to be reviewed by your university's IRB. During the review process, the researcher must answer specific questions regarding potential harm to participants and complete an application for review by the board. This sounds like a big undertaking, and some studies undergo a thorough and lengthy review, but the intent is important: to protect the participants in the research from any harm. Many studies, however, including those usually undertaken by undergraduates and master's students in the social sciences, qualify for an exemption from full review. This shortens the process considerably, and usually, you can gain approval in just a few days.

Exempt studies include:

- those conducted as a normal part of research on educational practices

- research using an educational test with confidentiality protection
- survey or interview methods on public behavior with the protection of confidentiality
- research using existing data without violating confidentiality
- research on federal demonstration projects
- survey or interview data when the respondents are elected or appointed officials or candidates for public office

Exemptions are generally not available when specific vulnerable populations are included in the study—children and prisoners, for example—or when there the deception participants are deceived or they are subject to unusual situations, particularly those that involve any harassment or discomfort.

Small agencies not receiving federal funding do not require IRB review, so in this situation, you need to be very careful that your research is ethically sound. Always seek the opinions of others on this issue.

Anonymity and Confidentiality

Both anonymity and confidentiality help participants avoid harm. Again, the NASW Code of Ethics (2021) states:

- Social workers engaged in evaluation or research should ensure the anonymity or confidentiality of participants and of the data obtained from them. Social workers should inform participants of any limits of confidentiality and when any records containing research data will be destroyed.

Anonymity means that the researcher cannot identify a given response with a given respondent. It was mentioned previously that an interview could never be anonymous. Anonymity is also jeopardized when identification numbers are put on questionnaires to facilitate follow-up and increase the response rate. Ensuring anonymity not only reassures the subjects but can also enhance the objectivity of the responses. For example, if you are asking questions about deviant behavior, the respondent is more likely to give an answer that accurately reflects their behavior if anonymity can be assured.

Confidentiality means that the researcher knows the identity of the respondents and their associated responses but takes care not to disclose this information to anyone else. Confidentiality becomes particularly critical when conducting interviews, for which anonymity is impossible to ensure. The principle of confidentiality should be explained to respondents either verbally or in a cover letter accompanying the questionnaires. Do not confuse confidentiality and anonymity; they are different and both extremely important.

Justification of the Research

The NASW Code of Ethics (2021) states:

- Social workers should never design or conduct evaluation or research that does not use consent procedures, such as certain forms of naturalistic observation and archival research, unless a rigorous and responsible review of the research has found it to be justified because of its prospective scientific, educational, or applied value and unless equally effective alternative procedures that do not involve waiver of consent are not feasible.

We discussed informed consent in Chapter 6. Using data not collected directly from the participants (such as client records and other secondary data) does not exempt the researchers from another ethical responsibility: ensuring that the research is needed and justified.

Human Diversity Issues in Collecting the Data

Awareness and knowledge of human diversity issues during the data collection stage of the research process are critical. Some of the central issues to which we need to pay attention are the selection of the data collection method for diverse populations, the relevance to diverse populations of the content of the data collection method, and the application of the data collection method to diverse populations.

Methodological Issues in Conducting Research with Diverse Groups

Mendez-Luck et al. (2008) examined how female caregivers in a suburb of Mexico City conceptualize the burden of taking care of their elders. They conducted semistructured interviews about giving care to older relatives with forty-one women. The participants described "burden" negatively as a weight on their shoulders and as a "positive sacrifice that involved love, initiative, and goodwill" (p. 265). The researchers stress the importance of understanding local definitions of the burden involved in caregiving and the need for culturally appropriate research methods to measure this burden, so policy recommendations for more institutional support can be made.

Selection of Data Collection Methods for Diverse Populations

The extent to which data collection methods may or may not apply to certain groups within a population needs to be considered. For example, some groups may be uncomfortable with being interviewed or administered a questionnaire; you need to be sensitive to how different cultural groups might regard different methods.

Relevance to Diverse Populations of the Content of the Data Collection Method

In addition to the appropriateness of a particular data collection instrument, taking account of human diversity requires you consider the content of that instrument and its suitability to the group under study. The most obvious situation is when research is conducted with populations who speak a language different from the researcher's primary language. Translations must be offered and undertaken. This sounds obvious, but often it is assumed that if a population appears to be fluent in

---

An Example of a Bilingual Interview

Nedjat-Haiem et al. (2018) conducted a qualitative study in Southern New Mexico to explore the experiences of older Latinos. The authors used motivational interviewing to encourage advance care planning among the participants in regards to their preferences for end-of-life care. All interviews were conducted in Spanish.

Participants ($n = 32$) were primarily women (74.3 percent). Half of them were born in the United States and the other half were from Mexico. The participants had been in the United States for an average of 31.75 years. Many had less than a sixth-grade education (31.3 percent) or had not completed high school (21.9 percent). Key themes indicated the following stages of change: (1) precontemplation, (2) contemplation, (3) preparation, (4) ACP action, and (5) maintenance.

English, for example, then no translation is necessary. Yet, specific segments of the population may not be as fluent in the assumed language as it appears, like elders for instance, or that translation may be a symbolic gesture by the researcher that indicates their acknowledgment and understanding of the population under study. For example, the author assisted in planning a "Talking Circle" (Community Forum) at the Zuni Pueblo in New Mexico. As a result, the "Participant Guide" was translated into Zuni, even though most of the population were English speakers.

Even if translations do not occur, certain words or phrases—whether in interview or questionnaire form, whether conducted under the auspices of a feminist or traditional research approach—may be interpreted by the respondent differently from how the researcher intended. In many cases, this divergence of interpretations may be due simply to the researcher's lack of understanding or insensitivity to the cultural group being studied. For example, some groups may interpret questions about mothers as including mothers-in-law. Serious validity problems can result since the researcher thinks of *mother* in one sense, and the subject defines *mother* differently. Reliability problems also arise.

Another perhaps less obvious problem might occur when conducting, for example, a research project concerned with methods of and difficulties with disciplining children. You would need to acknowledge the methods and problems experienced by gay and lesbian parents (unless we purposefully *intend* to exclude them) in addition to those of heterosexual parents because some of the issues gay and lesbian parents encounter might be different. Consequently, you would need to include questions relevant to this group so as not to exclude problems such parents might be experiencing and thus jeopardize the validity of your findings.

Earlier, we discussed the usefulness of rapid assessment instruments and other instruments that have already been developed. First, check whether the instruments have been used with diverse populations and whether their reliability and validity were tested with these groups.

Many of these issues are an extension of the discussion in Chapter 3 about the need to include relevant variables in the study. You must not only account for all the relevant variables but also be aware of human diversity issues in phrasing or constructing the data collection instrument.

Application of the Data Collection Method to Diverse Populations

Even if the data collection method and the structure and content of this method are sensitive to the needs of diverse populations, how the instrument is administered still may not be.

For example, you may be carrying out a needs assessment for socially isolated, recently immigrated Asian women. To obtain valid and reliable information, you would need to include questions relevant to this population and conduct the interviews to elicit the required information. This necessitates the use of people who are sensitive to the population under study as interviewers, administrators of questionnaires, and observers. For example, with the Asian women, an interviewer would need to be familiar with this group's language, gender role, and intergenerational role expectations to engage the subject in the interview and obtain valid and reliable data.

Summary

Quantitative approaches create categories of the phenomenon under study and assign numbers to these categories. Qualitative approaches examine the phenomenon in more detail. Data collection methods include interviews, questionnaires, observation, logs and journals, and secondary data. Scales can measure complex variables. There are several techniques for checking the reliability and validity of data collection methods. Ethical issues include considering potential harm to the subjects and the issues of confidentiality and anonymity. When considering human diversity issues, the data collection method's selection, relevance, and application need to be considered.

STUDY/EXERCISE QUESTIONS

1. Develop a questionnaire to assess the campus needs (such as parking, daycare, and so on) of students in your class. Include both open-ended and closed-ended questions.

   a. How do you decide what questions to include?

   b. How would you administer the questionnaire?

2. Have another student in the class critique your questionnaire and comment on its reliability and validity.

3. Search for a suitable instrument to measure adolescents' self-esteem.

   a. Report on its validity and reliability.

   b. Are there any groups for which the instrument may not be reliable or valid?

4. Your agency has asked you to participate in planning a program for adults with a history of childhood sexual abuse.

   a. How would you collect data that would demonstrate the need for such a program?

   b. How would you ensure confidentiality?

5. Design a structured interview to assess the satisfaction of clients who have just finished receiving services from a family service agency.

   a. Conduct this interview with a classmate.

   b. Would other data collection methods be more reliable or valid in this case?

6. Design a way of observing a Head Start student who is reported to be disruptive in the classroom.

   a. How would you check the validity and reliability of this method?

References

Abendstern, M., Wilberforce, M., Hughes, J., Arandelovic, A., Batool, S., Boland, J., Pitts, R., & Challis, D. (2022). The social worker in community mental health teams: Findings from a national survey. *Journal of Social Work, 22*(1), 4–25. https://doi.org/10.1177%2F1468017320979932

Birger, L., & Nadan, Y. (2022). Social workers and refugee service users (re)constructing their relationships in a hostile political climate. *Journal of Social Work, 22*(2), 402–421. https://doi.org/10.1177/14680173211009739

Cabrera-Nguyen, E. P. (2010). Author guidelines for reporting scale development and validation results in the *Journal of the Society for Social Work and Research*. *Journal of the Society for Social Work and Research, 1*, 99–103.

Cave, E., & Holm, S. (2003). Milgram and Tuskeegee—Paradigm research projects in bioethics. *Health Care Analysis, 11*(1), 27–40.

Currin-McCulloch, J., Stanton, A., Boyd, R., Neaves, M., & Jones, B. (2021). Understanding breast cancer survivors' information-seeking behaviours and overall experiences: A comparison of themes derived from social media posts and focus groups. *Psychology & Health, 36*(7), 810–827. https://doi.org/10.1080/08870446.2020.1792903

Duncan, S., & Fiske, D. (1977). *Face-to-face interaction.* Hillsdale, NJ: Erlbaum.

Fischer, J., Corcoran, K., & Fischer, J. (2020). *Measures for clinical practice: A sourcebook* (6th ed.). Oxford University Press.

Ferguson, H. (2018). Making home visits: Creativity and the embodied practices of home visiting in social work and child protection. *Qualitative Social Work, 17*(1), 65–80. doi:10.1177/1473325016656751

Graham, L. M., Sahay, K. M., Rizo, C. F., Messing, J. T., & Macy, R. J. (2021). The validity and reliability of available intimate partner homicide and reassault risk assessment tools: A systematic review. *Trauma, Violence, & Abuse, 22*(1), 18–40. https://doi.org/10.1177%2F1524838018821952

Gregg, R. (1994). Explorations of pregnancy and choice in a high-tech age. In C. Riessman (Ed.), *Qualitative studies in social work research.* Newbury Park, CA: Sage.

Heckemann, B., Schuttengruber, G., Wolf, A., Grobschadl, F., & Holmberg, C. (2021). Attitudes towards oldest-old adults (age ≥80 years): A survey and international comparison between Swedish and Austrian nursing students. *The Scandinavian Journal of Caring Sciences.*

Hong, J., Kim, D., Burlaka, V., Peguero, A., Padilla, Y., & Espelage, D. (2021). Bullying victimization and internalizing problems of foreign-born and US born Latino/Hispanic and Asian adolescents in the United States: The moderating role of parental monitoring. *Journal of the Society for Social Work and Research, 12*(3), 445–464. https://doi.org/10.1086/715891

Hudson, W., & McMurtry, S. L. (1997). Comprehensive assessment in social work practice: The multi-problem screening inventory. *Research on Social Work Practice, 7*(1), 79–88.

Kadushin, A., & Kadushin, G. (2013). *The social work interview: A guide for human service professionals* (6th ed.). Belmont, CA: Brooks Cole/Cengage Learning.

Karadzhov, D. (2021). Expanding the methodological repertoire of participatory research into homelessness: The utility of the mobile phone diary. *Qualitative Social Work, 20*(3), 813–831. https://doi.org/10.1177%2F1473325020913904

Karlsson, P., & Lundström, T. (2021). ADHD and social work with children and adolescents. *European Journal of Social Work, 24*(1), 151–161. https://doi.org/10.1080/13691457.2019.1592122

Kiehne, E., & Cadenas, G. (2021). Development and initial validation of the Latinx immigrant threat attitudes scale. *Journal of the Society for Social Work and Research, 12*(3), 521–544. https://doi.org/10.1086/715815

Kirst-Ashman, K. K., & Hull, G. H. (2017). *Understanding generalist practice*. Belmont, CA: Brooks Cole/Cengage Learning.

Littman, D., Bender, K., Mollica, M., Erangy, J., Lucas, T., & Marvin, C. (2021). Making power explicit: Using values and power mapping to guide power-diverse Participatory Action Research processes. *Journal of Community Psychology, 49*(2), 266–282. https://doi.org/10.1002/jcop.22456

McLaren, H. J., Wong, K. R., Nguyen, K. N., & Mahamadachchi, K. N. D. (2020). Covid-19 and women's triple burden: Vignettes from Sri Lanka, Malaysia, Vietnam, and Australia. *Social Sciences, 9*(5), 87. http://dx.doi.org/10.3390/socsci9050087

Meneses-Falcón, C. (2021). "Living in the brothel": Participant observation in hidden contexts. *The Social Science Journal, 58*(3), 27–285. DOI: 10.1016/j.soscij.2019.04.010

Menzies, K. (2019). Understanding the Australian Aboriginal experience of collective, historical, and intergenerational trauma. *International Social Work, 62*(6), 1522–1534. https://doi.org/10.1177%2F0020872819870585

Milgram, S. (1963). Behavioral study of obedience. *Journal of Abnormal and Social Psychology, 67*, 371–378. https://psycnet.apa.org/doi/10.1037/h0040525

National Association of Social Workers. (2021). NASW code of ethics. *NASW News, 25*, 25.

Nedjat-Haiem, F. R., Carrion, I. V., Gonzalez, K., Bennett, E. D., Ell, K., O'Connell, M., Thompson, B., & Mishra, S. I. (2018). Exploring motivational interviewing to engage Latinos in advance care planning: A community-based social work intervention. *American Journal of Hospice and Palliative Medicine, 35*(8), 1091–1098. https://doi.org/10.1177/1049909118763796

Oliveri, S., Lanzoni, L., Petrocchi, S., Janssens, R., Schoefs, E., Huys, I., Smith, M. Y., Smith, I. P., Veldwijk, J., de Wit, G. A., & Pravettoni, G. (2021). Opportunities and challenges of web-based and remotely administered surveys for patient preference studies in a vulnerable population. *Patient Preference and Adherence, 15*, 2509–2517. https://dx.doi.org/10.2147%2FPPA.S327006

Patton, M. (2014). *Qualitative research and evaluation methods* (4th ed.). Newbury Park, CA: Sage.

Taylor, S., Battis, C., Carnochan, S., Henry, C., Balk, M., & Austin, M. J. (2019). Exploring trauma-informed practice in public child welfare through qualitative data-mining of case records. *Journal of Public Child Welfare, 13*(3), 325–344, DOI: 10.1080/15548732.2018.1500967

Zhu, H., & Andersen, S. T. (2021, March 17). Digital competence in social work practice and education: Experiences from Norway. *Nordic Social Work Research*. Online https://www.tandfonline.com/doi/full/10.1080/2156857X.2021.1899967

10

Organizing the Data

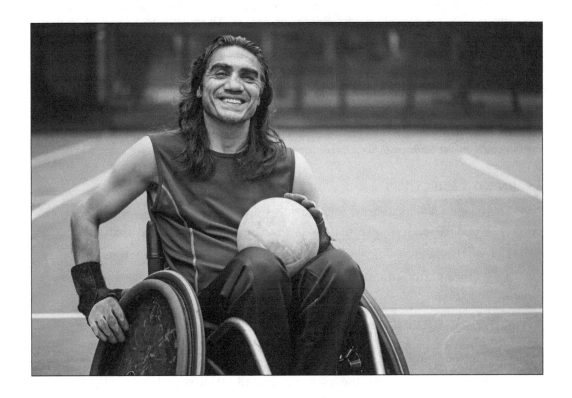

INTRODUCTION

Sometimes you get so caught up in designing the project and planning the data collection that once the data are in hand, you may wonder what to do with it all. The three types of research discussed in this book—practice evaluation, program evaluation, and needs assessment—all have the potential to overwhelm you with data.

This chapter is concerned with organizing the data once they are collected. This stage bridges the gap between data collection and data analysis. In generalist practice, data organization and data analysis are equivalent to the analyzing resource capabilities in practice.

How the data are analyzed depends significantly on whether the data are qualitative or quantitative. As discussed in Chapter 1, quantitative data are the result of fitting diverse phenomena into predetermined categories. These categories are then analyzed using statistical techniques. On the other hand, qualitative data produce a mass of detailed information in the form of words rather than numbers. Therefore, such data must be subjected to conditions of analysis that will help make sense out of these words.

Another essential step is finding out what software packages are available to you, either at your university or in the workplace. Some can be expensive and not particularly "user-friendly." There are some developed for analyzing both quantitative and qualitative data. Whatever you use, these different data also require different strategies for their organization before they can be analyzed.

LEARNING OBJECTIVES

This chapter will include the following learning objectives:

1. To understand how quantitative data can be organized prior to analysis

2. To understand how qualitative data can be organized before analysis

3. To articulate the ethical and human diversity issues in data organization

Organizing Quantitative Data

You work for a public agency that provides assistance to foster care families. Your supervisor has just asked you to develop a questionnaire to mail to all foster families in the area served by the agency to identify their unmet needs. There are 300 foster families in your area. You send a two-page questionnaire to all 300 families and receive 150 back. These questionnaires contain a considerable amount of valuable data for your agency.

These data are quantitative and in raw form; however, this is not very useful to you. Imagine tallying answers to 30 questions for 150 questionnaires by hand—a very time-consuming and tedious process.

Coding the Data

In the foster family study, you need to transfer the information from the questionnaire to the computer by coding it. Coding involves organizing the collected data so that it can be entered into the software. Coding is accomplished in three steps: (1) converting the responses to numerical codes; (2) assigning names to the variables; and (3) developing a codebook.

Converting the Responses to Numerical Codes

In the foster care example, one question on the questionnaire is: "How many times in the last month were you contacted by a worker in the agency?" The response to this type of question is very straightforward; it simply entails entering the number reported into the computer. Note that this response is at the ratio level of measurement and reflects the absolute magnitude of the value (see Chapter 3). The level of measurement determines the type of statistical analysis that we can perform. With ratio data, you have a great deal of latitude in that responses can be manipulated in various ways: They can be added, subtracted, multiplied, and divided. They represent real numbers and are not strictly codes.

When you look at the other types of questions and their responses, the number assigned to the response is a code, and there is a certain amount of arbitrariness in its assignment. This is the case with data at the nominal and ordinal levels of measurement. So, for example, the questionnaire might read: "How would you gauge your overall level of satisfaction with the services our agency provides? (Circle the most appropriate response.)"

very satisfied   satisfied   somewhat satisfied   not satisfied

This information can be entered more easily if you assign numeral codes to each of the possible responses—for example:

very satisfied	1
satisfied	2
somewhat satisfied	3
not satisfied	4

Note that the level of measurement of this variable is ordinal. The numbers are ranked, but the distance between the numbers is not necessarily equal. Thus, our use of these numbers in statistical analysis will be more limited than those in the previous question. Note that this satisfaction question constitutes one variable with four possible responses or values, coded 1 to 4.

Another question on the questionnaire is this: "Specifically, which services could be expanded to meet any of your needs more to your satisfaction? Please check all that apply."

_____ Individual counseling
_____ Family counseling
_____ Training and preparation for foster child
_____ Other, please specify: _____

For this question, more than one response could be checked. The easiest way to deal with this type of question is to divide it into three subquestions or three variables rather than one. The three would consist of individual counseling, family counseling, and training. Then, a number would be assigned (1 or 2) according to whether the respondent checked or did not check each item. Note that here we are dealing with variables at the nominal level of measurement. The numbers have been assigned arbitrarily to the responses, and they are not ranked in any way.

		Numerical Code
individual counseling	checked (yes)	1
	not checked (no)	2
family counseling	checked (yes)	1
	not checked (no)	2
training	checked (yes)	1
	not checked (no)	2

Another characteristic of this question that demands special attention is the "other" item, which directs respondents to write in an answer. One solution is to categorize the response to this subquestion or variable into finite (countable) groups (for example, individual services, group services, information and referral, and so on) and then assign numbers to each of these groups. Alternatively, you can fit the data into existing categories. We need to be careful not to lose the meaning intended by the respondent. An alternative strategy is to treat this item as qualitative data. After all, this is essentially a qualitative mode of collecting data. It attempts to seek information from the subject's perspective rather than imposing previously constructed categories on the subject's behaviors. We will discuss the organization of qualitative data later in this chapter.

Whatever type of question you are coding, you need to follow two guidelines: The coding categories should be mutually exclusive and exhaustive. When categories are mutually exclusive, you can code a given response in one way only for each variable. That is why in the last example, the question needed to be treated as several variables to accommodate the fact that more than one yes response was possible.

The codes should also be exhaustive; in other words, all the data need to be coded in some way. Coding is a tedious task in research. Do not omit coding some responses because you think you will not need them in the analysis (if this is the case, the questions should not have been asked). Moreover, it is challenging to perform coding later and add to the data set once data analysis has begun. So, although it can be tiresome, you must complete the coding with care. Any mistakes will lead to a misrepresentation of the results.

Assigning Names to the Variables

It is too cumbersome to enter the entire question into the computer. Also, the computer cannot read questions in this way. Consequently, the variables themselves need to be coded or named to be accessed by the computer. This means translating the questions into words of a certain length—for example, usually no more than seven characters. Generally, the first character must be a letter; it cannot be a numeral.

Next, it is helpful to pick a variable name related to the question. For example, say the question was this: "How would you gauge your overall level of satisfaction with the services our agency provides?" A possible variable name could be SATISFY. For the question about individual counseling, family counseling, and training services, these three variables could be denoted SERVICE1, SERVICE2, and SERVICE3.

Developing a Code Book

You use the codebook to record how responses are coded, and each variable is named. The codebook provides a reference for you and other researchers who need to know or remember what the codes originally referred to. Sometimes, particularly on smaller projects, you may not need a codebook because the codes are included on the questionnaire. When designing the questionnaire, bear this in mind; it can save work later. In the last example, you would need to note in the codebook that the code for a yes response to the question about expanding individual counseling, family counseling, and training services is 1; for a no response, the code is 2.

The next step is to enter the information into the computer.

Statistical Software

You can use statistical software packages to make data analysis an efficient and straightforward task—the most common and readily available is the Statistical Package for the Social Sciences (SPSS). In addition, there are student versions, which are compatible with both Windows and macOS.

Many of the programming principles are similar, no matter the software you use. For all of them, follow these general steps:

1. Data are usually entered in rows (although some statistical software does not require this). Then, columns are assigned to variables. The first few columns are usually assigned to the ID number of the questionnaire or interview schedule. In the previous example, if 150 questionnaires were returned, three columns will be needed for the ID number to cover ID numbers 001 to 150. The following variable, SATISFY, requires only one column since the codes range only from 1 to 4.

2. Names can be given to each of the variables. However, there are usually restrictions on the form and length of these variable names.

3. The program is run choosing from the menu of commands. Each command refers to a specific statistical test. You can also use the commands to decode the data, such as converting ratio level data into categories at the nominal level or giving instructions concerning what to do about missing data.

4. You will receive output from running the program, including the analysis results.

To gain familiarity and confidence with different software, check out university information technology services. They usually provide workshops and instruction in the use of specific software. These workshops, typically free to students, can be very helpful.

Organizing Qualitative Data

Organizing qualitative data can be even more overwhelming than organizing quantitative data simply because of the nature of this type of information.

Quantitative data, by definition, are pieces of information that fit into specific categories, which in most cases, you have previously defined. Consequently, organizing the data ensures that the data are correctly assigned to the categories and are in a form compatible with the appropriate software. On the other hand, qualitative data, once collected, are usually completely uncategorized to capture as much in-depth information as possible. Therefore, analysis becomes a much more complex process.

The use of the software is not confined to quantitative data but is equally helpful in organizing and analyzing qualitative data. Using any current writing and editing software allows different files to be maintained and cross-referenced with minimal effort. Software packages are designed specifically for analyzing qualitative data, such as CAQDAS, MAXQDA, and THE ETHNOGRAPHY. New ones are developed every year. Both O'Kane, Smith, and Lerman (2021) and St. John and Johnson (2000) discuss the pros and cons of using qualitative analysis software and conclude it can save significant time. However, they can tend to emphasize volume and breadth in the analysis rather than depth and meaning. In addition, it is essential to factor in the time spent on learning the software.

Before you start collecting data, it is good to decide what software you will be using. Then you will be able to organize your field notes and codes accordingly.

An Example of Using Qualitative Software

Oswald (2019) reports on his personal experience working with Qualitative Data Analysis Software, specifically MAXQDA 12, to support a more extensive study that explored the social lives of older gay men. This is one of the few studies that describe how this digital tool can work.

We will describe four elements involved in the organization of qualitative data: keeping notes, organizing files, coding notes, and identifying gaps in the data.

Note-Keeping

As discussed in Chapter 9, the primary mode of collecting qualitative data is observation or interviewing. This involves keeping a lot of notes. Sometimes, particularly in the case of participant observation or informal interviewing, these notes are haphazard. Consequently, one of the first steps is to organize and rewrite these field notes as soon as possible after you have taken them. Rewriting the notes will help jog your memory, and the result will be more detailed, comprehensive notes than you could have produced in the field. Bernard (2017), an anthropologist, suggested five basic rules in the mechanics of taking and managing field notes:

1. Don't put your notes in one long commentary; use plenty of paper and keep many shorter notes.

2. Separate your note-taking into physically separate sets of writing.

   a. Field jottings: notes taken in the field. These provide the basis of field notes.

   b. Field notes: write-ups from your jottings.

   c. Field diary: a personal record of your experience in the field, chronicling how you feel and how you perceive your relations with others in the field.

   d. Field log: a running account of how you plan to spend your time, how you spend it, and how much money you spend.

3. Take field jottings all the time; don't rely on your memory.

4. Don't be afraid of offending people when taking field jottings. (Bernard made an interesting point about this: Being a participant observer does not mean that you become a fully accepted member of the group, but instead, you experience the life of your informants to the extent possible.) Ask permission to take notes; usually, it will be given. You can also offer to share your notes with those being interviewed.

5. Set aside some time each day to write up your field notes.

Phillippi and Lauderdale (2018) also provide excellent guidelines for organizing field notes. Use current technology throughout this process whenever possible. For example, instead of using an actual notebook, record your notes using an iPad or tablet. Mobile phones can be used not only to take notes but to record (of course, make sure you have the participant's permission for this).

When collecting qualitative data, you can **transcribe** interviews or write down a recording of the interview verbatim. Transcriptions are incredibly time-consuming. It takes six to eight hours to transcribe a one-hour interview. Sometimes, in the case of process recordings (discussed in Chapter 7), you can complete a shorthand transcription, writing down the main interactions in sequence. This results in more than field notes but is less detailed than a full transcription.

Of course, there may be occasions when the transcription is necessary and central to the study. For example, Marlow (1983) transcribed a behavior therapy interview from a videotape to look at the relationship between nonverbal and verbal behaviors. The transcription included very small behaviors—for example, intonation, slight movements of the hands, and facial features. Nevertheless, descriptions can give critical, detailed information that can enrich our understanding of client and worker experiences.

Organizing Files

Your rewritten field notes will form your basic or master file. Always keep backup copies of these notes as a precautionary measure. As you proceed with the data collection, you will need different files or sets of notes. Generally, at a minimum, you will need five types of files: descriptive files, methodological files, biographical files, bibliographical files, and analytical files.

> **An Example of Using Transcriptions**
>
> Lynch et al. (2018) studied the different dimensions of empathy as a social work skill in a mixed-method study of 110 audio recordings of meetings in a child protection service between workers and parents, applying a coding framework for analysis. Findings indicate that workers who demonstrate higher levels of empathy skill use more open questions and reflections in their communication with parents. They also demonstrate curiosity about and make efforts to understand parents' often difficult experiences, including a focus on emotions. However, most workers were found not to demonstrate a high level of empathy.

> **An Example of an Alternative to a Transcription**
>
> Parameswaran et al. (2020) describe an alternative to coding with transcripts using a method called **live coding**. This allows for simultaneous manual coding while listening or watching audio or video recording. Live coding can be beneficial in preserving the participant's voice, especially within focus group data, allowing the researcher to both see and hear the participants, thus keeping the context of the interaction.

The descriptive file includes information on the topic being studied. For example, in the case of a program evaluation, this file would consist of information on the program itself, its history, its development, and so forth. Initially, this file will contain most of your notes.

The methodological file or set of notes deals with the techniques of collecting data. It allows you to record what you think has improved or damaged your interviewing and observation techniques.

The biographical file includes information on individuals interviewed or included in the study. For example, it might consist of information about clients or the director.

The bibliographical file contains references for the material you have read related to the study. This file is very similar to the type of file you might keep when completing a research term paper.

Finally, the analytical file provides the beginnings of the analysis proper. It contains notes on the kinds of patterns you see emerging from the data. For example, when interviewing the clients from a family service agency, you may have detected the relationship between their perceptions about the benefits of the program and the specific type of problem they brought to the agency. Consequently, you may start a file labeled "Benefit-Problem." Your analytical set of notes will initially be the smallest file. Further discussion on the analysis of qualitative data will be in Chapter 11.

Do not forget to cross-reference your files. For example, some materials in the "Benefit-Problem" file about a particular client may need to be cross-referenced with a specific biographical client file. A note in each will suffice. This preparation and organization will help the analysis later.

Coding Notes

In addition to cross-referencing the five main types of notes, additional coding will help when you come to the analysis stage. As you write up the field notes, use codes for categorizing the notes. These codes can be recorded at the top of each page or in the margin and can be numbers or letters. Don't forget, though, to keep a codebook just as you would for quantitative data.

These codes will vary in their precision and form depending on the purpose of the study. For example, in a program evaluation, the codes may refer to the different channels of authority within the organization, the different types of clients served, or any other aspect of the program that is of concern.

In a practice evaluation where you may be monitoring the application of an intervention, you can use the codes to categorize the content of the interview or meeting. We describe carrying out this coding in Chapter 11.

Identifying Gaps in the Data

Throughout the data organization, you need to keep notes on any missing information or gaps in the data. Keeping track of gaps is unnecessary in a quantitative study because you make decisions about data collection early in the study. However, with a qualitative study, you often do not know what data need to be collected until well into the project when new insights and ideas relating to the study become apparent.

Ethical Issues in Organizing the Data

Two ethical issues are involved in data organization—one for each data type, quantitative and qualitative. For quantitative data, ethical problems are minimized because most decisions about how to handle the data were made before this stage. The major problem is how to deal with the "other" responses.

As mentioned before, you can create categories for these responses or fit them into existing categories. In adopting the latter approach, you need to be careful to preserve the integrity of the data and that you do not try to put the data into categories that are inappropriate or that reflect your preferences.

Ethical issues relating to the organization of qualitative data are more pervasive. You must be careful that your biases do not overtly interfere at each stage.

For example, when compiling field notes from your field jottings, ensure that the field notes reflect as closely as possible your observations in the field and are not molded to fit your existing or developing hypothesis. This is difficult because one of the underlying principles governing the interpretive approach (which usually involves qualitative data) is that objectivity is not the overriding principle driving the research. Instead, the researcher recognizes the role of subjectivity. Namely, the data's nature is a product of the relationship between the researcher and the participant.

When coding the notes, be aware of the same issue. If you doubt your objectivity, you may want to consult with someone who can examine part of your notes or your coding scheme and give you some feedback. What you are doing here is conducting a reliability check, which can serve the purpose of ensuring that you are ethically conducting the research.

Another issue is that ensuring anonymity can be especially challenging when organizing and analyzing qualitative data. This is especially the case when conducting research in rural areas. Many community members are very familiar with their neighbors, and quotes can be easily attached to specific individuals.

Human Diversity Issues in Organizing the Data

The primary human diversity issue parallels the ethical issues concerning quantitative data. When ambiguous data are categorized, such as responses to "other" questions, attention needs to be paid to ensuring that the categorization adequately accounts for the various human diversity issues involved in the responses.

Human diversity issues arise in different stages in the organization of qualitative data. Field notes need to reflect any human diversity elements, although this depends on from whom you get your information. The coding also needs to tap into this dimension. And you may wish to pay particular attention to whether human diversity issues were addressed when trying to determine if gaps exist in your data. For example, when the research involves collecting data on clients' perceptions of the services they are receiving from a family service agency, it may be important to ask clients how significant their social worker's ethnicity is to them or whether clients feel that their social worker and the agency are sensitive to cultural differences.

An Example of the Challenge of Researcher Identity

Kanuha (2000) discusses the challenges involved in "native," "indigenous," or "insider" research in which scholars conduct studies with populations, communities, and identity groups of which they are also members. The author explores the challenge of being both an insider and an outsider and discusses the difficulty of maintaining these roles throughout the research process.

Summary

Organizing quantitative data includes coding the data and identifying statistical packages. Organizing qualitative data also involves identifying appropriate software and note-keeping, organizing the files, coding the notes, and identifying gaps in the data. Ethical and human diversity issues include ensuring that the integrity of the data is preserved.

STUDY/EXERCISE QUESTIONS

1. Construct a questionnaire of about five items to determine students' attitudes on combining research with practice. Administer the questionnaire to five students in the class.

   a. Create a codebook.

   b. Enter the data in a computer using a statistical package.

2. Interview five students in the research class about their opinions on the results of climate change. How would you organize these data?

REFERENCES

Bernard, H. R. (2017). *Research methods in cultural anthropology* (6th ed.). Lanham, MD: Rowman and Littlefield.

Kanuha, V. K. (2000). "Being" native versus "going Native": Conducting social work research as an insider. *Social Work, 45*(5), 439–447. https://doi.org/10.1093/sw/45.5.439.

Lynch, A., Newlands, F., & Forrester, D. (2018). What does empathy sound like in social work communication? A mixed-methods study of empathy in child protection social work practice. *Child and Family Social Work, 24*(1), 139–147.

Marlow, C. R. (1983). The organization of interaction in a behavior therapy interview. Unpublished doctoral dissertation, Chicago, IL: University of Chicago.

O'Kane, P., Smith, A., & Lerman, M. P. (2021). Building transparency and trustworthiness in inductive research through computer-aided qualitative data analysis software. *Organizational Research Methods, 24*(1), 104–139.

Oswald, A. G. (2019). Improving outcomes with qualitative data analysis software: A reflective journey. *Qualitative Social Work, 18*(3), 436–442.

Parameswaran, U. D., Ozawa-Kirk, J. L., & Latendresse, G. (2020). To live (code) or to not: A new method for coding in qualitative research. *Qualitative Social Work, 19*(4), 630–644.

Phillippi, J., & Lauderdale, J. (2018). A guide to field notes for qualitative research: Context and conversation. *Qualitative Health Research, 28*(3), 381–388.

St. John, W., & Johnson, P. (2000). The pros and cons of data analysis software for qualitative research. *Journal of Nursing Scholarship, 32*(4), 393–398.

11

Analysis of Qualitative Data

With Colin Collett van Rooyen,
M.Soc.Sc.

INTRODUCTION

Working with qualitative data can initially appear daunting. For the new qualitative researcher, Mason (2018) discusses in detail how overwhelming qualitative data can be. The amount of data and its apparent lack of order can become an unnecessary stressor, no matter how you collect qualitative data through interviews, open-ended questionnaires, or personal logs, whether using recordings, transcriptions, or field notes. However, this does not need to be the case because there are systems for organizing and managing the data to allow the producer and consumer of the data to interact with it in a meaningful way.

In this chapter, we describe ways that qualitative data can be analyzed. The primary focus of this chapter will be on analyzing data in interpretive studies, in which the data are usually qualitative. Although interpretive studies will be the focus here, you can also use some of the techniques used to analyze qualitative data as part of positivist studies.

LEARNING OBJECTIVES

This chapter will include the following learning objectives:

1. **To understand the similarities and differences between qualitative and quantitative data analysis**

2. **To understand how to plan for the analysis of qualitative data**

3. **To be able to identify categories within the qualitative data**

4. **To understand some basic concepts in interpreting qualitative data**

5. **To identify the principles of validating qualitative data**

6. **To understand the principles of writing qualitative research reports**

7. **To articulate the ethical and human diversity issues in practice evaluation**

Qualitative and Quantitative Data Analysis Compared

Analysis of qualitative data and quantitative data analysis differs in several important ways, and these differences will be discussed in this section (see Table 11.1). We will consider quantitative data analysis in the following chapter. The common conception is that qualitative data analysis is "easier" than quantitative, primarily because quantitative data are analyzed using statistical procedures. We all know that statistics are something we want to avoid, right? Wrong, as we will see in the next chapter. We will see that qualitative data analysis has its own difficulties, different from those confronted during statistical analysis, but equally if not more challenging. Let us now look at these differences.

First, the distinctions among data collection, organization, and analysis are much more difficult to define when the data are qualitative. For example, data analysis can often begin before data collection is completed. This *interim analysis* allows for the exposure of "layers of the setting" for the researcher, which influences further data collection (Miles, Huberman, & Saldana, 2019). Thus, the research process becomes more fluid and circular when a study involves primarily qualitative data. This flexibility can provide essential insights and discoveries throughout the project. Still, on the other hand, the lack of structure places considerable responsibility on the researcher to make decisions that are not guided by the research process itself.

Second, the methods of analysis themselves are also much less structured than they are with quantitative data. As a result, qualitative data analysis is much more challenging and, at times, challenging to complete successfully. Many decisions are left to the researcher's discretion. This raises important issues surrounding the impact of the researcher's values on the research. As we discussed in Chapter 1, the interpretive approach usually involves collecting qualitative data, focusing less on capturing an "objective" reality and more on the "subjective" experience. However, despite the emphasis on subjectivity, you need to be aware of your own values as a researcher and their possible impact on the data analysis. This stance is more challenging to maintain than at first it may appear.

A third way qualitative and quantitative data analyses differ is that the primary purpose of analyzing qualitative data is to look for patterns in the data, noting similarities and differences. Various techniques can be used to identify these patterns. In quantitative analysis, the emphasis is on establishing the statistical significance of the findings based on probability theory.

Fourth, one of the goals of quantitative data analysis is to "separate" the data and place it in discrete groups, which is the "cleaning" referred to in the last chapter. It is important to keep the data in context (McCurdy & Ross, 2018). Understanding the context within which an action took place and through which meaning was developed is central to the qualitative research process. Information interpreted or presented devoid of contextual content is thus seen as information lacking the ability to convey meaning and may present a distortion of an event or situation. Therefore, contextual analysis is central to qualitative research. Consequently, you must always present the data in context by referring to the specific situations, time periods, and persons around which the identified pattern occurred.

Fifth, qualitative data analysis tends to be inductive rather than deductive. Quantitative data is often used to test hypotheses derived from theoretical constructs. With qualitative analysis, careful observation leads to the description of connections and patterns in the data, enabling us to form hypotheses and ultimately develop them into theoretical constructs and theories. These theories evolve as the data are collected and as the process of interim analysis takes place. In this way, and given the cognizance afforded to contextual issues, the findings are grounded in real-life patterns—hence the term *grounded theory* first proposed by Glaser and Strauss (1967) and later developed by many researchers, including Timonen, Foley, and Conlon (2018) among others.

In this chapter, we will discuss five steps in the analysis of qualitative data. These steps include planning the analysis, interpreting the data, validating the data, and writing the qualitative report (see Figure 11.1).

Planning the Analysis of Qualitative Data

Organizing both qualitative and quantitative data was discussed in the last chapter. Qualitative data involves note-keeping, including transcribing, organizing the files, coding the data, and identifying gaps in the data. The next step, considered here, is to set up a plan for the data analysis. As we discussed earlier in this chapter, this is important because there are not as many prescribed rules or steps to follow as with quantitative analysis.

The first step is to read over all the transcribed material to get a sense of the data as a whole. As you proceed, take down some brief notes and jot down some beginning ideas. For example, in a study about female immigrants, you may see that the women use the term "safety" fairly consistently. When they talk about support, "family" is frequently mentioned.

This leads to the second important component of this planning stage. If you have not done so already, you need to start a research journal. This idea was introduced initially in Chapter 9 as a part of the data collection process. In the journal, you record the process of the study and record ideas and insights. For example, you might note that when safety is mentioned, it is often done so in the context of a discussion of housing. Make a note of this. Remember, context is essential. Don't worry about systematically recording observations at this point. Later in the analysis, you will need to be more systematic. Here the concern is noting insights and things that "jump out at you" from the data.

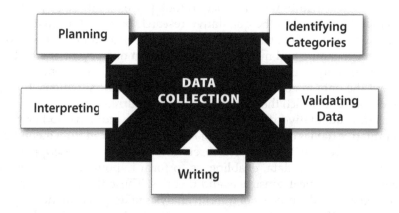

Figure 11.1 Dimensions of qualitative analysis

The journal not only helps you remember your ideas as they occur to you, but it also provides an audit trail. An audit trail is used if and when an outside person is brought in to review your work and ensure there are no serious problems or flaws with the analysis. This is particularly important with a qualitative study because of the lack of clear, precise, and regulated rules to guide the analysis.

Identifying Categories and Levels of Coding in Qualitative Data Analysis

As mentioned earlier, interpretive studies and analyses of qualitative data generally use an inductive rather than a deductive approach. Patterns emerge from the data rather than being developed before collection. The data are organized, classified, and edited into an accessible package. The researcher begins to sift out data relevant to the aims of the study and codes and categorizes these data to develop themes. Hence your next step in analyzing the data is to start creating these categories and coding them.

Austin, Grinnell, Rothery, and Tutty (2015) provide a valuable guide to understanding qualitative data analysis for social workers. In addition, Elliot (2018) wrote an excellent article on coding and stressed that it is entirely a decision-making process. Therefore, the researcher always needs to be aware of their own biases.

Austin et al. (2015) suggest there are two levels of coding and categorizing in qualitative data analysis and the following guide follows their recommendations.

The **first level of coding** involves identifying meaning units, fitting them into categories, and assigning codes to these categories. This happens as you read and re-read the data. This is time-consuming and involves five tasks:

1. *Identifying the meaningful experiences or ideas in the data, or "meaning units,"* i.e., finding out what pieces of data fit together. Ultimately these will develop into patterns that will provide the core of your interpretation (the next step). We can think of the meaning units as the building blocks of the analysis. A unit can be a word, a sentence, part of a sentence, a paragraph, or something else. This is the part of the analysis where you must be very aware of your possible biases and interests in the research. In the example of women immigrants, one type of meaning unit might be those relating to the women feeling vulnerable as their housing is temporary. Another might relate to their feelings of isolation because they are only in contact with a few family members.

2. *Fitting the meaning units into categories and assigning category names* to groups of similar meaning. This stage is quite challenging because you must decide how the meaning units interrelate with one another. No set number of categories will result from this process. The more you have, the more complex the study. Also, remember that these categories can change as you progress with the analysis. For example, possible categories in the women and immigration study may include feelings of safety and helplessness, how the women are gaining control of their lives, approaches to finding housing, types of family support, concerns about children's welfare, and relationships with their spouses. However, you

later decide that "ways in which they are gaining control of their lives" in fact includes two main types of meaning units: "ways of finding housing" and "types of family support." Later you may find more.

3. *Assigning codes or a form of shorthand to the categories.* Again, this is relatively straightforward, and the codes are made up of one or two letters—for example, G for gaining control, etc.

4. *Refining and reorganizing coding.* Before moving on to the next stage of analysis, review your work and do not hesitate to make changes. As you become more familiar with the data, your confidence in making the right kinds of decisions about the analysis will increase.

5. *Deciding when to stop.* One way of determining this is that their responses fit easily into the existing categories when you interview new participants.

First-level coding is relatively concrete. You are identifying properties of data that are clearly evident rather than undertaking interpretation.

An Example of Themes

Wachter et al. (2021) examined how refugees from the Democratic Republic of the Congo rebuilt their social networks when settling in the United States. The qualitative study involved in-depth individual interviews in 2016 with twenty-seven adult women who lived in a mid-size U.S. town. The qualitative study involved interviewing the women. The analysis disclosed five themes: (1) reconfiguring family support; (2) engaging multiple sources for practical support; (3) accessing mentorship; (4) attending places of worship; and (5) sustaining a relationship with God. Sources of social support included family and loved ones spanning local, national, and transnational geographies; God; neighbors; places of worship; and the resettlement agency.

The **second level of coding** is more abstract and involves interpreting the data. Here, you identify similarities and differences between the categories to find relationships. This involves two tasks:

1. *Sorting meaning units from each of the interviews into categories,* preferably using a computer program designed for this purpose, but if not, simply cutting and pasting using writing software. At this level, you are beginning to compare data across different respondents.

2. *Comparing and contrasting categories* with the goal of integrating the categories into themes. For example, "helplessness."

Relationships between categories are either based on similarity of content (the above example), or based on time (i.e., one category always precedes another), or on causality. This latter type of relationship is difficult to establish, though (remember all the conditions needed to establish causality?), as we will see later when the analysis is validated. Once you identify a theme, you assign it a code (as you did with the categories).

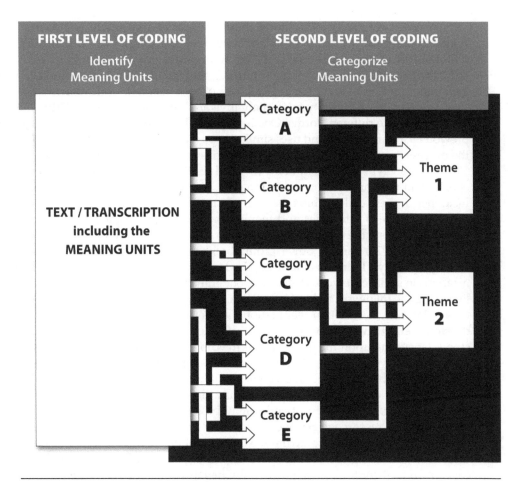

Figure 11.2 The process of coding

The Process of Coding

In their study of parenting and gender-based violence in Uganda, Wight et al. (2022) describe in detail how they coded their data from interviews and focus groups. Recordings were transcribed verbatim and translated into English. After becoming familiar with the data, the researchers developed a coding frame combining prior research topics and issues, using deductive and inductive approaches. After piloting with transcripts from two interviews, they were revised and then coded manually and summarized using framework analysis. Themes were identified and hypotheses were developed and tested systematically against all the relevant data.

A note here needs to be made about **content analysis**, which was first mentioned in Chapter 9 as a data collection method. For example, you can perform content analysis on transcribed or recorded interviews, process recordings on a case, published articles in newspapers or journals, and so forth, instead of the data being generated from interviews, focus groups, or other direct data collection methods.

Content analysis is a type of qualitative analysis in that it uses written material but can take two different forms. One is very similar to the type of analysis discussed previously in this chapter and uses similar steps (Faria-Schützer et al., 2021). However, the process is inductive here, and the categories and themes emerge from the data.

Another type of content analysis involves the researcher constructing the categories and then applying them to the data. Inferences are then made based on the incidence of these codes. This type of analysis is less concerned with looking at relationships between categories and themes and more with counting their incidences. The approach is more quantitative and descriptive in this form of content analysis.

Hollis (1972) carried out a groundbreaking historical content analysis using coding typology. Hollis was interested in describing and understanding the communications in social casework interviews. She transcribed interviews and coded line by line using the following codes: U—unclassified; A—sustainment; B—direct influence; C—exploration, description, ventilation; D—person-situation reflection; E—pattern-dynamic reflection; F—developmental reflection. Interviews could then be understood depending upon the frequency of the different types of communication. These codes were developed specifically for casework practice; thus, different categories would need to be developed to do content analysis on generalist practice interviews.

Although content analysis is often used in social work research, it has several problems. First, the validity of codes may be an issue if they are constructed previously by the researcher. Second, the coding of the text can be unreliable if only one coder does it. Therefore, intercoder reliability should be established, which often means training the coder. Third, the coding almost inevitably involves lifting concepts out of context, which essentially negates much of the value of qualitative research. However, these are not issues if the content analysis is conducted.

Content Analysis Using Researcher-Constructed Categories

Diaz-Strong, Roth, Velazquillo, and Zuch (2021) explored how social work research published in five leading social work journals—Health & Social Work, Research on Social Work Practice, Social Service Review, Social Work, and Social Work Research—*helps our* understanding of international migration and where it may be lacking. The authors focused on articles published between 2007 and 2016, analyzing content addressing immigrants and refugees. The results indicated that social work research is making a solid contribution to mental health but does not adequately address critical stratification dimensions including race, ethnicity, and legal status. The authors also found ambiguity in how "immigrant" is defined and in the addressed generation(s). They argued that maximizing social work's contributions requires offering more detailed definitions of the immigrant populations and paying greater attention to dimensions of inequality.

Interpreting Qualitative Data

This step is probably the most exciting stage in the qualitative analysis and goes to the heart of what you are trying to accomplish. With interpretation, you are looking at the relationships between variables and concepts. Again, Austin, Grinnell, Rothery, and Tutty's (2015) discussion of qualitative analysis identifies two steps in this process: developing classification systems and developing hypotheses and theories.

Developing Classification Systems

Again, different software packages will offer other options for the development of classification systems, but here are some options.

Cluster diagrams: Cluster diagrams involve drawing circles for each theme and arranging them in relation to one another. Some may overlap, and some may stand alone. Make larger circles for the themes that are most important. This is a good approach if you are a visual learner.

Matrices: Data can also be displayed and analyzed in a table or **matrix**. A table allows the researcher to organize data so that they are easily accessible, have some structure, and enable the identification of relationships. It also allows easy access to positive, negative, and neutral responses and helps link clients to responses.

Counts: You can use **counts** to track the occurrences of the meaning units, categories, or themes without your study becoming quantitative. It gives another dimension to the analysis and helps you detect any biases that might have influenced your handling of the data. These are often used in content analyses

Metaphors: These can be useful when thinking about relationships within the data. Cassell and Bishop (2018) present three different ways of analyzing qualitative data through their in-depth interviews with taxi drivers about their experiences of dignity at work. One of these approaches was metaphor analysis.

Missing links: These occur when two categories or themes seem to be related, but in fact, there may be a third variable linking them.

Contradictory evidence: This must always be accounted for and not simply ignored. This evidence can help validate data and will be discussed later in this chapter.

Developing Hypotheses and Theories

Interpretive research is primarily concerned with developing hypotheses rather than testing them. However, part of qualitative and interpretive analysis does involve speculation about causality and linkages. One way of representing and presenting causality is to construct **causal flowcharts**. These are visual representations of ideas that emerge from studying the data, seeing patterns, and seeing possible causes for phenomena. We have been using causal flowcharts in this text to illustrate some of the research methods. Often, causal flowcharts consist of a set of boxes connected by arrows. The boxes contain descriptions of states (attitudes, perceptions, ages, and so on) and the arrows tell how one state leads to another.

The development of hypotheses and causal statements should be firmly rooted in the data and not imposed on the data or overly influenced by the researcher's theoretical biases. For example, suppose a researcher uses a category previously defined theoretically. In this case, the qualitative nature of the research is ensured by the data collection methods and how the data are used to support or refute the categories. The context of the data must be taken into full consideration. The research should try to avoid the linear thinking associated with quantitative analysis. One strength of qualitative analysis is its potential for revealing contextual interrelationships among factors.

Validating Qualitative Data

Validation of qualitative data requires somewhat different processes than validation of quantitative data. Procedures for validation of qualitative data include consideration of rival or alternative hypotheses, negative cases, triangulation, preservation of the context of the data, and establishing your credibility.

Rival or Alternative Hypotheses

After a hypothesis is developed and proposed, **rival or alternative hypotheses** need to be explored and compared to the proposed hypothesis. Rival hypotheses can emerge from the literature or the data. The rival and proposed hypotheses are tested by looking at the data and considering which hypothesis reflects the data most closely. In some cases, both hypotheses appear to be supported.

Negative Cases

Patterns in data emerge when researchers look at what occurs most often. However, there are always exceptions, or **negative cases**, that do not fit the patterns. These need to be examined and explained. When you encounter a case that does not fit your theory, ask yourself whether it is the result of (1) normal social variation, (2) your lack of knowledge about the range of appropriate behavior, or (3) a genuinely unusual case. Force yourself to think creatively on this issue.

Triangulation

Triangulation involves using different research approaches to study the same research question. One way to use triangulation is to collect other kinds of data, such as interviews and observations, including qualitative and quantitative data. Another approach is to have different people collect and analyze the data or use other theories to interpret the data. Finally, data from various sources can be compared, for example by examining consistent and inconsistent information from different sources and consistent and conflicting information from other informants.

Using triangulation may result in what appears to be conflicting information. However, such conflicts do not automatically invalidate the proposed hypothesis.

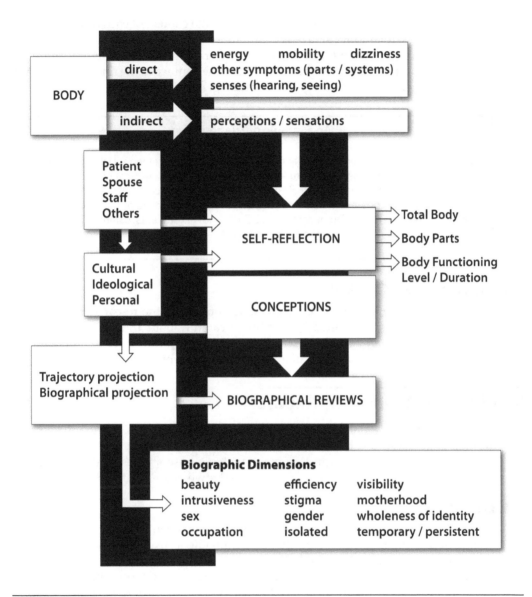

Figure 11.3   An example of a causal flowchart.

Instead, such conflicts may simply indicate that new and different information has been acquired, adding another dimension to our understanding of the studied phenomenon.

Preserving the Context of the Data

One central purpose of interpretive research and qualitative data analysis is to keep the data in context. This contextualization provides greater assurance that the findings are not distorted. Therefore, you need to consider the context of each response. Additionally, it is essential to recognize the limitations of the sampling method used, for these limitations can affect the external validity of the findings. Generally, sampling methods are purposive in interpretive studies. The context of the findings is limited; to put it another way, the findings have limited generalizability.

An Example of Triangulation

Kankaras et al. (2019) carried out a triangulated assessment of nineteen social and emotional skills of ten- and fifteen-year-old students across eleven cities and countries. This study assessed students' social and emotional skills combining three sources of information: students' self-reports and reports by parents and teachers. The authors looked at the similarities and differences between the different data sources and found that students', parents', and teachers' reports on students' skills overlapped substantially.

Establishing your Credibility

Because qualitative analysis depends so much on you as the researcher rather than the actual methods, you must be extremely careful about the records you keep. Therefore, keeping an accurate research journal is critical. In it, you can document the process and record any particular biases you think you might have.

Writing the Qualitative Report

You can write a qualitative report using different approaches. Although research writing is the focus of Chapter 13, we will discuss the different types of qualitative studies here. These types include content analyses, case studies, and ethnography. Bear in mind that there is considerable overlap between these different types.

Case Studies

A **case study** may be centered around the "case" of an event, an individual, an institution, or any other phenomenon that is identifiable in itself. The narrative can be **chronological or thematic** (or both) but is generally primarily descriptive. For example, the case study may take the form of an account that describes the immigrant's life since the day on which she arrived in her host country—touching on important events since this day. This would constitute a chronological narrative. A thematic narrative would use the themes emerging from the data as the framework for the report.

Analytical Studies

An **analytical study** is more concerned with looking at the relationships between variables (as discussed previously). In other words, it is more explanatory. It may take the form of a needs assessment or a program evaluation.

An Example of a Case Study

Martinez et al. (2018) described four case studies of research studies directly involving youths. First was a youth-led community health assessment that engaged youths of color in five U.S. cities to identify and assess health priority areas and health risk and protective factors affecting youths. Second, a participatory research effort between Boston-area youths and a social work researcher to understand youth perceptions of their neighborhood environment and its impact on their well-being. The third case study was of the first youth-led participatory budgeting project identifying the needs and priorities of Boston youths and developing capital projects to enhance the city for young people. Finally, the fourth case was a youth participatory research project that engaged youths in a metropolitan assessment, leading to a youth-led regional social justice community development initiative across eighteen community organizations.

Ethnographies

One type of qualitative report is an **ethnography**. As described in Chapter 9, an ethnography is a description of a culture. Ethnography is a specific approach to interpretive research. Historically, ethnography was the domain of anthropology. Anthropologists rely on participant observation to produce ethnographic studies or monographs of exotic cultures.

Social workers have recognized the value of this approach in describing the different cultures with which they are involved—for example, the culture of homelessness or gangs. Ethnographies are often long and detailed in anthropology, but social work researchers have produced mini ethnographies. Note that ethnographies (both full-length and short ethnographies) can also be a valuable resource for social workers and help acquaint them with different cultures.

An Example of an Analytical Qualitative Study

Gezinski et al. (2018) explored the experiences of commissioning parents (CPs) who travel abroad for surrogacy, paying attention to motivations, processes, and sources of social support. The authors recruited ten CPs and used semistructured, in-depth interviews to elicit storytelling. Data analysis revealed themes around CPs' experiences pre-surrogacy, during surrogacy, and post-surrogacy. International surrogacy was described as a long and arduous journey only undertaken after multiple failed attempts at "natural" conception. Before traveling abroad, the CPs weighed their reproductive assistance options. CPs were primarily motivated to undertake international surrogacy by health complications and legal restrictions in their home country. CPs emphasized difficult relationships in both the destination country and at home and worried about disclosing the surrogacy to family, friends, and children. The mental health and social needs of CPs were neglected throughout the process and should be incorporated in future interventions to address stigmatization.

An Example of Ethnography in Social Work

Ferguson et al. (2020) conducted an ethnographic study of two social work departments in England. Researchers spent fifteen months observing practice and organizational life to understand how social workers maintained long-term relationships with families. The findings indicated that counter to customary thinking that relationship-based casework is rarely achieved, the qualitative data indicated that some of the time, social work has a significant amount of involvement with some service users. However, families at one research site received a much more substantial, reliable service due to the additional input of family support workers and having a stable workforce who had their own desks and were colocated with managers in small team offices. This arrangement provided more support than at the second site, which was a large open plan "hot-desking" office.

Ethical Issues in Qualitative Analysis

There are ethical issues in the analysis of qualitative data that you don't encounter in quantitative data analysis. Quantitative analysis is protected by the nature of statistical analysis and the rules that govern whether findings are statistically significant. Without this kind of objective guide, the interpretation and analysis of qualitative data depend more on judgment; thus, the possibility that ethical standards might be violated increases.

Personal, intellectual, and professional biases are more likely to interfere with qualitative data analysis, despite validation controls. For example, sometimes, it can be tempting to ignore negative cases, implying more agreement among the findings to make the proposed hypothesis or argument appear stronger. A negative case may not have been examined because the researcher did not see it as an exception but interpreted it as supporting the proposed hypothesis.

As discussed earlier, keeping a research journal can help identify any possible biases. In addition, you may consider using "member checking"—getting feedback from the research participants and asking them to confirm your conclusions. Ethical issues are also raised when analyzing social media data, which is becoming increasingly common. How much should sharing between the participants and the researchers occur?

Qualitative analysis can sometimes expose distortions in previous research. Consequently, qualitative studies can make an important ethical contribution to our knowledge.

Human Diversity Issues in Qualitative Analysis

As with ethical issues, qualitative data analysis provides more opportunities to ignore human diversity issues than the analysis of quantitative data. Data can be analyzed and hypotheses generated that directly reflect the researcher's biases, negatively reflecting upon certain groups. Although such biases can also appear in quantitative

---

An Example of Ethical Issues

Hennell et al. (2020) point out that social media platforms that enable users to create and share online content with others are used increasingly in social research. This article explored the ethical issues of using social media for data collection and subsequent analysis. It also looked at the alcohol consumption practices of young people. The article concluded by recommending that researchers who face ethical dilemmas associated with the use of social media maintain an ongoing dialogue with their relevant ethics committees and other researchers to identify potential solutions and share their findings.

---

research, they are more likely in qualitative research, and so additional precautions must be taken. Researchers conducting qualitative analysis should constantly use self-examination to determine whether they are perpetuating stereotypical or negative images of the participants in their studies. The purpose of the validation procedure is partly to ensure that stereotyping and other forms of bias do not occur.

Qualitative analysis can also be a great asset in recognizing human diversity issues. The qualitative approach can provide a richer and fuller picture of the complexity of how certain groups are viewed and treated in the research.

Overcoming biases can be a difficult task, even through the use of careful qualitative strategies. Sometimes it is tough for us to identify these biases in our thinking; even the definition of a bias can be problematic. As social workers, we know that the environment and society in which we live profoundly affect how we think, including how we think about different groups. For example, our upbringing and social environment may result in our unconscious exclusion of certain groups. This effect provides the foundation for **discourse analysis.**

Discourse analysis focuses on how all analyses are embedded in the researcher's biographical and historical location. This perspective relates to our discussion in Chapter 1 concerning the difficulty of achieving true objectivity and the impact of values on how science is conducted.

An Example of Discourse Analysis

Reyes-Menendez et al. (2020) studied the key indicators of social identity in the #MeToo movement on Twitter. They studied 31,305 tweets. Using discourse analysis, they identified keywords, topics, and frequency to understand the social identity of the #MeToo movement. Social identity is particularly strongly correlated with women and the workplace.

Summary

The primary mission of qualitative data analysis is to look for patterns in the data while focusing on the importance of the study's context. Approaches to qualitative analysis include identifying categories for coding, content analysis, interpreting the data, developing classification systems, hypotheses, theories, and validating the data. Also included in this chapter is how to write the report, human diversity, and ethical issues.

Although qualitative data analysis is naturally compatible with social work practice, the myth persists that it is unduly time-consuming, unsophisticated, and nonproductive. Researchers in agency settings have the responsibility of dispelling this myth. Indeed, most of them are unknowingly gathering and analyzing qualitative data and are thus well placed for dispelling the myths that exist. Because qualitative data are less structured than quantitative data, it is vital in order to ensure that personal, intellectual, and professional biases do not interfere with the processor that steps are taken to minimize the extent to which they might interfere. It is also essential that diverse and underrepresented groups are recognized at this stage and throughout the research process.

STUDY/EXERCISE QUESTIONS

1. Conduct an interview with a fellow student, gathering information on what they consider to be their family's culture.

   a. Use the category approach discussed in this chapter.

   b. Compare your findings with others in the class.

   c. Is it possible to propose a hypothesis based on these findings?

   d. How would you validate your findings?

2. Carry out a content analysis on ethics and research using social work journals. Note that you will need to define ethics and research and specify the number and type of journal. What conclusions can you draw from your findings?

REFERENCES

Austin, C. D., Grinnell, R. M., Rothery, M. A., & Tutty, M. (2015). *Qualitative research for social workers: Phases, steps, and tasks*. Boston, MA: Crane Publishers.

Cassell, C., & Bishop, V. (2018). Qualitative data analysis: Exploring themes, metaphors, and stories. *European Management Review, 16*(1), 195–207. https://doi.org/10.1111/emre.12176

Diaz-Strong, D. X., Roth, B. J., Velazquillo, A., & Zuch, M. (2021). Social work research on immigrants: A content analysis of leading journals from 2007 to 2016. *Social Work, 66*(2), 111–118.

Elliott, V. (2018). Thinking about the coding process in qualitative data. *The Qualitative Report, 23*(11), 2850–2861.

Faria-Schützer, D. B., Surita F. G., Alves, V. L. P., Bastos, R. A., Campos, C. J. G., & Turato, E. R. (2019). Seven steps for qualitative treatment in health research: The Clinical-Qualitative Content Analysis. *Ciéncia and Saûde Colectiva, 26*(1), 265–274. https://doi.org/10.1590/1413-81232020261.07622019

Ferguson, H., Warwick., Cooner, T. S., Leigh, J., Beddoe., Disney, T., & Plumridge, G. (2020). The nature and culture of social work with children and families in long-term casework: Findings from a qualitative longitudinal study. *Child and Family Social Work, 25*(3), 694–703.

Gezinski, L. B., Karandikar, S., Huber, S., & Levitt, A. (2018). Commissioning parents' experiences with international surrogacy: A qualitative study. *Health & Social Work, 43*(3), 175–184. https://doi.org/10.1093/hsw/hly018

Glaser, B. G., & Strauss, A. L. (1967). *The discovery of grounded theory strategies for qualitative research.* New York: Aldine de Gruyter.

Hennell, K., Limmer, M., & Piacentini, M. (2020). Ethical dilemmas using social media in qualitative social research: A case study of online participant observation. *Sociological Research Online, 25*(3), 473–489.

Hollis, F. (1972). *Casework: A psychosocial therapy.* New York: Random House.

Kankaraš, M., Feron, E., & Renbarger, R. (2019). Assessing students' social and emotional skills through triangulation of assessment methods. *OECD Education Working Papers*, No. 208, OECD Publishing, Paris. https://doi.org/10.1787/717ad7f2-en.

Martinez, L. S., Richards-Schuster, K., Teixeira, S., & Augsberger, A. (2018). The power of prevention and youth voice: A strategy for social work to ensure youths' healthy development. *Social Work, 63*(2), 135–143. https://doi.org/10.1093/sw/swx059

Mason, J. (2018). *Qualitative researching* (3rd ed.). London: Sage Publications.

McCurdy, S. A., & Ross, M. W. (2018). Qualitative data are not just quantitative data with text but data with context: On the dangers of sharing some qualitative data: Comment on Dubois et al. (2018). *Qualitative Psychology, 5*(3), 409–411.

Miles, M. B., Huberman, A. M., & Saldana, J. (2019). *Qualitative data analysis: A methods sourcebook.* Thousand Oaks, CA: Sage.

Reyes-Menendez, A., Saura, J. R., & Thomas, S. B. (2020). Exploring key indicators of social identity in the #MeToo era: Using discourse analysis in UGC. *International Journal of Information Management, 54*, 102–129. https://doi.org/10.1016/j.ijinfomgt.2020.102129.

Timonen, V., Foley, G., & Conlon, C. (2018). Challenges when using grounded theory: A pragmatic introduction to doing GT research. *International Journal of Qualitative Methods, 17*(1), 1–10.

Wachter, K., Gulbas, L. E., & Snyder, S. (2021). Connecting in resettlement: An examination of social support among Congolese women in the United States. *Qualitative Social Work, 21*(2), 349–366.

Wight, D., Sekiwunga, R., Namutebi, C., Zalwango, F., & Siu, G. E. (2022). A Ugandan parenting programme to prevent gender-based violence: Description and formative evaluation. *Research on Social Work Practice, 32*(4), 448–464.

12

Analysis of Quantitative Data

INTRODUCTION

This chapter describes how to analyze quantitative data. As we discussed in Chapter 1, these are data that can be counted or quantified. The analysis stage of the research process makes some sense out of the information collected. This research stage compares to the practice step of evaluation (see Chapter 2 for a discussion of the different steps in generalist practice). In research, this often elicits considerable anxiety. This text attempts to describe and explain statistics as straightforwardly as possible.

Meaning can be derived from quantitative data in two ways. One is through descriptive statistics, which summarize the characteristics of the sample or the relationship among the variables. During this process, you want to get as complete a picture of the data as possible. Several different statistical techniques allow you to do this, including frequency distributions, measures of central tendency, variability, and association. You can also use inferential statistics, which are techniques for determining whether generalizations or inferences about the population can be made using the data from your sample. Inferential statistics involve using statistical tests to evaluate hypotheses. You can also use this approach for data derived from practice evaluations. We will discuss both the descriptive and inferential statistics in this chapter.

The focus of this chapter is twofold. First, it focuses on understanding which statistics are useful for which purpose. Some statistics are simply not appropriate and are meaningless when used with certain types of data. This approach to statistical understanding prepares you to become an informed and observant consumer of research—a critical role for the generalist social worker. Using findings for practice involves understanding and interpreting statistical data analysis in various studies and understanding any biases that may distort the results.

The second focus of this chapter is on how to run different statistical tests using statistical software. While many different statistical software packages that use similar procedures are available, the most commonly used is SPSS, which is also available in a student version. This text does not examine how to compute each statistic in great detail because whole texts are devoted to this. However, the statistical formulas are included in the appendices.

LEARNING OBJECTIVES

The learning objectives in this chapter are to understand the following:

1. Key concepts in statistical analysis

2. Frequency distributions

3. Measures of central tendency

4. Measures of variability or dispersion

5. Measures of association

6. Sources of error, hypotheses, and significance levels

7. Types of statistical tests

8. Ethical and human diversity issues in statistical analysis

Key Concepts in Statistical Analysis

Types of Statistical Methods

Methods of quantitative analysis may be categorized as either descriptive or inferential. **Descriptive methods** analyze and summarize data to describe what is found in an existing dataset. An example of descriptive analysis would be to take everyone's grades in a research class, summarize them, and compute an average score for the class. **Inferential methods** analyze and summarize data to make estimates about a larger body of data and test hypotheses to draw conclusions about populations. An example of inferential analysis would be to take a sample of incomes of persons from around the country and estimate, or infer, from those sample data the mean income of the larger population of people in the country and look at the relationship between income and ethnicity.

Levels of Measurement

We first discussed this in Chapter 4. The different levels of measurement are **nominal**, **ordinal**, **interval**, and **ratio**. The level of measurement determines the type of statistical procedure used.

Discrete and Continuous Variables

A **discrete variable** is one in which its values are countable, such as the number of children in a family, the number of trips one has taken, or the number of appointments a client has with a social worker. We have 0, 1, 2, or some other whole number of children, we have taken 0, 1, 2, or some other number of trips, and a client has had 1, 2, 3, or some other number of appointments. A family does not have 3.2 children, we have not taken 9.4 trips, and the client cannot have had 6.8 appointments. Although one may perform statistical analysis, such as calculating a mean, resulting in a fractional value, the actual instances are countable for all three variables.

Continuous variables are when actual instances can take on values that must be expressed in whole numbers. Two possible continuous variables are a person's level of happiness and the intensity of one's fear of spiders. It is certainly possible to categorize levels of happiness as *not at all, mildly, somewhat, quite,* and *ecstatically happy,* but we know that levels of happiness are not like the steps of a staircase. Instead, they are more like an incline, in which every point along that incline indicates some decreasing or increasing level of happiness. Even if we elect to number those levels—not at all = 0, mildly = 1, somewhat = 2, quite = 3, and ecstatically = 4—we understand that the numbers are convenient markers but do not capture all of the possible levels of happiness. Likewise, the intensity of a fear of spiders may range from none to extreme. Every point between those two ends of the continuum marks some degree of that fear.

Frequency Distributions

As discussed in Chapter 4, each variable possesses values. The variables' names and their values are adopted in whatever software package is used, as described in Chapter 10. Therefore, one of the first things you need to do in statistical analysis is to understand how these values are distributed for each variable. To do so, you use **frequency distributions**. These are descriptions of the number of times values of a variable occur in a sample.

For example, say you have collected data on the need for a daycare center on a local university campus. Let's assume that twenty-five students with preschool-aged children were interviewed. Each of these students represents one observation or case, equivalent to a unit of analysis. The variables included the number of preschool-aged children, ethnicity, expressed need for daycare on campus, and miles from campus. Codes represent the ethnic groups: 1 for white non-Hispanic, 2 for Hispanic, and 3 for African American. Expressed need for daycare on campus is coded on a 4-point scale, with 4 representing greatest need and 1 the least need. The number of preschool children in a family and miles from campus are represented by the actual numbers of children and miles. We could present the data as in Table 12.1.

Simply reviewing this table does not make it easy to understand how the data really look. You can construct several frequency distributions for the previous example: one for the variable ethnicity (see Table 12.2), one for the expressed need for daycare (see Table 12.3), and one for the number of preschool-aged children (see Table 12.4). One can also be constructed for miles from campus (see Table 12.5); rather than list each distance separately, you can categorize values to make data more readable. Try to use categories that make some intuitive or theoretical sense. You also need to ensure that categories are of the same size.

For example, you might use categories such as "less than 5 miles,""5–9 miles,""10–14 miles," and "15 miles and over." However, some information is inevitably lost by grouping data points into categories.

Often frequency distributions are displayed as graphs or charts; we give more examples in Chapter 13.

Measures of Central Tendency

Another important factor in describing the data is the location of the middle of the distribution or the average value. There are three different types of averages, each determined in a slightly different way. These three types are the mode, median, and mean.

TABLE 12.1   Data from Four Different Variables by Each Observation

Observation Number	Number of Children	Ethnicity	Need for Daycare	Miles from Campus
1	2	1	3	2
2	1	1	4	1
3	1	3	4	10
4	1	1	4	23
5	1	2	3	4
6	1	1	3	2
7	2	2	4	1
8	2	1	3	1
9	1	2	2	6
10	3	1	4	40
11	2	1	3	2
12	1	2	1	1
13	1	1	2	3
14	2	1	4	7
15	2	1	4	8
16	1	3	4	9
17	1	1	3	15
18	2	1	4	12
19	1	2	1	23
20	2	1	1	1
21	2	1	4	2
22	1	2	4	1
23	2	1	4	3
24	1	1	4	1
25	2	1	3	6

Mode

The **mode** is the value possessed by the greatest number of observations. In Table 12.2, non-Hispanic white is the mode for ethnicity because this category or value occurred most often. In Table 12.3, "great need" is the mode for the expressed need for daycare, and in Table 12.5, "less than 5 miles" is the mode for the distance from campus. The mode can be used regardless of the level of measurement. It can be used for ethnicity (a nominal level of measurement), expressed need for daycare (an ordinal level of measurement), and for miles from campus (a ratio level of measurement). In contrast, other measures of central tendency and other

TABLE 12.2   Frequency Distribution of Ethnicity

Label	Value	Frequency	%
Non-Hispanic white	1	17	68
Hispanic	2	6	24
African American	3	2	8
	Total	25	100

statistics discussed in this chapter (measures of variability and measures of association) are restricted in terms of levels of measurement that they can use.

Median

The **median**, another type of average, can be used only with ordinal, interval, and ratio level data. Median is that value at which 50 percent of observations lie above and 50 percent lie below. The median is thus the value that divides the distribution in half.

The median cannot be used for nominal levels of measurement because it has meaning only with ranked data. Nominal data cannot be ranked, and consequently, it cannot be determined whether cases lie above or below a particular nominal value. Numbers are often assigned to nominal data, but these numbers do not have any inherent meaning. For example, we cannot rank the values of ethnicity from highest to lowest, and thus we cannot determine the middle or median value. The median is a popular measure of central tendency primarily because it is not influenced by extreme values that can be a problem with the mean (see the following section). In addition, the median is more stable than the mode, although less stable than the mean. Salaries are often described using the median. (See Appendix B for the formula for the median.)

TABLE 12.3   Frequency Distribution of Need for Daycare

Label	Value	Frequency	%
No need	1	3	12
A Little Need	2	2	8
Some Need	3	7	28
Great Need	4	13	52
	Total	25	100

TABLE 12.4   Frequency Distribution of the Number of Preschool Children in the Household

Value	Frequency	%
1	13	52
2	11	44
3	1	4
Total	25	100

TABLE 12.5   Frequency Distribution of Miles from Campus

Value	Frequency	%
Less than 5	14	56
5–9 miles	5	20
10–14 miles	2	8
15 miles and over	4	16
Total	25	100

Mean

The **mean**, the third type of measure of central tendency, is even more restrictive in the level of measurement that can be used. It can be computed only from interval and ratio levels of measurement (although some will argue that it can also be used with ordinal level data). The mean results from adding the values of observations and

An Example of a Bar Graph

Krings et al. (2020) did a study summarizing peer-reviewed articles ($N = 497$) on environmental topics in social work journals between 1991 and 2015. The authors found that theoretical and empirical scholarship on environmental social work is growing, though this growth remains limited to specific geographical regions and topics. Some of the results are presented in the bar chart in Figure 12.1.

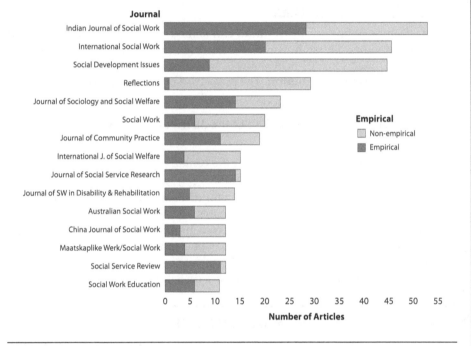

Figure 12.1   Example of a bar graph

then dividing by the total number of observations. For example, the mean miles from campus for the participants in the needs assessment (Table 12.1) is 7.36 miles. (See Appendix B for the formula for the mean.)

The major strength of the mean is that it considers each value for each observation. Extreme values, however, either high or low, can distort the mean, particularly if the sample size is relatively small. Let's look at the example of miles from campus again but substitute one high value (60 miles) for a middle-range value (6 miles). The mean now becomes 9.52 (238/25 =9.52), a two-mile difference in the mean as a result of one observation. The mean is the most stable measure of central tendency and is the prerequisite for the computation of other statistics.

To determine which measure of central tendency to apply, you need to consider how to use the information. For example, means are appropriate when you are interested in totals. If you know the national average is 2.3 children per family, you can guess that a town of 100 families should have about 230 children. If you know that the mode is 1 child per family, then any family you choose at random will probably have 1 child. The average household income is often reported as the median rather than the mean because we are usually interested in an individual comparison of our financial situation to other normal-range incomes. The mean is inflated by the few unusual persons who make millions. Mean income, however, is more helpful in comparing different countries' gross national product (GNP).

Visual Distribution of Data

Data from a frequency distribution can sometimes be presented as a chart, as discussed previously. First, however, we need to see if the data are evenly or symmetrically distributed for statistical analysis. In this case, the chart will take on the shape of a bell, or a **normal distribution**. The properties of a normal distribution are as follows:

1. The mean, median, and mode have the same score value.

2. It is symmetrical: The right half of the distribution is the mirror image of the left half.

3. Most scores are concentrated near the center.

   The assumption that a distribution is normally distributed underlies many inferential statistical tests, which we will discuss later in this chapter. For example, sometimes distributions have most scores concentrated at one end of distribution rather than at the middle. This is referred to as a **skewed distribution** (see Figure 12.2) rather than a normal distribution. Consequently, the mean, median, and mode will be different. Nevertheless, displaying data in this form can help gain a visual and almost intuitive sense of how the data are distributed.

Measures of Variability or Dispersion

Another dimension for describing data is the extent to which scores vary or are dispersed in distribution. For example, Figure 12.3 depicts three distributions. They have the same measure of central tendency, but they differ in the extent to which they are spread out, or in their variability.

Like measures of central tendency, measures of variability differ, with each one more appropriate in some situations than others. We discuss two types of measures of variability here: the range and the standard deviation.

Range

The **range** is the most straightforward measure of variability to compute and understand—it is simply the distance between the largest or maximum value and the smallest or minimum value. The range is calculated by subtracting the lowest value from the highest value. You can use the range with interval and ratio levels of data because it assumes equal intervals.

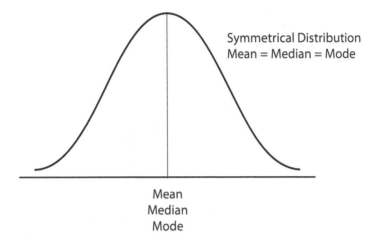

Symmetrical Distribution
Mean = Median = Mode

Mean
Median
Mode

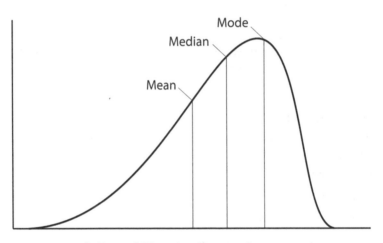

Mode

Median

Mean

Left-Skewed (Negative Skewness)

Figure 12.2   Normal and skewed distributions

The problem with the range is its extreme instability. Different samples drawn from the same population may have very different ranges. Consequently, the range does not give you a very reliable view of what the variability is in the population. For example, the range for the miles from campus variable in Table 12.1 is 39 (40 minus 1). If you changed the highest or lowest score to an extreme value, the range would be dramatically affected.

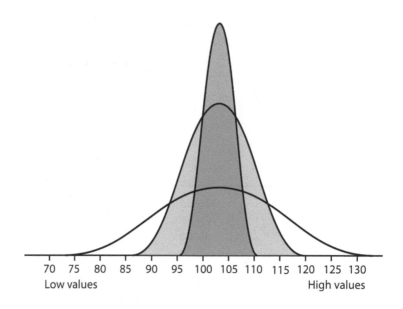

70 75 80 85 90 95 100 105 110 115 120 125 130
Low values   High values

Figure 12.3   Three distributions with the same measure of central tendency but different variabilities or dispersions

Standard Deviation

The **standard deviation** is a measure that averages each value's distance from the mean. Calculating the standard deviation involves the following steps:

1. Calculate the mean.

2. Measure the distance of each score from the mean.

3. Square these distances (to eliminate negative values).

4. Add the squared differences from the mean.

5. Divide by the n, thus calculating a mean of the differences from the mean.

6. Take the square root of the result.

(See Appendix B for the formula for the standard deviation.)

   Because the standard deviation uses the mean and is similar to the mean in many respects, it can be used only with interval and ratio level data. As a result, the standard deviation is the most stable of the measures of variability, although extreme scores can also affect it because it uses the mean.

Example of a Mean, Standard Deviation, Range and Median

Gredig and Bartelsen-Raemy (2018) studied social work students' attitudes to the social work research course. The following table shows each construct variable's range, mean, standard deviation, and median.

Construct Variable	Scale	Range	Mean	SD	Median
Interest in research course	1–5	3.5	3.6	.55	3.67
Perceived importance of research	1–5	4	3.12	.49	3.20
Attributed usefulness of research	1–5	3	3.34	.51	3.40
Perceived unbiased nature of research	1–5	3.17	3.28	.49	3.30
Fear of research courses	1–5	4	3.01	.68	3.00

Measures of Association

Up to this point, we have been looking only at **univariate measures**, which measure one variable at a time. We have been trying to develop a picture of how that one variable is distributed in a sample. In addition, we often want to measure the relationship between two or more variables; such measures are, respectively, **bivariate** and **multivariate measures**.

When carrying out a program evaluation, you are often interested in the relationship between two or more variables. For example, you may want to study the effect of a special program for high school students on their self-esteem. You would need to look at the relationship between the independent variable (the special program) and the dependent variable (self-esteem). Or you may wish to compare the dependent variables of an experimental and control group—outcomes from two different programs. To do so, you need to use bivariate statistics.

Similarly, in needs assessments, sometimes you are interested in examining the relationship among variables. For example, in investigating a community's need for a recycling center, you want to know how many people express this need and the characteristics of these individuals—ages, size of households, transportation, etc.

Multivariate analysis involves examining the relationships among more than two variables. This text does not discuss this type of analysis, but you should be able to find plenty of statistics texts and courses on this topic.

We discuss two bivariate measures of association in this section: cross tabulation and correlation.

Cross Tabulation

Cross tabulation (or crosstab) is probably the most widely used bivariate statistic because it is versatile and straightforward. Cross tabulations are also known as **contingency tables**. You can use cross tabulations with any level of measurement. For example, suppose interval and ratio (and sometimes ordinal) levels of measurement are used. If this is the case, they must be collapsed into a smaller number of categories (the meaning of *smaller* here is discussed a little later).

An example of a cross tabulation , shown in Table 12.6, is from a study that examined the workplace service needs of women employees. This contingency table looks at the relationship between how the women perceived their husband's participation in household chores (CHORE) and their need for flexible work hours (FLEX).

Generally, the dependent variable (in this case, the need for flexible work hours) is displayed in columns, and the independent variable (husband's participation in chores) is shown in the column totals plus percentages are written at the end of each row and column, respectively.

CHORE has three values (low, medium, and high participation) and FLEX has two values (yes, a need; no, no need). Consequently, we have a 3 by 2 (3 values by 2 values) contingency table with 6 cells or boxes. If the variables had more values, the table would be larger. You need to make sure the table is not too large; we also cannot let the number of cases in any of the cells get too low (five or fewer) because then there are problems in using inferential statistics. (We will discuss inferential statistics

TABLE 12.6   Relationship between CHORE and FLEX

		FLEX		
CHORE	Count Row Percent Col. Percent Total Percent	YES	NO	Row Total
Low Participation 1		75 83.3 65.8 53.6	15 16.7 57.7 10.7	90 64.3
Medium Participation 2		15 83.3 13.2 10.7	3 16.7 11.5 2.1	18 12.9
High Participation 3		24 75.0 21.1 17.1	8 25.0 30.8 5.7	32 22.8
Column Total		114 81.4	26 18.6	140 100.0

later in this chapter.) Sometimes several values need to be combined to reduce the number of values and reduce the table's size. As a result, the number of cases in each cell increases.

Continue reading the table. The top number in each cell refers to the number of cases. For example, in the top left cell in Table 12.6, cases are 75. The second number is the row percentages—that is, for the percentage of women who stated their husbands were low participants in household chores, 83.3 percent requested flexible work hours. The third number in the cell is the column percentage: In our example, this represents the percentage of women who asked for flexible work hours—65.8 percent reported low participation of their husbands in household chores. Finally, the bottom number in the cell is the total percentage.

In other words, the number of cases in the cell, 75, is 53.6 percent of the total number of cases. The total number of cases can be found in the lower right corner. In Table 12.6, this number is 140 and, as is recorded immediately below 140 in the cell, represents 100 percent of cases. You can go through and read each of the cells in this manner. The row totals and percentages are to the extreme right, and at the bottom of the table are the column totals and percentages. Note that the labels on the table help guide your interpretation.

The availability of percentages allows you to compare groups of unequal size. A sense of association can be gained by comparing these percentages. For example, a slightly lower proportion of those reporting high participation of their husbands in household chores requested flexible work hours (75 percent) than those who reported medium and low participation (83.3 percent for both). Is this difference big enough to signify a relationship between the variables, or is it simply due to chance? This question is answered later in this chapter when we discuss inferential statistics.

Correlation

Correlation is another common way of looking at the relationship between variables, which can be used only with interval and ratio level data. In our example of a study investigating the impact of a program directed at increasing the adolescent participants' self-esteem, it was hypothesized that the number of sessions adolescents attended would affect their level of self-esteem measured on an equal-interval scale. Ten adolescents were tested on their level of self-esteem before and after the program (see Table 12.7).

We can plot these data on a chart called a **scattergram** (Figure 12.4). The

TABLE 12.7   Self-esteem Scores and Number of Weeks in the Program ($n = 10$)

Client ID	Self Esteem Score	# of Weeks in Program
1	8	1
2	10	2
3	12	3
4	14	4
5	16	5
6	18	6
7	20	7
8	22	8
9	24	9
10	26	10

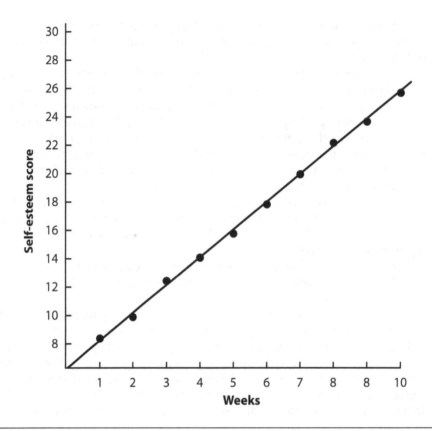

Figure 12.4 Scattergram showing a perfect positive correlation

horizontal axis (X) represents the client's length of time in the program, and the vertical axis (Y) represents the difference in the client's level of self-esteem before and after participation in the program.

In Figure 12.4, the line connecting the dots is perfectly straight. In this case, there is a **perfect correlation** between the two variables: When one variable increases or decreases, the other does so at the same rate. A perfect correlation rarely occurs; usually, you find that the dots do not perfectly follow the line but are scattered around it. The direction of the relationship can vary. Figure 12.4 demonstrates a **positive correlation** between the number of sessions attended and the level of self-esteem. As the number of sessions attended increased, so did the level of self-esteem. A **negative correlation** can also occur. Here the high values of one of the variables, self-esteem, are associated with the low values of the other variable, the number of sessions attended. The test to determine the strength of the correlation is discussed later in this chapter. Therefore, instead of sloping to the right, the scattergram would slope to the left, essentially a mirror image of the positive scattergram in Figure 12.4.

Sources of Error, Hypotheses, and Significance Levels

Sources of Error

Throughout the research process, there are possibilities for errors in our conclusions. Errors can come from three different sources, and specific strategies can address each source of error.

First, a measurement error may affect data collection; this possibility can be assessed by checking the reliability and validity of the data collection instrument (see Chapter 9 for a discussion). Second, other variables might be responsible for the relationship and must be controlled. Variables can be controlled by the research design or, as we discussed in the last chapter, statistically. The third source of error is chance. Chance has to do with sampling variability, as was discussed in Chapter 8. A randomly drawn sample and a population may differ due to chance. The role of chance factors can be assessed through inferential statistics, which relies on probability theory. (The specific statistical tests involved are described later in this chapter.) These three sources of error and the strategies for their assessment are illustrated in Table 12.8.

TABLE 12.8   Sources of and Corrections for Error

Type of Error	Correction
Measurement	Test reliability and validity
Other variables	Research design and statistical control
Chance in sampling and random assignment	Inferential statistics

Types of Hypotheses

A hypothesis suggests that two or more variables are associated in some way.

There are two types of hypotheses. First, the **two-tailed or nondirectional hypothesis** simply states that there is an association between two or more variables but predicts nothing about the nature of the direction of the association. One such example would be the hypothesis that gender impacts the likelihood of hospitalization for depression. A **one-tailed** or **directional hypothesis** specifies the associated variables and the nature or direction of the relationship or association, whether positive or negative. For example, we might hypothesize that women are more likely than men to be hospitalized for depression. The state of prior knowledge drawn from the literature and theory will determine whether we develop one-tailed or two-tailed hypotheses. When developing hypotheses, you need to draw on existing knowledge; hypotheses should not be based on impulse or initial impressions.

A central hypothesis in inferential statistics is the **null hypothesis**, which is derived from either the one-tailed or two-tailed hypothesis. The null hypothesis states there is no association between the variables. The null hypothesis is formulated only for testing purposes. Using our previous example of a one-tailed hypothesis, the null hypothesis would be that women are not more likely than men to be hospitalized for depression or that there is no relationship between gender and hospitalization.

Statistical analysis then allows the null hypothesis to fail to be rejected. If the null hypothesis is not rejected, then it is concluded that no relationship exists between the variables. On the other hand, if the null hypothesis is rejected, there does appear to be a relationship between the variables that is not a result of chance.

An Example of a Hypotheses

Gredig and Bartelsen-Raemy (2018) studied social work students' attitudes toward the social work research course in Switzerland. They hypothesized that:
- students' interest in research courses was predicted directly by student's fear of research courses and their research orientation
- their fear of research courses predicted student's research orientation
- the implied control variables (age, gender, study modality, the type of credentials allowing admittance to the program, and campus) influenced fear of research courses and research orientation.

This process may seem unnecessarily complicated. Yet the concept of the null hypothesis is essential; because it reminds us that statistical tests are intended to determine to what extent a relationship is due to chance, rather than whether or not the hypothesis is true.

Sometimes decision errors can be made in either failing to reject or rejecting the null hypothesis. These two errors are referred to as Type I and Type II errors.

Type I error is the rejection of the null hypothesis and the false conclusion that a relationship exists between the variables when no "real" relationship exists. Type II error is the failure to reject the null hypothesis and thus the failure to identify any "real" relationship between the variables (see Table 12.9). These errors can present some serious problems.

TABLE 12.9 Type I and Type II Errors

	True	False
Accept	Correct Decision	Type II Error
Reject	Type I Error	Correct Decision

A statistical test's ability to correctly reject a null hypothesis is referred to as **statistical power.** The test's power also increases in tandem with increases in the level of measurement. In other words, tests using ratio level data will be more powerful than nominal level data. Also, note that our sampling error is reduced with a larger sample size, as discussed in Chapter 8. Similarly, the sample size affects the power of the statistical test. As the sample size increases, the power of the statistical test also increases. Findings can be generalized more confidently from a large sample, even if the relationship between the variables does not appear very strong.

Significance Levels

When data are first examined, it is impossible to draw clear conclusions based on the findings. For example, in the question relating to gender and hospitalization for depression, the results may disclose that of the people hospitalized for depression, 55 percent were women versus the 45 percent that were men. However, these results do not reveal whether this 10 percent difference between the men and women is simply due to chance or is due to the program's effect or some other variable. Therefore, a statistical test must be used for this purpose.

A finding is statistically significant when the null hypothesis is rejected. This is because the probability the result is due to chance in the sample or population (or, in other words, sampling error) falls at or below a certain cutoff point. This cutoff point has been established by statistical convention to be .05. In other words, if a relationship occurs due to chance no more than five times out of one hundred, the null hypothesis is rejected. In this case, it is doubtful that the relationship is based on chance, and the hypothesis acknowledges that the variables named in it are having an impact on the outcome. Sometimes the significance level is set at lower levels (for example, .01) or, under special circumstances, higher levels (.10). The critical thing to remember is that the significance level is set before the statistical testing.

The observed level of significance is signified by $p = .05$ (or $p = .01$), and any level below .05 (or .01) is regarded as statistically significant. Establishing statistical significance at the .05 level or lower does not mean there is a proven relationship between the variables. Instead, there is only a 5 percent probability that the relationship results from chance occurrence. Therefore, avoid stating that a hypothesis has been proved. A more accurate statement is that the hypothesis is statistically significant at the .05 level.

It is essential to distinguish between significance levels and the confidence levels discussed in Chapter 8. Both involve probability, but confidence levels relate to how close the samples match the actual population. In contrast, significance levels relate to the outcomes of statistical tests and whether the findings are due to chance or a "real" relationship between the variables.

Types of Statistical Tests

Before discussing specific statistical tests, we will describe the common steps you need to take. They are as follows:

1. Identify the appropriate test and its formula.

2. Enter the raw data into the formula and compute the statistical score. (The formulas for the statistical tests can be found in Appendix B.)

3. Compute the degree of freedom, which is related to the size of the sample and the power of the test.

4. Use the probability tables, which can be found in many statistics textbooks (or online), to assess the statistics score's probability level and statistical significance.

These steps are completed rapidly and accurately by whichever statistical software you may be using. Generally, the statistical result and its statistical significance are reported.

This section will describe the most common statistical tests encountered in the social work literature and those needed to analyze most of your data. We will discuss four tests: *t*-tests, analysis of variance (ANOVA), correlational analysis (including regression analysis), and chi-square analysis.

Each test is appropriate only under certain conditions. When selecting a test, you need to consider four factors: first, the structure of the null hypothesis; second, the need to use specific tests only with certain levels of measurement; third, the size of the sample; fourth, the distribution of the responses—whether or not the distribution is normal. We present a summary table of the tests and their conditions for use in Table 12.10.

TABLE 12.10   Types of Statistical Tests and Some Conditions for the Use of Correlational Analysis

	t-test	ANOVA	Pearson's *r*	Chi-Square
Comparing means of two populations	Yes	No	No	No
Comparing means of more than two populations	No	Yes	No	No
All variables at interval/ratio level of measurement	No	No	Yes	No
One variable only at interval/ratio level of measurement	Yes	Yes	No	No
All variables at ordinal/nominal level of measurement	No	No	No	Yes

t-tests

Conditions of Use

The *t*-test is used under the following conditions:

1. You are interested in testing a null hypothesis to find whether two groups have the same mean.

2. The dependent variable is at least at the interval level of measurement(although some argue that the ordinal level of measurement is acceptable). The other variable (usually the independent variable) is at the nominal level of measurement.

3. The sample size can be small.

4. The observations are independent.

These conditions often occur in social work. Many program evaluation designs include comparison groups. Each group that is compared represents a value at the nominal level of measurement. Program evaluations often measure the outcome or dependent variable (the number of months an individual has held a job or the score on a standardized test) at the interval or ratio level. The null hypothesis in such a program evaluation could be that the intervention had no effect; in other words, the two groups had similar outcomes or mean scores. Just based on probability, though, outcomes are likely to be different. The *t*-test discloses whether this difference could be due to chance. Similarly, you would want to use this test when comparing two groups, such as males and females, urban and rural residents, or married and unmarried people, and their differing outcome variables. This type of *t*-test is an independent samples *t*-test or a groupwise comparison *t*-test.

Another type of *t*-test is the paired samples or pairwise comparison *t*-test. Also commonly used in social work research, the paired samples *t*-test compares two means at different points in time for the same sample. For example, such a test might compare academic and cognitive scores for children at the beginning of a Head Start program with their scores at the end of a year.

The degrees of freedom for the *t*-test is accomplished by subtracting 2 from the *n* (the total number of participants in both groups).

An Example of the Use of *t*-tests

Bostock et al. (2019)investigated whether a mindfulness meditation program delivered via a smartphone application could improve psychological well-being, reduce job strain, and reduce ambulatory blood pressure during the workday. The sample consisted of 238 healthy employees from two large companies in the United Kingdom. Random assignment was made to a mindfulness meditation practice app or a wait-list control condition. The app offered forty-five prerecorded ten- to twenty-minute guided audio meditations. Participants were asked to complete one meditation per day. The researchers used Psychosocial measures and measured blood pressure throughout one working day at baseline and eight weeks later; a follow-up survey was also emailed to participants sixteen weeks after the intervention started. Using *t*-tests, the two groups were compared. The intervention group reported significant improvement in well-being, distress, job strain, and perceptions of workplace social support compared to the control group. In addition, the intervention group had a small significant decrease in self-measured workday systolic blood pressure from pre- to post-intervention. Positive effects in the intervention group were found for well-being and job strain at the sixteen-week follow-up assessment.

Analysis of Variance (ANOVA)

Conditions of Use

We use the analysis of variance statistical test (ANOVA) under these conditions:

1. You are interested in testing a null hypothesis to find whether the means in more than two groups are the same.

2. The dependent variable is at least the interval level of measurement, and the other variable, usually the independent variable, is measured at the nominal level.

3. The sample size can be small.

4. The observations are independent.

Does this sound familiar? The *t*-test is, in fact, a special case of ANOVA, and the conditions of the use of ANOVA are consequently very similar to those of the *t*-test, except that ANOVA is used to compare more than two groups. The ANOVA results in an *F*-test statistic.

ANOVA is useful if, for example, you compare the outcomes of three or more programs in different parts of the state and the outcome is being measured at the interval level or above.

An Example of the Use of ANOVA

Hortigüela-Alcalá et al. (2019) posed the following research hypothesis: Does Twitter and Instagram's pedagogical use improve students' motivation and learning? The sample consisted of 197 students from two different classes, all of whom received tuition in a subject known as *Physical Education and its Didactics*. A quasi-experimental design was used, involving a pretest and a posttest with an experimental group ($n = 100$) and a non-equivalent control group ($n = 97$). The data was collected using a questionnaire. In addition, factor analysis and an ANOVA were applied. The results indicated that the use of Twitter and Instagram bore a significant influence, increasing both student motivation and involvement and their degree of achievement.

Correlational Analysis (Pearson's *r*)

Conditions of Use

The correlation coefficient indicates the strength of the correlation between two variables. It is used under the following conditions:

1. You are interested in testing the null hypothesis to determine whether two variables are not correlated.

2. Both variables are at the interval level of measurement or a higher level.

3. A normal distribution of responses is not required.

Earlier in this chapter, we discussed the use of the scattergram to look at the relationship between two variables. This relationship was described as a correlation. The correlation coefficient examines the strength and direction of the relationship between two variables and discloses whether the relationship is statistically significant. The correlation coefficient statistic is represented by *r*, also referred to as Pearson's *r*. The coefficient is in the range of –1.0 to +1.0. The –1.0 represents a perfect negative correlation, and +1.0 represents a perfect positive correlation.

The degree of freedom for the Pearson's *r* is simply the *n*. You need to remember that the *r* statistic merely looks at the strength and relationship between two variables; under no circumstances is it to imply causation.

The level of self-esteem and performance on an aptitude test for social work might be highly correlated, but this does not mean that one causes the other; the other conditions of causality still need to be met (see Chapter 3).

An Example of Correlational Analysis

Cerrato and Cifre (2018) carried out a correlational study using a questionnaire applied to 515 subjects (63 percent men) in two independent samples of Spanish men and women without an emotional relationship who lived with their heterosexual partners. First, results showed unequal involvement in household chores by women and men. It is higher in women than in men, and the perception of partner involvement is lower in women than in men. Second, those unequal involvements relate differently to men and women in terms of work-family interaction. They do not increase work-family conflict (WFC) in women compared to men, but there are some significant differences in work conflict (WC) and family conflict (FC). Third, perception of partner involvement in household chores increases WFC both in men and women but not WC nor FC.

Nevertheless, an increase in marital conflict (MC) by domestic tasks did not significantly affect WFC in women nor in men, but increased WC in both women and men and FC only in women. Results confirm that involvement in household chores is not a significant predictor of WFC in women or men. MC by domestic tasks is a statistically significant predictor in women of WFC and FC, but not in men. Thus, results show that traditional gender roles still affect how men and women manage work and family interaction. However, the increased WFC due to involvement in housework is not exclusive to women but also occurs in men.

Multiple Regression Analysis

Multiple regression analysis is another statistical test that, like ANOVA, allows us to look at the relationship between more than two variables. It uses as a base the correlation coefficient and looks at the overall correlation between different independent variables and a variable dependent on an interval or ratio level of measurement. The multiple correlation coefficient is represented by R and explains the proportion of variation explained by the entire set of independent variables(rather than just one). Multiple regression analysis also computes the standardized regression coefficient or beta weight, which allows each independent variable's relative contribution and statistical significance to be assessed while controlling for the others. In this way, the contribution of each variable to the prediction of a particular outcome can be evaluated both for the direction and the amount of change.

For example, we know that scores on various academic tests (e.g., the SAT or ACT) are related to the parent's educational level, ethnicity, and parental income, among other factors. Regression analysis allows us to assess the contribution of each of these independent variables to test scores. For example, a regression coefficient of +2 points on the ACT for the variable "years of parents' education" indicated that one more year of parents' education is worth two more points on the ACT (assuming that the other independent variables are held constant).

Multiple regression analysis can become quite complex, and more details are beyond the scope of this text. However, you can see that it is a necessary test in contributing to our understanding of how certain variables contribute and can predict changes in a dependent variable or outcome.

An Example of Multiple Regression Analysis

Gyan et al. (2021) examined barriers to women's involvement in community development in Ghana. The data were subject to regression analysis from a sample of 210 who completed a questionnaire containing scales. The major barriers for the women were found to be the patriarchal norms of Ghanaian society and factors related to their socialization. The authors recommended that future community development emphasize the participation of women to promote greater equality, freedom, and advancement of local women.

Chi-Square Analysis

Conditions of Use

Chi-square analysis is one of the most widely used statistical tests in social work research, in part because it is a test that can be used with the ordinal or nominal levels of measurement.

You can use the chi-square under these conditions:

1. You are interested in testing the null hypothesis to find whether there is no relationship between the two variables.

2. The variables are both measured at the nominal or ordinal level. Although chi-square analysis can be used with data at any level of measurement, often at the interval or ratio level of measurement the data will need to be collapsed into categories.

Earlier in this chapter, cross tabulation was discussed to describe the relationship between two variables measured at the nominal or ordinal level. With cross tabulation, we are eyeballing or estimating the relationship. The chi-square statistic can be applied to cross tabulation to give us a more accurate reflection of the significance of the relationship between two variables. Chi-square analysis assesses the extent to which the frequencies in our cross tabulation, called the observed frequencies, differ from what we might expect to observe if the data were distributed in the cross tabulation according to chance. These chance frequencies are called the expected frequencies. The more the actual or observed frequencies vary from the expected frequencies, the more likely there is an association between the two variables.

X^2 represents the chi-square statistic. The degrees of freedom for the chi-square are related to the number of cells rather than the n. They are computed using the following formula: $df = (r-1)(c-1)$, with r indicating number of rows and c indicating number of columns. Exercise caution when using chi-square analysis. If the sample is too small or one or more of the cells has an expected value of less than 5, chi-square analysis should not be used.

An Example of Chi-Square Analysis

Chaturvedi et al. (2021) looked at the impact of the COVID-19 pandemic on students' lives. A survey was conducted on 1,182 individuals of different age groups from various educational institutes in Delhi-National Capital Region (NCR), India. The researchers used chi-square analysis to examine the relationship between the age of the students and time spent on online classes and self-study (the medium used for learning), sleeping habits, daily fitness routines, and the effects on weight, social life, and mental health. The participants adopted different coping mechanisms and engaged with social media at different rates according to age.

Ethical Issues and Statistical Analysis

One major ethical issue in using statistical analysis is ensuring that the correct—that is, the appropriate—statistic and statistical test is being used to present and analyze the data. In addition, you must avoid distorting the data to fit any preconceived ideas. Be careful not to leave out data that do not support your hypothesis—this is completely unethical. Accurate reporting of the methods you use and the results you obtain is the backbone of good science. Only in this way can we replicate studies and add to the knowledge base of social work. The NASW Code of Ethics (2021) states: "Social workers should report evaluation and research findings accurately. They should not fabricate or falsify results and should take steps to correct any errors later found in published data using standard publication methods."

Another issue is recognizing that statistical significance is not a concrete entity or property of a particular set of data. The presence of statistical significance may or may not indicate strong relationships and depends on a number of factors, many of which we have already discussed, including sample size, type of question being asked, and the influence of other factors. Consequently, we need to be careful in presenting results and how we draw conclusions when referring to statistical significance.

Weinbach (1989) stated: "If practitioners are to make intelligent and informed discussions regarding whether a finding is meaningful for them, they must know more than just whether a relationship between variables is statistically significant" (p. 35). He stressed the importance of responsible reporting of results, including a statement of the sample size and whether this size falls within the usual size range for which the test is best suited. Such reporting would help the reader assess the appropriateness of the particular test for the research.

The strength of the relationship should be presented as clearly as possible—as a percentage difference or an actual correlation. Weinbach concluded: "The ethical researcher who invites replication and feels comfortable in the use of statistical testing should not object to any of these requirements" (p. 35).

Although reports from the outcomes of agency-based research studies may contain descriptive statistics, a more in-depth analysis is often missing. This is probably a result of two factors: first, the tendency to focus on practical over statistical significance; second, the lack of knowledge about statistics and statistical software.

The focus on practical significance is understandable in an agency setting. Often, this practical significance can be thought of as political significance. For example, suppose an agency is carrying out a program evaluation. In that case, the agency may not be concerned with whether the results are statistically significant, but rather whether the program's goals have been met. Demonstrating statistical significance, however, could enhance practical findings considerably and strengthen the agency's case.

Unfortunately, a lack of statistical and statistical software knowledge in agency settings is all too common. This overview of statistics has given you some basic knowledge that you can build on by enrolling in statistics courses or exploring the many available statistics texts. If you still feel at a loss when confronted with your data analysis, seek consultation. Universities often have statistical consultants, or you can look in your community for someone with statistical know-how. If you are writing a grant or research proposal, budget in the cost of a statistical consultant. Whenever possible, bring in the consultant early in the planning stage.

As we have seen, the type of analysis you carry out is contingent upon other aspects of the research process—the levels of measurement, design, and sample size. Thus, utilizing the consultant from the start will ultimately help the data analysis itself.

Human Diversity Issues and Statistical Analysis

In categorizing values—to construct frequency distribution tables or for cross tabulations—you must take care that differences between groups of individuals are respected. For example, the number of subjects in some minority groups is often small, and there is a temptation to collapse these groups into one. However, we may lose critical information about human diversity in doing so. Consequently, it is essential to devise a means to retain this information. One strategy would be to add a qualitative or interpretive dimension to your study. In addition, care must be taken in how you interpret and understand statistical findings, however clearly and responsibly they are reported. Occasionally, findings can seduce us into believing that something is related to something else when actually the findings are partial or otherwise open to question. Therefore, you must be careful that you use these results responsibly and that you have acknowledged your potential bias against certain groups. As discussed throughout this book, the sources of these biases can exist at each stage of the research process.

Summary

Descriptive statistics summarize the characteristics of a sample, whereas inferential statistics analyze data and make estimates about a larger body of data. Frequency distributions are descriptions of the number of times the values of a variable occur in a sample. The measures of central tendency are the mode, median, and mean. Data can be distributed in a normal or bell-shaped curve or a skewed pattern. Measures of variability are the range and standard deviation. The measures of association are cross tabulation and correlation.

One possible source of error in research is chance. The role of chance factors can be assessed with inferential statistics and probability theory. Hypotheses can be two-tailed, one-tailed, or null. A finding is statistically significant when the null hypothesis is rejected, and the probability that the finding will occur due to chance falls at or below a certain cutoff point. The ability of a statistical test to correctly reject a null hypothesis is the power of the test.

Four statistical tests are t-tests, ANOVA, correlational analysis, regression analysis, and chi-square analysis.

STUDY/EXERCISE QUESTIONS

1. Look for articles in social work journals that use

   a. the mean/median or mode

   b. the standard deviation

   c. correlation

   d. cross tabulations

2. One of the Study/Exercise Questions in Chapter 10 asked you to develop a questionnaire to measure student attitudes on combining research and practice, administer the questionnaire, and construct a codebook. Construct a frequency distribution table for two of the variables included in this questionnaire.

REFERENCES

Bostock, S., Crosswell, A., Prather, D., Aric, A.,& Steptoe, A. (2019). Mindfulness on-the-go: Effects of a mindfulness meditation app on work stress and well-being. *Journal of Occupational Health Psychology*, 24(1), 127–138.

Cerrato, J., & Cifre, E. (2018). Gender inequality in household chores and work-family conflict. *Frontiers in Psychology, 9*, 1330. https://doi.org/10.3389/fpsyg.2018.01330

Chaturvedi, K., Vishwakarma, D. K., &Singh, N. (2021).COVID-19 and its impact on education, social life and mental health of students: A survey. *Children and Youth Services Review,*121. https://doi.org/10.1016/j.childyouth.2020.105866.

Gredig, D.,& Bartelsen-Raemy, A.(2018). Exploring social work students' attitudes toward research courses: Predictors of interest in research-related courses among first-year students enrolled in a bachelor's programme in Switzerland. *Social Work Education, 37*(2), 190–208. DOI: 10.1080/02615479.2017.1389880

Gyan, C., Malik, M.,& Siddique, A. (2021). Barriers to the participation of women in community development process in rural Ghana: A regression analysis. *Development in Practice, 32*(4), 448–459. DOI: 10.1080/09614524.2021.1937541

Hortigüela-Alcalá, D., Sánchez-Santamaría, J., Pérez-Pueyo, A., & Abella-García, V. (2019). Social networks to promote motivation and learning in higher education from the students' perspective. *Innovations in Education and Teaching International, 56*(4), 412–422. DOI: 10.1080/14703297.2019.1579665

Krings, A., Victor, B. G., Mathias, J., & Perron, B. E. (2020). Environmental social work in the disciplinary literature, 1991–2015. *International Social Work, 63*(3), 275–290. https://doi.org/10.1177/0020872818788839

Manolov, R., Losada, J. L., Chacón-Moscoso, S., & Sanduvete-Chaves, S. (2016). Analyzing two-phase single-case data with non-overlap and mean difference indices: Illustration, software tools, and alternatives. *Frontiers in Psychology, 7*(32). https://doi.org/10.3389/fpsyg.2016.00032

Weinbach, R. W. (1989). When is statistical significance meaningful? A practice perspective. *Journal of Sociology and Social Welfare, 16*(1), 31–37.

13

Research Writing

INTRODUCTION

You've analyzed the research results, and on your screen in front of you are the results, whether the research was qualitative, quantitative, or both. Now is the time to write up your research results. Writing the research report is necessary both for yourself—particularly when you are evaluating your own practice—and for others. In fact, for needs assessments and program evaluations, the writing of the report is a critical research stage; as a generalist social worker, you may be more involved in this stage than any other. In addition, you may be asked to assist with developing research proposals, often as part of larger grant proposals. Alternatively, as a student, you will need to write up research reports and, in a graduate program, a thesis or dissertation. Finally, you may decide to submit an article, based on a completed research project, for presentation at a conference or publication in one of the many professional journals in social work or a related field.

Writing about research is the focus of this chapter. The two basic types of research writing—proposal writing and reporting research results—are analogous to similar steps in practice: first, the writing of an assessment and intervention plan; and second, the reporting of the results of the intervention.

LEARNING OBJECTIVES

This chapter includes the following learning objectives:

1. To understand the general principles of research writing

2. To learn how to reference and cite library resources

3. To be able to write a research proposal and report

4. To understand the skills needed to write grants

5. To understand how to disseminate the findings from research

6. To understand the role of the agency in research writing

7. To articulate ethical and human diversity issues in research writing

General Principles of Research Writing

Four general principles of research writing are addressed here: knowing your audience; using appropriate citations and references; the structure of the report or proposal; and, finally, the process of writing.

Knowing Your Audience

One of the basic principles of writing, whether it be research or otherwise, is to identify your audience. The content and style of the written product should differ according to your intended readers. For example, in writing a research proposal for a needs assessment to establish a date rape prevention program on a university campus, clarify from the outset to whom the proposal is directed—the university administration, a local chapter of NASW, or some other audience. Obviously, audiences are very different. The university administration might need considerable information about the phenomenon of date rape and a discussion of its potential impact on student recruitment, whereas the NASW chapter might require more emphasis on the social and psychological costs of the problem, such as date rape's impact on women's self-esteem.

Your audience influences not only the content of your proposal or report but also the style you adopt. If writing for the university administration, your writing style would be more formal than if you were writing a report for a group of parents in the community.

Referencing Sources of Information

When you are writing any type of report that refers to work by other authors, whether quoting them directly or through indirect reference, it is critical that you appropriately cite your sources of information. Although you can use a number of different referencing styles, the one most widely used in social work literature is the American Psychological Association (APA) referencing method. This is the style used in this book.

The *Publication Manual of the American Psychological Association, 5th edition* (2020) is the guidebook for the APA style. This book contains a great deal of information. Some examples will follow:

Quotations from a Source

The authors stated "Interview data indicated that women perceived physical and mental health issues as barriers to full-time employment. Women reported a struggle to maintain housing even when they had employment" (Groton and Rady, 2021, p. 92).

Referencing Citations in the Text

Groton and Rady (2021) studied employment opportunities for homeless women with children.

Referencing Citations from Electronic Sources

Often electronic sources do not provide page numbers. If paragraph numbers are visible, then use them rather than page numbers. Use the ¶ symbol or the abbreviation "para."If neither page numbers nor paragraph numbers are available, cite the heading and the number of the ¶ following the heading.

These citations in the text, whether direct quotes or ideas, are then listed in a bibliography. The sources are listed alphabetically by author, using the following format:

Listing References in the Bibliography

Journal articles:

Mensinga, J. (2021). A narrative inquiry exploring social workers' understanding of yoga and its application in professional practice. *Australian Social Work, 74*(2), 134–145.

Johnstone, M., & Lee, E. (2021). Epistemic injustice and indigenous women: Toward centering indigeneity in social work. *Affilia, 36*(3), 376–390.

Books:

Marlow, C. R. (2023). *Research methods for generalist social work.* Long Grove, IL: Waveland Press.

Articles or chapters in edited books:

Guendelman, S. (2003). Immigrant families. In M. A. Mason, A. Skolnick, & S. D. Sugarman (Eds.). *All our families* (pp. 244–264). New York: Oxford University Press.

Refer to Szuchman and Thomlison (2009), who specifically discuss APA style and social work.

The Structure of the Proposal or Report

This section outlines some general principles relating to the structure of the report. (The specifics of the content of both the proposal and the report are discussed in the following section.) Again, the APA manual is useful since it not only contains details about referencing sources but also describes each component of the report or proposal.
    In general, these conventions should be followed:

- *Title.* Use a clear and concise title.

- *Authorship and sponsorship.* Credits should be inclusive. Don't forget anyone!

- *Abstract.* An overview of the contents of the report or proposal is provided in the form of an abstract to prepare the reader for what follows. Abstracts are often included at the beginning of journal articles.

- *Body of the report/proposal.* Details on this are included in this chapter.

- *Appendices.* Sometimes the report may include material that is relevant but too bulky to include in the text of the proposal or report. These materials are then included as appendices. Common materials to place in the appendices are the data collection instruments and statistical tables that do not relate directly to the findings.

- *Bibliography and referencing.* As was discussed in the previous section, be sure to cite all your sources appropriately.

    Remember that your report or proposal should maintain a consistent style. For instance, if you use the APA style for references, you should also use this manual for instructions on how to structure titles and abstracts.

The Process of Writing

Research reports and proposals should be written as clearly and as concisely as possible. This is not the place for flamboyant writing. Remember that you want others, possibly from very diverse backgrounds, to read and understand the results of your research. A long and convoluted report may not only cloud readers' comprehension of the findings but also discourage some from even trying to read the report. Be as straightforward in your writing as possible. The following suggestions can help you achieve this clarity:

- Keep a research log to facilitate the process of the report or proposal writing as well as the process and development of the research itself. A research log is an informal but systematic record of ideas and progress relating to the research. Once the research is completed, it may be difficult to remember exactly why one research strategy was adopted over another or what doubts there were about a particular approach. The research log can help jog the memory.

- Prepare an outline (details will be discussed in the next section). You may not end up following your outline exactly, but that's OK. The idea is to at least have a rough idea in your mind and on paper of how the report or proposal is structured. The outline helps avoid a written product that wanders from one topic to another.

- Write a first draft, then revise and revise and revise, if necessary. Do not expect your first draft to be anything like the final one.

- Ask colleagues, faculty, or students to read early drafts and give their comments.

  Do not be afraid of criticism at this point. Generally, the more input you receive, the higher the quality of the written product. Have your readers comment on structure, content, style, grammar, and spelling.

- Have someone proof the final copy—primarily for grammar and spelling.

The Research Proposal

A **research proposal** is a paper proposing the undertaking of a specific type of research. This is often necessary to obtain permission and funds to conduct the study.

Writing the proposal can also directly assist the researcher in conceptualizing the research. By systematically thinking through each step of the research process, as is required in the research proposal, the researcher can gain new insights and clarifications regarding the research itself.

The format required for a research proposal varies depending upon the specific conditions under which the proposal is being written. These include the following:

- The funding agency may provide application forms that specify the information being requested.

- The funding agency may request a letter of intent, which requires the researcher to describe the proposal briefly. The funding source, based on this letter, may or may not ask the researcher to submit a full-fledged proposal.

- Sometimes, funding agencies send out requests for proposals (RFPs) that specify what they are interested in funding and how proposals should be submitted.

Taking these conditions into consideration, generally a standard outline is used for writing research proposals. The different components include these:

- statement of the research topic
- literature review
- research questions and hypotheses
- research design
- sampling strategy
- data collection
- data analysis
- presentation of the results
- administration and budget
- credentials of the researcher and other relevant personnel

These outlines tend to have a quantitative or positivist bias. Although it could be argued that the outline could also accommodate an interpretive or qualitative study, many funding agencies are, in reality, still primarily interested in more traditional approaches. As discussed in Chapter 1, however, researchers are increasingly adopting a number of different methods of inquiry, which will eventually influence the format and expectations of RFPs.

Each step of the outline has been explained sequentially in this book. A few items should be clarified, though. First, the literature review varies according to what type of research is being proposed (as was also discussed in Chapter 4). In the case of a program evaluation, this section would report why the program is being evaluated and would include findings from the evaluations of similar programs. For a needs assessment, this section would include a description of prior research that has reported on the extent of the social problem to be investigated. Some of this information could be found in the social work literature, but it may also be found in various government document depositions or in agencies' archives. The literature review for a less applied study—for instance, looking at the impact on a child's self-image of one parent being physically challenged (a possible thesis topic)—would be different. Here the literature review would include a discussion of the various theories that have suggested a relationship may occur, in addition to reporting similar research and their findings. This information could be found in the social work and social science literature in university libraries.

In the data collection section, you are generally required only to state the method you will use to collect data. For example, if the data collection requires the development of an instrument—such as an interview schedule or a questionnaire—typically, this does not need to be completed for the proposal, but you will need to state what types of variables you will be including. If you plan to use scales or other instruments that have already been developed, then you would include these in an appendix to the proposal.

The data analysis section clearly cannot be discussed in any detail in the proposal except to indicate which statistical tests or other forms of analysis will be used. The presentation of results section should include a discussion of how and to whom the results will be presented. The budget section should itemize all expenses, including supplies, personnel costs, mailing costs, computer costs, and so forth. Finally, you usually need both to summarize your credentials as they relate to the project and to include a curriculum vitae.

Writing Grants

Social workers often find themselves in the position of needing to seek funding for specific projects or programs and in many cases to help support the entire agency. Consequently, grant-writing skills are essential for the social worker. As discussed above, research proposals vary in their format according to the requirements of the funding source, similar to a **grant proposal**. Careful attention needs to be paid to the guidelines for the letter of application, the letter of intent, and the request for proposals.

Types of Funding

There are three categories of grant funding:

- **Federal Agencies:** A good source for funding opportunities can be found in the Catalog of Federal Domestic Assistance https://cfda.symplicity.com/. This site provides funding opportunities for over 1,800 programs, including over 500 from the Department of Health and Human Services and the Department of Education. A search for "Indian Child Welfare" produced 738 possible courses. Usually, formal RFPs are issued with very strict guidelines and deadlines. The Federal Register is another important source of opportunities: http://www.archives.gov/federal-register.

- **State Government:** The types and availability of state funds varies from state to state. Sometimes these are in the form of **block grants** awarded to states according to a specific formula and funded by legislative appropriations. As with federal funding opportunities, state agencies usually issue formal RFPs with specific guidelines.

- **Foundations:** Foundations are nonprofit organizations specifically devoted to dispersing funds. There are a few very large foundations but most foundations issue quite small grants. Applications for foundation funding are usually more informal and less complicated than applying for federal or state funds and usually involve writing a letter of application. However, it is very important that you carefully investigate the types of programs the foundation funds and the amount usually awarded, otherwise you can waste a great deal of time. The Foundation Directory (http://fconline.foundationcenter.org) is an important source to explore, although a subscription is required.

Other sources of grant opportunities are various grant databases, where monthly updates and notices are available. Check with the grants and research office on your campus.

Components of a Grant Proposal

Just as a research proposal has specific requirements, so does a grant proposal. Generally, these include the following:

- **The Cover Letter:** a letter to the funding agency
- **Title Page:** (or Contact Information Page)
- **Summary or Abstract:** usually about a paragraph
- **Problem or Needs Statement:** why this project is necessary
- **Goals and Objectives:** be very specific here and add measurable objectives whenever possible
- **Implementation and Activities:** specifically what will be undertaken as a part of the project
- **Evaluation:** tie to the measurable objectives
- **Sustainability of the Project:** how will the project be funded after the grant funds run out
- **Dissemination:** how will information about the program and its benefits be distributed to the appropriate constituencies
- **Budget:** tie to the activities of the project and include personnel costs
- **Attachments and Appendices:** these may or may not be allowed, so check the RFP carefully as they could include letters of support

Guidelines for Writing Grants

The following are some guiding principles in grant writing.

- For first time grant writers, try to get help by assisting someone (a professor or the director of an agency) who has experience with grant writing. This will help you learn some of the necessary skills.
- Carefully research funding opportunities, especially when seeking foundation funding, and make sure that your requests are in line with the mission and purpose of the funding agency.
- Carefully study the requirements for the letter of application or the RFP.
- When writing the proposal, use simple, jargon-free language.
- Always abide by any page limits.
- Look at the criteria the reviewers will use to assess the proposal and write the proposal accordingly.

- Make sure the budget corresponds to the objectives in the proposal and that it is within the limits provided.
- Always meet the deadlines—there are no exceptions.
- Be patient. It often takes several attempts at submitting proposals before you receive an award.
- Good Luck!

The Research Report

As with the research proposal, the organization of the research report depends in part upon the demands of the agency or the funding source. In general, however, this outline is followed:

- statement of the research topic
- literature review
- research questions and hypotheses
- research design
- sampling strategy
- data collection method(s)
- results
- discussion
- limitations
- recommendations for future research
- implications for practice

These sections apply whether you are reporting on a practice evaluation, needs assessment, or program evaluation study and regardless of whether the study employs a primarily quantitative or qualitative approach.

Obviously, this outline is very similar to the proposal. In fact, if you have a well-structured and well-informed proposal, the research report will be much easier to complete.

Some differences do exist between the proposal and the report. The report includes four additional sections: the results of the study, a discussion of the findings, the limitations of the study, and suggestions for future research.

Results Section

Regardless of your audience and the type of research, the focus of your report will be on the results. How results or findings are reported depends on whether the study has adopted a quantitative or qualitative approach, and reference will be made to this distinction throughout the following sections. Reporting findings often involves the use of tables, graphs, and pie charts. These visual representations are particularly useful for presenting quantitative data. In the following section, we will describe some forms visual representations can take.

Tables

Statistical tables are the most common form of reporting quantitative findings and are essentially types of frequency distributions. Several principles need to guide the presentation of the data. First, clearly display the data and do not clutter the table with unnecessary details. Second, make the table as complete as possible, usually by including both raw numbers and percentages (percentages facilitate comparison). Third, provide a summary of the statistical tests at the bottom of the table when appropriate. Finally, clearly label the table, including footnotes where appropriate. There are some good examples of tables in Chapter 12.

Graphs

Graphs are an alternative or a supplement to tables that present the data more visually. Similar guidelines apply to graphs as apply to tables. One drawback of graphs is that they lack the detail of tables; but their advantage is that they present a visual image of the data that makes the results apparent at a glance. Graphs are particularly useful in presenting data from practice evaluation studies. Some of the principles of graphing were discussed in Chapter 7.

Various types of graphs can be used. The **line graph** connects various data points with lines. These types of graphs are used extensively for the evaluation of individual practice.

Another type of graph is the **bar graph**. Bar graphs are useful visual means of displaying data at the nominal level of measurement. There is an example of a bar graph in Chapter 12.

Pie Charts

A final type of pictorial or visual presentation of data is the **pie chart.** Pie charts can be used when we want to show the relative contributions of each value to the whole variable. Pie charts are particularly useful for displaying a budget. If too many values need to be included, however, pie charts can look cluttered and be confusing.

Graphs and charts are fairly easily generated electronically. Remember when constructing these visual aids that the goal is to make the data more accessible and clearer to the reader.

Apart from reporting the results using visual aids, the other part of presenting findings is to describe them in writing. This description need not be extensive and can simply consist of translating the findings as straightforwardly as possible. When describing the findings, it is important to avoid interpreting the data; simply report the information and, when necessary, the statistical tests and their results.

Sometimes studies include both qualitative and quantitative results. The quantitative results might be presented followed by a description of the qualitative findings. A discussion section would then integrate the two. Chapter 12 provides many examples of how the results from quantitative studies can be presented.

Example of a Line Graph

Zhang et al. (2021) carried out research examining how the COVID-19 pandemic affected teens' social media engagement and psychological well-being, comparing teens both with and without mental health concerns. Data were collected on the frequency of posting on Reddit using a time series research design.

The results indicated that both teens with and without mental health concerns reversed the trend in posting frequency and negative emotion from declining to increasing right after the pandemic outbreak, and teens with mental health concerns had a more rapidly increasing trend in posting/commenting. The findings suggest that teens' social media engagement and emotion expression reflect the pandemic evolution. Figure 13.1 is a line graph showing the weekly mean number of posts/comments per participant made in the r/Teenagers subreddit by youth who visited and never visited the mental health subreddits.

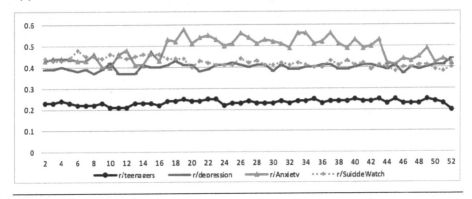

Figure 13.1 Example of a line graph

Example of a Pie Chart

Rabia et al. (2019) investigated the thoughts of men and women on gender inequality in Pakistan. The data were collected using the survey method, and 63 percent of people gave opinions that women are not treated fairly, while 71 percent felt there is discrimination between men and women in education, and 57 percent said that parents give more importance to their sons as compared to their daughters in Pakistan. The ages of the participants sampled were displayed in pie charts. See Figure 13.2.

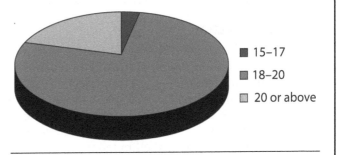

Figure 13.2 Example of a pie chart

Discussion Section

Unlike a research proposal, a research report always contains some kind of discussion section. The discussion section follows and is closely linked to the results section, and it provides an explanation of the results. This section is important whether you are discussing the results of an evaluation of your own practice, a needs assessment, or a program evaluation.

Reporting Results in a Qualitative Study

Benoit et al. (2022) investigated how children and teenagers manage their *ecological grief* and *eco-anxiety* and how they can leverage it into *environmental action*. In a scoping review, the authors analyzed newspaper content between 2018 and 2021 in six of the top ten American newspapers by circulation about young people during the climate crisis. The 131 articles selected addressed the attitudes of children, adolescents, and parents toward the climate crisis. A qualitative analysis was carried out. The authors summarized the results as follows:

Newspaper articles commonly categorized children, adolescents, and their respective perspectives and experiences around climate change along four patterns of discourse: (a) fierce young activists; (b) *adultified* children; (c) innocent victims; and/or (d) ultimate saviors. In turn, articles considered parents and adults in one of four paradigmatic ways: (a) experiencing eco-anxiety through parenthood; (b) taming children's eco-anxiety; (c) criticizing youth-led activism; and/or (d) reimagining climate action as a source of meaning in the lives of young people. (p. 47)

The findings are related to the hypotheses (if there are any) and to the theoretical premise of the study itself. Part of this process involves comparing your research findings to findings from comparable research in the literature and pointing out similarities and differences in the results and conclusions. In this way, you can make connections among various empirical findings, thereby providing collective support and evidence for theories.

In qualitative studies, the distinction between describing the results and discussing the findings can be fuzzy. In part, this fuzziness may result from our attempt to provide an insightful description of the phenomenon under study. We still need to make a careful distinction between the description and the interpretation.

Limitations Section

By now, it should be very evident that no research is perfect. Flaws and limitations may result from the nature of the question being asked, but often—and particularly in social work research—these imperfections simply reflect the social and political context of the studies. For example, random assignment into the experimental and control groups is not always feasible, as discussed in Chapter 6. Sometimes there simply is not time to carry out in-depth interviews with as many people as you would like. In reporting the limitations, go through the research process and point out the drawbacks of the method at each stage. Some common limitations have been discussed in previous chapters, but here is a summary of these problems:

A Discussion Section from a Quantitative Study

Retzer et al. (2020) investigated the effect of disclosing a parental intellectual disability (PID) upon child welfare workers' risk assessment. They included 191 social workers' risk assessments using hypothetical child safeguarding scenarios.

> This research has found that rather than a widely held negative view of parents with ID, the defining factor that determines the assessment of cases appears to be the other factors that are present. The perceived risk assessed to be presented by these factors affects the extent to which PID contributes to the overall risk assessment. Where PID presents along with high risk factors, it does not affect the risk assessment, whereas where PID presents along with low risk factors, it does affect the risk assessment and results in a greater assessment of risk. Rather than an active form of discrimination as is suggested by the wider literature, this study illustrates a different pattern of assessment. This provides a basis for further research into the specifics of how PID is considered alongside other factors. (p. 1196)

- *Problems associated with the research strategy or approach:* The study's approach—descriptive, explanatory, qualitative, or quantitative—needs to be made explicit, and the approach's drawbacks need to be acknowledged.

- *Limitations of the sampling method:* Nonprobability sampling will result in limited generalizability of the findings; but probability sampling may not yield information-rich cases.

- *Limited response rate:* A response rate of less than 50 percent limits generalizations even if probability sampling is used.

- *The reliability and validity of the data collection methods:* These need to be specified.

- *The problems associated with internal and external validity:* Validity problems can occur when the research is explanatory (rather than descriptive) and often result from the lack of a comparison group, particularly one that has been randomly assigned. These problems need to be acknowledged.

- *The problems associated with the interpretation of the results:* It is important to point out that interpretations are just that—interpretations; other people may interpret the results rather differently. Interpretive problems may arise whether statistical tests have been used or the data are qualitative.

The extent to which you discuss limitations depends on your audience. You must devote at least a paragraph to addressing these issues. If you are writing up the results of a needs assessment or a program evaluation, the limitations section can be minimal. But if your audience is more knowledgeable about research, you must provide a more extensive limitations section.

A Limitations Section—Descriptive Research

Franchino-Olsen et al. (2022), in their study of domestic minor sex trafficking (DMST) and commercial sexual exploitation of children (CSEC) in the United States clearly stated the limitations of the research:

> Nonetheless, our review is not without limitations. Firstly, we only include estimates of the number or prevalence of DMST/CSEC cases in a given population. We did not include publications of reported, suspected, or identified cases. We acknowledge that many cases of DMST/CSEC go unidentified, leading to an undercount of the problem of trafficking when using identified case statistics. Secondly, our study only considers cases of domestic sex trafficking of minors. Labor trafficking of domestic minors and trafficking non-U.S. nationals into or within the United States remain grave issues as well that are not reflected in these prevalence values. That said, research on the prevalence of these forms of human trafficking is scant and is an area of future work. (p. 192)

A Limitations Section—Explanatory Research

O'Toole et al. (2018) studied the effectiveness of homeless-tailored patient-centered medical homes (PCMHs) for homeless veterans. They examined the impact of enrollment in a Veterans Health Administration (VHA)homeless-tailored PCMH on health services use, cost, and satisfaction compared with enrollment in a traditional, nontailored PCMH.

> Our study has several limitations. Although the quasi-experimental study design is an improvement over the design of previous studies, unmeasured differences between the groups might have been controlled for in a randomized controlled trial study design, which was not chosen for reasons noted. The study population was limited to predominantly male homeless veterans and may not be generalizable to other population groups such as nonveterans, women, and younger persons, who may have different obstacles to access, treatment engagement, or drivers of poor health outcomes. "Basing the study in VHA and using electronic medical records allowed us to more efficiently capture data on care use across the continuum of services and events for the entire sample, although we may not have captured all data on care received in other health systems. Recording of non-VA care events was subject to recall bias. Further research is needed to determine whether our findings are reproducible. Finally, our study was conducted in urban centers on the East and West coasts and may not be generalizable to rural communities or settings with fewer homeless persons, where adequate economies of scale may not exist to concentrate care and services in this type of model. (p. 5)

Recommendations Section

The next section of the report consists of recommendations for further study and explicitly states the questions that have arisen from the research itself. Think carefully about the groups or constituencies to which you want and need to communicate. These constituencies might include the community, policy makers, or funders.

Implications for Practice

A section on implications for practice is critical to many reports and central when the research is a needs assessment or a program evaluation. After all, these implications are a central purpose of the research.

The order and structure of these last few sections can vary. Often the discussion section includes the implications for practice section, the limitations section, and the suggestions for further research section.

Recommendations for Further Research

Jackson et al. (2021), in their study exploring police neglect and psychological, physical, and sexual violence perpetrated by police, examined how these forms of police violence relate to perceptions of police legitimacy/trust, police effectiveness, and police performance.

Additional research and evaluation is needed to provide empirical evidence on the effectiveness and overall effects of social work–police partnerships—compared to existing approaches and community-driven innovations—in addressing police violence. In the context of reimagining policing and the criminal legal system and defunding or even eliminating the police, it is vital to maintain a continued awareness of the historical roots of policing, the militarization of law enforcement, and the associated rise in police violence—in all its forms—that continues to disproportionately impact minority groups. (p. 322)

Implications for Practice Section: Program Evaluation

Griffen (2022) used a participatory approach to evaluate the presence of the Inclusion Wheel Model across programs on a variety of public health topics in which people with disabilities were intentionally included. The author conducted a qualitative analysis using virtual meetings, meeting notes, and the series of feedback surveys as data across settings and topics.

This examination has critical implications for public health trainers, leaders, and program designers on the inclusion of people with disabilities and other underserved populations in health promotion efforts. Public health practitioners must serve the whole community, including underserved and marginalized demographic groups, like the one in four Americans living with a disability. The Inclusion Wheel may be used as a model to guide disability inclusion training among public health partners and leaders in nonprofit, corporate, and government sectors, as well as to prioritize involvement of marginalized and underserved population groups in planning health promotion efforts.

Implications for Practice Section: Needs Assessment

Miller et al. (2022) examined service needs and barriers to accessing services among autistic adults by gender identity (man, woman, and other gender). Data were generated from a statewide needs assessment survey that included quantitative and qualitative data.

    The results of this study documented barriers to service access reported by autistic adults. This study also found that other gender autistic adults were more likely to report unmet needs for counseling services than autistic men, and both autistic women and other gender adults in this sample reported multiple barriers to receiving needed services as compared to their male counterparts. Both women and other gender adults were more likely to report multiple barriers to needed services than men including transportation and scheduling. This study indicated the needs to provide targeted services that are gender specific.

Disseminating the Report

Disseminating or distributing the research report is an essential prerequisite to incorporation of research into practice and is key to the whole concept of evidence-based practice. Research findings must be accessible to practitioners. The dissemination of a report can take several forms: Reports can be presented orally, distributed internally in written form, and published in journals. As with writing, think about your audience when disseminating the report and plan accordingly.

Oral Presentation

You may be required to present your research results orally at a community meeting, at a meeting of the agency's board of directors, or to legislators. In the case of practice evaluations, usually the results are discussed more informally with the client and others who might be involved. When presenting orally at a formal meeting, keep the following items in mind:

- Know how much time you have to give the report and stick to this time. Rehearsing your presentation will help.

- Allow time for questions and discussion. Know in advance how much time will be allocated for discussion.

- Use visual aids (PowerPoint presentations, for example) and handouts (containing a summary of the results and perhaps some charts and scales) when appropriate.

- Try not to become defensive about the research if someone criticizes it during discussion or question time. Simply answer the questions as clearly and as straightforwardly as possible. You should already be aware of the limitations and have thought them through, but you may have missed some.

A Note on PowerPoint

Microsoft PowerPoint (PP) is a great tool to use for oral presentations. However, a few cautions:

- Remember the PowerPoint is to help your audience rather than you (you might want to compose a PP presentation for your own consultation and guide and use another for the audience)
- Keep it simple and use a large font (24-point or greater)so it is readable, and use no more than six lines of text and no more than six words per line
- Include photographs and simple graphs whenever possible—the purpose of using PP is to focus on the visual, not the written
- When presenting using a PP remember not look at the PP but at the audience—engagement is the name of the game
- Test the equipment before the presentation

A Poster Session

Occasionally conferences include "poster sessions" or you may be required to complete a poster for a class. Posters usually include displays of about 4 by 6 feet. The idea is that the research is displayed visually, usually with a mix of writing, charts, and pictures/photographs, and that this enables the audience to visit a number of posters and ask questions of the researchers. The advantages over a standard presentation are that those that are interested in the topic can stop and engage in conversation with the researcher and ask specific questions. Another advantage is that poster sessions are much less intimidating for the presenter.

Szuchman and Thomlison (2011) give some guidelines for poster sessions:

- The poster must be readable from a distance of 3 feet away
- Posters are true to the spirit of APA format, but the rules of presentation are relaxed
- Make the Introduction section no longer than three large typed pages
- Consider posting parts and photos of the actual materials
- Posters usually have conclusions, presented in bulleted or numbered highlights, in place of a discussion section
- Make it easy for the reader to understand the sequence in which pages should be read

Distributing Written Reports Internally

The appearance of the report is important even if it is only to be distributed in-house. The term *in-house* can encompass anything from a small agency to a large government department. Be sure that the original report is clear and will reproduce good copies; it can be frustrating to read a report that has been poorly copied. Make sure that everyone who is meant to receive the report actually does.

Publishing the Report

You should strive to publish whenever possible. Publication undoubtedly allows the professional the best access to research findings. Social work journals are making a conscious effort to solicit and publish articles written by practitioners.

As a practitioner, you have important contributions to make that can be very different from those of academicians.

There are some ways to assess whether or not your report has potential for publication. Consider the following:

- Is it investigating a problem that has received little attention in the past in the research literature? Many journals devote entire issues to research on a newly explored topic.

- Does it have a new slant or perspective on a problem? For example, there may have been many program evaluations on the effectiveness of parent training on reducing the incidence of child abuse and neglect. But if your agency has a program that serves a large number of Puerto Rican clients and you have been involved in evaluating the program, you might have excellent material for publication if none has previously been published on this type of intervention with this particular client group.

- Is it an innovative research method or combination of methods?

Use participatory principles in disseminating the report. The possibilities for sharing research results are endless, from distributing pamphlets to presenting on the radio. Foster (2007) used a participatory approach to study women's experiences as mothers in an impoverished community in England and presented results to "an audience of local residents, academics and practitioners in the form of poetry readings and displays of visual art work and short-film. In addition, we performed two short plays based on interview data" (p. 370).

If you are considering publishing, you should know that different journals are interested in different types of articles. To get a sense of who is interested in what, refer to the *NASW Guide to Social Work Authors*. This gives information on many journals and lists their specific requirements in terms of length of article, reference style, number of copies, and so on.

Very often the agency for which you are completing the research will give you specific requirements on how to write the report. Usually, an in-house report on a program evaluation or needs assessment will focus on the results section. A needs assessment may also concentrate on the implications of the findings for practice. If you are writing the report for publication and wider distribution, you may want to emphasize the methods section over the results and devote some attention to a discussion of how the results support or reject previous research. This will enable other researchers to replicate or augment your study.

As a generalist social worker employed in an agency, you will most often write reports on individual cases. These are also research reports if you used some type of evaluation as part of your practice. So start now—combine research and practice and contribute to social work knowledge.

Also, don't forget that another important way in which you can contribute is to give presentations at conferences. For example, your state NASW chapter probably holds conferences every year and strongly encourages practitioners to contribute.

Ethical Issues in Research Writing

Two major ethical issues arise in research writing. The first issue is appropriately referencing material included in a report. The second is confidentiality of results. We will discuss each of these issues in turn.

Referencing Appropriately

Existence of Previous Work

Whenever research is being planned and conducted, it is imperative that you consult other work that has been completed in the target area. For example, you may have been asked by your supervisor to conduct a needs assessment for an afterschool program in your community. You are excited about the opportunity to show off some of your newly acquired research skills. But the next day an ex-classmate calls you from a neighboring city; after you tell her about your assignment, she tells you she has just finished conducting such a study in her community.

You are tempted to ignore this piece of information and continue with your own plans because that way you could do your survey alone and collect the credit. Ethically, however, you need to acknowledge your friend's information as useful assistance in the development of your needs assessment; perhaps you may even be forced to recognize that there is no need for this type of study in your community at this time.

Citing References Appropriately

Given that you do decide to use information from your friend's study, it is imperative that you give her credit for her work. This applies to a study published locally as a report, as well as to more widely distributed publications. Recognizing others' contributions can present dilemmas. It would be impossible to credit everyone who has contributed to our intellectual and professional development.

In the case of specific research endeavors, however, you must recognize the contributions of others; otherwise, you may be guilty of plagiarism.

Confidentiality of Results

Just as confidentiality needs to be ensured during the data collection phase, you also need to preserve confidentiality when writing and disseminating the report.

Subjects' identities should not be disclosed without their permission. Confidentiality may be problematic in qualitative reports with extensive quotes that inadvertently reveal the subject's identity. It is also an issue with practice evaluations.

The NASW Code of Ethics (2021) states:

- Social workers engaged in the evaluation of services should discuss collected information only for professional purposes and only with people professionally concerned with this information.
- Social workers who report evaluation and research results should protect participants' confidentiality by omitting identifying information unless proper consent has been obtained authorizing disclosure.

Another related issue is copyright. Copyright law applies not only to published materials but also to in-house reports. Be sure to check on the restrictions that might pertain to distribution and publishing before you disseminate a report more widely.

Negative Findings

Quite often a research study will result in either unanticipated findings or findings that are "negative." In the case of explanatory research, it may be that the hypothesis was not supported. It is important to remember that these findings can be equally as useful for practice as the "positive" findings and should be disseminated as much as possible.

An Example of "Negative Findings"

Miller and Grise-Owens (2020) investigated the perception that millennials, who by 2025 will make up 75 percent of the world's workforce, are overly focused on self-care, which negatively impacts their work duties. This study examined the self-care practices of social work practitioners ($N = 3079$) in the United States. Researchers investigated self-care practices in the following categories: Professional Support, Professional Development, Life Support, Cognitive Awareness, and Daily Balance.

> Overall, data suggest that social workers in all generations engaged in moderate amounts of self-care. Analyses revealed that millennials engaged in significantly fewer self-care practices related to Professional Support and Daily Balance, when compared to Generation X and Baby-boomer participants. While not statistically significant, millennials scored lower across all other self-care domains. (p. 1400)

Human Diversity Issues in Research Writing

Three human diversity issues are involved in research writing. First, you must ensure that bias against certain groups is not contained in the report. Second, you should avoid using exclusive language. Third, you must consider to whom the results are being disseminated.

Bias Against Certain Groups

Be careful to exclude biases in the writing that tend to stereotype groups in our society. You are less at risk for this if you paid careful attention to human diversity issues throughout the research process. Then you simply ensure the data are accurately presented and equitably and nonjudgmentally discussed.

Exclusive Language

The issue of exclusive language involves acknowledging our differences and avoiding sexism. Although the predominant use of the male pronoun as a generic pronoun is becoming increasingly less acceptable, we do need to ensure that nonsexist terms are employed consistently. This involves not only the appropriate use of male, female, and plural pronouns, but also the use of terms that are gender neutral, such as *chair* instead of *chairman*.

We also need to ensure that terms do not reflect ethnic or cultural biases or a lack of sensitivity to human diversity. Use a descriptor of a cultural group that is recognized by the group itself. For example, using the term *Mexican American* in New Mexico to refer to Hispanics or Latino/a people could be offensive to some individuals who view themselves as Spanish Americans with minimal connections to Mexico. Accuracy often requires that we not lump groups of people together under one label.

Disseminating the Results to the Participants

The final human diversity issue relating to research writing is the question of who should receive the results. There is a growing argument in favor of giving the findings to the participants included in the research rather than just to the practitioners and other researchers. This is of course critical when conducting participatory or action research.

This does not necessarily entail making the entire research report available to the participants, particularly if it is extensive or excessively technical. Instead, a smaller report can be written specifically for those participating in a needs assessment or program evaluation, in which the results could potentially influence an entire community. One advantage of practice evaluations is that the results are routinely shared with the client (usually verbally).

Giving participants access to findings is viewed as an important issue, not just in social work but in many fields of enquiry. It is being recognized that research results can be empowering to subjects. Historically, minority subjects have often been used by the researcher and have reaped no benefits. Apart from making the results accessible to the participants, researchers need to pay more attention to repaying the participants. Of course, in social work research, the results of needs assessments, program evaluations, and practice evaluations all directly contribute to the development or improvement of interventions designed to assist those who are studied. Sometimes, though, benefits can be extended further—for example, by returning a proportion of the royalties from book sales to the community or by paying participants for the time they spend being interviewed.

One approach to disseminating the results to the participants is through a community forum. A community forum involves publicizing a meeting or series of meetings to which community members are invited. Online forums can be carried out via Zoom, as a Webinar, or by using other platforms. The community forum can serve a number of different functions; it can be used to get input for the initial development of a research question and project, apart from its use as a venue for the dissemination of findings.

Collecting and Sharing Data Together

McConnell et al. (2019) addressed the issue of empowerment for people with dementia (PWD). Initially the researchers carried out a scoping review to identify previous literature defining empowerment specifically for PWD. A list of terms was then shared in three workshops/forums consisting of academic team members and nine members of Dementia NI (an organization founded and led by people with dementia). The findings of the research were reviewed together and coproduced in an agreed definition they felt best described empowerment for them.

Summary

Four general principles of research writing are to know your audience, to use appropriate citations and references, to structure your research report or proposal correctly, and to write the report as clearly and as concisely as possible. The research proposal is a paper proposing a specific type of research. The funding agency may have requests for proposals (RFPs) that list the projects they are interested in funding and how the proposals should be submitted. Like the research proposal, the research report should follow an outline structure: statement of the research topic, theoretical framework, research questions and hypotheses, data collection methods, sampling strategy, research design, results, discussion, limitations, recommendations for future research, and implications for practice. Reports may be presented orally, distributed internally (in-house), distributed electronically, and/or published.

The ethical issues involved in research writing include appropriately referencing material and ensuring confidentiality of the results. Human diversity issues of concern in research writing are eliminating stereotyping of certain groups, avoiding exclusive language, and disseminating results to subjects.

STUDY/EXERCISE QUESTIONS

1. Request sample grant applications from organizations in your city or state that fund research efforts related to social work. Share these in class and discuss their similarities and differences.

2. Select a social work journal article and critique it, using the structure of a research report presented in this chapter as a guide.

3. Select research articles from social work journals that contain tables or charts.

   a. Do they clearly illustrate the results of the research?

   b. What changes would you make to improve them?

4. Find a request for proposals from the Federal Register.

5. Search for a foundation that provides support for battered family services.

REFERENCES

American Psychological Association (2020). *Publication manual of the American Psychological Association* (7th ed.). Washington, DC: Author.

Benoit, L., Thomas, I.,& Martin, A. (2022). Review: Ecological awareness, anxiety, and actions among youth and their parents—A qualitative study of newspaper narratives. *Child and Adolescent Mental Health, 27*(1) 47–58. http://dx.doi.org/10.1111/camh.12514

Foster, V.(2007)."Ways of knowing and showing": Imagination and representation in feminist participatory social research. *Journal of Social Work Practice, 21*(3), 361–376.

Franchino-Olsen, H., Chesworth, B. R., Boyle, C., Rizo, C. F., Martin, S. L., Jordan, B., Macy, R. J., & Stevens, L. (2022). The prevalence of sex trafficking of children and adolescents in the United States: A scoping review. *Trauma, Violence, & Abuse, 23*(1), 182–195.

Griffen, A. K. (2022, January 19). Exploratory evaluation of Inclusion Wheel Model for public health practice to include people with disabilities: Implications for leadership and training to serve the whole community. *Health Promotion Practice.* https://doi.org/10.1177/15248399211070809

Groton, D., & Radey, M. (2021)."I've been through it": Assessing employment barriers among unaccompanied women experiencing homelessness. *Social Work Research, 45*(2), 88–100.

Jackson, A. N., Fedina, L., DeVylder, J., & Barth, R. P. (2021). Police violence and associations with public perceptions of the police. *Journal of the Society for Social Work and Research, 12*(2), 303–326.

McConnell, T., Sturm, T., Stevenson, M. McCorry, N., Donnelly, M., Taylor, B. J., & Best, P. (2019). Co-producing a shared understanding and definition of empowerment with people with dementia. *Research Involvement and Engagement, 5*(19). https://doi.org/10.1186/s40900-019-0154-2

Miller, J. J., & Grise-Owens, E. (2021). Assessing the "millennial self-care obsession" among social workers: #notsomuch. *Journal of Social Work, 21*(6), 1399–1412.

Miller, K., Cooper, D., Song, W., & Shea, L. (2022). Self-reported service needs and barriers reported by autistic adults: Differences by gender identity. *Research in Autism Spectrum Disorders, 92.* https://doi.org/10.1016/j.rasd.2022.101916

National Association of Social Workers. (2021). NASW Code of Ethics. *NASW News, 25,* 24–25.

O'Toole, T., Johnson, E. E., Borgia, M., Noack, A., Yoon, J., Gehlert, E., & Lo, J. (2018). Population-tailored care for homeless veterans and acute care use, cost, and satisfaction: A prospective quasi-experimental trial. *Preventative Chronic Disease, 15.*

Rabia, M., Tanveer, F., Gillani, M., Naeem, H., & Akbar, S. (2019). Gender inequality: A case study in Pakistan. *Open Journal of Social Sciences, 7,* 369–379. doi: 10.4236/jss.2019.73031.

Retzer, A., Kaye, J., & Gray, R. (2020). A factorial survey investigating the effect of disclosing parental intellectual disability on risk assessments by children's social workers in child safeguarding scenarios. *The British Journal of Social Work, 50*(4), 1185–1200.

Rhodes, S. D., Mann-Jackson, L., Alonzo, J., Garcia, M., Tanner, A. E., Smart, B. D., Horridge, D. N., Van Dam, C. N., & Wilkin, A. M. (2021). A rapid qualitative assessment of the impact of the COVID-19 pandemic on a racially/ethnically diverse sample of gay, bisexual, and other men who have sex with men living with HIV in the US South. *AIDS and Behavior, 25*(1), 58–67.

Szuchman, L., & Thomlison, B. (2011). *Writing with style: APA style for social work* (4th ed.). Pacific Grove, CA: Brooks/Cole Publishing.

Zhang, S., Liu, M., Li, Y., & Chung, J. E. (2021). Teens' social media engagement during the COVID-19 pandemic: A time series examination of posting and emotion on Reddit. *International Journal of Environmental Research and Public Health, 18*(19), 10079.

Appendix A

Recommended Resources for Online Research

Compiled by Joe Buenker, M.S.
Associate Librarian
Arizona State University
ASU Library

A. Social Work's Professional Organizations

B. Social Work Magazines and News Sites

C. Consumer Health Information Websites

D. Data and Statistics

E. Associations and Organizations

F. United States: Federal, State, Local, and Tribal Government Websites

G. Current Social Work Journals

H. Current Social Work Book Series

I. Recent Books on Social Work with Specific Populations

J. Library of Congress Subject Headings

Even though this appendix emphasizes freely available web resources more than it does fee- or subscription-based resources licensed by academic libraries, this has been done only because the resources (research databases, journal article indexes, electronic book packages, electronic journal collections, streaming video collections, etc.) at each academic library is going to vary according to that library's funding for research materials, the size and needs of the student and faculty populations, and the various academic programs and their levels (bachelor's, master's or doctoral) it supports. Social work students are strongly encouraged to begin **all of their research** at their academic library building or their academic library's website, and to use free search tools (i.e., Google Scholar) as supplementary sources of information.

When a library licenses or subscribes to a research database, it must pay the database provider (vendor) an agreed-upon amount of money and ensure that it is restricting access to this copyrighted material to just those persons authorized by the licensing agreement (current university students, faculty, and staff). While a university student you have access—via your university login and password—to online resources and content that your university library system has licensed or purchased. It is to your advantage to use these materials to support your learning and writing.

In addition to the breadth and depth of high-quality resources provided by academic libraries, academic libraries also are staffed by librarians and other professionals who are available for no-cost research consultations. Part of our work as liaison/research/subject librarians focuses on enhancing and supporting student learning—via classroom instruction visits, online research tutorials and quizzes, and individual or group research consultations. Most academic libraries provide an *Ask a Librarian* service that promotes the various ways for you to contact the library for collection, policy, or technology questions, as well as for research assistance on assignments or projects. For example, the ASU Library's service is located at https://askalibrarian.asu.edu.

Again, while the number of search tools or research databases available from academic libraries varies, most offer both a single highly comprehensive search tool (the ASU Library's is called *Library One Search*—https://search.lib.asu.edu) as well as an "A-Z Databases" module (https://libguides.asu.edu/az.php). In almost all cases, anyone can view the list of available databases and see how their library has classified them (by subject, resource type and publisher/vendor). Access to research databases, and the ability to search, download/email/print/save full-text content from them, however, is restricted to current students and faculty of the university as required by the licensing agreements. Unlike the individual research databases, *Library One Search* discovery platforms generally can be searched by anyone, but again, because of licensing contracts with publishers/vendors, the ability to download/email/print/save most content is restricted to current students and faculty of the university.

If you have questions about your library's collections, databases, and services, use the library's *Ask a Librarian* service to ask if there is a specific librarian assigned to support the social work program, and if there are online research guides focused on social work research.

What follows are resources recommended to help you gain familiarity with the social work profession and online searching in support of your social work coursework.

A. Social Work's Professional Associations

Association for Gerontology Education in Social Work
(AGESW)
https://agesw.org/
American Academy of Social Work & Social Welfare
https://aaswsw.org/
American Board of Clinical Social Work
https://www.abcsw.org/
Association of Baccalaureate Social Work Program
Directors
https://www.bswpdonline.org/
Association of Oncology Social Work (AOSW)
https://aosw.org/
Association of Social Work Boards
https://www.aswb.org/
Clinical Social Work Association
https://www.clinicalsocialworkassociation.org/
Council on Social Work Education
https://www.cswe.org/
Global Social Service Workforce Alliance
https://www.socialserviceworkforce.org/
International Association for Social Work with Groups,
Inc. (IASWG)
https://www.iaswg.org/
The International Association of Schools of Social Work
https://www.iassw-aiets.org/
International Association of Veterinary Social Work
https://veterinarysocialwork.org/
International Council on Social Welfare
https://www.icsw.org/
International Federation of Social Workers
https://www.ifsw.org/

National Association of Black Social Workers
https://www.nabsw.org/
National Association of Deans and Directors of Schools
of Social Work
http://www.naddssw.org/
National Association of Social Workers (NASW)
https://www.socialworkers.org/
NASW Code of Ethics:
https://www.socialworkers.org/about/ethics/
code-of-ethics
National Organization of Forensic Social Work
https://www.nofsw.org/
National Rural Social Work Caucus
https://ruralsocialwork.org/
National Social Work Enrichment Program
https://nsepscholars.org/
The Network for Social Work Management
https://socialworkmanager.org/
Professional Association of Social Workers in HIV/
AIDS (PASWHA)
https://paswha.org/
Phi Alpha Honor Society
https://phialpha.org/
School Social Work Association of America
https://www.sswaa.org/
Social Work Policy Institute (NASW Foundation)
https://www.naswfoundation.org/Our-Work/
Social-Work-Policy-Institute
Society for Social Work and Research
https://secure.sswr.org/
Society for Social Work Leadership in Health Care
https://sswlhc.org/

B. Social Work Magazines and News Sites

Children's Voice. CWLA (Child Welfare League of
America), 1991– .
https://www.cwla.org/childrens-voice/
Council on Social Work Education (CSWE) News
https://www.cswe.org/news-landing/
Equality Magazine. Human Rights Campaign, (2003–)
https://www.hrc.org/magazine
Grand Challenges for Social Work
https://grandchallengesforsocialwork.org/
See the 2019 book *Grand Challenges for Society:
Evidence-Based Social Work Practice*:
https://naswpress.org/product/53465/grand-
challenges-for-society.
Influencing Social Policy
https://www.influencingsocialpolicy.org/

*Intersectionalities: A Global Journal of Social Work Analysis,
Research, Polity, and Practice*
https://journals.library.mun.ca/ojs/index.php/IJ
My Social Work News
https://www.mysocialworknews.com/
NASW News
https://www.socialworkers.org/News
NASW Social Work Talks Podcast (2018–)
https://www.socialworkers.org/News/Social-
Work-Talks-Podcast/
The New Social Worker. White Hat Communications
(1994–)
An online-only magazine focused on social work
education.
https://www.socialworker.com/

Open Social Work
https://opensocialwork.org/
"Building information equity in social work with open educational resources and open access to research."

Social Dialogue. International Association of Schools of Social Work (2011–)
https://socialdialogue.online/

Social Welfare History Project. Virginia Commonwealth University (VCU).
The Social Welfare History Project encompasses contemporary scholarship and historic documents. Articles on this site come from a broad range of sources, including materials that are offensive or contain negative stereotypes. VCU Libraries provides access to these items to support research and inquiry.
https://socialwelfare.library.vcu.edu/

Social Work Advocates. National Association of Social Workers (2018–)
https://www.socialworkers.org/News/Social-Work-Advocates

Social Work Blog. National Association of Social Workers.
http://www.socialworkblog.org/

Social Work Today. Great Valley Publishing Company (2010–)
https://www.socialworktoday.com/

Social Work News. Sanctuary Social Care (2017–)
"The magazine for social workers, by social workers."
https://www.mysocialworknews.com/magazine
https://issuu.com/socialworknews

SWHelper
https://swhelper.org/

Voting is Social Work
https://votingissocialwork.org/

C. Consumer Health Information Websites

Assistant Secretary for Planning and Evaluation (ASPE)
https://aspe.hhs.gov/topics

Centers for Disease Control and Prevention: A–Z Index
https://www.cdc.gov/az/a.html

Eunice Kennedy Shriver National Institute of Child Health and Human Development (National Institute of Health): A–Z Topics Index
https://www.nichd.nih.gov/health/topics

Food and Drug Administration: For Consumers
https://www.fda.gov/consumers

Health and Human Services: A–Z Index
https://www.hhs.gov/az/a/index.html

Healthy People 2030
https://health.gov/healthypeople

Mayo Clinic: Patient Care and Health Information
https://www.mayoclinic.org/patient-care-and-health-information

MedlinePlus®: Trusted Health Information for You
https://medlineplus.gov/

MyHealthfinder
https://health.gov/myhealthfinder

National Center for Health Statistics: FastStats!
https://www.cdc.gov/nchs/fastats/default.htm

National Institute on Aging: Health Information
https://www.nia.nih.gov/health

National Institutes of Health: Health Information
https://www.nih.gov/health-information

National Institute of Mental Health: Mental Health Information
https://www.nimh.nih.gov/health

U.S. Department of Health & Human Services: A–Z Index
https://www.hhs.gov/az/a/index.html

D. Data and Statistics

Administration for Children & Families (ACF): Data & Research
https://www.acf.hhs.gov/acf-data-research

Assistant Secretary for Planning and Evaluation (ASPE): Data
http://aspe.hhs.gov/statinfo/

Bureau of Economic Analysis (BEA)
https://www.bea.gov/data

Cochrane: Trusted evidence. Informed decisions. Better health.
https://www.cochrane.org/

Council on Social Work Education: Research & Statistics
https://www.cswe.org/research-statistics

Data.gov
https://data.gov/

Food and Nutrition Service (U.S. Department of Agriculture): Data & Research
https://www.fns.usda.gov/data-research

Google Public Data Explorer
https://www.google.com/publicdata/directory

HealthData.gov
https://www.healthdata.gov/

Inter-University Consortium for Political and Social Research (ICPSR)
https://www.icpsr.umich.edu/web/pages/

ICPSR (Open)
https://www.openicpsr.org/openicpsr/

Kids Count Data Center (Annie E. Casey Foundation)
https://datacenter.kidscount.org/

National Association of Social Workers (NASW): Research & Data
https://www.socialworkers.org/News/Research-Data

National Center for Health Statistics (Centers for Disease Control and Prevention)
http://www.cdc.gov/nchs/

National Center for Health Statistics: FastStats
https://www.cdc.gov/nchs/fastats/default.htm

National Neighborhood Indicators Partnership: Data Sources
https://www.neighborhoodindicators.org/data-tech/sources

National Prevention Information Network (Centers for Disease Control and Prevention)
https://npin.cdc.gov/

National Criminal Justice Reference Service (NCJRS) Office of Justice Programs, U.S. Department of Justice
https://www.ojp.gov/ncjrs/virtual-library

Occupational Outlook Handbook: Social Workers
https://www.bls.gov/ooh/community-and-social-service/social-workers.htm

Organization for Economic Cooperation and Development (OECD): Statistics
https://stats.oecd.org/

UNdata
http://data.un.org/

U.S. Bureau of Labor Statistics: Databases, Tables & Calculations by Subject
https://www.bls.gov/data/

U.S. Census Bureau: Explore Census Data
https://data.census.gov/cedsci/

U.S. Department of Education: Data & Statistics
https://www2.ed.gov/rschstat/landing.jhtml

U.S. Department of Health & Human Services. Substance Abuse and Mental Health Administration (SAMSHA): Data and Dissemination
https://www.samhsa.gov/data/

The World Bank: Data Catalog
https://datacatalog.worldbank.org/home

E. Associations and Organizations

American Association of People with Disabilities (AAPD)
https://www.aapd.com/

American Association of Retired Persons (AARP)
https://www.aarp.org/

Aging Life Care Association
https://www.aginglifecare.org/

Alcoholics Anonymous
https://www.aa.org/

Alliance for Aging Research
https://www.agingresearch.org/

American Association on Intellectual and Developmental Disabilities
https://www.aaidd.org/

American Council of the Blind
https://www.acb.org/

American Geriatrics Society
https://www.americangeriatrics.org/

American Health Care Association and the National Center for Assisted Living (AHCA/NCAL)
https://www.ahcancal.org/

American Society of Addiction Medicine
https://www.asam.org/

American Society on Aging
https://www.asaging.org/

American Public Human Services Association (APHSA)
https://aphsa.org/

Battered Women's Justice Project
https://www.bwjp.org/

Canadian Society for Spirituality & Social Work
https://www.spiritualityandsocialwork.ca/

Caregiver Action Network (National Family Caregivers Association)
https://www.caregiveraction.org/

Center for Effective Public Policy
https://cepp.com/

CHANGE: Sexual & Reproductive Health & Rights for All
https://srhrforall.org/

CLASP: The Center for Law and Social Policy
https://www.clasp.org/

Children's Defense Fund
http://www.childrensdefense.org/
Coalition Against Trafficking in Women
https://catwinternational.org/
Child Welfare League of America (CWLA)
http://www.cwla.org/
Directory of Accredited Programs (Council on Social
Work Education)
https://www.cswe.org/accreditation/directory/
Disability Rights Education & Defense Fund
https://dredf.org/
Disability Social History Project
https://disabilityhistory.org/
Everytown for Gun Safety
https://www.everytown.org/
Evident Change
https://www.evidentchange.org/
Family Caregiver Alliance
https://www.caregiver.org/
Feeding America
https://www.feedingamerica.org/
The Gerontological Society of America
https://www.geron.org/
The Grantsmanship Center
https://www.tgci.com/
Human Rights Campaign
https://www.hrc.org/
Human Rights Watch
https://www.hrw.org/
Human Trafficking Search
https://humantraffickingsearch.org/
The Hunger Project
https://thp.org/
INCITE!
https://incite-national.org/
Institute for Women's Policy Research
https://iwpr.org/
Institute on Violence Abuse and Trauma
https://www.ivatcenters.org/
International Child Resource Institute
https://www.icrichild.org/
International Society for Prevention of Child Abuse
and Neglect
https://www.ispcan.org/
Joyful Heart Foundation
https://www.joyfulheartfoundation.org/
Justice in Aging: Fighting Senior Poverty Through Law
https://justiceinaging.org/
Learning for Justice
https://www.learningforjustice.org/
Mental Health America
https://www.mhanational.org/

Narcotics Anonymous World Services (NA)
https://na.org/
National Association for the Advancement of Colored
Persons (NAACP)
https://naacp.org/
National Association for Alcoholism and Drug Abuse
Counselors (NAADAC)
https://www.naadac.org/
National Alliance on Mental Illness (NAMI)
https://www.nami.org/
National Association of State Units on Aging (NASUA)
https://nasua.org/
National Association for Home Care & Hospice
https://www.nahc.org/
National Center for Children in Poverty (Bank Street
Graduate School of Education)
https://www.nccp.org/
National Center for Public Policy Research
https://nationalcenter.org/
National Center for School Safety
https://www.nc2s.org/
National Center for Victims of Crime
https://victimsofcrime.org/
National Center for Youth Development
https://www.nationalyouthdevelopment.org/
National Center on Deaf-Blindness
https://www.nationaldb.org/
National Children's Alliance
https://www.nationalchildrensalliance.org/
National Clearinghouse for the Defense of Battered
Women
https://www.ncdbw.org/
National Clearinghouse on Abuse in Later Life
(NCALL)
https://www.ncall.us/
National Coalition Against Domestic Violence
https://ncadv.org/
National Coalition for the Homeless
https://nationalhomeless.org/
National Committee to Preserve Social Security and
Medicare
https://www.ncpssm.org/
National Council on Child Abuse and Family Violence
https://www.preventfamilyviolence.org/
National Council on Family Relations
https://www.ncfr.org/
National Council on Independent Living
https://ncil.org/
National Council on Aging
https://www.ncoa.org/
National Crime Prevention Council
https://www.ncpc.org/
National Domestic Violence Hotline
https://www.thehotline.org/

National Federation of the Blind
   https://nfb.org/
National Hispanic Council on Aging (NHCOA)
   https://nhcoa.org/
National Indian Council on Aging (NICOA)
   https://www.nicoa.org/
National LGBTQ Task Force (Lesbian, Gay, Bisexual,
   Transgender, Queer)
   https://www.thetaskforce.org/
National Low Income Housing Coalition
   http://www.nlihc.org/
National Organization on Disability
   https://www.nod.org/
National Rehabilitation Information Center
   https://www.naric.com/
National Resource Center on Children and Families of
   the Incarcerated
   https://nrccfi.camden.rutgers.edu/
National Resource Center on Domestic Violence
   https://www.nrcdv.org/
National Sexual Violence Resource Center
   https://www.nsvrc.org/
National Hospice and Palliative Care Organization
   (NHPCO)
   https://www.nhpco.org/
North American Council on Adoptable Children
   https://nacac.org/
Office on Violence Against Women (The United States
   Department of Justice)
   https://catwinternational.org/
OutRight Action International
   https://outrightinternational.org/
Partnership Against Domestic Violence (PADV)
   https://www.padv.org/
Parents, Families, and friends of Lesbians And Gays
   (PFLAG)
   https://pflag.org/
Planned Parenthood
   https://www.plannedparenthood.org/

Prevent Child Abuse America
   https://preventchildabuse.org/
Prevention Institute
   https://www.preventioninstitute.org/
Public Citizen
   https://www.citizen.org/
Rape, Abuse & Incest National Network (RAINN)
   https://www.rainn.org/
SeniorNet
   https://seniornet.org/
Shriver Center on Poverty Law
   https://www.povertylaw.org/
Southern Poverty Law Center
   https://www.splcenter.org/
Spaulding for Children
   https://spaulding.org/
UN Women
   https://www.unwomen.org/en
United Nations Children's Fund (UNICEF)
   https://www.unicef.org/
United Nations
   https://www.un.org/en/
Urban Institute
   https://www.urban.org/
Violence Policy Center
   https://vpc.org/
VolunteerMatch
   https://www.volunteermatch.org/
Volunteers of America
   https://www.voa.org/
Women's International League for Peace and Freedom
   https://www.wilpf.org/
World Childhood Foundation USA
   https://www.childhood-usa.org/
World Health Organization
   https://www.who.int/en/
World Institute on Disability
   https://wid.org/
World Resources Institute
   https://www.wri.org/

F. United States: Federal, State, Local, and Tribal Government Websites

Federal Government Websites of Relevance to Social Work

AboutFace: National Center for PTSD
   https://www.ptsd.va.gov/apps/aboutface/
   index.html
Americans with Disabilities Act (ADA) Information
   and Technical Assistance
   https://www.ada.gov/

Administration for Children & Families
   https://www.acf.hhs.gov/
Administration for Community Living
   https://acl.gov/
Administration for Native Americans
   https://www.acf.hhs.gov/ana

Agency for Healthcare Research and Quality
https://www.ahrq.gov/
AMBER Alert (America's Missing: Broadcast Emergency Response)
https://amberalert.ojp.gov/
AmeriCorps
https://americorps.gov/
Bureau of Justice Statistics
https://bjs.ojp.gov/
Center for Nutrition Policy and Promotion
https://www.fns.usda.gov/cnpp
Centers for Disease Control and Prevention
https://www.cdc.gov/
Centers for Medicare & Medicaid Services
https://www.cms.gov/
Child Welfare Information Gateway
https://www.childwelfare.gov/
Children's Bureau (Administration for Children & Families)
https://www.acf.hhs.gov/cb
ChildStats.gov
https://www.childstats.gov/
COVID-19
https://www.cdc.gov/coronavirus/2019-ncov/
DisasterAssistance.gov
https://www.disasterassistance.gov/
Elder Justice Initiative
https://www.justice.gov/elderjustice
Eldercare Locator
https://eldercare.acl.gov/Public/Index.aspx
Education Resources Information (ERIC)
https://eric.ed.gov/
Explore Census Data
https://data.census.gov/cedsci/
Federal Bureau of Prisons
https://www.bop.gov/
Federal Emergency Management Agency (FEMA)
https://www.fema.gov/
Food and Nutrition Service
https://www.fns.usda.gov/
Genetic and Rare Diseases Information Center
https://rarediseases.info.nih.gov/
girlshealth.gov
https://www.girlshealth.gov/
Health Resources & Services Administration
https://www.hrsa.gov/
Health.gov (Office of Disease Prevention and Health Promotion)
https://health.gov/
HealthCare.gov
https://www.healthcare.gov/
Healthy People 2030
https://health.gov/healthypeople

Health and Human Services (HHS) (U.S. Department of Health & Human Services)
https://www.hhs.gov/
Human Immunodeficiency Virus (HIV)
https://www.hiv.gov/
HIVinfo.NIH.gov
https://hivinfo.nih.gov/
Housing and Urban Development (HUD) (U.S. Department of Housing and Urban Development)
https://www.huduser.gov/portal/home.html
Individuals with Disabilities Education Act (IDEA)
https://sites.ed.gov/idea/
Immigrant and Employee Rights Section
https://www.justice.gov/crt/immigrant-and-employee-rights-section
Indian Affairs
https://www.bia.gov/
Indian Health Service
https://www.ihs.gov/
Institute of Education Sciences
https://ies.ed.gov/
InsureKidsNow.gov
https://www.insurekidsnow.gov/
Job Corps
https://www.jobcorps.gov/
Library of Congress
https://www.loc.gov/
Maternal & Child Health Bureau
https://mchb.hrsa.gov/
Medicare.gov
https://www.medicare.gov/
MedlinePlus: Trusted Health Information for You
https://medlineplus.gov/
Missing and Murdered Indigenous People
https://www.bia.gov/service/mmu
Morbidity and Mortality Weekly Report
https://www.cdc.gov/mmwr/publications/index.html
National Center for Education Statistics
https://nces.ed.gov/
National Center for Health Statistics
https://www.cdc.gov/nchs/
National Center for Homeless Education
https://nche.ed.gov/
National Center on Law & Elder Rights
https://ncler.acl.gov/
National Clearinghouse for English Language Acquisition
https://www.ncela.ed.gov/
National Clearinghouse of Rehabilitation Training Materials
https://ncrtm.ed.gov/
National Council on Disability
https://ncd.gov/

National Center on Elder Abuse
https://ncea.acl.gov/

National Clearinghouse on Homeless Youth & Families
https://rhyclearinghouse.acf.hhs.gov/

National Criminal Justice Reference Service
https://www.ojp.gov/ncjrs

National Data Archive on Child Abuse and Neglect
https://www.ndacan.acf.hhs.gov/

National Foster Care & Adoption Directory Search
https://www.childwelfare.gov/nfcad/

National Gang Center
https://nationalgangcenter.ojp.gov/

National Institute for Occupational Safety and Health
https://www.cdc.gov/niosh/

National Institute of Corrections
https://nicic.gov/

National Institute of Justice
https://nij.ojp.gov/

National Institute of Mental Health
https://www.nimh.nih.gov/

National Institute of Neurological Disorders and Stroke
https://www.ninds.nih.gov/

National Institute on Aging
https://www.nia.nih.gov/

National Institute on Deafness and Other Communication Disorders
https://www.nidcd.nih.gov/

National Institute on Drug Abuse
https://nida.nih.gov/

National Institutes of Health
https://www.nih.gov/

National Library of Medicine
https://www.nlm.nih.gov/

National Library Service for the Blind and Print Disabled
https://www.loc.gov/nls/

National Prevention Information Network
https://npin.cdc.gov/

Eunice Kennedy Shriver National Institute of Child Health and Human Development (NICHD)
https://www.nichd.nih.gov/

National Institute on Drug Abuse for Teens (NIDA)
https://teens.drugabuse.gov/

Nutrition.gov
https://www.nutrition.gov/

Occupational Outlook Handbook
https://www.bls.gov/ooh/

Occupational Safety and Health Administration (OSHA)
https://www.osha.gov/

Office of Career, Technical, and Adult Education
https://www2.ed.gov/about/offices/list/ovae/index.html

Office of Disability Employment Policy
https://www.dol.gov/agencies/odep

Office of Elementary & Secondary Education
https://oese.ed.gov/

Office of Juvenile Justice and Delinquency Prevention (OJJDP)
https://ojjdp.ojp.gov/

Office of Minority Health
https://minorityhealth.hhs.gov/

Office of Minority Health Resource Center Online Catalog
https://1455.sydneyplus.com/final/Portal.aspx

Office of Population Affairs
https://opa.hhs.gov/

Office of Refugee Resettlement
https://www.acf.hhs.gov/orr

Office of Special Education and Rehabilitation Services
https://www2.ed.gov/about/offices/list/osers/index.html

Office on Violence Against Women
https://www.justice.gov/ovw

Office on Women's Health
https://www.womenshealth.gov/

Post Traumatic Stress Disorder (PTSD) publications database
https://www.ptsd.va.gov/ptsdpubs/search_ptsdpubs.asp

Public and Indian Housing
https://www.hud.gov/program_offices/public_indian_housing

PubMed, National Library of Medicine. National Center for Biotechnology Information
https://pubmed.ncbi.nlm.nih.gov/

Substance Abuse and Mental Health Services Administration (SAMHSA)
https://www.samhsa.gov/

Smokefree.gov
https://smokefree.gov/

Smoking & Tobacco Use
https://www.cdc.gov/tobacco/

Statistical Abstract of the United States
https://catalog.data.gov/dataset/statistical-abstract-of-the-united-states

StopBullying.gov
https://www.stopbullying.gov/

Supreme Court of the United States
https://www.supremecourt.gov/

United States House of Representatives
https://www.house.gov/

United States Institute of Peace
https://www.usip.org/

United States Interagency Council on Homelessness
https://www.usich.gov/

United States Mission to the United Nations
https://usun.usmission.gov/
United States Parole Commission
https://www.justice.gov/uspc
United States Senate
https://www.senate.gov/
United States Social Security Administration
https://www.ssa.gov/
U.S. Access Board
https://www.access-board.gov/
U.S. Bureau of Labor Statistics
https://stats.bls.gov/
U.S. Census Bureau
https://www.census.gov/
U.S. Census Bureau Index A–Z
https://www.census.gov/about/index.html
U.S. Citizenship and Immigration Service
https://www.uscis.gov/
U.S. Department of Education
https://www.ed.gov/
U.S. Department of Health and Human Services
See HHS.gov
U.S. Department of Housing and Urban Development
https://www.hud.gov/

U.S. Department of Justice
https://www.justice.gov/
U.S. Department of Labor
https://www.dol.gov/
U.S. Food & Drug Administration
https://www.fda.gov/
U.S. Government Bookstore
https://bookstore.gpo.gov/
USA.gov
https://www.usa.gov/
Veterans Affairs (VA) (U.S. Department of Veterans' Affairs)
https://www.va.gov/
Vaccines & Immunizations
https://www.cdc.gov/vaccines/
Veterans' Employment and Training Service
https://www.dol.gov/agencies/vets
The White House
https://www.whitehouse.gov/
Women's Bureau
https://www.dol.gov/agencies/wb
Youth.gov
https://youth.gov/

State, Local, and Tribal Government Websites of Relevance to Social Work

https://www.usa.gov/state-tribal-governments
This is a great resource for the identification of federal, state, local, and tribal government websites.

G. Current Social Work Journals

To determine if your library provides online full-text access to and/or has any print holdings of the following social work-related journals, perform a journal title search from your *Library Catalog* or *Library One Search*. You will need to learn how to do this type of research because very few journal article indexes or research databases are comprised entirely of full-text articles. Most journal indexes offer full-text for some journal titles (as arranged by the journal publisher and the database provider) and the percentage of journals in full-text format can vary from almost zero (citation-only indexes) to near complete full-text (JSTOR).

Most American academic libraries provide full-text access to journal titles either through agreements with individual publishers or by licensing journal indexes/databases that contain full-text articles. Library catalogs typically provide within the journal title's catalog record hyperlink(s) when full-text is available (noting volumes and issues, available years, databases, or publisher names). And the *Library One Search* tool generally provides a "Journal Search" (by title or ISSN, as you can see below) for electronic and print journals, as well as a subject-based browsable directory of all electronic journals. If you are unsure if your library has access to specific journal titles, try the above recommendations, or contact your *Ask a Librarian* service.

To briefly return to the idea of Library of Congress Subject Headings (LCSHs), a good number of the below titles will be classified as either:

* Social Service—Periodicals

* Social Service—United States—Periodicals

ISSN: International Standard Serial Number

See "What is an ISSN?":
https://www.issn.org/understanding-the-issn/what-is-an-issn/

If you are interested in learning more about a particular journal, check to see if your library licenses the *Ulrichsweb*™ database:
https://about.proquest.com/en/products-services/Ulrichsweb.

Alphabetical List of Active Social Work Journals

Sample:

ISSN	Journal Title (Year Publication Began–) Homepage for Journal (online)
1360-0443	*Addiction* (1993–) https://onlinelibrary.wiley.com/journal/13600443
2330-314X	*Administration in Social Work* (1977–) https://www.tandfonline.com/toc/wasw21/current
1740-469X	*Adoption & Fostering* (1976–) https://us.sagepub.com/en-us/nam/journal/adoption-fostering
2331-4125	*Advances in Social Work* (2000–) https://journals.iupui.edu/index.php/advancesinsocialwork All content is open access.
1552-3020	*AFFILIA: Journal of Women & Social Work* (1986–) https://us.sagepub.com/en-us/nam/journal/affilia
1544-4538	*Alcoholism Treatment Quarterly* (1984–) https://www.tandfonline.com/loi/watq20/current
1573-2770	*American Journal of Community Psychology* (1973–) https://onlinelibrary.wiley.com/journal/15732770
1447-0748	*Australian Social Work* (1971–) https://www.tandfonline.com/loi/rasw20
1873-622X	*Behaviour Research and Therapy* (1963–) http://www.elsevier.com/locate/brat/
1468-263X	*The British Journal of Social Work* (1971–) https://academic.oup.com/bjsw

1873-7757	*Child Abuse & Neglect* (1977–) https://www.journals.elsevier.com/child-abuse-and-neglect
1573-2797	*Child & Adolescent Social Work Journal* (1984–) https://www.springer.com/journal/10560
1365-2206	*Child & Family Social Work* (1996–) https://onlinelibrary.wiley.com/journal/13652206
1552-6119	*Child Maltreatment* (1996–) https://journals.sagepub.com/home/cmxa
0009-4021	*Child Welfare* (1948–) https://www.cwla.org/child-welfare-journal/
1545-682X	*Children & Schools* (2000–) https://naswpress.org/content/1406/children-schools https://academic.oup.com/cs
1873-7765	*Children and Youth Services Review* (1979–) https://www.journals.elsevier.com/children-and-youth-services-review
1573-3343	*Clinical Social Work Journal* (1973–) https://www.springer.com/journal/10615
1469-3615	*Community, Work & Family* (1998–) https://www.tandfonline.com/loi/ccwf20
2049-8675	*Critical and Racial Social Work* (2013–) https://policy.bristoluniversitypress.co.uk/journals/critical-and-radical-social-work
1468-2664	*European Journal of Social Work* (1998–) https://www.tandfonline.com/journals/cesw20

1945-1350   *Families in Society* (1990–)
https://alliance1.org/web/resources/
families-society/web/resources/pubs/
families-society-online.aspx

1741-3729   *Family Relations* (1952–)
https://onlinelibrary.wiley.com/jour-
nal/17413729

1758-5341   *The Gerontologist* (1961–)
https://gerontologist.gerontologyjour-
nals.org/

1365-2524   *Health and Social Care in the Community*
(1993–)
https://onlinelibrary.wiley.com/jour-
nal/13652524

1545-6854   *Health & Social Work* (1976–)
https://naswpress.org/content/1410/
health-social-work
https://academic.oup.com/hsw

1468-2397   *International Journal of Social Welfare*
(1999–)
https://onlinelibrary.wiley.com/jour-
nal/14682397

1461-7234   *International Social Work* (1958–)
https://journals.sagepub.com/home/
isw

1095-9254   *Journal of Adolescence* (1978–)
https://onlinelibrary.wiley.com/jour-
nal/10959254

1547-0679   *Journal of Child Sexual Abuse* (1992–)
https://www.tandfonline.com/loi/
wcsa20

1099-1298   *Journal of Community & Applied Social
Psychology*
https://onlinelibrary.wiley.com/jour-
nal/10991298

1520-6629   *Journal of Community Psychology* (1973–)
https://onlinelibrary.wiley.com/jour-
nal/15206629

1531-3212   *Journal of Ethnic and Cultural Diversity in
Social Work* (2000–)
https://www-tandfonline-com.
ezproxy1.lib.asu.edu/loi/wecd20

1540-4072   *Journal of Family Social Work* (1995–)
https://www.tandfonline.com/loi/
wfsw20

1540-4048   *Journal of Gerontological Social Work*
(1978–)
https://www.tandfonline.com/loi/
wger20

1049-2089   *Journal of Health Care for the Poor and
Underserved* (1990–)
https://www.press.jhu.edu/journals/
journal-health-care-poor-and-under-
served

1540-3602   *Journal of Homosexuality* (1974–)
https://www.tandfonline.com/loi/
wjhm20

1540-3556   *Journal of Human Behavior in the Social
Environment* (1998–)
https://www.tandfonline.com/loi/
whum20

1532-0863   *The Journal of Nephrology Social Work*
(1996–)
All content is open access.
https://www.kidney.org/profession-
als/CNSW/JNSWOnline

1540-7616   *Journal of Progressive Human Services*
(1990–)
https://www.tandfonline.com/loi/
wphs20

1542-6440   *Journal of Religion and Spirituality in
Social Work* (2004–)
https://www.tandfonline.com/loi/
wrsp20

1469-7823   *Journal of Social Policy* (1972–)
https://www.cambridge.org/core/jour-
nals/journal-of-social-policy

1540-7314   *Journal of Social Service Research* (1977–)
https://www.tandfonline.com/loi/
wssr20

1043-7797   *Journal of Social Work Education* (1985–)
https://www.cswe.org/Publications/
Journal-of-Social-Work-Education

1465-3885   *Journal of Social Work Practice* (1983–)
https://www.tandfonline.com/loi/
cjsw20

1533-2578   *Journal of Social Work Practice in the
Addictions* (2001–)
https://www.tandfonline.com/loi/
wswp20

1949-7652   *Journal of Sociology and Social Welfare*
(1973–)
https://wmich.edu/socialworkjournal
All but most recent two years is open
access content.

1540-7349   *Journal of Teaching in Social Work* (1987–)
https://www.tandfonline.com/loi/
wtsw20

1522-8991   *Journal of Technology in Human Services*
(1999–)
https://www.tandfonline.com/loi/
wths20

1948-822X   *Journal of the Society for Social Work and
Research* (2010–)
https://www.journals.uchicago.edu/
loi/jsswr

1742-4909   *Practice: Social Work in Action* (1987–)
https://www.tandfonline.com/loi/
cpra20

1522-9033   *Psychoanalytic Social Work*
https://www.tandfonline.com/loi/wpsw20

1741-3117   *Qualitative Social Work* (2002–)
https://journals.sagepub.com/home/qsw

1552-7581   *Research on Social Work Practice* (1991–)
https://journals.sagepub.com/home/rsw

1553-0426   *Smith College Studies in Social Work* (1930–)
https://www.tandfonline.com/loi/wscs20

1573-0921   *Social Indicators Research* (1974–)
https://www.springer.com/journal/11205

1537-5404   *Social Service Review* (1927–)
https://www.journals.uchicago.edu/loi/ssr

1545-6846   *Social Work* (1956–)
https://naswpress.org/content/1405/social-work
https://academic.oup.com/sw

1070-5317   *Social Work Abstracts* (1994–)
https://naswpress.org/product/53644
https://www.ebsco.com/products/research-databases/social-work-abstracts

1944-7779   *Social Work and Christianity* (1979–)
https://www.nacsw.org/publications/journal-swc/

1470-1227   *Social Work Education* (1981–)
https://www.tandfonline.com/loi/cswe20

1541-034X   *Social Work in Health Care* (1975–)
https://www.tandfonline.com/loi/wshc20

1533-2993   *Social Work in Mental Health* (2002–)
https://www.tandfonline.com/loi/wsmh20

1545-6838   *Social Work Research* (1994–)
https://naswpress.org/content/1412/social-work-research
https://academic.oup.com/swr

1540-9481   *Social Work with Groups* (1978–)
https://www-tandfonline-com.ezproxy1.lib.asu.edu/loi/wswg20

H. Current Social Work Book Series by Publisher

These book series and their individual titles may be available in electronic and/or print format at your academic library. To identify if your library has a particular resource, perform a title or series title search of the *Library Catalog* or discovery service (often branded as *One Search* or *Library One Search*).

Routledge: Social Work and Social Policy Titles
https://www.routledge.com/search?sb=SCHS85

Contemporary Social Work Studies
https://www.routledge.com/Contemporary-Social-Work-Studies/book-series/ASHSER1007

Essential Clinical Social Work Series
https://www.springer.com/series/8115

Indigenous and Environmental Social Work
https://www.routledge.com/Indigenous-and-Environmental-Social-Work/book-series/IESW

New Directions in Social Work
https://www.routledge.com/New-Directions-in-Social-Work/book-series/NEWDIREC

Routledge Advances in Social Work
https://www.routledge.com/Routledge-Advances-in-Social-Work/book-series/RASW

Student Social Work
https://www.routledge.com/Student-Social-Work/book-series/SSW

SAGE Publishing: Social Work
https://us.sagepub.com/en-us/nam/collegesocialwork

Social Work Series, A-Zs
https://us.sagepub.com/en-us/nam/a-zs-in-social-work-series

Social Work in the New Century
https://us.sagepub.com/en-us/nam/series/Series1309

Springer
https://www.springer.com/us

Transforming Social Work Practice Series
https://us.sagepub.com/en-us/nam/transforming-social-work-practice-series

I. Recent Books on Social Work with Special Populations

Social workers and social work faculty have long been involved in the promotion of what is now commonly called justice, equity, diversity, and inclusion (JEDI) initiatives. These issues, as well as demands to have individual identities acknowledged and respected, have become increasingly commonplace in 21st-century America, and are important factors in how to approach social work with specific populations.

The following is a list of English-language books published since 2016 that focus on one or more of the Library of Congress Subject Headings related to social workers (see section J below).

Alldred, Pam, Fin Cullen, Kathy Edwards and Dana Fusco, eds. *The SAGE Handbook of Youth Work Practice.* London; Thousand Oaks, CA: SAGE Publications, 2018. xxxvi, 635 pages. ISBN: 9781473939523 (hardback). https://us.sagepub.com/en-us/nam/the-sage-handbook-of-youth-work-practice/book245391.

Arguëllo, Tyler M., ed. *Queer Social Work: Cases for LGBTQ+ Affirmative Practice.* New York, NY: Columbia University Press, 2019. xv, 223 pages. ISBN: 9780231194006 (hardback), 9780231194013 (paperback). https://cup.columbia.edu/book/queer-social-work/9780231194013.

Baldrige, Bianca J. *Reclaiming Community: Race and the Uncertain Future of Youth Work.* Stanford, CA: Stanford University Press, 2019. xii, 258 pages. ISBN: 9781503606975 (hardback), 9781503607897 (paperback). https://www.sup.org/books/title/?id=25699.

Baobaid, Mohammed and Lynda M. Ashbourne. *Enhancing Culturally Integrative Family Safety Response in Muslim Communities.* New York, NY: Routledge, Taylor & Francis Group, 2017. 119 pages. ISBN: 9781138948730 (hardback), 9781138948747 (paperback). https://www.routledge.com/Enhancing-Culturally-Integrative-Family-Safety-Response-in-Muslim-Communities/Baobaid-Ashbourne/p/book/9781138948747.

Bell, Melissa M. and Sherie L. Edenborn. *Reproductive Decision Making: Acting to Help Clients.* Washington, DC: NASW Press, 2018. viii, 147 pages. ISBN: 9780871015327 (paperback). https://naswpress.org/product/53467/reproductive-decision-making.

Betton, Victoria and James Woollard. *Teen Mental Health in an Online World: Supporting Young People Around Their Use of Social Media, Apps, Gaming, Texting and the Rest.* London, UK; Philadelphia, PA: Jessica Kingsley Publishers, 2019. 294 pages. ISBN: 9781785924682 (paperback). https://us.jkp.com/products/teen-mental-health-in-an-online-world.

Bland, Robert, Gabrielle Drake and John Drayton. *Social Work Practice in Mental Health: An Introduction.* 3rd ed. Abingdon, Oxon, UK; New York, NY: Routledge, Taylor & Francis Group, 2021. 294 pages. ISBN: 9780367710040 (hardback), 9781760529499 (paperback). https://www.routledge.com/Social-Work-Practice-in-Mental-Health-An-Introduction/Bland-Drake-Drayton/p/book/9781760529499.

Brottman, Mikita. *The Maximum Security Book Club: Reading Literature in a Men's Prison.* New York, NY: Harper, 2016. xxix, 230 pages. ISBN: 9780062384331 (hardback), 9780062384348 (paperback). https://www.harpercollins.com/products/the-maximum-security-book-club-mikita-brottman?variant=32122710392866.

Carlozzi, Alfred F. and Kurt T. Choate, eds. *Transgender and Gender Diverse Persons: A Handbook for Service Providers, Educators, and Families.* New York, NY: Routledge, Taylor & Francis Group, 2019. xvi, 222 pages. ISBN: 9780815382959 (hardback), 9780815382966 (paperback). https://www.routledge.com/Transgender-and-Gender-Diverse-Persons-A-Handbook-for-Service-Providers/Carlozzi-Choate/p/book/9780815382966.

Choudrey, Sabah. *Supporting Trans People of Colour: How to Make Your Practice Inclusive.* London, UK: Jessica Kingsley Publishers, 2022. 203 pages. ISBN: 9781787750593 (paperback). https://us.jkp.com/products/supporting-trans-people-of-colour

Church, Wesley T., II and David W. Springer, eds. *Serving the Stigmatized: Working Within the Incarcerated Environment.* New York, NY: Oxford University Press, 2018. xvii, 380 pages. ISBN: 9780190678753 (hardback). https://global.oup.com/academic/product/serving-the-stigmatized-9780190678753?cc=us&lang=en&.

Delgado, Melvin. *Social Work with Latinos: Social, Economic, Political, and Cultural Perspectives.* 2nd ed. New York, NY: Oxford University Press, 2017. x, 338 pages. ISBN: 9780190684792 (paperback). https://global.oup.com/academic/product/social-work-with-latinos-9780190684792?cc=us&lang=en&.

De Montigny, Gerald A. J. *Conversation Analysis for Social Work: Talking with Youth in Care.* Abingdon, Oxon, UK; New York, NY: Routledge, 2019. 283 pages. Routledge Advances in Social Work. ISBN: 9780815391807 (hardcover), 9780367585341 (paperback). https://www.routledge.com/Conversation-Analysis-for-Social-Work-Talking-with-Youth-in-Care/Montigny/p/book/9780367585341.

Denato, Michael P., ed. *Social Work Practice with the LGBTQ Community: The Intersection of History, Health, Mental Health, and Policy Factors.* New York, NY: Oxford University Press, 2018. xxvi, 570 pages. ISBN: 9780190612795 (paperback). https://global.oup.com/academic/product/social-work-practice-with-the-lgbtq-community-9780190612795?cc=us&lang=en&.

Dente, Claire, L., ed. *Social Work Practice with LGBTQIA Populations: An Interactional Perspective.* New York, NY; London, UK: Routledge, Taylor & Francis Group, 2019. xiv, 301 pages.9781138672420 (hardback), 9781138672437 (paperback). https://www.routledge.com/Social-Work-Practice-with-LGBTQIA-Populations-An-Interactional-Perspective/Dente/p/book/9781138672437.

Dettlaff, Alan J. and Rowena Fong, eds. *Immigrant and Refugee Children and Families: Culturally Responsive Practice.* New York, NY: Columbia University Press, 2016. xvii, 524 pages. ISBN: 9780231172844 (hardback), 9780231172851 (paperback). https://cup.columbia.edu/book/immigrant-and-refugee-children-and-families/9780231172851.

Dewey, Susan and Tonia St. Germain. *Women of the Street: How the Criminal Justice-Social Services Alliance Fails Women in Prostitution.* New York: New York University Press, 2016. ix, 275 pages.9781479854493 (hardback), 9781479841943 (paperback). https://nyupress.org/9781479841943/women-of-the-street.

Diaz, Mery F. and Benjamin Shepard, eds. *Narrating Practice with Children and Adolescents.* New York, NY: Columbia University Press, 2019. ix, 369 pages. ISBN: 9780231184786 (hardback), 9780231184793 (paperback). https://cup.columbia.edu/book/narrating-practice-with-children-and-adolescents/9780231184793.

Galambos, Colleen M., Roberta R. Greene, Nancy P. Kropf, and Harriet L. Cohen. *Foundations of Social Work Practice in the Field of Aging: A Competency-Based Approach.* 2nd ed. Washington, DC: NASW Press, 2018. viii, 287 pages. ISBN: 9780871015242 (paperback). https://naswpress.org/product/53470/foundations-of-social-work-practice-in-the-field-of-aging.

Glass, Cathy. *Finding Stevie: A Dark Secret: A Child in Crisis.* London: Harper Element, 2019. 306 pages. ISBN: 9780008324292. https://www.harpercollins.com/products/finding-stevie-a-dark-secret-a-child-in-crisis-cathy-glass?variant=32181573451810.

Grandin, Temple and Debra Moore. *Navigating Autism: 9 Mindsets for Helping Kids on the Spectrum.* New York, NY: W.W. Norton & Company, 2021. xiv, 362 pages. ISBN: 9780393714845 (paperback). https://wwnorton.com/books/9780393714845.

Gratton, Finn V. *Supporting Transgender Autistic Youth and Adults: A Guide for Professionals and Families.* London, UK; Philadelphia, PA: Jessica Kingsley Publishers 2020. 239 pages. ISBN: 9781785928031 (paperback). https://us.jkp.com/products/supporting-transgender-autistic-youth-and-adults.

Greene, Roberta R., Nicole M. Dubus, Michael A. Wright, Taunya S. Cole, Harriet L. Cohen, and Nancy A. Greene. *Social Work Practice with Older Adults: A Resilience-Enhancing Guide.* Washington, DC: NASW Press, 2021. iii, 174 pages. ISBN: 9780871015624 (paperback). https://naswpress.org/product/53656/social-work-practice-with-older-adults.

Hamilton, Tracy Brown. *Substance Abuse Counselors: A Practical Career Guide.* Lanham, MD: Rowman & Littlefield, 2021. xi, 93 pages. Practical Career Guides. ISBN: 9781538159224 (paperback). https://rowman.com/ISBN/9781538159231/Substance-Abuse-Counselors-A-Practical-Career-Guide.

Hitchcock, Laurel Iverson, Melanie Sage, and Nancy J. Smyth. *Teaching Social Work with Digital Technology.* Alexandria, VA: CSWE Press, 2019. x, 713 pages. ISBN: 9780872931954 (paperback). https://www.cswe.org/products/teaching-social-work-with-digital-technology/

Jaffe, Miriam, Megan Conti, Jeffrey Longhofer, and Jerry Floersch, eds. *The Social Work and LGBTQ Sexual Trauma Casebook: Phenomenological Perspectives.* New York, NY: Routledge, Taylor & Francis Group, 2020. xiv, 198 pages. 9781138351035 (hardback), 9781138351042 (paperback). https://www.routledge.com/The-Social-Work-and-LGBTQ-Sexual-Trauma-Casebook-Phenomenological-Perspectives/Jaffe-Conti-Longhofer-Floersch/p/book/9781138351042.

Johnston, Tim R. *Welcoming LGBT Residents: A Practical Guide for Senior Living Staff*. Abingdon, Oxon, UK; New York, NY: Routledge, Taylor & Francis Group, 2020. xi, 107 pages. ISBN: 9780367027322 (hardback), 9780367027346 (paperback). https://www.routledge.com/Welcoming-LGBT-Residents-A-Practical-Guide-for-Senior-Living-Staff/Johnston/p/book/9780367027346.

Joyner, Mildred C. and Angelo McClain. *Social Work Speaks: National Association of Social Workers Policy Statements 2021-2023*. 12th ed. Washington, DC: NASW Press, 2021. xii, 402 pages. ISBN:9780871015648 (spiral-bound). https://www.naswpress.org/product/53653/social-work-speaks-12th-edition.

Kaplan, Mary. *The Practice of Social Work with Older Adults: Insights and Opportunities for a Growing Profession*. Baltimore, MD: Health Professions Press, Inc., 2020. xi, 211 pages. ISBN: 9781938870866 (paperback). https://www.healthpropress.com/product/the-practice-of-social-work-with-older-adults.

Kattari, Shanna K., M. Killian Kinney, Leonardo Kattari and N. Eugene Walls, eds. *Social Work and Health Care Practice with Transgender and Nonbinary Individuals and Communities: Voices for Equity, Inclusion, and Resilience*. London, UK; New York: Routledge, Taylor & Francis Group, 2021. xxxix, 394 pages. ISBN: 9781138336216 (hardback), 9781138336223 (paperback). https://www.routledge.com/Social-Work-and-Health-Care-Practice-with-Transgender-and-Nonbinary-Individuals/Kattari-Kinney-Kattari-Walls/p/book/9781138336223.

Kourti, Marianthi, ed. *Working with Autistic Transgender and Non-Binary People*. Philadelphia, PA: Jessica Kingsley Publishers, 2021. 200 pages. ISBN: 9781787750227 (paperback). https://us.jkp.com/products/working-with-autistic-transgender-and-nonbinary-people.

Linton, Kristen Faye, Heidi Adams Rueda, and Lela Rankin Williams. *Disability, Intimacy, and Sexual Health: A Social Work Perspective*. Washington, DC: NASW Press, 2017. x, 133 pages. ISBN: 9780871015228 (paperback). https://naswpress.org/product/53472/disability-intimacy-and-sexual-health.

Lutnick, Alexandra. *Domestic Minor Sex Trafficking: Beyond Victims and Villains*. New York, NY: Columbia University Press, 2016. xiii, 181 pages. ISBN: 9780231169202 (hardback), 9780231169219 (paperback). https://cup.columbia.edu/book/domestic-minor-sex-trafficking/9780231169219.

Mallon, Gerald P. *Strategies for Child Welfare Professionals Working with Transgender and Gender Expansive Youth*. London, UK; Philadelphia, PA: Jessica Kingsley Publishers, 2021. 207 pages. ISBN: 9781787753884 (paperback). https://us.jkp.com/products/strategies-for-child-welfare-professionals-working-with-transgender-and-gender-expansive-youth.

Mallon, Gerald P., ed. *Social Work Practice with Lesbian, Gay, Bisexual, and Transgender People*. London, UK; New York, NY: Routledge, Taylor & Francis Group, 2018. xiii, 256 pages. ISBN: 9781138909885 (hardback), 9781138909892 (paperback). https://www.routledge.com/Social-Work-Practice-with-Lesbian-Gay-Bisexual-and-Transgender-People/Mallon/p/book/9781138909892.

Marsiglia, Flavio Francisco, Stephen S. Kulis and Stephanie Lechuga-Peña. *Diversity, Oppression, and Change: Culturally Grounded Social Work*. 3rd ed. New York: Oxford University Press, 2021. xxvi, 398 pages. ISBN: 9780190059507 (paperback). https://global.oup.com/academic/product/diversity-oppression-and-change-9780190059507?cc=us&lang=en&.

Marrs Fuchsel, Catherine Luz. *Yes, I can, (si, yo puedo): An Empowerment Program for Immigrant Latina Women in Group Settings*. New York, NY: Oxford University Press, 2017. xvi, 172 pages. ISBN: 9780190672829 (paperback). https://global.oup.com/academic/product/yes-i-can-s-yo-puedo-9780190672829?cc=us&lang=en&.

Matthew, Jonny. *Working with Troubled Children and Teenagers*. London, UK; Philadelphia, PA: Jessica Kingsley Publishers, 2018. 142 pages. ISBN: 9781785923937 (paperback). https://us.jkp.com/products/working-with-troubled-children-and-teenagers.

Nichols, Andrea J., Tonya Edmond, and Erin C. Heil, eds. *Social Work Practice with Survivors of Sex Trafficking and Commercial Sexual Exploitation*. New York: Columbia University Press, 2018. xvii, 423 pages.9780231180924 (hardback), 9780231180931 (paperback). https://cup.columbia.edu/book/social-work-practice-with-survivors-of-sex-trafficking-and-commercial-sexual-exploitation/9780231180931.

Nicotera, Nicole and Julie Anne Laser-Maira. *Innovative Skills to Support Well-Being and Resiliency in Youth*. New York, NY: Oxford University Press, 2017. xiii, 151 pages. ISBN: 9780190657109 (paperback). https://global.oup.com/academic/product/innovative-skills-to-support-well-being-and-resiliency-in-youth-9780190657109?cc=us&lang=en&.

Obeng, Cecilia Sem and Samuel Gyasi Obeng, eds. *Invisible Faces and Hidden Stories: Narratives of Vulnerable Populations and Their Caregivers*. New York: Berghahn Books, 2021. xi, 145 pages. Studies in Public and

Applied Anthropology, vol. 12. ISBN: 9781789209334 (hardback). https://www.berghahnbooks.com/title/ObengInvisible.

Payne, Malcolm. *Older Citizens and End-of-Life Care: Social Work Practice Strategies for Adults in Later Life.* London; New York: Routledge, Taylor & Francis Group, 2017. 187 pages. Routledge Key Themes in Health and Society. ISBN: 9781409440840 (hardback), 9781138288720 (paperback). https://www.routledge.com/Older-Citizens-and-End-of-Life-Care-Social-Work-Practice-Strategies-for/Payne/p/book/9781138288720.

Pitts, Byron. *Be the One: Six True Stories of Teens Overcoming Hardship with Hope.* New York, NY: Simon & Schuster BFYR, 2017. 119 pages. ISBN: 9781442483828 (hardback); 9781442483835 (paperback). https://www.simonandschuster.com/books/Be-the-One/Byron-Pitts/9781442483835.

Potocky, Miriam and Mitra Naseh. *Best Practices for Social Work with Refugees and Immigrants.* 2nd ed. New York: Columbia University Press, 2019. x, 426 pages. ISBN: 9780231181389 (hardback), 9780231181396 (paperback). https://cup.columbia.edu/book/best-practices-for-social-work-with-refugees-and-immigrants/9780231181396.

Ricciardelli, Lauren A., ed. *Social Work, Criminal Justice, and the Death Penalty.* New York, NY: Oxford University Press, 2020. xxviii, 281 pages. ISBN: 9780190937232 (hardback). https://global.oup.com/academic/product/social-work-criminal-justice-and-the-death-penalty-9780190937232?cc=us&lang=en&.

Richardson, Brent. *Working with Challenging Youth: Seven Guiding Principles.* 2nd ed. New York, NY: Routledge, 2016. xiii, 207 pages. ISBN: 9781138886452 (hardback), 9781138886445 (paperback). https://www.routledge.com/Working-with-Challenging-Youth-Seven-Guiding-Principles/Richardson/p/book/9781138886445.

Roberts, Dorothy. *Torn Apart: How the Child Welfare System Destroys Black Families--and How Abolition Can Build a Safer World.* New York, NY: Basic Books, 2022. ISBN: 9781541675445 (hardback). https://www.basicbooks.com/titles/dorothy-roberts/torn-apart/9781541675452.

Rymer, Sally and Valentina Cartei. *Working with Trans Survivors of Sexual Violence: A Guide for Professionals.* London, UK; Philadelphia, PA: Jessica Kingsley Publishers, 2019. 181 pages. ISBN: 9781785927607 (paperback). https://us.jkp.com/products/working-with-trans-survivors-of-sexual-violence.

Sanders, Sara, Stacey R. Kolomer, Cheryl Waites Spellman, and Victoria M. Rizzo, eds. *Gerontological Social Work and the Grand Challenges: Focusing on Policy and Practice.* Cham, Switzerland: Springer, 2019. xx, 186 pages. ISBN: 9783030263331 (hardback), 9783030263362 (paperback). https://link-springer-com.ezproxy1.lib.asu.edu/book/10.1007/978-3-030-26334-8.

Shelton, Jama and Gerald P. Mallon, eds. *Social Work Practice with Transgender and Gender Expansive Youth.* 3rd ed. New York, NY: Routledge, 2022. [xviii], 253 pages. ISBN: 9780367277499 (hardback), 9780367277482 (paperback). https://www.routledge.com/Social-Work-Practice-with-Transgender-and-Gender-Expansive-Youth/Shelton-Mallon/p/book/9780367277482.

Shelton, Kimber, Michelle King Lyn, and Mahlet Endale, eds. *A Handbook on Counseling African American Women: Psychological Symptoms, Treatments, and Case Studies.* Praeger, 2022. 325 pages. ISBN: 9781440875953 (hardback). https://www.abc-clio.com/products/a6308c/

Smith, Andrew. *Counselling Male Sexual Offenders: A Strengths-Focused Approach.* London, UK; New York, NY: Routledge, Taylor & Francis Group, 2018. 204 pages. ISBN: 9781138062856 (hardback), 9781138067653 (paperback). https://www.routledge.com/Counselling-Male-Sexual-Offenders-A-Strengths-Focused-Approach/Smith/p/book/9781138067653.

Spencer, Michael S., ed. *Microaggressions and Social Work Research, Practice, and Education.* London: Routledge, Taylor & Francis Group, 2019. xiv, 277 pages. ISBN: 9781138624719 (hardback), 9780367730079 (paperback). https://www.routledge.com/Microaggressions-and-Social-Work-Research-Practice-and-Education/Spencer/p/book/9781138624719.

Springer, David W. and Albert R. Roberts, eds. *Social Work in Juvenile and Criminal Justice Systems.* 4th ed. Springfield, IL: Charles C. Thomas, Publisher, Ltd., 2017. xxix, 387 pages. ISBN: 9780398091552 (paperback). https://www.ccthomas.com/details.cfm?P_ISBN13=9780398091552.

Sumser, Bridget, Meagan Lyon Leimena, and Terry Altilio, eds. *Palliative Care: A Guide for Health Social Workers.* New York, NY: Oxford University Press, 2019. xx, 285 pages. ISBN: 9780190669607 (paperback). https://global.oup.com/academic/product/palliative-care-9780190669607?cc=us&lang=en&.

Tascón, Sonia M. and Jim Ife, eds. *Disrupting Whiteness in Social Work.* London, UK; New York, NY: Routledge, Taylor & Francis Group, 2020. vii, 204 pages. ISBN: 9780367247508 (hardback), 9781032083612 (paperback). https://www.routledge.com/Disrupting-Whiteness-in-Social-Work/Tascon-Ife/p/book/9781032083612.

Ukockis, Gail. *Women's Issues for a New Generation: A Social Work Perspective.* Oxford, UK; New York, NY: Oxford University Press, 2016. xx, 467 pages. ISBN: 9780190239398 (paperback). https://global.oup.com/academic/product/womens-issues-for-a-new-generation-9780190239398?cc=us&lang=en&.

Ungar, Michael. *Working with Children and Youth with Complex Needs: 20 Skills to Build Resilience.* 2nd ed. New York, NY; London, UK: Routledge, Taylor & Francis Group, 2021. 233 pages. ISBN: 9780367355333 (hardback), 9780367355364 (paperback). https://www.routledge.com/Working-with-Children-and-Youth-with-Complex-Needs-20-Skills-to-Build-Resilience/Ungar/p/book/9780367355364.

Waegemakers Schiff, Jeannette. *Working with Homeless and Vulnerable People: Basic Skills and Practices.* Oxford; New York: Oxford University Press, 2016. xxiii, 440 pages.   https://global.oup.com/academic/product/working-with-homeless-and-vulnerable-people-9780190615574?cc=us&lang=en&

Waites, Matthew. *Supporting Young Transgender Men: A Guide for Professionals.* London, UK; Philadelphia, PA: Jessica Kingsley Publishers, 2018. 168 pages. ISBN: 9781785922947 (paperback). https://us.jkp.com/products/supporting-young-transgender-men.

Wong, Nga-Wing Anjela. *Opening Doors: Community Centers Connecting Working-Class Immigrant Families and Schools.* New York, NY: Peter Lang, 2018. xv, 160 pages. Social Justice Across Contexts in Education, vol. 7. ISBN: 9781433146855 (hardback), 9781433146862 (paperback). https://www.peterlang.com/document/1055967.

Zufferey, Carole. *Homelessness and Social Work: An Intersectional Approach.* Abingdon, Oxon, UK; New York, NY: Routledge, 2017. 160 pages. Routledge Advances in Social Work. ISBN: 9781138858770 (hardback), 9780367152192 (paperback). https://www.routledge.com/Homelessness-and-Social-Work-An-Intersectional-Approach/Zufferey/p/book/9780367152192.

J. Library of Congress Subject Headings (LCSHs)

When performing literature searches, beginning researchers almost exclusively rely on keyword searching. When using the library to identify available books, journals, and video recordings, please realize that you are not limited to just the default keyword search option. Compared to much of what is posted on the open web, records within library catalogs are highly organized and structured.

To optimize the relevancy of results from a library catalog search, you should review the results from your keyword searchso that you can identify the most relevant records. Research is a process. Do not expect to produce highly relevant results with your first few attempts at searching the library catalog. Instead, when you identify what you consider to be an especially relevant or useful result, scroll to the "Subjects" portion of its record, and note which subject headings have been assigned to describe its intellectual content. It is actually good practice to create a log of relevant subject headings. Just as you will be learning the terminology of the social work profession, it is likewise important to learn some of the terminology of academic libraries and library catalogs.

In addition to keyword searching, library catalogs provide field-specific search options including author, title, subject, etc. Make time to explore the different fields that comprise a library catalog record. Also, take advantage of the hyperlinked [Library of Congress] **Subject Headings** to connect to similarly focused resources through the controlled vocabulary, which is the backbone of a library catalog.

Library of Congress Classification Outline:
        https://www.loc.gov/aba/cataloging/classification/lcco/
Class H—Social Sciences
Subclass HV   = Social pathology. Social and public welfare. Criminology.
HV40-69   = Social service. Social work. Charity
        https://www.loc.gov/aba/cataloging/classification/lcco/lcco_h.pdf

With your list of Library of Congress Subject Headings (LCSHs), perform a subject search of the library catalog—instead of the keyword search—and you will normally retrieve better or more useful results.

Also, take advantage of the search limits offered by catalogs and library indexes. Common limits include limiting by language of publication, type of materials (book or video recording, etc.), and the range of publication years of interest to you.

A quick note about Library of Congress Subject Headings and social work: the phrase "social work" is not recognized as an official LCSH, but when you enter a subject search of "social work," most academic library catalogs will direct you to the preferred LCSH—which is "social service."

It is not uncommon for a 500-page book to receive just 4–5 subject headings. This is because the LCSHs are often very broad or general concepts—such as "social service." With searching experience, however, you will learn that part of the power of library catalogs comes from the use of what are called *subheadings*. Subheadings are indicated by double-dashes in catalogs, and in the below examples you can see that besides the general subject of "social services," there are also subject headings that point to the more focused and specific topics of "Social Service—Moral and Ethical Issues" and "Social Service—United States—History."

Examples of Library of Congress Subject Headings for Social Service

Social Service—Handbooks, manuals, etc.
Social Service—Library resources
Social Service—Literature
Social Service—Methodology
Social Service—Moral and Ethical Issues
Social Service—Psychological aspects
Social Service—Research

Social Service—Research Methodology
Social Service—Statistical Methods
Social Service—Teamwork
Social Service—United States
Social Service—United States—History
Social Service—Vocational Guidance

Examples of Library of Congress Subject Headings Focused on Social Work

African American social workers
Child welfare
Child welfare workers
Communication in social work
Confidential communications—Social case work
Evidence-based social work
Family social work
Gay social workers
Group social work
Hispanic American social workers
Male social workers

Medical social work
Medical social work—Handbooks, manuals, etc.
Medical social work—United States
Military social work
Police social work
Private practice social work
Psychiatric social work
Racism in social services
School social work
Schools of social work
Social advocacy

Social case work
Social case work reporting
Social case work with alcoholics
Social case work with children
Social case work with older people
Social case work with teenagers
Social case work with youth
Social group work
Social service—Research
Social service—Sociological aspects
Social service—Teamwork
Social service literature
Social work
Social work administration
Social work education
Social work with African American children
Social work with African American teenagers
Social work with African Americans
Social work with alcoholics
Social work with bisexuals
Social work with children
Social work with children with disabilities
Social work with children with mental disabilities
Social work with criminals
Social work with drug addicts
Social work with gay youth
Social work with gays
Social work with gender-nonconforming youth
Social work with Hispanic Americans
Social work with human trafficking victims
Social work with immigrants
Social work with Indians
Social work with Indigenous peoples
Social work with juvenile delinquents
Social work with lesbian youth
Social work with lesbians
Social work with men
Social work with minorities
Social work with older people
Social work with older sexual minorities
Social work with people with disabilities

Social work with people with mental disabilities
Social work with people with social disabilities
Social work with prostitutes
Social work with refugees
Social work with sex offenders
Social work with sexual minorities
Social work with sexual minority youth
Social work with single parents
Social work with single people
Social work with teenagers
Social work with the deaf
Social work with the homeless
Social work with the terminally ill
Social work with the unemployed
Social work with transgender people
Social work with transgender youth
Social work with widows
Social work with women
Social work with youth
Social workers—Attitudes
Social workers—Biography
Social workers—Certification
Social workers—In-service training
Social workers—Interviews
Social workers—Job stress
Social workers—Legal status, laws, etc.
Social workers—Mental health
Social workers—Professional ethics
Social workers—Professional relationships
Social workers—Psychology
Social workers—Religious life
Social workers—Supervision of
Social workers—Training of
Social workers—United States
Social workers—United States—Biography
Task-centered social work
Women in social work education
Women social workers
Women social workers—United States—Biography
Youth workers

Additional Related Library of Congress Subject Headings

Adolescence—Encyclopedias
Adolescent psychology—Encyclopedias
African Americans—Statistics
Aged—Economic conditions
Aged—Encyclopedias
Aged—Government Policy
Aging—United States—Encyclopedias

AIDS (Disease)—Encyclopedias
Alcoholism—Encyclopedias
American Sign Language—Dictionaries
Asian Americans—Statistics
Charities
Charities—United States
Child abuse—Dictionaries

Child development—Encyclopedias
Child psychology—Encyclopedias
Child sexual abuse
Child welfare
Child welfare workers
Children—Health and hygiene
Church charities
Church group work
Counseling
Demographic surveys
Deviant behavior—Encyclopedias
Disability studies—Handbooks, manuals, etc.
Drinking of alcoholic beverages—Encyclopedias
Drug abuse—Encyclopedias
Family—United States—Statistics
Gays—Bibliography
Gerontology—Encyclopedias
Health services administration
Helping behavior
Hispanic Americans—Statistics
Hispanic Americans—Economic conditions
Hospitals—After care
Hospitals—Case management services
Household Surveys—United States
Human Services—research
Indians of North America—Population
Indians of North America—Statistics
Interviewing in child abuse
Interviewing in social service
Lesbians—Bibliography
Medical care—Dictionaries
Minority aged—Care
Minority aged—Counseling of
Minority aged—Health and hygiene
Minority aged—Services for
Old age
Pacific Islander Americans—Statistics
People with disabilities—Rehabilitation
Psychiatry—Dictionaries
Public health
Public welfare
Retirees
Social history—Encyclopedias
Social problems
Social reformers
Social sciences

Social sciences—Dictionaries
Social sciences—Methodology
Social sciences—Research
Social sciences—Statistical methods
Social service—Dictionaries
Social service—Moral and ethical aspects
Social service—Research
Social service—Research—Methodology
Social service—United States
Social service—United States—Dictionaries
Social service—Vocational guidance—United
    States
Social Work with Narcotic Addicts
Social Work with the Aged
Social Workers
Social workers—Professional ethics
Social workers—United States
Social workers—United States—Statistics
Sociology
Sociology of disability
Spanish Americans—Statistics
Statistics—Methodology
Substance abuse—Encyclopedias
Transsexuals—Services for
United States—Economic conditions
United States—Politics and government
United States—Population—Statistics
United States—Social conditions—Encyclope-
    dias
United States—Social conditions—Statistics
United States—Social life and customs
United States—Social policy
United States—Statistics
United States—Statistics, Vital
United States Census—21st, 1990
United States Census—22nd, 2000
United States—Census
United States—Population
Violence—United States
Violence in the workplace
Violent crimes—United States
    Voluntary health agencies
Women—Crimes against
Women Social Workers
Youth—Services for

Appendix B

Useful Formulas

Mean

$$\bar{x} = \frac{\sum x_1}{N}$$ where $\sum$ = scores added together
X_1 = score for subjects
N = number of subjects

Median

Given an ordered list of n values, the median equals the value at position $\frac{(n+1)}{2}$. If n is odd, a single value occupies this position. If n is even, the median equals the mean of the two middle values.

Standard Deviation

$$S = \sqrt{\frac{\sum(x-\bar{x})}{n-1}}$$ where S = sample standard deviation
n = sample population
$\bar{x}$ = sample mean
x = total scores

Chi-Square

$$x^2 = \sum \frac{(O-E)^2}{E}$$ where x^2 = chi-square value
x = total scores
O = observed frequency
E = expected frequency
$\sum$ = sum of (for all cells)

$$E = \frac{(R)(C)}{(N)}$$ where E = Expected frequency in a particular cell
R = Total number in that cell's row
C = Total number in that cell's row
N = Total number of cases

Pearson r

$$r = \frac{e - \dfrac{(a)(b)}{N}}{N\left[e - \left(\dfrac{a^2}{N}\right)\right]\left[d - \left(\dfrac{b^2}{N}\right)\right]}$$

where r = correlation coefficient
a = sum of values of x
b = sum of values of y
c = sum of values of x^2
d = sum of values of y^2
e = sum of values of x and y
N = number of cases

t-test

$$t = \frac{Ma - Mb}{\sqrt{\left(\dfrac{(Sa)^2 + (Sb)^2}{Na + Nb - 2}\right)\left(\dfrac{Na + Nb}{(Na)(Nb)}\right)}}$$

where t = t value
Na = Number of cases in Group A
Nb = Number of cases in Group B
Sa = Sum of squares of raw scores in Group A
Sb = Sum of squares of raw scores in Group B

Appendix C

NASW Code of Ethics (2021) Section 5.02: Evaluation and Research

5.02 Evaluation and Research

(a) Social workers should monitor and evaluate policies, the implementation of programs, and practice interventions.

(b) Social workers should promote and facilitate evaluation and research to contribute to the development of knowledge.

(c) Social workers should critically examine and keep current with emerging knowledge relevant to social work and fully use evaluation and research evidence in their professional practice.

(d) Social workers engaged in evaluation or research should carefully consider possible consequences and should follow guidelines developed for the protection of evaluation and research participants. Appropriate institutional review boards should be consulted.

(e) Social workers engaged in evaluation or research should obtain voluntary and written informed consent from participants, when appropriate, without any implied or actual deprivation or penalty for refusal to participate; without undue inducement to participate; and with due regard for participants' well-being, privacy, and dignity. Informed consent should include information about the nature, extent, and duration of the participation requested and disclosure of the risks and benefits of participation in the research.

(f) When using electronic technology to facilitate evaluation or research, social workers should ensure that participants provide informed consent for the use of such technology. Social workers should assess whether participants are able to use the technology and, when appropriate, offer reasonable alternatives to participate in the evaluation or research.

(g) When evaluation or research participants are incapable of giving informed consent, social workers should provide an appropriate explanation to the participants, obtain the participants' assent to the extent they are able, and obtain written consent from an appropriate proxy.

(h) Social workers should never design or conduct evaluation or research that does not use consent procedures, such as certain forms of naturalistic observation and archival research, unless rigorous and responsible review of the research has found it to be justified because of its prospective scientific, educational, or applied value and unless equally effective alternative procedures that do not involve waiver of consent are not feasible.

(i) Social workers should inform participants of their right to withdraw from evaluation and research at any time without penalty.

(j) Social workers should take appropriate steps to ensure that participants in evaluation and research have access to appropriate supportive services.

(k) Social workers engaged in evaluation or research should protect participants from unwarranted physical or mental distress, harm, danger, or deprivation.

(l) Social workers engaged in the evaluation of services should discuss collected information only for professional purposes and only with people professionally concerned with this information.

(m) Social workers engaged in evaluation or research should ensure the anonymity or confidentiality of participants and of the data obtained from them. Social workers should inform participants of any limits of confidentiality, the measures that will be taken to ensure confidentiality, and when any records containing research data will be destroyed.

(n) Social workers who report evaluation and research results should protect participants' confidentiality by omitting identifying information unless proper consent has been obtained authorizing disclosure.

(o) Social workers should report evaluation and research findings accurately. They should not fabricate or falsify results and should take steps to correct any errors later found in published data using standard publication methods.

(p) Social workers engaged in evaluation or research should be alert to and avoid conflicts of interest and dual relationships with participants, should inform participants when a real or potential conflict of interest arises, and should take steps to resolve the issue in a manner that makes participants' interests primary.

(q) Social workers should educate themselves, their students, and their colleagues about responsible research practices.

Appendix D

Universal Declaration of Human Rights

The Universal Declaration of Human Rights (UDHR) is a milestone document in the history of human rights. Drafted by representatives with different legal and cultural backgrounds from all regions of the world, the Declaration was proclaimed by the United Nations General Assembly in Paris on 10 December 1948 (General Assembly resolution 217 A) as a common standard of achievements for all peoples and all nations. It sets out, for the first time, fundamental human rights to be universally protected and it has been translated into over 500 languages. The UDHR is widely recognized as having inspired, and paved the way for, the adoption of more than seventy human rights treaties, applied today on a permanent basis at global and regional levels (all containing references to it in their preambles).

Preamble

Whereas recognition of the inherent dignity and of the equal and inalienable rights of all members of the human family is the foundation of freedom, justice and peace in the world,

Whereas disregard and contempt for human rights have resulted in barbarous acts which have outraged the conscience of mankind, and the advent of a world in which human beings shall enjoy freedom of speech and belief and freedom from fear and want has been proclaimed as the highest aspiration of the common people,

Whereas it is essential, if man is not to be compelled to have recourse, as a last resort, to rebellion against tyranny and oppression, that human rights should be protected by the rule of law,

Whereas it is essential to promote the development of friendly relations between nations,

Whereas the peoples of the United Nations have in the Charter reaffirmed their faith in fundamental human rights, in the dignity and worth of the human person and in the equal rights of men and women and have determined to promote social progress and better standards of life in larger freedom,

Whereas Member States have pledged themselves to achieve, in co-operation with the United Nations, the promotion of universal respect for and observance of human rights and fundamental freedoms,

Whereas a common understanding of these rights and freedoms is of the greatest importance for the full realization of this pledge,

Now, therefore,

The General Assembly,

proclaims

this Universal Declaration of Human Rights

as a common standard of achievement for all peoples and all nations, to the end that every individual and every organ of society, keeping this Declaration constantly in mind, shall strive by teaching and education to promote respect for these rights and freedoms and by progressive measures, national and international, to secure their universal and effective recognition and observance, both among the peoples of Member States themselves and among the peoples of territories under their jurisdiction.

Article 1

All human beings are born free and equal in dignity and rights. They are endowed with reason and conscience and should act towards one another in a spirit of brotherhood.

Article 2

Everyone is entitled to all the rights and freedoms set forth in this Declaration, without distinction of any kind, such as race, colour, sex, language, religion, political or other opinion, national or social origin, property, birth or other status. Furthermore, no distinction shall be made on the basis of the political, jurisdictional or international status of the country or territory to which a person belongs, whether it be independent, trust, non-self-governing or under any other limitation of sovereignty.

Article 3

Everyone has the right to life, liberty and security of person.

Article 4

No one shall be held in slavery or servitude; slavery and the slave trade shall be prohibited in all their forms.

Article 5

No one shall be subjected to torture or to cruel, inhuman or degrading treatment or punishment.

Article 6

Everyone has the right to recognition everywhere as a person before the law.

Article 7

All are equal before the law and are entitled without any discrimination to equal protection of the law. All are entitled to equal protection against any discrimination in violation of this Declaration and against any incitement to such discrimination.

Article 8

Everyone has the right to an effective remedy by the competent national tribunals for acts violating the fundamental rights granted him by the constitution or by law.

Article 9

No one shall be subjected to arbitrary arrest, detention or exile.

Article 10

Everyone is entitled in full equality to a fair and public hearing by an independent and impartial tribunal, in the determination of his rights and obligations and of any criminal charge against him.

Article 11

1. Everyone charged with a penal offence has the right to be presumed innocent until proved guilty according to law in a public trial at which he has had all the guarantees necessary for his defence.
2. No one shall be held guilty of any penal offence on account of any act or omission which did not constitute a penal offence, under national or international law, at the time when it was committed. Nor shall a heavier penalty be imposed than the one that was applicable at the time the penal offence was committed.

Article 12

No one shall be subjected to arbitrary interference with his privacy, family, home or correspondence, nor to attacks upon his honour and reputation. Everyone has the right to the protection of the law against such interference or attacks.

Article 13

1. Everyone has the right to freedom of movement and residence within the borders of each state.
2. Everyone has the right to leave any country, including his own, and to return to his country.

Article 14

1. Everyone has the right to seek and to enjoy in other countries asylum from persecution.
2. This right may not be invoked in the case of prosecutions genuinely arising from non-political crimes or from acts contrary to the purposes and principles of the United Nations.

Article 15

1. Everyone has the right to a nationality.
2. No one shall be arbitrarily deprived of his nationality nor denied the right to change his nationality.

Article 16

1. Men and women of full age, without any limitation due to race, nationality or religion, have the right to marry and to found a family. They are entitled to equal rights as to marriage, during marriage and at its dissolution.
2. Marriage shall be entered into only with the free and full consent of the intending spouses.
3. The family is the natural and fundamental group unit of society and is entitled to protection by society and the State.

Article 17

1. Everyone has the right to own property alone as well as in association with others.

2. No one shall be arbitrarily deprived of his property.

Article 18

Everyone has the right to freedom of thought, conscience and religion; this right includes freedom to change his religion or belief, and freedom, either alone or in community with others and in public or private, to manifest his religion or belief in teaching, practice, worship and observance.

Article 19

Everyone has the right to freedom of opinion and expression; this right includes freedom to hold opinions without interference and to seek, receive and impart information and ideas through any media and regardless of frontiers.

Article 20

1. Everyone has the right to freedom of peaceful assembly and association.

2. No one may be compelled to belong to an association.

Article 21

1. Everyone has the right to take part in the government of his country, directly or through freely chosen representatives.

2. Everyone has the right of equal access to public service in his country.

3. The will of the people shall be the basis of the authority of government; this will shall be expressed in periodic and genuine elections which shall be by universal and equal suffrage and shall be held by secret vote or by equivalent free voting procedures.

Article 22

Everyone, as a member of society, has the right to social security and is entitled to realization, through national effort and international co-operation and in accordance with the organization and resources of each State, of the economic, social and cultural rights indispensable for his dignity and the free development of his personality.

Article 23

1. Everyone has the right to work, to free choice of employment, to just and favourable conditions of work and to protection against unemployment.

2. Everyone, without any discrimination, has the right to equal pay for equal work.

3. Everyone who works has the right to just and favourable remuneration ensuring for himself and his family an existence worthy of human dignity, and supplemented, if necessary, by other means of social protection.

4. Everyone has the right to form and to join trade unions for the protection of his interests.

Article 24

Everyone has the right to rest and leisure, including reasonable limitation of working hours and periodic holidays with pay.

Article 25

1. Everyone has the right to a standard of living adequate for the health and well-being of himself and of his family, including food, clothing, housing and medical care and necessary social services, and the right to security in the event of unemployment, sickness, disability, widowhood, old age or other lack of livelihood in circumstances beyond his control.

2. Motherhood and childhood are entitled to special care and assistance. All children, whether born in or out of wedlock, shall enjoy the same social protection.

Article 26

1. Everyone has the right to education. Education shall be free, at least in the elementary and fundamental stages. Elementary education shall be compulsory. Technical and professional education shall be made generally available and higher education shall be equally accessible to all on the basis of merit.

2. Education shall be directed to the full development of the human personality and to the strengthening of respect for human rights and fundamental freedoms. It shall promote understanding, tolerance and friendship among all nations, racial or religious groups, and shall further the activities of the United Nations for the maintenance of peace.

3. Parents have a prior right to choose the kind of education that shall be given to their children.

Article 27

1. Everyone has the right freely to participate in the cultural life of the community, to enjoy the arts and to share in scientific advancement and its benefits.

2. Everyone has the right to the protection of the moral and material interests resulting from any scientific, literary or artistic production of which he is the author.

Article 28

Everyone is entitled to a social and international order in which the rights and freedoms set forth in this Declaration can be fully realized.

Article 29

1. Everyone has duties to the community in which alone the free and full development of his personality is possible.

2. In the exercise of his rights and freedoms, everyone shall be subject only to such limitations as are determined by law solely for the purpose of securing due recognition and respect for the rights and freedoms of others and of meeting the just requirements of morality, public order and the general welfare in a democratic society.

3. These rights and freedoms may in no case be exercised contrary to the purposes and principles of the United Nations.

Article 30

Nothing in this Declaration may be interpreted as implying for any State, group or person any right to engage in any activity or to perform any act aimed at the destruction of any of the rights and freedoms set forth herein.

Glossary

AB design   A single-system design in which there is a comparison between the baseline (A) and an intervention period (B).

ABAB design   A single-system design that is also known as a withdrawal or reversal design where the AB design is duplicated in order to increase the validity of the results.

ABC design   A single-system design in which the baseline (A) is followed by one intervention period (B) and a second intervention period (C). Also known as successive intervention design.

Alternate form   A method of testing an instrument's reliability in which different but equivalent forms of the same test are administered to the same group of individuals, usually close in time, and then compared.

Alternative hypothesis   A means of validating findings when analyzing qualitative data (also referred to as a rival or alternative hypothesis).

Anonymity   A condition in which the researcher cannot identify a given response with a given respondent.

Applicability   Whether or not a measuring instrument is appropriate and suitable for a particular type of problem.

Applied research   Research that produces practical outcomes and is directed at solving problems encountered in social work practice.

Authority   Referring to outside sources of knowledge.

Autocorrelation   The relationship between the outcome or dependent variable scores in single-system studies.

Availability sampling (convenience sampling)   A nonprobability sampling method in which available or convenient elements are included in the sample.

Bar graph   A visual means of displaying data at the nominal level of measurement.

Baseline   Repeated measurement before the introduction of the intervention that allows the comparison of target behavior rates before and after the intervention.

Baseline comparison   A strategy for comparing the equivalency between experimental and comparison groups in which the comparison group is composed of cases handled prior to the introduction to the program.

Bivariate measure   A method of measuring the relationship between two variables.

Case studies   A description of the application of an intervention.

Causal flowcharts   A visual means of representing causal connections of qualitative data.

Causality   A principle that involves meeting three conditions: first, two factors are empirically related to one another; second, the cause precedes the effect in time; and third, the relationship between the factors cannot be explained by other factors.

Client satisfaction survey   A design used to ask clients how they experienced or perceived a program.

Clinical significance (practical significance)   Significance level that is achieved when the specified goal of the intervention has been reached.

Closed-ended question   Questions that provide respondents with a fixed set of alternatives from which they choose.

Cluster sampling   A form of probability sampling that involves randomly sampling a larger unit containing the elements of interest and then sampling from these larger units the elements to be included in the final sample.

Coding   A means of organizing and collecting information so that it can be entered into a computer.

Cohort groups   A strategy for increasing the equivalency between experimental and comparison groups in which the comparison groups move through an organization at the same time as those in the program being evaluated but do not receive program services.

Cohort studies   Cohort studies examine specific subgroups as they change over time.

Community forum   A public meeting or series of meetings where individuals are briefed on the issues and then asked for input—a form of purposive sampling.

Comparison groups   Subjects who receive another type of intervention or who receive no type of bona fide intervention and who have not been randomly assigned. Comparison groups can be used to increase the internal and external validity of group designs.

Confidence level   How often you would expect to find similar results if the research were repeated.

Confidentiality   A state in which the researcher knows the identity of the respondents and their associated responses but guarantees not to disclose this information.

Construct validity   A means of testing an instrument's validity; involves examining the extent to which an instrument measures a theoretical construct.

Contamination   The difficulty of distinguishing between the experimental and comparison groups, either due to contact between the subjects of each group or due to no clear distinction between the program experiences of the clients in each group.

Content analysis   A method of coding written communication to a systematic quantifiable form.

Content validity   A method of testing an instrument's validity that involves ensuring the content of the instrument corresponds to the concepts being measured.

Contingency table   A measure of association, also known as cross-tabulation.

Control group   Subjects who do not receive the intervention being evaluated and who have been randomly assigned.

Convenience sampling (availability sampling)   A nonprobability sampling method in which available or convenient elements are included in the sample.

Copyright   Laws that apply not only to published material but also to in-house reports.

Correlation   A measure of association used with interval- or ratio-level data.

Correlation coefficient   A statistic that measures the extent to which the comparisons are similar or not similar, related or not related.

Cost-benefit analysis   Program costs compared with the dollar value of the program results; a way of computing the ratio of costs to benefits.

Cost-effectiveness study   Program costs compared to some measure of program output; a way of calculating cost per unit.

Cover letter   Sent with a questionnaire to briefly describe the purpose of the study and the principle of confidentiality.

Criterion sampling   Selecting all cases that meet some criterion; a type of nonprobability sampling.

Criterion validity   The extent to which a correlation exists between the measuring instrument and another standard.

Cross-classification   A method of qualitative data analysis that creates categories by crossing one dimension or typology with another.

Cross-sectional design   A method of measuring behavior as it occurs at one point in time or over a relatively short period of time.

Cross-tabulation   A measure of association, also known as a contingency table.

Data (datum)   Information collected for research.

Deductive reasoning   A process of drawing conclusions from the general to the particular; opposite of the process of induction.

Dependent variable   The outcome variable that has been presumably affected by the independent variable.

Descriptive research   A process of recording and reporting phenomena; not primarily concerned with causes.

Descriptive statistics   A means of summarizing the characteristics of a sample or the relationship among the variables.

Developmental research (intervention research)   Research specifically focused on developing innovative interventions by actually using research to design the interventions, test their effectiveness, and modify them based on recommendations that emerge from testing.

Directional hypothesis (one-tailed hypothesis)   A hypothesis that specifies not only that there is an association between variables but also predicts whether the relationship is negative or positive.

Discontinuity   A difference in data levels between the baseline and intervention periods.

Discourse analysis   A way of understanding how the researcher's social context can influence how data are understood and analyzed.

Drifts   Trends that occur across the intervention and baseline periods.

Ecological fallacy   The danger of reaching conclusions in your study using a unit of analysis other than that used by the study.

Element   The item under study in the population and sample; in social work, a client system.

Emic   A system of organizing and developing categories of qualitative data that are derived from those being studied rather than constructed by the researcher.

Empiricism   Observation through use of the senses.

Ethnography   A method of describing a culture or society.

Ex post facto design ("after the fact")   Refers to designs in which subjects already possess the independent variable of interest before the study begins.

Expected frequencies   Cross-tabulations that are what one might expect to observe according to probability.

Experience   A form of knowledge that includes firsthand, personal participation in events.

Experimental designs   Group research designs that randomly assign participants to the control group and experimental group.

Experimental group   In a program evaluation, the group that receives the intervention being evaluated.

Explanatory research   Studies directed at providing explanations of events to identify causes.

Exploratory research   A form of research that generates initial insights into the nature of an issue and develops questions to be investigated by more extensive studies.

Exploratory single-system design   A design focused on assessing an intervention's impact on a target behavior.

External validity   The extent to which research results are generalizable to the wider population.

Feasibility studies (needs assessment)   Another term for a needs assessment.

Feedback   An important way of testing the validity of data from interpretive studies and making certain that the data are understandable to and relevant to the participants in the research.

Feminist research   An approach to research that argues that a relationship is formed between the researcher and participant, which results in the formation of a constructed reality between them.

Focus group   A group formed to help develop the research question, or as a form of non-probability sampling.

Formative program evaluation   An examination of the planning, development, and implementation of a program.

Frame elicitation   A means of framing questions to elicit from subjects what they include in a particular topic or category.

Frequency distribution   A description of the number of times the values of a variable occur in a sample.

Front-end analyses (needs assessment)   Another term for a needs assessment.

Generalist social work practice   A form of social work practice taught in B.S.W. programs that involves practice with different-size client systems and uses a number of different interventions and practice roles.

Generalization   The application of research findings to other situations.

Generalize   The ability to apply the findings gained from studying the sample to the population.

Goal attainment scales (GAS)   Scales used in single-system studies that reflect the achievement of outcomes; they both set client goals and assess whether the goals have been met.

Group design   The effect of a variable or variables on another variable or variables for a number of different client systems or elements.

History   A threat to the internal validity; those events that occur, other than the intervention, to affect the outcome.

History-treatment interaction   A threat to the external validity.

Human diversity   The whole spectrum of differences among people, including but not limited to gender, ethnicity, age, and sexual orientation.

Human subjects committees   Committees that review the ethical implications of research.

Hypothesis   A probability statement about the relationships among certain factors.

Independent variable   The presumed causal variable in a relationship.

Inductive reasoning   The use of observation to examine the particular and then develop a generalization to explain the relationship among many of the particulars; the opposite of deduction.

Inferential statistics   A means to determine whether an observed relationship is due to chance or in fact reflects a relationship among factors; allows us to generalize the findings to the wider population.

Information-rich sampling (purposive sampling)   Picking cases from which you can learn about the issues central to the research question—the sampling method of choice in interpretive studies.

Informed consent   Subjects' permission, obtained after fully informing potential participants of their research role and the consequences of their participation.

Institutional review boards   Boards that review the ethical implications of research being conducted at that institution.

Instrumentation   A threat to internal validity; the way in which the variables are measured may change when measures are taken more than once.

Internal validity   The extent to which the changes in the dependent variable(s) are a result of the introduction of the independent variable(s) rather than other factor(s).

Interpretism   An approach to science that emphasizes the subjective, descriptive, inductive, and qualitative aspects of inquiry, also known as the qualitative approach to research.

Interval measures Measures that classify observations into mutually exclusive categories in an inherent order and with equal space between the categories.

Intervention research (developmental research) Research specifically focused on developing innovative interventions by actually using research to design the interventions, test their effectiveness, and modify them based on recommendations that emerge from testing.

Intuition A form of insight not based on specialized training or reasoning.

Key informant sampling Picking someone in the community identified as an expert in the field of interest; a form of nonprobability sampling.

Level of measurement The extent to which a variable can be quantified and subsequently subjected to mathematical or statistical procedures.

Likert scale A common measurement scale consisting of a series of statements with five response alternatives.

Limited probability sample A sample whose characteristics are compared with the characteristics of a sample drawn from a larger population, allowing some tentative generalizations of the findings to be made.

Line graph A graph that uses a line to connect the data points.

Literature review A resource for consulting with the written material relevant to the research problem.

Logical analysis In qualitative data analysis, the process of looking at the relationships between the variables and concepts.

Longitudinal design A study that tracks behavior over a significant period of time.

Margin of error Measure of the precision the researcher needs.

Matching A strategy for increasing the equivalency of experimental and comparison groups; certain characteristics thought to be important in impacting outcomes are selected, and these characteristics are equally represented in each group.

Maturation A threat to internal validity; a change that is not a result of the intervention but of the subject's becoming more mature with the passage of time.

Mean A measure of central tendency; the result of adding all values of the observations and then dividing by the total number of observations.

Measuring instrument The method or means by which data are collected.

Median A measure of central tendency; a value where 50 percent of the cases lie above the value and 50 percent of the cases lie below the value.

Missing values Incomplete data.

Mode A measure of central tendency; the value possessed by the greatest number of observations.

Monitoring client progress Examining and reflecting on client progress; used in practice evaluation.

Monitoring interventions Examining and reflecting on interventions used in practice evaluation.

Mortality A threat to internal validity; subjects dropping out of groups, resulting in a lack of equivalency between the groups.

Multiple baseline design A replication of the AB design in which the same intervention is applied to two or more target problems, to two or more clients, or in two or more settings at different points in time.

Multivariate analysis Involves examining relationships between more than two variables.

Multivariate measure A method of measuring the relationship of two or more variables.

Needs assessment (feasibility studies and front-end analysis) Questions concerned with discovering the nature and extent of a particular social problem to determine the most appropriate type of response.

Negative cases A means of validating findings from qualitative research.

Negative correlation A relationship between two variables; as the values of one variable increase, the values of the other variable decrease.

Neutrality When the researcher does not seek a particular perspective in order to draw conclusions.

Nominal measures Measures that clarify observations into mutually exclusive categories with no ordering to the categories.

Nondirectional hypothesis (two-tailed hypothesis) A hypothesis that states there is an association between two or more variables but predicts nothing about the direction of that association.

Nonprobability sampling The process of selecting a sample in which each element in the population has an unknown chance of being included in the sample.

Normal distribution A symmetrical bell-shaped curve; the mean, median, and mode are the same, and most of the scores cluster around the mean, median, and mode.

Null hypothesis A hypothesis that there is no association between the variables.

Objectivity The condition in which to the greatest extent possible, the researcher's values and biases do not interfere with the study of the problem.

Observation A way of collecting information separate from philosophizing or speculating.

Observed frequencies Frequencies in a cross-tabulation derived from the sample.

Observer reliability The comparison of different administrations of the same instrument by different observers or interviewers.

One-group posttest-only design A type of quasi-experimental group design.

One-group pretest/posttest design A type of quasi-experimental group design.

One-tailed hypothesis (directional hypothesis) A hypothesis that specifies not only that there is an association between variables but also predicts whether the relationship is negative or positive.

Open-ended questions   Questions that do not provide respondents with responses, leaving them free to formulate their own responses.

Operationalize   A means of specifying the manner by which the variable is to be measured.

Ordinal measures   Measures that classify observations into mutually exclusive categories with an inherent order.

Output   The final product obtained from submitting a computer program to the computer; this can be displayed on the screen or as hard copy (printout).

Overflow comparison groups   A strategy for increasing the equivalency of comparison and experimental groups in which the comparison groups are those who are referred to a program but who cannot be served at that time.

Panel studies   Studies that look at the same set of people over time.

Participant observation   An observation method involving the observer fully submerging himself or herself to become one of the observed group.

Participatory action research   An opportunity for the subjects' involvement in the research process—an approach to research that has several aims, all intended to empower participants.

Perfect correlation   A relationship between two variables in which the values of each variable increase or decrease at the same rate as one another.

Pie charts   A visual representation of data used to show the relative contributions of each of the values to the whole variable.

Population   All possible cases of interest to the researcher.

Positive correlation   A relationship between two variables in which, as the values of one variable increase, the values of the other variable also increase.

Positivism   An approach to science that adheres to the principles of objectivity, causality, deduction, collecting quantitative data, and producing generalizable results. Also referred to as the quantitative approach to research.

Posttest-only control-group design   A type of experimental design.

Power   The probability of correctly rejecting a null hypothesis.

Practical significance (clinical significance)   Significance level that is achieved when the specified goal of the intervention has been reached.

Practice evaluation   The type of research that assesses an individual social worker's practice.

Practice logs   A type of process recording in which the practitioner keeps an ongoing record of their practice.

Pre-experimental designs   Group designs that use comparison groups rather than control groups, or that use no type of comparison group or control group, and thus have limited internal and external validity.

Pretest/posttest comparison-group design   A type of preexperimental group design.

Pretest-posttest control-group design   A type of experimental design.

Probability sampling   The process of selecting a sample in which each element in the population has a known chance of being included in the sample.

Process recording (process analysis)   A written record of what transpired with a client system.

Program evaluation   A type of research concerned with the assessment of a program's overall functioning.

Provisionality   A scientific principle involving the realization that all scientific findings are tentative and that no ultimate truths can be established.

Pure research   Research centered on answering questions about human behavior to satisfy intellectual curiosity with little concern for the practical benefits that might result.

Purposive sampling   A form of non probability sampling in which the characteristics are defined for a purpose relevant to the study.

Qualitative   The nonnumerical examination of phenomena focusing on the underlying meanings and patterns of relationships. Can denote a specific approach to research.

Quantitative   The creation of categories of phenomena under study prior to investigation and the assignment of numbers to these categories. Can denote a specific approach to research.

Quasi-experimental designs   Designs that eliminate more threats to internal and external validity than preexperimental designs, and use comparison groups rather than control groups, and thus still have limited internal and external validity.

Quota sampling   A nonprobability sampling method that includes a certain proportion of elements with specific characteristics in the sample.

Random assignment   The process by which every subject has an equal chance of being assigned to a control group or the experimental group.

Range   A measure of variability; the distance between the largest and the smallest value.

Rapid assessment instrument (RAI)   A standardized series of questions or statements to connect data in single-system studies.

Rates under treatment   A type of secondary data that uses existing data from agencies to determine the needs of the community.

Ratio measures   Measures that classify observations into mutually exclusive categories with an inherent order and equal spacing between the categories; the ratio measure reflects the absolute magnitude of the value (and has an absolute zero point).

Reactive effect   The degree to which the researcher's presence affects the behavior being observed.

Reductionism   The extreme limitation of the kinds and numbers of variables to be considered when explaining or accounting for broad types of behavior.

Regression analysis   A statistical analysis that allows an estimate of how much change in the dependent variable is produced by a given change in the independent variable or variables.

Regression to the mean   A threat to external validity; the tendency of test scores to regress to the mean.

Reliability   The extent to which a measure reveals actual differences in what is being measured, rather than differences that are inherent in the measuring instrument itself.

Replicate   To repeat a study in order to determine if the same results are found.

Representative sample   A sample that accurately represents the distribution of relevant variables in the population.

Research log   Informal but systematic records of ideas and progress relating to a research study.

Research methods   Means of systematically organizing observations and replicating studies.

Research proposal   A paper proposing to undertake a specific type of research.

Response rate   The proportion of the sample that responds to a questionnaire or interview.

Reversal design   A design that is the same as an ABAB single-system design.

Rival hypothesis   A means of validating findings when analyzing qualitative data (also referred to as an alternative hypothesis).

Sample   A group of subjects chosen from the population.

Sampling   A means of determining the subjects of the study.

Sampling error   The extent to which the values of a sample differ from those of the population.

Sampling frame   A list of all the elements in the population from which the sample is selected.

Scales   A measurement technique that combines a number of items into a composite score.

Scattergram   A means of plotting the relationships between two-interval or ratio-level data.

Science   A system for producing knowledge as well as the knowledge produced from that system.

Scoping reviews   A preliminary review of the literature to assess the extent of a topic.

Secondary data   Existing forms of information that have been previously collected.

Selection   A threat to internal validity; the possibility that the group of people selected for one group will differ from those selected for the other group.

Selection-treatment interaction   A threat to external validity.

Self-monitoring   A process in which a client collects data on his or her own behavior.

Semistructured interview   An interviewing situation in which the interviewer is freer to pursue hunches and improvise in asking questions.

Simple random sampling   A form of probability sampling in which the population is related as a whole unit and each element has an equal chance of being included in the sample.

Single-system design or study   The type of design used in practice evaluation.

Skewed distribution   A distribution in which most of the scores are concentrated at one end of the distribution rather than in the middle.

Split half method   Items on the instrument are divided into comparable halves.

Slopes   Trends that occur in the data within the baseline or within the intervention period.

Snowball sampling   A form of nonprobability sampling that identifies some members of the population and then has those individuals contact others in the population.

Social indicators   A form of secondary data collection that involves selecting demographic data from existing records to predict a community's needs.

Standard deviation   A measure of variability that averages the distance of each value from the mean.

Standardized scales   Uniform scales that are tested extensively.

Static-group comparison design   A type of quasi-experimental group design.

Statistically significant   Characteristic of a finding when the null hypothesis is rejected and the probability that the result was due to chance falls at or below a certain cutoff point—usually 5 percent, or the .05 significance level.

Stratified random sampling   A form of probability sampling in which the population is divided into strata, and subsamples are randomly selected from each stratum.

Structured interview   An interviewing situation in which the interviewer knows ahead of time the questions to be asked and in many cases is simply verbally administering a questionnaire.

Structured observation   Behaviors are categorized prior to the observation according to their characteristics, including their frequency, direction, and magnitude. These categories can then be quantified.

Subjective   Reality as perceived by the subject; the researcher's biases and values are explicitly stated.

Successive intervention design   A design that is the same as the ABC single-system design.

Summative program evaluation   An assessment that determines whether goals and objectives have been met and the extent to which program efforts are generalizable to other settings and populations.

Survey research   Studies focusing on describing the characteristics of a group.

Systematic random sampling   A form of probability sampling in which every nth element of the sampling frame is selected for the sample.

Target problem scales   Scales used in single-system studies to track the changes in a client system's target behavior.

Task forces   Representatives of the agency or community, used to help formulate research questions.

Testing   A threat to internal validity; the effect the testing itself may have on the subject.

Test-retest   The repeated administration of the instrument to the same set of people on separate occasions.

Theories   Scientific descriptions and explanations of logical relationships among phenomena.

Time series design   A type of quasi-experimental design in which a number of measurements are made both before and after the intervention.

Transcribe   The act of writing down verbatim a recording of the interview.

Treatment diffusion   The act of ensuring that there are no interferences over the course of the evaluation that may affect either the equivalence of the groups or the representativeness of the sample.

Trend studies   Multiple samplings from the same population over months or years to monitor changes or trends.

Triangulation   A means of validating findings from qualitative research.

Two-tailed hypothesis (nondirectional hypothesis)   A hypothesis that states that two or more variables are associated but does not predict whether the association is negative or positive.

Type I error   An erroneous rejection of the null hypothesis—the conclusion that a relationship exists between the variables when no relationship in fact exists.

Type II error   An erroneous failure to reject the null hypothesis—a failure to identify a relationship between variables.

Typical case sampling   The most often-used type of nonprobability sampling. Typical cases are sought using the literature, previous research, or consultation with relevant groups.

Unit of analysis   The situation or person who is the object of the study.

Univariate measures   Measures that examine variables one at a time.

Unstructured interviews   Interviews that are similar to conversations except that the interviewer and interviewee know that an interview is being conducted and the interviewee is privy to information of interest to the interviewer.

Unstructured observation   Observation that is used when little is known about the behaviors being observed and no categorization of the behaviors has been done before the interview.

Validity of a measuring instrument   The extent to which we are measuring what we think we are measuring.

Value   The quantitative measure attached to a variable.

Variable   Characteristic of a phenomenon; something that varies and subsequently has different values.

Vignettes   Hypothetical situations either drawn from a source or developed by the researcher for the purpose of eliciting certain responses from the participants.

Visual significance   A state that occurs when the visual presentation of results from a single-system study looks significant.

Withdrawal design   A design that is the same as an ABAB single-system design.

Index